Foreign Direct Investment in China

Location Determinants, Investor Differences and Economic Impacts

Chunlai Chen

The Australian National University

Edward Elgar
Cheltenham, UK • Northampton, MA, USA

Published by
Edward Elgar Publishing Limited
The Lypiatts
15 Lansdown Road
Cheltenham
Glos GL50 2JA
UK

Edward Elgar Publishing, Inc.
William Pratt House
9 Dewey Court
Northampton
Massachusetts 01060
USA

A catalogue record for this book
is available from the British Library

Library of Congress Control Number: 2011929459

ISBN 978 1 84980 388 5

Typeset by Servis Filmsetting Ltd, Stockport, Cheshire
Printed and bound by MPG Books Group, UK

Contents

Foreword

Chunlai Chen has written an important book about the Chinese economy. Here he documents the growth of foreign direct investment (FDI) flows into China, their determinants and their effects, not only in China but also in the rest of the world.

The China FDI story is a remarkable one. As Dr Chen writes, not so long ago FDI was banned in China. Today the accumulated inflow is around $US1000 billion. The annual growth of the inflow was over 30 per cent a year in the 30 years since 1979. During 2000 to 2009, China accounted for 6 per cent of world total inflows and 17 per cent of FDI inflows into developing countries. China has become the largest recipient among developing countries.

This transformation certainly deserves attention, and Dr Chen brings his life's research together in this volume for that purpose. He does that with good organization and great clarity, and with the application of powerful research methods.

The book covers some of the big questions in the study of FDI flows – is China too big as a recipient, why does the sectoral distribution look odd, why is the source of the inflows unusual and why have some provinces missed out?

The book contains some remarkable findings. Dr Chen identifies the uneven patterns of FDI inflows across regions of China and comes up with an explanation for that. He analyses the sources of the inflows: he finds that over three-quarters come from other countries and economies in the region, such as Hong Kong, Taiwan, South Korea and Singapore. The role of the big developed countries is less than might have been expected. The growth in FDI is a manufacturing phenomenon, but is increasingly in technology intensive activities. Dr Chen provides an explanation of these trends. He designs an index of attractiveness at provincial level that will be of great interest to policy-makers working on their country's FDI strategy. Dr Chen also examines and identifies differences in behaviour of investors of different origins. This, too, will be important reading for FDI agencies.

There has been a concern that China has attracted 'too much' FDI. By studying the determinants of FDI flows and applying that analysis to China, Dr Chen finds that, on the contrary, China's performance was only moderately above what might have been expected. He also finds that inflows into China are associated with a positive effect on inflows into other developing countries. Dr Chen identifies a couple of contributors to this result.

With respect to impacts of FDI, Dr Chen looks at the effects on growth at the aggregate level, on productivity at the firm level and on exports. The book reports on empirical work on a series of linkages between foreign and domestic firms which is not often studied.

With this background, Dr Chen also draws out some policy lessons. He refers to the questions of national treatment, regional development strategies, incentives for investment in particular industries, and mechanisms for enhancing the positive effects on domestic firms.

This book is written by a researcher in touch with the big questions about China and about FDI. It is also written by someone who is a great teacher. The skills of the teacher to mobilize interest in a topic and then explain and digest material which is relevant are all evident here.

Christopher Findlay
School of Economics
University of Adelaide
14 April 2011

Preface

Foreign direct investment in China has been one of the most successful aspects of China's economic reform and opening up to the outside world. The gradual liberalization of restrictions on FDI since 1979, the government's commitments for further opening up, particularly the commitments to the World Trade Organization in trade and investment liberalization, have greatly improved the overall investment environment in China. Foreign firms have been attracted by the huge domestic market and pool of relatively well-educated, low-cost labour, which has made China one of the most attractive destinations for FDI in the world.

Over the course of the past three decades, FDI became well established in China's economy, and the activities of multinational enterprises came to assume increasing importance in capital formation, labour training, technology transfer, international trade, and in accelerating the transition of China from a planned economy to a market economy. As a result, FDI has increasingly integrated the Chinese economy into the world economy.

This book presents a comprehensive analysis of FDI in China. It provides a remarkable background of information on the growth of FDI inflows and the evolution of China's FDI policies for the past 30 years; a thorough analysis of the leading theoretical explanations of FDI and a series of rigorous empirical examinations of the location determinants of FDI; a comprehensive analysis of the differences in investment and production behaviour between the major investors; and an in-depth investigation of the impacts of FDI on China's economy.

The results of this study provide us with much insight into the general issues of FDI in developing countries. In particular, this study extends our knowledge in three main ways: (1) greater understanding of the general causes of FDI from the aspect of the 'demand-side' factors by focusing on investigating the location determinants affecting inter-country and inter-region distributions of FDI; (2) better knowledge of the differences between the developing source economies and the developed source economies in their investment relationships with China, and the distinctive features of the investments from the overseas Chinese investors as compared to those from the foreign country investors; and (3) further evidence of the impact of FDI on economic growth, the spillover effects of FDI on productivity and exports of domestic firms in the case of FDI in China.

I hope this book will be a valuable source for scholars and students who are interested in FDI studies in general and in Chinese economic studies in particular, and also be of interest to a wide range of readers.

Chunlai Chen
The Australian National University
Canberra, Australia

Acknowledgements

This book was completed with the support of many people. First, I am very grateful to Professor Christopher Findlay, who inspired my research interest in foreign direct investment when I was a PhD student under his supervision, and that of Professor Andrew Watson during 1994 to 1998 in the University of Adelaide, Australia. Their profound knowledge both of economic theory and of China greatly benefited my study. I sincerely thank Professor Findlay for his encouragement, valuable comments and substantive advice on drafting and publishing this book.

I would like to thank Dr Yu Sheng for his technical assistance with the regressions in Chapters 9 and 10.

I wish to thank the Crawford School of Economics and Government at the Australian National University for providing the excellent research facilities. I also wish to thank the China Economic and Business Program in the Crawford School of Economics and Government, particularly Associate Professor Lignag Song for providing me with financial assistance in editing this book. I would like to thank Dr Nicola Chandler for her excellent editing of the work. And I also would like to thank Edward Elgar Publishing for publishing the book.

Finally, I would like to give my special thanks to my family – my father Hongjin Chen, my wife Tessia Deng and my son Christopher Chen – for their love, encouragement and support. The understanding and support, especially from my wife Tessia, were of immeasurable value throughout the course of my writing of this book.

Chunlai Chen
Canberra, Australia
March 2011

Abbreviations

ACFTA	ASEAN-China Free Trade Area
ASEAN	Association of South-East Asian Nations
BOA	Bank of America
BOC	Bank of China
CCB	China Construction Bank
CERC	China Enterprise Registration Code
CPI	consumer price index
DOEs	domestic enterprises
EDZs	Economic Development Zones
ETDZs	Economic and Technological Development Zones
EU	European Union
FCAs	foreign country affiliates
FD	first differential
FDI	foreign direct investment
GDP	gross domestic product
ICBC	Industrial and Commercial Bank of China
ILO	International Labour Organization
IMF	International Monetary Fund
ISIC	International Standard Industrial Classification
M&As	mergers and acquisitions
MFN	most favoured nation
MNEs	multinational enterprises
MOFCOM	Ministry of Commerce (of China)
NBS	National Bureau of Statistics (of China)
NIEs	newly industrializing economies
OCAs	overseas Chinese affiliates
OECD	Organisation for Economic Co-operation and Development
OLI	ownership advantage, location advantage and internalization advantage
OLS	ordinary least squares
R&D	research and development
RBS	Royal Bank of Scotland
RMB	renminbi, the name of the Chinese currency
SEZs	Special Economic Zones

SOEs	state-owned enterprises
SPV	special purpose vehicle
TDZ	Technology Development Zone
TFP	total factor productivity
TRIMs	General Agreement on Trade-Related Investment Measures
TRIPs	General Agreement on Trade-Related Aspects of Intellectual Property Rights
TRQ	tariff-rate quotes
UBS	United Bank of Switzerland
UNCTAD	United Nations Conference on Trade and Development
WTO	World Trade Organization
yuan	the unit of the Chinese currency

In memory of my mother

1. Introduction

Foreign direct investment (FDI) is international investment in the financial or non-financial corporate sectors of the economy in which the non-resident investor purchases 10 per cent or more of the voting power of an incorporated enterprise or has the equivalent ownership in an enterprise operating under another legal structure (IMF, 2004). Allowing FDI into its domestic economy is one of the most dramatic features of China's move from a planned economy towards a market economy. Since the passing, in late 1979, of the Equity Joint Venture Law which granted legal status to FDI in Chinese territory, China has gradually liberalized its FDI regime, and an institutional framework has been developed to regulate and facilitate such investments. The liberalization of the FDI regime together with the improved investment environment has greatly increased the confidence of foreign investors to invest in China. Consequently, FDI inflows into China increased rapidly after 1979, particularly during the early 1990s and after China's entry into the World Trade Organization (WTO) in 2001.

The total accumulative amount of FDI inflows at 2000 US dollar prices rose from the initial US$0.22 billion in 1979 to reach US$934 billion in 2009, at an annual growth rate of 32.11 per cent.[1] As a result, since 1993, China has become the largest FDI recipient in the developing world. Over the course of the past three decades, from 1979 to 2009, FDI became well established in China's economy, and the activities of multinational enterprises (MNEs) came to assume increasing importance in capital formation, labour training, technology transfer, international trade, and in accelerating the transition of China from a planned economy to a market economy. As a result, FDI has increasingly integrated the Chinese economy into the world economy.

WHY STUDY FDI IN CHINA?

Owing to its fast growth and huge amount of inflows, FDI in China has received increasing attention both within China and abroad. There are several key reasons to study FDI in China.

First, China is the world's largest developing country and one of its fastest growing economies, with the annual real growth rate of gross domestic product (GDP) averaging around 10 per cent for the past three decades. China's participation and growing role in the world economy, particularly after China's entry into the WTO, calls for a careful study of the pattern and process of China's internationalization. Undoubtedly, FDI in China's economy will play a very important and increasing role in the process of China's integration with the world economy. Therefore, studying FDI in China has a strategic significance not only for China but also for the whole world economy.

Second, China has a particular political and economic environment. It is moving from a planned economy towards a market economy. Its experience with FDI is thus of relevance to many other developing countries, especially to the former socialist countries of Eastern Europe, not only because of the magnitude of FDI inflows it has attracted but also because the essential elements of the policy environment are replicated there.

Third, China is the largest FDI recipient in the developing world. As a result, China has increasingly become more significant in influencing not only the flows of international FDI, but also the division of labour and specialization in global production. Therefore, studies of FDI cannot afford to ignore China.

Fourth, the fast growth rate of FDI inflows into China during the past three decades has caused increasing concern in other developing countries about their own efforts in attracting FDI inflows. Has the fast growth of FDI inflows into China caused a diversion of FDI away from other developing countries? One cannot answer this question without a careful study of the location determinants affecting FDI inflows and the relative performance of China in attracting FDI inflows as compared with other developing countries.

Fifth, one of the prominent features of FDI in China is the overwhelming dominance of investments from developing source countries and economies, particularly from the overseas Chinese investors. The existing theories of FDI have been mainly drawn from studies of developed source countries. Little work has been done on the investment behaviour and characteristics of developing source countries. Fortunately, FDI in China provides a valuable opportunity for economists not only to test the adequacy of existing theories of FDI but also to compare the particular characteristics of developing source countries with developed source countries in their investment behaviour.

Sixth, it is hypothesized that because FDI firms possess firm-specific ownership advantages, such as advanced technology and know-how, mature marketing and managerial skills, well-organized international distribution channels, coordinated relationships with suppliers and good reputation, FDI firms can compete locally with more informed domestic firms. Since both FDI firms and domestic firms can imitate each other in the same market, domestic firms are usually expected to increase their productivity and competitiveness in international markets. This positive impact of foreign presence on domestic firms' productivity and exports is referred to as 'spillovers of FDI', which is an important channel through which developing countries can close the technology gap with developed countries. China, as the largest developing country with a huge amount of FDI inflows, provides a valuable case for the empirical study of spillovers of FDI on domestic firms' productivity and exports of developing countries.

Finally, there is a considerable and a growing number of studies on FDI in China. These studies can be broadly classified into three groups. The first has mainly focused on China's FDI policies, legal and institutional framework, the impacts of trade and investment liberalization of China on FDI inflows and the characteristics of FDI in China. This includes, for example: Chen (1982), Chu (1987), Harrold and Lall (1993), Liu et al. (1993), Shirk (1994), Wei (1994), Chen (1996, 1997a, 2002, 2007, 2010a), McKibben and Wilcoxen (1998), Branstetter and Feenstra (1999), Li and Li (1999), Walmsley and Hertel (2001), Breslin (2003), Huang (2003a), Xiao (2004), Blanchard (2007), Liu (2008), Oxelheim and Ghauri (2008), Cole et al. (2009), Lo and Tian (2009), Wilson (2009) and Huang (2010).

The second group has mainly focused on location determinants of FDI, sources of FDI and the impacts of China on FDI inflows into other countries. This includes, for example: Pomfret (1989), Thoburn et al. (1990), Ash and Kueh (1993), Qi and Howe (1993), Zhang (1994), Croix et al. (1995), Wei (1995), Chen (1996), Broadman and Sun (1997), Chen (1997b, 1997c, 2003, 2010b), Dees (1998), Wu et al. (2002), Chantasasawat et al. (2004), Eichengreen and Tong (2005), Mercereau (2005), Zhou and Lall (2005), Cravino et al. (2007), Kang and Lee (2007), Wang et al. (2007), Amiti and Javorcik (2008) and Resmini and Siedschlag (2008).

The third group has mainly focused on the impacts of FDI on China's economy, including, for example: Kamath (1990, 1994), Pomfret (1991, 1994, 1997), Fan (1992), Kueh (1992), Zhan (1993), Chen et al. (1995), Lardy (1995), Sun (1995), Wei (1996a), Chen (1997d, 1999), Tse et al. (1997), Henley et al. (1999), Hu and Ma (1999), Liu et al. (2001), Sun and Parikh (2001), Buckley et al. (2002), Huang (2003b), Li (2003), Zheng et al. (2004), Ma (2006), Zhang (2006), Buck et al. (2007), Y. Chen (2007), Ran et al. (2007), Sung (2007), Li and Zhou (2008), Tang et al. (2008), Vu et al. (2008), Yu and Zhao (2008), Sun (2009), Tuan et al. (2009), Xu and Lu (2009), Cheung (2010), Ramasamy and Yeung (2010) and Whalley and Xin (2010).

Although these studies have made considerable contributions to the study of FDI in China, there still is a lack of, and therefore a need for, a systematic and comprehensive theoretical and empirical study covering the aspects of policy and the legal system governing FDI, location determinants of FDI, sources of FDI and the economic impacts of FDI in China. It is aimed in this study to fill this gap.

FDI INFLOWS INTO CHINA BETWEEN 1979 AND 2009

The Growth of FDI Inflows into China

During the past three decades, China has attracted a large amount of FDI inflows. As shown in Figure 1.1, the growth of FDI inflows into China from 1979 to 2009 can be broadly divided into three phases: the experimental phase from 1979 to 1991; the boom phase from 1992 to 2001; and the post-WTO phase from 2002 to 2009.

In the initial stage of the experimental phase, following the establishment of the four Special Economic Zones (SEZs) in Guangdong and Fujian provinces,[2] accompanied by the special incentive policies for FDI

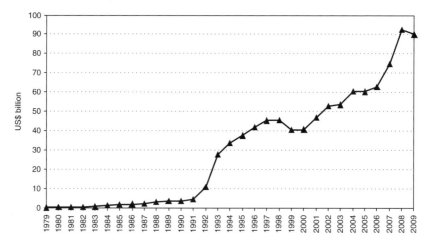

Note: The data do not include FDI inflows into the financial sector.

Sources: National Bureau of Statistics of China (various issues), *China Statistical Yearbook*, Beijing: China Statistics Press.

Figure 1.1   FDI inflows into China (current US$)

offered by the Chinese government in these SEZs, FDI inflows into China were highly concentrated in Guangdong and Fujian provinces, and particularly in the four SEZs. For example, Guangdong and Fujian provinces absorbed more than 70 per cent of total FDI inflows in 1983. However, since the Chinese government was very cautious about introducing FDI into its domestic economy, foreign investors were also cautious about making investments in China in the initial stage of China's opening up to the outside world. During this period, therefore, China's performance in attracting FDI inflows was not very impressive. The inflows of FDI were only US$0.11 billion in 1979 and US$0.64 billion in 1983, averaging US$0.35 billion annually.

In 1984, Hainan Island and 14 coastal cities across ten provinces were opened to FDI. As in the SEZs, a series of special economic policies were introduced in these open coastal cities. Consequently, in 1984 the inflows of FDI into China doubled the amount of those in 1983, reaching US$1.26 billion, indicating a new stage in attracting FDI inflows into China. The momentum of FDI inflows into China continued from 1984 to 1988. However, in 1989, mainly due to the Tiananmen event, the growth rate of FDI inflows into China fell sharply from 38 per cent in 1988 to 6 per cent in 1989. The downturn continued in 1990, until it recovered in 1991. During the period from 1984 to 1991, the Chinese government made a significant effort to attract FDI inflows. This included opening more and more areas and regions to FDI, such as the Yangzi River Delta, the Pearl River Delta, the Min Nan Delta, the Shanghai Pudong New Development Zone and the entire coastal areas, and introducing a series of laws and regulations to encourage FDI inflows. As a result, FDI inflows into China continued to increase in absolute terms during the whole period from 1984 to 1991.

The second phase began in 1992, when Deng Xiaoping made a tour to China's southern coastal economically opened areas and SEZs, and made a speech, which subsequently became famous. His aim was first to push China's overall economic reform process forward, and second to emphasize China's commitment to the open door policy and market-oriented economic reform in order to increase the confidence of foreign investors to invest in China. His speech explicitly declared his support for the successful economic development assisted by FDI in the economically opened areas and SEZs, and expressed a desire to see the pace of liberalization quickened. Deng Xiaoping's tour, which turned out to be a landmark, set the scene for China's move away from the uneven regional priority towards nationwide implementation of open policies for FDI. The Chinese government then adopted and implemented a series of new policies and regulations to encourage FDI inflows into China.[3] The results were astounding. In 1992 the inflows of FDI into China reached US$11.01

billion, doubling the figure of 1991. In 1993 the inflows of FDI again doubled the figure of 1992, reaching US$27.52 billion. The high growth of FDI inflows continued during 1994 to 1996.

Foreign direct investment inflows slowed down after 1997 and declined in 1999 and 2000, followed by a moderate recovery in 2001. The slow-down from 1997 to 2000 could be explained by several factors. First, there was a slow-down in transfers of labour-intensive activities from neighbouring Asian economies. In addition, the East Asian financial crisis weakened substantially the outward investment abilities of East and South-East Asian economies. As a result, FDI flows into China from East and South-East Asia declined substantially since 1997. Second, informal relationships and corruption still hinder many business transactions by foreigners. In addition, inefficient state-owned enterprises (SOEs) continue to dominate many key sectors of economy, especially the service sector. Third, there are still restrictions on FDI, such as on ownership shares, modes of entry, business operations, and regional and sectoral restrictions.

The third phase began in 2002 after China's entry into the WTO in 2001. China's accession to the WTO came at a critical time, when the country was facing difficulties sustaining a high level of FDI inflows. After China's accession to the WTO, with the implementation of its commitments and broader and deeper liberalization in trade and investment, FDI inflows presented an increasing trend. Foreign direct investment inflows increased from US$46.88 billion in 2001 to US$92.40 billion in 2008. However, because of the global financial and economic crisis, FDI inflows into China declined to US$90.03 billion in 2009.

There has long been an issue of 'round-tripping' of FDI in the case of China. Round-tripping involves the circular flow of capital out of China and the subsequent reinvestment of this 'foreign' capital in China for the purpose of benefiting from fiscal entitlements accorded to foreign investors. Because the funds originate in the host country itself, round-tripping inflates actual FDI inflows. According to the UNCTAD (2007), a significant share of FDI inflows into China is round-tripping, mainly via Hong Kong and more recently and increasingly via some tax-haven islands – Virgin Islands, Cayman Islands and Samoan Islands. Some estimates suggest that round-tripping inward FDI accounted for 25 per cent of China's FDI inflows in 1992 (Harrold and Lall, 1993)[4] and accounted for 40 per cent of China's total FDI inflows during 1994 to 2001 (Xiao, 2004).

Round-tripping is driven by a number of incentives. In the case of China, preferential treatments offered for FDI are one of the main incentives for round-tripping FDI. Since the beginning of economic reform, the Chinese government has used tax incentives, tariff concessions and various preferential treatments intensively and selectively to attract FDI

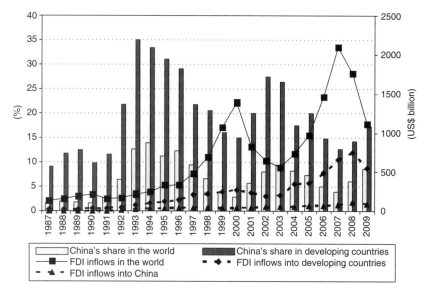

Note: Data for China include FDI inflows into the financial sector after 2005.

Sources: Compiled from United Nations Conference on Trade and Development (various issues), *World Investment Report*, New York and Geneva: United Nations Publication.

Figure 1.2 China's FDI inflows in global perspective (current US$)

flowing into the designed areas and industries.[5] These preferential treatments offered for FDI are the primary incentives for domestic firms to do round-tripping FDI.

Since China's accession to the WTO, China has gradually introduced national treatment of FDI firms. In March 2007 China passed the new corporate income tax law, unifying the corporate income tax rates for foreign and domestic enterprises at 25 per cent. The unification of the corporate income tax rate and the elimination of preferential treatment of FDI firms will reduce the incentives for FDI round-tripping.

China's FDI Inflows in Global Perspective

Since the 1980s, world FDI inflows have experienced two massive waves of ups and downs. As shown in Figure 1.2, the first large increase of world FDI inflows started in the mid-1990s. World FDI inflows increased from US$331 billion in 1995 to US$1393 billion in 2000. Following a sharp decline in 2001 to 2003, world FDI inflows increased again and experienced a period of high growth during 2003 to 2007, reaching a historical record of US$2100 billion in 2007. However, the growing trend of world FDI inflows came to an end in 2008. World FDI inflows dropped sharply to US$1771 billion, declining by 15.71 per cent in 2008, and further dropped to US$1114 billion in 2009, declining by 37.29 per cent, caused by the global financial crisis, which was in turn triggered by the USA's sub-prime crisis which began in summer 2007 and led to a rapid deterioration of the global investment environment. However, as compared to the large fluctuations in world FDI inflows, FDI inflows into China have been rela-tively stable, presenting a steady growing trend with minor fluctuations.

What has been the position of China in world FDI inflows? As shown in Figure 1.2, during the 1980s China's share in FDI inflows in the world and in developing countries was around 2 per cent and 11 per cent respectively, with minor annual fluctuations. However, in the 1990s China's share in FDI inflows in the world and in developing countries increased dra-matically, reaching 7.5 per cent and 23 per cent respectively. In the 2000s China's share in FDI inflows in the world and in developing countries declined slightly due to the massive increase in world FDI inflows during the period of 2004 to 2007. However, during the period from 2000 to 2009, China still accounted for 6 per cent of total world FDI inflows and 17 per cent of total FDI inflows into developing countries.

The Regional Distribution of FDI within China

Although at the national level the aggregate FDI inflows into China have grown steadily over the past 30 years, the distribution of inward FDI among China's regions and provinces has been very uneven. By the end of 2008, as shown in Figure 1.3, FDI in China was overwhelmingly concen-trated in the eastern region, which accounted for 86.26 per cent of the total accumulative FDI inflows, while the central region and western region accounted for only 9.16 per cent and 4.58 per cent of the total respectively.

As a single province Guangdong has been the largest FDI recipient in China among all the provinces. Its share of accumulative FDI inflows from 1983 to 2005 was over a quarter of the national total (see Table 1.1),[6] followed by Jiangsu (14.41 per cent), Shanghai (8.94 per cent), Shandong (8.44 per cent), Fujian (7.99 per cent), Liaoning (5.06 per cent), Zhejiang (5.01 per cent), Beijing (4.25 per cent) and Tianjin (3.62 per cent).

Who are the Major Investors in China?

Since 1979 more than 170 countries and economies have invested in China. However, of interest is to determine who are the major investors. By the end of 2008, as shown in Table 1.2, FDI in China was overwhelmingly

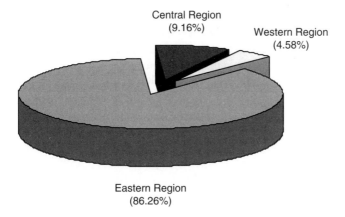

Note: The calculation is based on 2000 US$.

Sources: Compiled from National Bureau of Statistics of China (various issues), *China Statistical Yearbook*, Beijing: China Statistics Press; Ministry of Commerce of China (various issues), *China Foreign Investment Report*, Beijing: MOFCOM.

Figure 1.3   Shares of accumulative FDI inflows into China by region, 1983–2008 (total = 100)

dominated by developing countries and economies, which accounted for 75.38 per cent of the total accumulative FDI inflows, while developed countries accounted for only 24.62 per cent of the total. Among the developing countries and economies, as a group the Asian newly industrializing economies (NIEs)[7] has been the largest investor, accounting for 56.64 per cent of the total. Within the Asian NIEs, Hong Kong has held the dominant position, accounting for 41.75 per cent of the total, followed by Taiwan (5.76 per cent), South Korea (4.74 per cent) and Singapore (4.39 per cent). The four Association of South-East Asian Nations (ASEAN) economies[8] accounted for 1.48 per cent of the total.

One notable feature is the large shares held by the tax-haven economies. Foreign direct investment inflows into China from the tax-haven economies increased dramatically in the 1990s and particularly in the 2000s. As a result, their combined shares in total FDI inflows increased to 13.64 per cent by the end of 2008. The Virgin Islands took the dominant position, accounting for 9.78 per cent of the total, followed by the Cayman Islands (1.78 per cent) and the Samoan Islands (1.30 per cent).

Among the developed countries, Japan and the USA are the most important investors in China, accounting for 7.78 per cent and 7.18 per cent of the total, while the combined share of the European Union (15) was 7.19 per cent. Apart from the UK, Germany, the Netherlands and France,

*Table 1.1   Accumulative FDI inflows in China by region and selected
provinces, 1983–2005 (2000 US$)*

Regions	Accumulative FDI inflows 1983–2005 (US$ million)	Share 1983–2005 (%)
Eastern Region	535 940	86.26
Guangdong	157 037	25.28
Jiangsu	89 519	14.41
Shanghai	55 545	8.94
Shandong	52 428	8.44
Fujian	49 617	7.99
Liaoning	31 438	5.06
Zhejiang	31 589	5.01
Beijing	26 380	4.25
Tianjin	22 870	3.62
Central Region	56 902	9.16
Hubei	13 120	2.11
Hunan	10 551	1.70
Jiangxi	8634	1.39
Henan	6807	1.10
Western Region	28 462	4.58
Guangxi	8748	1.41
Sichuan	5844	0.94
Shaanxi	4639	0.75
Chongqing	3744	0.60
Provincial total	612 304	100.00

Sources: Compiled from National Bureau of Statistics of China (various issues), *China
Statistical Yearbook*, Beijing: China Statistics Press.

whose shares are 1.89 per cent, 1.76 per cent, 1.06 per cent and 1.03 per
cent respectively, no other individual developed country has contributed
more than 1 per cent of the total accumulative FDI inflows into China.

Sectoral Distribution of FDI in China

By the end of 2008, the sectoral distribution of FDI in China was characterized by a high concentration in the manufacturing sector. As shown in
Figure 1.4, the manufacturing sector attracted 62.72 per cent, the service
sector attracted 34.74 per cent, while the primary sector attracted only
2.54 per cent of the total accumulative FDI inflows into China during the
period from 1997 to 2008.[9]

How important are FDI firms in China's manufacturing sector? As

*Table 1.2   Accumulative FDI inflows into China by developing and
developed countries and economies, 1983–2008 (2000 US$)*

	1983–2008	
	(US$ million)	(%)
Developing countries and economies	620925	75.38
NIEs	466542	56.64
Hong Kong	343888	41.75
Taiwan	47423	5.76
South Korea	39043	4.74
Singapore	36188	4.39
ASEAN (4)	12225	1.48
Tax-haven economies	112372	13.64
Other developing countries	29787	3.62
Developed countries	202814	24.62
Japan	64114	7.78
USA	59172	7.18
EU (15)	59262	7.19
UK	15561	1.89
Germany	14480	1.76
Netherlands	8715	1.06
France	8474	1.03
Other developed countries	20266	2.46
Total	823739	100.00

Sources: Compiled from National Bureau of Statistics of China (various issues), *China
Statistical Yearbook*, Beijin: China Statistics Press; Ministry of Commerce of China, Invest
in China, FDI Statistics.

shown in Table 1.3, in terms of total assets, the share of FDI firms in the
manufacturing sector has increased from 18.93 per cent in 1995 to 32.10
per cent in 2008. In other words, one-third of the total assets of manufacturing sector were held by FDI firms in 2008. This is significant, especially
when we take into account the large aggregate scale and overall fast
growth rate of China's manufacturing sector in the last 30 years.

Among the three industry groups of manufacturing, FDI firms in
the technology-intensive sector gained more share, and therefore more
importance, than FDI firms in the labour-intensive sector and the capital-
intensive sector in manufacturing. By 2008, the share of FDI firms in
the technology-intensive sector reached 42.15 per cent, increasing 20.11
percentage points compared with that in 1995. The share of FDI firms in
the labour-intensive sector increased to 33.79 per cent in 2008, rising by

Foreign direct investment in China

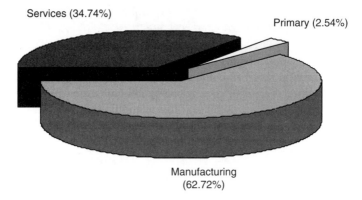

Services (34.74%)

Primary (2.54%)

Manufacturing
(62.72%)

Note: The calculation is based on 2000 US$.

Sources: Compiled from National Bureau of Statistics of China (various issues), *China Statistical Yearbook*, Beijing: China Statistics Press; Ministry of Commerce of China, Invest in China, FDI Statistics.

Figure 1.4   Sectoral distribution of accumulative FDI inflows in China, 1997–2008 (total = 100)

Table 1.3   Shares of FDI firms in manufacturing by total assets (%)

Sector	1995	2008
Labour intensive	25.19	33.79
Capital intensive	10.75	24.01
Technology intensive	22.04	42.15
Total	18.93	32.10

Sources: Compiled form National Bureau of Statistics of China (various issues), *China Statistical Yearbook*, Beijing: China Statistics Press.

8.60 percentage points above that in 1995. The share of FDI firms in the capital-intensive sector is still relatively low compared with those in the technology-intensive sector and the labour-intensive sector. However, it increased to 24.01 per cent in 2008, rising by 13.26 percentage points over that in 1995.

Since the manufacturing sector is the main recipient of FDI inflows, its industrial distribution has special significance. In the early stage of FDI inflows into manufacturing, FDI firms were overwhelmingly concentrated in the labour-intensive sector. By the end of 1995, as shown in Table 1.4, in terms of the total assets of FDI firms in manufacturing, 50.91 per cent

Table 1.4   Industrial structure of FDI firms in manufacturing by total assets (%)

Sector	1995	2008
Labour intensive	50.91	31.11
Capital intensive	21.71	31.28
Technology intensive	27.38	37.61
Total	100.00	100.00

Sources: Compiled from National Bureau of Statistics of China (various issues), *China Statistical Yearbook*, Beijing: China Statistics Press.

were in the labour-intensive sector while only 21.71 per cent and 27.38 per cent were in the capital-intensive sector and the technology-intensive sector respectively.

With the fast economic growth, high level of capital accumulation, large improvement in human capital development and technology progress, China's comparative advantage has changed rapidly. Though China still has strong comparative advantage in labour-intensive activities owing to its huge population and abundant labour supply, China has greatly increased its comparative advantages in capital-intensive and technology-intensive activities. As a result, FDI flows into Chinese manufacturing have gradually shifted from a high level of concentration in the labour-intensive sector towards increasing investment in the capital-intensive sector and the technology-intensive sector. By the end of 2008, as shown in Table 1.4, the investment structure of FDI firms in Chinese manufacturing has changed fundamentally. The technology-intensive sector has become the most important and largest sector receiving FDI, and the capital-intensive sector has also surpassed the labour-intensive sector receiving FDI. In terms of the total assets of FDI firms, the shares of the technology-intensive sector and the capital-intensive sector have increased to 37.61 per cent and 31.28 per cent respectively, while the share of the labour-intensive sector has fallen to 31.11 per cent.

The Contribution of FDI to China's Economy

In the FDI literature, FDI is believed to have played some major roles in the development process of a host country's economy, via capital formation, the creation of employment opportunities, promotion of international trade, technology transfer and spillovers to the domestic economy

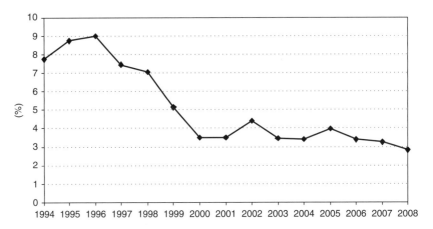

Sources: Compiled from National Bureau of Statistics of China (various issues), *China
Statistical Yearbook*, Beijing: China Statistics Press.

*Figure 1.5   FDI inflows as a percentage of total investment in fixed assets
           in China, 1994–2008*

(Caves, 1996; Dunning, 1993; Markusen and Venables, 1999; UNCTAD,
World Investment Report, 1999, 2004). Over the past three decades, China
has attracted a huge amount of FDI inflows, and FDI firms have made
some important impacts on China's economy.

Capital formation
How important have FDI inflows been in China's domestic capital formation? To evaluate the contribution of FDI to China's domestic capital
formation, we use the share of FDI in China's total investment in fixed
assets. As shown in Figure 1.5, the share reached the highest level of 9 per
cent in 1996. Since then it fell to around 3.5 per cent or less after 2000. This
suggests that FDI made an important contribution to China's domestic
capital formation during the 1990s. However, since 2000, the role of FDI
in China's domestic capital formation has been declining. Nevertheless,
for a large and fast-growing economy like China – average annual GDP
growth around 10 per cent for the past three decades – FDI has provided
an important supplementary source of finance to its domestic capital
formation.

Employment creation
In the developing countries, where capital is relatively scarce but labour
is abundant, one of the most prominent contributions of FDI to the local

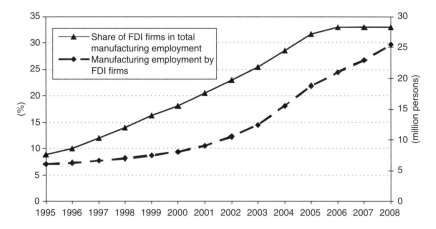

Sources: Data for 1995, 1999–2001, 2003, and 2005–2008 are compiled from National Bureau of Statistics of China (various issues), *China Statistical Yearbook*, Beijing: China Statistics Press; data for the other years are estimated by the author.

Figure 1.6   FDI firms' manufacturing employment in China, 1995–2008

economy is the creation of employment opportunities. Figure 1.6 shows FDI firms' employment in the manufacturing sector during 1995 to 2008 and indicates that FDI firms' manufacturing employment increased significantly after 2001. While they employed 6.05 million workers or 8.9 per cent of China's manufacturing employment in 1995, the figures have increased to 25.45 million workers or 32.97 per cent in 2008. In other words, by the end of 2008, FDI firms employed one-third of China's manufacturing labour force.

Export promotion
There is considerable evidence that FDI contributes to the growth of host countries' international trade. In the case of China, the most prominent contribution of FDI perhaps is expanding China's exports. Figure 1.7 presents the export performance of FDI firms from 1980 to 2008. FDI firms' exports rose from US$0.01 billion in 1980 to US$119 billion in 2000 and to US$791 billion in 2008. As a result, the importance of FDI firms in China's exports has increased from only 0.05 per cent in 1980 to 47.93 per cent in 2000 and further to 58.30 per cent in 2005, before falling slightly to 55.25 per cent in 2008. One reason for this is that China's FDI policy has been deliberately biased towards export-oriented FDI. As a result, FDI firms have rapidly become a major exporting group.

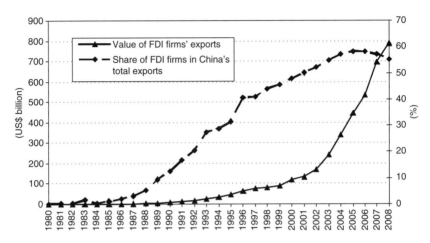

Sources: Compiled from National Bureau of Statistics of China (various issues), *China Statistical Yearbook*, Beijing: China Statistics Press; National Bureau of Statistics of China (various issues), *China Foreign Economic Statistical Yearbook*, Beijing: China Statistics Press; Ministry of Commerce of China, Invest in China, FDI Statistics.

Figure 1.7   FDI firms' export performance, 1980–2008 (current US$)

THE MAIN ISSUES TO BE STUDIED

The above section has outlined the key features of FDI in China. They are characterized by fast growth and a huge amount of inflows, uneven regional distribution, overwhelming dominance by developing source countries and economies, concentration in the manufacturing sector and significant contributions to China's economy. What are the underlying causes for these special features of FDI in China? This study aims to answer these questions by focusing on analysing three main issues. These are the location determinants, the investor differences and the economic impacts of FDI on China's economy. For each of these issues, we analyse some specific questions.

Before addressing each of the main issues to be studied, we first clarify the use of FDI data in this study. In China's official statistics, there are two types of FDI data. One is the contracted FDI data based on the approvals of FDI projects, and the other is the realized FDI data based on the actual investments of FDI projects. The contracted FDI data are a relatively poor indicator when we use them to analyse FDI inflows into China, since some of the approved FDI projects failed to be implemented and some investments are less than specified in the contracts. To avoid such a problem and to increase the credibility of our analysis, all FDI data used in the analysis of this study are actual realized FDI data. In addition, China did not publish the data for FDI inflows into its financial sector until 2005. To keep data consistency in the analysis, the data for FDI inflows into China used in this study are FDI inflows into non-financial sectors unless otherwise stated.

Location Determinants

The first issue is related to the causes of FDI. Because this study is focused on inward FDI into China, our interest mainly lies in examining the location determinants of FDI. In this study we analyse this from two different levels.

First, in order to compare the relative performance of China in attracting FDI inflows with that of other developing countries and to investigate the impact of FDI inflows into China on FDI inflows into other developing countries, we examine and test the location factors determining FDI inflows into developing countries. At this level of analysis, we ask: what location factors determine the country distribution of FDI inflows from all source countries into developing host countries; what is the relative performance of China in attracting FDI inflow as compared with other developing countries; and what is the impact of FDI inflows into China on FDI inflows into other developing countries?

Second, the provincial distribution of FDI inflows into China has been very uneven. This may reflect the regional variations in economic reform policies introduced by the central government and the regional differences in attracting FDI inflows caused by the local investment environment. The latter includes the differences in economic and social development levels, in the quality and costs of labour, and in natural resource endowments. It is, therefore, necessary to analyse and test the location determinants affecting the provincial distribution of FDI inflows. At this level of analysis, our interest lies in answering the questions: what location factors determine the provincial distribution of FDI inflows across the provinces within China and why have FDI inflows been mainly concentrated in the eastern coastal region?

Investor Differences

One of the prominent features of FDI in China in terms of sources is the overwhelming dominance of the developing source countries and economies, particularly the overseas Chinese investors from Hong Kong and Taiwan. Constrained by their own levels of innovatory capability, productive technology and overall economic development, the ownership advantages they possess should be different compared with those of developed source countries. As a result, one needs to ask the questions why FDI in China has been dominated by the developing countries and economies, and whether the developing source countries and economies behave differently from the developed source countries. Therefore, in this study we examine the questions: are the developing and developed source countries different in their investment behaviour in terms of investment intensity, patterns of investment, type of entry, market orientation, factor intensity and labour productivity? If they are, then what are the general characteristics of investments by the developing source countries and economies compared with the developed source countries, and what factors explain these differences?

Economic Impacts

What are the impacts of FDI on China's economy? Foreign direct investment brings into a host country a package of capital and other financial resources; advanced technology and know-how, modern enterprise management and mature marketing skills, well-organized international distribution channels, coordinated relationships with suppliers and clients, good reputation and other intangible assets. Therefore, it will have both direct and indirect impacts on a host country's economy. On the one hand, FDI can directly contribute to China's domestic capital formation, creation of employment and expansion of exports, thus increasing China's economic growth. On the other hand, FDI can also have indirect impacts on China's domestic firms' productivity and exports through either horizontal or vertical spillovers. It is expected that through the knowledge spillovers such as learning by doing (demonstration effects), research and development (R&D), human resource movement, training courses, technical assistance and exposure to fierce competition, FDI improves productivity and increases exports of local firms of host countries. Therefore, this study seeks to investigate empirically the following issues: what are the impacts, with a particular emphasis on the spillover effects, of FDI on China's regional economic growth? What are the technology spillovers of FDI on China's domestic firms' productivity? What are the export spillovers of FDI on China's domestic firms' exports?

THE THEORETICAL FRAMEWORK

Foreign direct investment is formally defined as ownership of assets by foreign residents for purposes of controlling the use of those assets

(Graham and Krugman, 1991).[10] To analyse and understand FDI, a theoretical framework is necessary. Therefore, in this section we first briefly review some of the leading theories used in explaining FDI, and then discuss the implications of the existing literature for this study.

The Theory of FDI

There are many theories seeking to explain FDI, and the most recent and comprehensive surveys can be found in Dunning (1993), Dunning and Lundan (2008) and Caves (1996, 2007). Among these theories, however, the most influential are those based on industrial organization explanations.

The industrial organization explanations of FDI originate from Hymer's celebrated 1960 doctoral thesis (published in 1976). In his thesis, Hymer first distinguished the difference between portfolio investment and direct investment, and then argued that the capital-arbitrage hypothesis explaining international capital movements was inconsistent with several obvious patterns in the behaviour of MNEs and was unable to explain the causes of FDI. In particular, he gave three reasons for his arguments. First, Hymer argued that once risk and uncertainty, volatile exchange rates and the costs of acquiring information and making transactions were incorporated into portfolio capital-arbitrage theory, many of its predictions, for example, with respect to the cross-border movements of money capital in response to interest rate changes, became invalid. This was because such market imperfections altered the behavioural parameters affecting the conduct and performance of firms and, in particular, their strategy in serving foreign markets. Second, Hymer asserted that FDI involved the transfer of a package of resources including not only capital but also technology, management skills and entrepreneurship. As a result, MNEs were motivated to produce abroad by the expectation of earning an economic rent on the totality of their resources. Third, unlike portfolio investment, the most fundamental characteristic of FDI was that it involved no change in the ownership of resources or rights transferred.

Hymer not only swept aside the capital-arbitrage explanation for FDI but also laid the foundation for a microeconomic explanation of FDI by pointing out that FDI is not randomly distributed among industries, and competitive conditions, in particular those in product markets, clearly influence FDI. Applying industrial organization theory, Hymer pointed out that if foreign MNEs are identical to domestic firms, they will not find it profitable to enter the domestic market, since there are added costs of doing business in another country, including communications and transport costs, higher costs of stationing personnel abroad, language barriers, customs, and being outside the local business and government networks. Therefore, Hymer argued that for MNEs to conduct foreign production, they must possess some kind of firm-specific ownership advantages, such as superior technology or lower costs due to scale economies, which is sufficient to outweigh the disadvantages they face in competing with indigenous firms in the country of production. The ownership advantages may range from the possession of superior technology to ownership of a brand name. Whether the firm will exploit such advantages through licensing or FDI depends on the nature of the advantages and the degree of imperfections in the markets for the advantages it possesses. The higher the imperfections, the greater will be the tendency to undertake FDI and control operations rather than engage in arm's-length transactions.

Following Hymer, many economists have made contributions to the industrial organization explanations of FDI. Among them the work of Kindleberger (1969, 1970, 1974), Caves (1971, 1974a, 1974b, 1982, 1996, 2007) and Dunning (1977, 1980, 1981a, 1981b, 1986, 1988a, 1988b, 1993) is particularly worthy of note. Their studies concentrated on trying to identify and assess the origins and significance of the firm-specific ownership advantages which drive FDI, such as technological capacity, labour skills, industrial structure, product differentiation, marketing skills and organizational capabilities.

Another earlier influential approach in explaining FDI was that of Vernon's product cycle hypothesis (1966). The product cycle hypothesis states that, based on the comparative advantage arising from the pattern of factor endowments, initially a product was invented in the home country with comparative advantage in technology and innovatory capabilities, and produced for the home market in the home country near to both its innovatory activities and markets. At a latter stage of the product cycle, because of a favourable combination of innovation and production advantages offered by the home country, the product was exported to other countries most similar to the home country in demand patterns and supply capabilities. Gradually, as the product becomes standardized or mature and labour becomes a more important ingredient of production costs, the attractions of locating value-adding activities in a foreign, rather than in a domestic, location increase. Eventually, if conditions in the host country are right, the subsidiary could replace exports from the parent company or even export back to the home country. The product cycle hypothesis was the first dynamic interpretation of the determinants of, and relationship between, international trade and foreign production.

In the mid-1970s some economists, for example Buckley and Casson (1976), Lundgren (1977) and Swedenborg (1979), proposed the application of internalization theory to explain the growth of MNEs based on a theory of transactions costs. As Buckley and Casson observed, for MNEs to serve foreign markets through direct investment rather than alternative modes of doing business, such as exporting or licensing, there must have been some internalization advantages for the firm to do so. That is, there must be economies associated with a firm exploiting a market opportunity through internal operations rather than through external arm's-length transactions such as the sale of rights to the firm's intangible assets to other firms. These economies might be associated with costs (including opportunity costs) of contract enforcement or maintenance of quality or other standards. Buckley and Casson noted that, where these costs are absent, firms very often do use licensing or franchising as a means of serving international markets. For example, Coca-Cola franchises the right to market its products in many nations where contract enforcement is not a problem, but the firm directly controls operations in nations where enforcement is a problem.

The internalization approach incorporates the idea of market imperfections identified by Hymer and extends it to provide an explanation for the existence of MNEs across national boundaries. In general, it argues that, faced with imperfections in the markets for intangible assets and imperfect information, firms tend to internalize operations to minimize costs of transactions and increase productive efficiency. While this approach emphasizes the importance of transaction costs resulting from market imperfections, both Buckley (1987) and Casson (1987) have acknowledged the need to integrate location-specific variables with internalization variables to explain the MNE activities.

One organizing framework was proposed by Dunning (1977, 1980, 1981a, 1981b, 1986, 1988a, 1988b, 1993), who synthesized the main elements of various explanations of FDI, and suggested that three conditions all need to be present for a firm to have a strong motive to undertake direct investment. This has become known as the 'OLI' framework: *ownership advantage*, *location advantage* and *internalization advantage*.

A firm's *ownership advantage* could be a product or a production process to which other firms do not have access, such as a patent or blueprint. It could also be some specific intangible assets or capabilities such as technology and information, managerial, marketing and entrepreneurial skills, organizational systems and access to intermediate or final goods markets. Whatever its form, the ownership advantage confers some valuable market power or cost advantage on the firm sufficient to outweigh the disadvantages of doing business abroad. Although ownership advantages are firm specific, they are closely related to the technological and innovative capabilities and the economic development levels of source countries.

In addition, the foreign market must offer a *location advantage* that makes it profitable to produce the product in the foreign country rather than simply produce it at home and export it to the foreign market. Location advantages include not only resource endowments, but also economic and social factors, such as market size and structure, prospects for market growth and the degree of development, the cultural, legal, political and institutional environment, and government legislation and policies.

Finally, the multinational enterprise must have an *internalization advantage*. If a company has a proprietary product or production process and if it is advantageous to produce the product abroad rather than export it, it is still not obvious that the company should set up a foreign subsidiary. Another alternative is to license a foreign firm to produce the product or use the production process. However, because of market failures in the transaction of such intangible assets, the product or process is exploited internally within the firm rather than at arm's length through markets. This is referred to as an internalization advantage.

The generalized predictions of the OLI framework are straightforward. At any given moment in time, the more a country's enterprises – relative to those of other countries – possess ownership advantages, the greater the incentive they have to internalize rather than externalize their use, the more they find it in their interest to exploit them from a foreign location, then the more they are likely to engage in foreign production. The framework also can be expressed in a dynamic form. Changes in the outward or inward direct investment position of a particular country can be explained in terms of changes in the ownership advantages of its enterprises relative to those of other nations; changes in its location advantages relative to those of other countries; and changes in the extent to which firms perceive that these assets are best organized internally rather than by the market (Dunning, 1993).

The Main Implications of Existing Theory for the Present Study

In the above discussion we have reviewed the leading theories of FDI. From Hymer's seminal work to Dunning's OLI paradigm, scholars have made great contributions to the theory of FDI. Among them, Dunning's OLI framework has been the most ambitious and comprehensive explanation of FDI. It is a very useful theoretical framework for this study.

What are the main implications of the existing theories of FDI for this study? According to Dunning's eclectic OLI paradigm, which synthesizes the main elements of the various explanations for FDI, the determinants of FDI can be classified into two groups: supply-side factors and demand-side factors. The supply-side factors are the ownership advantages and the internalization advantages, and the demand-side factors are location advantages.

In terms of the supply-side factors, the investment potential and investment patterns of enterprises are determined by the nature and extent of their possession of ownership advantages and the incentive to internalize the use of their ownership advantages. However, the creation and development of the ownership advantages of enterprises are closely related to their home countries' technological and innovative capabilities and the overall economic development levels. In other words, differences in their technological and innovative capabilities and in their levels of economic development will lead to differences in the ownership advantages of the enterprises of different countries. In general, enterprises from developed source countries with high technological and innovative capabilities and high overall economic development levels will possess not only more ownership advantages in general but also more ownership advantages in the forms of advanced technology, product differentiation, managerial and entrepreneurial skills, and knowledge-based intangible assets in particular. In contrast, for developing source countries, because they have relatively lower technological and innovative capabilities and are at the mid-level of economic development, the ownership advantages possessed by their enterprises not only are relatively fewer in general but also are more concentrated in the forms of labour-intensive production technology, standardized manufactured products and well-established export market networks.

The incentives for enterprises to internalize the use of their ownership advantages through FDI depend on the nature of the ownership advantages and the degree of imperfections in the markets for the ownership advantages they possess. Therefore, the more technology-intensive and the higher the imperfections of the markets are, the stronger the incentives for the enterprises to internalize the use of their ownership advantages through FDI and control operations. Since enterprises in the technology-intensive sector and capital-intensive sector possess more advanced technology and knowledge-based intangible assets than enterprises in the labour-intensive sector, foreign investors in the technology-intensive sector and capital-intensive sector have more incentives to set up wholly owned enterprises than foreign investors in the labour-intensive sector. Also, as pointed out above, since enterprises from the developed source countries possess more technology-intensive and knowledge-based intangible assets than enterprises from the developing source countries, we may expect that enterprises from the developed source countries have greater incentives to internalize the use of their ownership advantages and a stronger tendency to secure control over the business than enterprises from the developing source countries.

One of our main interests in this study is to compare and analyse the differences between the developed and developing source countries and economies investing in China. Therefore, the main implication of this discussion for our present study is that in the case of the developed source countries, which have high technological and innovative capabilities, high overall levels of economic development and possess more ownership advantages in high technology and knowledge-based intangible assets, their investments in China should:

- be relatively more in the technology-intensive and capital-intensive sectors;
- adopt more capital-intensive technologies in production;
- have higher labour productivity;
- be more domestic-market oriented; and
- have a higher propensity to set up wholly owned enterprises.

By comparison, for the developing source countries and economies, being relatively low in technological and innovatory capabilities and overall level of economic development, and possessing more ownership advantages in labour-intensive production technology, standardized manufactured products and well-established international export market networks, their investments in China should:

- be mainly concentrated in the labour-intensive sector;
- use more labour-intensive technologies in production;
- have lower labour productivity;
- be more export oriented; and
- have lower propensity to set up wholly owned enterprises.

In terms of the demand-side factors, a host country's overall attractiveness to FDI is determined by the location advantages it possesses. Because resource endowments are not evenly distributed among countries, and social and economic factors as well as government policies are also different among countries, the attractiveness of host countries to FDI is different. This implies that given the supply-side factors the differences in location advantages of host countries are crucial in determining the distribution of FDI inflows into host countries.

To facilitate the discussion of the location factors affecting FDI inflows, from the host country's point of view, we classify total FDI into two types: market-oriented FDI and export-oriented FDI.

Market-oriented FDI aims to set up enterprises in a particular country to supply goods and services to the local market. This kind of FDI may be undertaken to sustain or protect existing markets or to exploit or promote new markets. The most frequently cited reason for market-oriented FDI is tariff barriers imposed by host country governments. However, studies of the causes of FDI, such as Caves (1971, 1974a, 1974b), have shown that market-oriented FDI is most likely to originate from, and to be found in, those industries characterized by high product differentiation, high absolute capital costs (high barriers to entry), high economies of scale, high multi-plant economies and high entrepreneurial requirements. According to these characteristics, the market size, prospects for market growth and the degree of development of host countries are very important location factors for market-oriented FDI. The general implication is that host countries with larger market size, faster economic growth and a higher degree of economic development will provide more and better opportunities for these industries to exploit their ownership advantages and, therefore, will attract more market-oriented FDI.

Export-oriented FDI aims to use particular and specific resources at a lower real cost in foreign countries and then to export the output produced to the home country or to third countries. The most important location factors for export-oriented FDI are resource endowments. In general, the explanation for export-oriented FDI can be found in an extension of international trade theory. The principle of comparative advantage in international trade theory seeks to explain the commodity composition of trade. It assumes complete immobility of factors of production and finds an explanation of commodity composition of trade in the factor endowment ratios and preference characteristics in different countries. However, factor endowments should not be considered as rigid, especially in developing countries. Many studies have shown that a country's comparative advantage changes over time in the process of its economic development, depending on its relative performance in physical capital and human capital accumulation compared with other countries in the world (Anderson, 1990; Leamer, 1984; Song, 1996). The frequently cited successful examples are the Asian NIEs (Hong Kong, Singapore, South Korea and Taiwan). Modifying the traditional theory of comparative advantage and allowing for the international mobility of some factors of production, for example, capital and technology, and not others like natural resources and human labour, enables location theory to determine the location decisions of FDI. In particular the differential endowment of immobile factors strongly influences such location decisions: those countries endowed with a relative abundance of a particular immobile factor will be the location choice of the production of those commodities that use that factor intensively.

For the developing countries, being relatively abundant in labour resources, FDI will tend to locate in them in order to benefit from the lower wage rates. However, it should be realized that it is not low absolute wages that matter, but low efficiency wages.[11] Thus, it is those developing countries which have put great efforts into investing in and developing human capital that will tend to attract more export-oriented FDI.

Whether export-oriented FDI will tend to produce the final product or just some input depends on the degree of product standardization and the degree to which all stages in the production process of the industry are or can become labour intensive.

This discussion of export-oriented FDI implies:

- export-oriented FDI will tend to be high in developing host countries where efficiency wages are low;
- export-oriented FDI will tend to be high in developing host countries which have a comparative advantage in labour-intensive manufacturing; and
- export-oriented FDI will tend to be high in the industries whose production is relatively labour intensive.

In addition to the location factors discussed above, other location factors such as relative distance, culture, language, government policy, and financial and political stability of host countries, are very important in influencing the distribution of FDI inflows into developing host countries. These will be explained further in the course of our analysis.

In terms of the spillovers of FDI, the supply-side factors – the owner-ship advantages and the internalization advantages – are the main sources of spillovers from FDI to host countries' economies. The general implication is that the more ownership advantages, the more spillovers would be generated from FDI to host countries' economies. However, whether domestic firms of host countries will benefit from spillovers of FDI will also depend on the absorptive capabilities of host countries – the demand-side factors, such as the level of local innovative capacity, the level of infrastructure development (telecommunications and transportation) and particularly the quality of human resources. Therefore, the implication is that, given the supply-side factors (the sources of spillovers of FDI), the higher the level of local absorptive capabilities, the more the benefit received by domestic firms of host countries from spillovers of FDI will be.

By applying mainly the theoretical framework of Dunning's OLI paradigm in explaining FDI, together with the theories of international trade and economic development, we have considered a number of key implications for our study. These implications will enable us to develop a set of hypotheses that may be expected to explain the distribution of FDI inflows into developing countries in general and to explain the location determinants, the investor differences and the economic impacts of FDI in China in particular. These hypotheses will be developed and tested in the following chapters of this study.

STRUCTURE OF THE STUDY

Chapter 2 analyses China's FDI policies. It aims to provide a general policy background for the study of FDI in China. China's FDI policies are very wide-ranging and complex, and it is difficult to cover all aspects in one chapter. Therefore, this chapter mainly focuses on several key policy aspects, including regional open policies, FDI laws and regulations, industrial policies for FDI, foreign exchange management and tax policies for FDI. These reflect not only the evolving changes but also the main features of China's FDI policies during the past three decades.

The eight core chapters are grouped into three parts, each focusing on a specific issue raised in this study, namely, location determinants (Part I), investor differences (Part II) and economic impacts (Part III).

Part I comprises Chapters 3 to 5 and focuses on the investigations and tests of location determinants affecting FDI inflows into developing countries, the impact of FDI inflows into China on FDI inflows into other developing countries, and the provincial distribution of FDI within China.

The study of location determinants in Chapter 3 is at the level of developing countries. At this level the country is the basic unit of analysis to examine the location determinants of FDI and to explain the differences of country distribution of FDI inflows into developing countries. This chapter starts with an introduction to China's performance in attracting FDI inflows during the past three decades and compares this with other developing countries. By doing so it raises the questions: which location factors determine FDI inflows into developing countries; what is the relative performance of China in attracting FDI inflows compared with other developing countries; and has China attracted excessive FDI inflows based on its location characteristics?

To facilitate the analysis and answer these questions, a 'modified' gravity model is developed, which establishes and provides a theoretical norm for FDI inflows from all source countries into each of the developing host countries. Following the principle of the theoretical model, a set of hypotheses which are thought to be important location factors determining FDI inflows and are expected to explain the country distribution of FDI inflows into developing countries is developed. Based on the modified gravity model and the hypotheses, a regression equation is established and then an econometric test of the hypotheses is conducted by using a multiple regression technique with panel data for 50 developing countries over 17 years from 1992 to 2008. Consequently, against the statistically tested empirical norm, the relative performance of China in attracting FDI inflows is evaluated. The issues of whether China's performance in attracting FDI inflows has been especially outstanding as compared with those of other developing countries, and whether China has attracted excessive FDI inflows into its economy are examined and discussed.

Chapter 4 focuses on investigating the impact of FDI inflows into China on FDI inflows into other developing countries. By incorporating the variable of the 'China effect' – FDI inflows into China – into the empirical model developed and tested in Chapter 3, a regression equation is established and the China effect is empirically tested by using a multiple regression technique, first with panel data for 49 developing countries and then with panel data for 18 Asian developing economies over 17 years from 1992 to 2008. Based on the empirical regression results, the impact of FDI inflows into China on FDI inflows into other developing countries and economies is examined, the possible causes of the China effect on FDI inflows into Asian developing economies are explained and, finally, the implications for future FDI inflows into China and Asian developing economies are discussed.

Chapter 5 also adopts the same analytical method developed in Chapter 3, but it focuses the analysis of location determinants of FDI inflows at the level of China's provinces. At this level, the analysis takes each province as the basic location for hosting FDI inflows in order to examine the provincial location determinants and to explain the differences in provincial distribution of FDI inflows within China. The chapter starts with an examination of the provincial distribution of inward FDI, and reveals a situation of significantly uneven provincial distribution. Why has this happened and what are the location factors determining the provincial distribution of FDI inflows into China? To answer these questions, a set of hypotheses relating to the provincial location factors affecting FDI inflows is developed and discussed. An econometric test of the hypotheses is conducted by using a multiple regression technique with panel data for 30 provinces over 20 years from 1986 to 2005. Based on the regression results, the inward FDI attractiveness index is developed for each province and region, and the uneven provincial distribution of FDI inflows is explained. Finally, some policy suggestions are proposed in order to reduce the degree of the uneven provincial distribution of FDI within China.

Part II consists of Chapters 6 and 7 and is devoted to the sources of FDI into China. The analysis focuses on examining and comparing the investor differences in their investment and production behaviour, and seeks to explain the reasons causing these differences among the major investors.

Chapter 6 shifts the analysis of FDI in China from examining the location determinants towards examining the investor differences. It starts with identifying the major investors by examining the composition of FDI sources in China, and then proceeds to examine and explain the variations of the investment intensities of the major source countries and economies in China. The investment intensity index reveals a sharp difference between the developed source countries and the developing source countries and economies in terms of the relative importance of China as a host for their investments as compared with the rest of the world. Which factors explain the variations of the investment intensities of the major source countries and economies in China? Mainly based on the theory of transactions costs, a number of hypotheses are developed to explain the variations of the investment intensities. The hypotheses are tested by applying the pooled ordinary least squares (OLS) and random effects regression techniques with panel data of 34 source countries and economies over the period 1992 to 2008. Finally, based on the regression results, the chapter gives the explanations for the variations of the investment intensities of the major source countries and economies in China.

Chapter 7 continues the investigation and analysis of investor differences started and developed in Chapter 6. However, it turns the analysis towards examining and explaining the differences in investment and production behaviour of the major investors in China. It starts with an examination of the sectoral distribution of FDI in China's economy, and an analysis of the development and structural changes of FDI in China's manufacturing sector, then proceeds to compare and analyse the differences among the major investors in their investment and production behaviours in China's manufacturing sector. To facilitate the analysis, based on data availability and the technological and economic development levels, the major investors are divided into two groups: the overseas Chinese investors (from Hong Kong, Macao and Taiwan) and the foreign country investors (mainly from the Organisation for Economic Co-operation and Development countries). Based on the above groupings, this chapter reveals several main differences in terms of investment pattern, mode of entry, export propensity, capital intensity and labour productivity between the overseas Chinese affiliates and the foreign country affiliates in China's manufacturing sector.

Part III contains Chapters 8 to 10 and is devoted to the impacts of FDI on China's economy. However, among the many possible consequences resulting from FDI, the analysis focuses on examining the contributions of FDI on China's economic growth, the spillover effects of FDI on productivity and exports of China's domestic firms.

Chapter 8 shifts the study of FDI in China from searching for the location determinants of FDI inflows into China and the investor differences in investment and production behaviour to assessing the consequences of the rapid growth of FDI on China's economy, with a particular emphasis on the spillover effects of FDI on China's economic growth. The chapter starts with an overview of the contributions of FDI to China's economy in terms of capital formation and employment creation. Then it identifies the possible channels through which FDI may affect China's economic growth. By using an augmented growth model with a panel dataset containing China's 30 provinces over the period 1986 to 2005, the direct effects (for example, raising output and productivity) and spillover effects (for example, diffusing technology and management skills) of FDI on China's regional economic growth are empirically tested and analysed. Finally, based on the empirical regression results, the contribution of FDI to China's regional economic growth is calculated and the implications for enhancing and accelerating the diffusion of positive spillovers from FDI to China's economy are discussed.

Chapter 9 deepens the analysis of the impacts of FDI on China's economy to the firm level by examining the spillover effects of FDI on domestic firms with a particular emphasis on examining the horizontal technology spillovers of FDI to China's domestic firms' productivity. This chapter first presents a literature review on the productivity spillovers of FDI for domestic firms and reveals the inconsistency between the theoretical prediction and what has been found in many previous empirical studies. Then it discusses the channels through which horizontal technology spillovers of FDI could take place and proposes that there may be a non-linear relationship between horizontal FDI presence and domestic firms' productivity. As a result, an empirical regression equation, with a non-linear function between horizontal FDI presence and domestic firms' productivity, based on the production function is specified and established. After dealing with the selection bias problem from firms' exit and entry with the neighbourhood matching technique and the endogeneity problem with first differencing regression, and controlling the inter-industry linkages between FDI presence and domestic firms (the backward and forward spillovers of FDI), the different sources of FDI (the ratio of the capital from Hong Kong and Taiwan to the capital from other foreign investors), and regional, industrial and time dummy variables, the horizontal spillovers of FDI on the productivity of China's domestic firms are empirically tested and investigated by using the manufacturing firm-level panel data for China during the period 2000 to 2003. Finally, based on the regression results, the turning point (the critical value) of the horizontal industrial FDI share, where the positive horizontal spillovers of FDI will peak, is calculated and the implications for enhancing the positive horizontal spillovers of FDI on China's domestic firms' productivity are discussed.

Chapter 10 continues the investigation of the impact of FDI on China's economy at the firm level, but it turns the analysis towards examining the impacts of FDI on China's exports by focusing on investigating the spillover effects of FDI on China's domestic firms' exports. The chapter starts with a presentation of the remarkable contribution of FDI to China's export expansion during the past three decades. This is followed by a discussion of the main channels by which FDI may promote domestic firms' export activities and a review of empirical studies on export spillovers of FDI on domestic firms' exports. Then it proceeds to investigate the spillover effects of FDI on China's domestic firms' exports. First, the variables of horizontal spillovers, backward spillovers and forward spillovers of FDI at the industry level are specified. Second, to control for firms' entry and exit and their possible impact on the relationship between FDI and domestic firms' exports, the neighbourhood matching technique is used to sort out those domestic firms with the same exporting behaviour. Then an empirical model for the investigation of the spillover effects of FDI on China's domestic firms' exports is specified, in particular, a Heckman two-step procedure regression is combined with the first differencing regression technique to deal with the endogeneity problem associated with firms' fixed effects and the sample selection problem due to domestic firms' non-random selection between exporting and non-exporting behaviours.

Based on the above specifications and the empirical model, using the firm-level census data of China's manufacturing industries during the period 2000 to 2003, after controlling for the impact of firm-specific characteristics of productivity, capital to labour ratio, R&D activities, scale, age and indirect foreign investment of domestic firms, the chapter carries out a series of regressions to investigate the impacts of FDI on China's domestic firms' exports. In searching for the export spillovers from FDI to domestic firms, the study not only examines the horizontal impact but also investigates the impact through backward and forward industrial linkages. In addition, the study examines the impact of different FDI firms in terms of the market orientation on domestic firms' exports. Finally, the chapter provides the interpretations of the regression results and presents some implications for promoting the diffusion of the positive export spillovers from FDI to China's domestic firms.

Chapter 11 serves as the conclusion of this study. It summarizes the main findings of this study, provides some policy implications for China's attraction and utilization of FDI in the near future, and discusses the prospects for FDI inflows into China amid the current global financial and economic crisis.

NOTES

1. However, we should note that this high annual growth rate is also partly because of the very low base of FDI in China in 1979.
2. The four special economic zones are Shenzhen, Zhuhai and Shantou in Guangdong Province, and Xiamen in Fujian Province.
3. See Chapter 2 for more detailed discussion of China's FDI policies and regulations.
4. Dr Guonan Ma from the International Settlement Bank informed the author that he estimated in 1993 that the round-tripping FDI accounted for 25 per cent of China's total FDI inflows in 1992.
5. We discuss the tax incentives and preferential treatments offered by various levels of Chinese governments to FDI in more detail in Chapter 2.
6. Data for provincial FDI inflows are not available after 2005.
7. The Asian NIEs include Hong Kong, Singapore, South Korea and Taiwan.
8. The four ASEAN economies include Indonesia, Malaysia, the Philippines and Thailand.
9. Data for actual FDI inflows by sectors are not available before 1997.
10. According to China's official statistics, foreign direct investment includes foreign investments in equity joint ventures, contractual joint ventures, wholly foreign owned ventures, and joint exploitation, and the minimum share of foreign investment should be equal or above 25 per cent.
11. We discuss the implication of efficiency wages in more detail in Chapter 3.

2. The evolution and main features of China's FDI laws and policies

INTRODUCTION

Since 1979, China has carried out massive economic reforms aimed at the establishment of an open market economy. One of the prominent features of these reforms has been the removal of restrictions on inward FDI in the Chinese economy. From the very beginning, policy reform for FDI has been one of the most important aspects of China's overall economic reforms. For historical and ideological reasons, FDI in China was highly restricted prior to 1978. In order to achieve new objectives of industrialization and economic development, however, China began to relax restrictions on FDI into its domestic economy at the end of 1978. Since 1979, the FDI regime has been liberalized gradually, and a series of policies and laws for FDI has been implemented, aimed at attracting a high level of FDI inflows and accelerating the transfer of technology and modern management skills, as well as at providing foreign exchange.

China's success in attracting FDI inflows into its domestic economy has been closely related to the formation and development of its legal framework and policies for FDI. To understand that success, one must first analyse and understand the evolving changes of China's legal framework and policies towards FDI. Given the total opposition to FDI during the Cultural Revolution period, this policy shift involved the abandonment of established orthodoxy and the development of an entirely new policy framework. Therefore, this chapter analyses several key aspects reflecting the evolving changes to China's FDI policies and laws during the past three decades.

THE BACKGROUND OF CHINA'S OPENING UP TO FDI

The changes to China's policies to inward FDI reflect important political changes.[1] In 1975, when Deng Xiaoping re-emerged from political obscurity, he commissioned the drafting of a series of economic development documents designed to achieve the four modernizations.[2] Some major political initiatives of Deng Xiaoping were particularly expressed in one of the documents, 'Some questions on accelerating industrial development' (Deng, 1984), which was drafted by the State Planning Commission and highlighted by Deng Xiaoping at a State Council meeting held to discuss the document in 1975. The document emphasized three main points. First, there was the need for China to adopt advanced technology from foreign countries and expand international trade. Second, China should introduce and improve modern industrial management methods. Third, China should import technology and equipment for natural resource exploitation by paying with coal and petroleum. The document elaborated that:

> to accelerate the exploitation of coal and petroleum in our country, we may sign long-term contracts with foreign countries and fix several locations of production under conditions of equality and mutual benefit and according to common practices in international trade . . . so that the foreign countries can supply us with complete sets of modern equipment suitable to our needs and we can repay them with coal and petroleum which we produce. (Deng, 1984, p. 47)

These and other major initiatives, as the drafters and particularly Deng Xiaoping believed, were absolutely crucial to China's successful pursuit of the four modernizations. However, these efforts were fiercely attacked by the radicals as 'capitalist' and, eventually, Deng Xiaoping was removed from all his party and government posts.

It is no surprise that Deng Xiaoping reintroduced these ideas immediately after his return to power in 1978. Furthermore, under his leadership, in late 1978 China launched its economic reforms, in which reform of the system of foreign economic interaction was, from the very beginning, one of the most integral parts. The ideas proposed by Deng Xiaoping in 1975 to introduce and acquire advanced technology and management methods from foreign countries were further developed to allow inward FDI into China's domestic economy. Drawing on the experience of other developing countries, particularly those of the East and South-East Asian economies, in attracting and utilizing FDI to accelerate the transfer of advanced technology and therefore to speed up the development of domestic economies, the Chinese leadership recognized that FDI is an effective way to quickly acquire and master advanced technology and equipment from foreign countries without having to make the heavy outlay of foreign exchange that would be involved in outright purchase. Foreign direct investment is also a means of better utilizing China's resources in the absence of domestic capital. Furthermore, FDI is a means of providing the Chinese with valuable experience of modern economic management skills. As a result, the Central Committee of the Chinese Communist Party and the State

Council repeatedly pointed out that China would adopt any methods commonly used in the world to utilize foreign capital to accelerate domestic economic development (Liu et al., 1993). It is clear that the Chinese leadership was politically sincere in its desire to attract FDI, even though FDI might also bring some capitalist influence into China. However, as Deng Xiaoping confidently stated: 'For example, technology, science – even advanced production management is also a sort of science – will be useful in any society or country. We intend to acquire advanced technology, science and management skills to serve our socialist production. And these things as such have no class character' (Deng, 1984, p. 333).[3]

The political endorsement for allowing inward FDI into China in the late 1970s was rationalized by the necessity of achieving a recovery from the economic disruption caused by the Cultural Revolution, and the necessity to capitalize the industrialization programme, which was launched by Mao's successor Hua Guofeng in early 1978 but later substantially revised due to 'overambitious' goals. Although China had made impressive progress in the technical level of its industry after 1949 (especially the phenomenal achievements made in the aerospace industry), in 1980 the general technological level in basic industries was still 15 to 20 years behind that of the USA, Japan and Western Europe. In other specific fields, such as the aircraft and automotive industries, the gap was as much as 20 to 30 years. All this prompted the adoption of what is termed the 'Great Leap Outward' (*Yang Yuejin*) policy, a massive acquisition of Western machinery and technology which, unfortunately, produced the largest trade deficit in China's history. As the trade deficit built up, foreign exchange reserves were scaled down. China's foreign reserves dropped sharply from US$6.22 billion (including holdings of gold) in June 1978 to only US$1.3 billion, plus an estimated value of US$2.23 billion of holdings of gold, at the end of 1979. This was equivalent to approximately five and a half months' imports from the non-communist world in 1978 (Chen, 1982). In addition, the profits of state enterprises dropped dramatically, and problems generated by the shortage of experienced engineers and the lack of infrastructure, which limited China's capacity to absorb technologies, began to surface.[4] The search for foreign capital seemed to be inevitable. A package deal that provides technology, management skills and access to international markets, as well as capital, was naturally the best choice for China's decision-makers in resolving these immediate problems.

Evidently, the fundamental shift of the Communist Party's political dominance from 'class struggle' towards 'socialist economic construction' and, even more significantly, the urgent demand for economic development, greatly facilitated the initial changes of China's policy to inward FDI into its domestic economy. As a result, at the Second Session of the Fifth National People's Congress in July 1979, the Law of the People's Republic of China on Joint Ventures Using Chinese and Foreign Investment[5] was passed, granting FDI a legal status in China.

THE EVOLUTION OF CHINA'S OPENING POLICIES TO FDI

Uneven Regional Opening Policies to FDI

Following the adoption of the 'open door policy' in late 1978 and the issue of the Equity Joint Venture Law in 1979, China established four SEZs, Shenzhen, Zhuhai, Xiamen and Shantou, located in Guangdong and Fujian Provinces in 1980. The creation of the four SEZs not only symbolized the beginning of China's economic reform but also constituted an integral part of the overall open door policy. However, the interesting question is why was it necessary to set up SEZs when China had decided to implement the open door policy nationwide? First, one of the political purposes of the Chinese government to promote the SEZs lay in its strategic plans to resume sovereignty over Hong Kong, which is adjacent to Shenzhen, by 1997. It was believed that the SEZs could contribute positively to the peaceful handover of Hong Kong to China. Second, the geographic proximity of the SEZs, which are the original home of many overseas Chinese, to Hong Kong, Macao, Taiwan and ASEAN, makes it possible for China to exploit national advantages by using the overseas Chinese business network to accumulate capital, productive technology and management skills, and to get access to the international market. Third, at the very beginning of carrying out market-oriented economic reforms, the establishment of a small number of selected SEZs also served as a laboratory for China's overall economic reforms. The idea was to introduce the successful experience drawn from the actual practice of market-oriented economic reforms in a small number of SEZs into other areas and, meanwhile, to make it easily controlled if something went wrong by keeping the effects within bounds. In addition, from the perspective of their spatial diffusion effect, the establishment of the SEZs could be viewed as a pioneering effort for the more extensive operation of the uneven development strategy that was implemented in 1988. Fourth, the creation of SEZs was also aimed at providing a favourable investment environment for foreign investors, while trying out preferential foreign investment policies to be implemented at a later stage in the rest of the country. Finally, but equally important, was the reformers' strategic consideration of reducing possible political resistance from the conservatives against market-oriented economic reforms in order to carry out the overall economic reform scheme more smoothly and effectively.

Drawing on the experience of the export-processing zones established in Taiwan, South Korea, and other developing countries and economies, the SEZs in China have the multiple functions of free-trade zones and export-processing zones. The main objective of the SEZ policy was to attract FDI by offering favourable terms and a good business climate. As an initial experiment in the market-oriented economic reform, the SEZs were granted unique freedoms to manage and operate their economies on a market basis and were allowed to offer concessionary tax policies to foreign investors. Among the preferential policies for FDI firms in the SEZs, for example, all FDI firms were granted 15 per cent reduction of income tax, and FDI firms engaged in production and scheduled to operate for a period of ten years or more were exempted from income tax in the first and second profit-making years and allowed a 50 per cent reduction of income tax in the following three years. The FDI firms were also granted exemption from income tax on the remitted share of profits, exemption from export duties and from import duties for equipment, instruments and apparatus for producing export products, and the easing of entry and exit formalities (Liu et al., 1993). With the establishment and implementation of a series of laws, regulations, and special open policies, especially those concerning FDI firms, the SEZs were granted the highest priority and freedom for economic development.

In addition to the concessionary tax policies for foreign investors, the four SEZs and their home provinces, Guangdong and Fujian, were also awarded financial subsidies in the form of fiscal and foreign exchange revenue contracts. Beginning in 1980, Guangdong and Fujian were awarded five-year fiscal contracts permitting them to retain almost all of the taxes and industrial profits generated by firms in their jurisdiction. In contrast, the three provincial-level cities of Beijing, Tianjin and Shanghai were still required to turn over between 63 and 88 per cent of their revenues. In terms of the special policy of foreign exchange retention, the SEZs were allowed to retain all of the hard currency they earned from trade, in contrast to the average of 25 per cent allowed to other localities. Guangdong and Fujian also were granted special foreign exchange retention rates higher than those for other provinces (Shirk, 1994). The special financial incentives for SEZs, Guangdong and Fujian provinces not only motivated local officials to develop their local economies in a profit-oriented manner, but also greatly facilitated the export expansion and overall rapid economic growth of the SEZs and Guangdong and Fujian provinces.

The economic success and the experience with FDI in the SEZs greatly increased the confidence of the Chinese government. However, owing to the small size and the specific location of the four SEZs, the desired diffusion effect was geographically limited. In addition, the pressure from other provinces in demanding the same special policies granted to SEZs increased. In February 1984 when Deng Xiaoping visited Shenzhen, Zhuhai and Xiamen SEZs, he pointed out: 'for us to establish SEZs and adopt open door policies, we must have a clear guiding ideology that is not to constrain but to release'. He also said: 'in addition to the existing SEZs, we can consider opening several more areas and port cities, such as Dalian and Qingdao. These areas will not be named SEZs but can apply some of the special policies implemented in SEZs' (Liu et al., 1993, p. 865). In order to implement Deng's speech, to prove further the government's commitment to the stability, continuity and long-term nature of the open door policy, and to tap fully the comparative advantage in encouraging the inflows of FDI, advanced technology and management skills, in May 1984 the Chinese government announced the opening up and extension of the concept of SEZs to another 14 coastal cities and Hainan Island.[6] These coastal open cities and the SEZs virtually form a coastal belt which, from a geographical viewpoint, is important not only for linkage with foreign markets but also for its wider connection with the massive domestic inland areas. First, this coastal belt physically constitutes a significant portion of the Pacific Rim, which makes it well positioned, from north to south, to attract FDI from Japan, South Korea, Taiwan and the South-East Asian countries, as well as from the USA, Canada and Europe. With their relatively more sophisticated existing labour force, technical capabilities and infrastructures, it was hoped that quicker, better and more sustainable returns in terms of capital formation, technological progress, structural transformation and overall economic development would be gained, and at lower cost (Wei, 1994).

The coastal open cities were permitted to offer tax incentives for FDI firms similar to, but less generous than, those offered in the SEZs. The coastal open cities, however, were encouraged to establish Economic and Technological Development Zones (ETDZs) that could offer terms as generous as those offered in the SEZs. The tax incentives offered to the FDI firms in the coastal open cities include mainly: (1) 15 per cent income tax reduction which is only to FDI firms that are technology or knowledge intensive and intend to develop energy, transportation and ports construction, to those that have an investment exceeding US$30 million with a low profit margin, or to those productive-type projects set up within the ETDZs; (2) 20 per cent income tax reduction that applies to those FDI firms that do not meet the foregoing requirements yet are involved in one of the categorized sectors, including machine building, electronics, metallurgy, chemicals, building materials, light industry, textiles, packaging, medical equipment, pharmaceuticals, construction, agriculture, forestry, animal husbandry, aquaculture, and related processing industries; (3) exemption from customs duties, import taxes and value-added tax with respect to production and management equipment, raw and semi-finished materials, components, spare parts and packaging materials for producing export products, and telecommunications and office equipment (Liu et al., 1993). These tax incentives plus the local government's infrastructure investments, in areas such as transport, water and electricity, telecommunications and special land use privileges, proved to be a great inducement to foreign investors.

The encouragement to establish the ETDZs in the coastal open cities has several basic considerations. First, drawing from the experience of the first four SEZs, the ETDZs were encouraged to build infrastructure and provide energy, telecommunications and other basic public facilities necessary for production and new technology development enterprises. This can greatly improve the investment environment and facilitate the economic development of the open cities. Second, by offering parallel investment incentives in the ETDZs along the coastline from north to south, foreign investors were provided more opportunities to locate their ventures where the transaction cost was least. Third, by expressly designating the goals of the ETDZs, the Chinese government wanted to make it clear that, while the coastal open cities should effectively utilize FDI and foreign technologies to improve and upgrade the industrial and technical capabilities of the existing firms and gradually spread out to the inland areas, their primary objective was to concentrate on the establishment of more technology-intensive productive projects through FDI.

From the perspective of regional development and the intended eventual diffusion effect, the coastal belt is believed able to spread its direct and indirect influence to the immediate inland and to more regions. Indeed, for all inland provinces, the coastal belt provides a window through which economic vitality in utilizing FDI can be transmitted back to the home provinces in the form of investment, technology transfer, information services and the training of personnel.

In order to attract further FDI and to speed up the diffusion process, in May 1985, three 'development triangles' – the Yangzi River Delta region (around Shanghai), the Pearl River Delta region (around Guangzhou) and the Min Nan Delta region (around Xiamen) – were designated as coastal economic open areas and granted most of the FDI preferential policies implemented in the 14 coastal open cities. Following the trend, the expansion continued to include Liaodong and Shandong peninsulas as coastal economic open areas in 1988 (Liu et al., 1993). These developments were intended primarily to spread benefits from SEZs and coastal open cities to the surrounding regions. It was also an effort to accommodate the growing interest of foreign investors, either because of simple proximity or because of historical linkages, to establish or expand their operations in China. Indeed, the major foreign investors do show strong regional investment biases. In the Pearl River Delta region, ethnic ties play an important part in the location decisions of investors from Hong Kong, Macao and the South-East Asian countries, while in the Min Nan Delta region, more Taiwanese investors are involved. On the other hand, South Korean and Japanese companies apparently find both the Liaodong and Shandong peninsulas more attractive, while the Yangzi River Delta region, with its relatively more developed economy and superior foreign connections, is the destination of most large corporations of the USA, Western Europe and Japan.

In order to realize further the potential in attracting FDI and develop an externally oriented economy, in early 1988 another large step towards expanding the open policies for FDI, termed the 'coastal development strategy', was taken by the Chinese government to extend the open policy to the entire coastal areas, with a total population of over 200 million. The document on Coastal Development Strategy jointly issued by the Chinese Communist Party Central Committee and the State Council states: 'we must continue to expand the open policies, accelerate the development of externally-oriented economy in the coastal areas, and actively participate in international exchange and competition, so that the economic development and prosperity of the coastal areas can bring the development of the whole national economy' (Liu et al., 1993, p. 866). In this policy, the then Party General Secretary Zhao Ziyang defended the concept of unbalanced growth by arguing that economic and cultural differences between the coastal and inland areas made it impossible for all parts of the country to develop at the same speed; therefore, the coastal areas should be allowed to move ahead by using their better labour, communications and infrastructure, and scientific and technological capacity to attract foreign business and expand exports (Shirk, 1994). The coastal development strategy stressed two main points. First, it would develop labour-intensive industries in the coastal areas and, second, these labour-intensive processing industries must base their products for export on imported raw materials. This is described by Zhao Ziyang as 'two heads outside, massive flow in and massive flow out' (*liangtuo zai wai, da jin da chu*). This strategy effectively brought all 11 coastal provinces and municipalities together to acquire foreign capital, technology, raw materials and international market opportunities. It enabled China to take advantage of its abundant cheap labour endowment and to increase significantly the ability of its manufacturing sector to compete in the international market.

With the implementation of the coastal development strategy, many special open zones were established in the coastal provinces and municipalities. In particular, Hainan Island became a province and China's fifth – and the largest – SEZ in April 1988, and later the concepts of SEZ and ETDZ were extended to the Shanghai Pudong New Economic and Technological Development Zone in June 1990 (Liu et al., 1993).

The implementation of the uneven regional open strategy for FDI, from the SEZs to coastal cities and then to the entire coastal areas, has enabled the coastal region to gain more benefits than other regions, not only in the form of fiscal priority and foreign exchange earnings, but also in the acquisition of capital, technology, modern management skills and the opportunity to access the international market. It is also true that there have been some beneficial effects on the inland economy. However, not only has the process of diffusion from the coastal region to the inland areas been slow, but also the outflow of skilled workers, technical personnel and capital from the inland areas to the coastal region has been increasing. Perhaps, more important is that the coastal region has been getting more freedom in economic decision-making from the central government than the inland regions. Consequently, the gap in economic development and income level between the coastal region and the inland areas has enlarged since the late 1980s. To deal with these problems, in the 1990s the Chinese government gradually moved the implementation of the open policies for FDI towards a more level playing field throughout China. This major policy move was especially enhanced by Deng Xiaoping's call for deeper, faster and wider economic reform and liberalization.

Nationwide Implementation of Opening Policies to FDI

In the spring of 1992, during his famous tour to the southern coastal economically opened areas and SEZs, Deng Xiaoping explicitly declared his support for the successful economic development assisted by FDI and expressed a desire to see the pace of liberalization quickened. Deng Xiaoping's landmark visit set the scene not only for a decisive move away from a command economy in favour of a market-oriented economy, but also for a move from the uneven regional priority towards nationwide implementation of open policies to FDI. Consequently, the Chinese government reaffirmed the adherence of the open door policy and launched another massive drive to attract FDI.

To facilitate the implementation of this policy, a series of measures with regard to FDI have been taken not only to address the existing unfair competition between the coastal and inland regions, but also to make more concessions to attract foreign investors. First, the application of preferential policies to FDI will gradually shift from regional priority to accommodating national and local industrial development policies. For example, as long as they are in line with state or local industrial policy and involve high or new technology, any FDI project is entitled to the same preferential treatment as applied in the ETDZs, regardless of its location. Second, 52 cities, including all the inland provincial capitals (except Lhasa in Tibet and Urumqi in Xinjiang) and the major cities along the Yangzi River, became open to foreign investors. The preferential policies granted to the 14 coastal cities will also be applied in these cities. Third, more than 15 border cities and counties in the south-west, north-west, north and north-east of China were declared open border cities. Some were authorized to offer coastal FDI preferential policies, while others were mandated to reopen or expand their existing border trade ties with neighbouring countries or to set up Economic Development Zones (EDZs). Fourth, some services industries, such as aviation, telecommunications, banking and retail trade, were opened to FDI participation in a limited and experimental fashion. For example, some designated coastal cities are allowed to host FDI banking, finance and retail entities. Shanghai, as a major commercial centre, is also permitted to host an FDI insurance company. Fifth, to develop further foreign trade and processing industries in the coastal areas, more duty-free zones are to be established. Sixth, the government allows foreign business people, either those with an intention to set up FDI firms in a later stage or land developers, to buy land use rights for building infrastructure facilities, including residential, commercial, industrial and recreational real estate (Liu et al., 1993; UNCTAD, *World Investment Report*, 1994; Wei, 1994). As a result, with the implementation of these new policies, during the first nine months of 1992, almost 2000 EDZs were set up, and a large proportion of them were located in inland areas (Shirk, 1994).

The EDZ policy was extremely popular throughout China, since the local officials saw it not only as a way to gain access to international business but also as a means of gaining benefit and privilege. As a result, the establishment of EDZs eventually went out of control. The uncontrolled spread of EDZs created some unintended negative consequences, such as economic overheating, shortages of funds, energy, transport and raw materials, the appropriation of good farmland for factories, and competitive cutting of tax rates and land prices to attract foreign investors (Shirk, 1994). All of these led to the 1993 rectification of all existing EDZs and the requirement of central approval for all new EDZs in order to solve the above-mentioned problems and ensure the healthy development of FDI.

To boost economic growth and, therefore, to reduce the gap of economic development between the coastal region and the central and western regions, the Chinese government launched the 'west development strategy' in 1998. According to the west development strategy, the areas include 12 provinces, municipality and autonomous regions, which are Sichuan, Chongqing, Guizhou, Yunnan, Gansu, Shaanxi, Qinghai, Ningxia, Xinjiang, Tibet, Guangxi and Inner Mongolia, and two prefectures, which are Enshi of Hubei Province and Xiangxi of Hunan Province.

The west development strategy emphasizes infrastructure development, environmental protection, industrial structural readjustment, development of sciences and education, and economic reform and openness. To realize these goals, four concrete measures are to be implemented. First, the central government will dramatically increase investment in the central and western regions, especially to increase transfer payment from central government budget. Second, the central and western regions will increase the degree of openness and implement more open policies, especially open more areas and sectors to FDI. Third, enterprises, especially FDI firms, in the coastal region are encouraged to invest and to do business in the central and western regions. Fourth, the central and western regions will enhance the development of sciences and education in order to attract and to improve human resources.

To improve the investment environment and accelerate economic growth in the western region, China will invest heavily in infrastructure development in the western region. According to the west development strategy, the major infrastructure projects include, for example, investing 120 billion yuan in highway and road construction from 2000 to 2020, investing 100 billion yuan in large and medium railway projects from 2000 to 2005, creating a hydro-electricity generation base in the western region and constructing a national electricity supply network in order to transport electricity from the western region to the eastern region from 2000 to 2015, investing 300 billion yuan in a gas pipeline construction to transport natural gas from the western region to the eastern region from 2000 to 2007, and constructing more airports in the western region.

To attract more FDI inflows into the central and western regions, the Chinese government has issued a series of preferential policies. These preferential policies for FDI in the central and western regions are summarized in Box 2.1.

Undoubtedly, the west development strategy and the further opening up of the central and western regions not only provide great opportunities for foreign investors, but also will accelerate economic growth in the central and western regions.

The Chinese approach of gradually extending regional openness to

BOX 2.1 PREFERENTIAL POLICIES FOR FDI IN THE CENTRAL AND THE WESTERN REGIONS

(1) FDI which can utilize the advantages of human and natural resources of the central and the western regions and is consistent with national industrial development policy can be classified as an encouraged category, and therefore, enjoy the preferential treatment of tariff free and value added tax exemption for imported equipment and technology.

(2) Approval conditions and degree of market openness for FDI projects under the restricted category or subject to foreign ownership control can be more open in the central and the western regions than in the coastal region.

(3) Central government will prioritize the establishment of a group of key projects in the central and western regions, including agriculture, water conservancy, transport, energy, raw materials and environment protection, to attract FDI, and will provide full support for complementary funds and other related measures.

(4) Large- and medium-sized state-owned enterprises and military enterprises transferring to civilian purpose in the central and western regions are encouraged to attract FDI to participate in technology innovation.

(5) FDI firms in the coastal region are encouraged to invest in the central and western regions. The invested enterprises can enjoy corresponding preferential treatment if the share of foreign investors' investment exceeds 25 per cent.

(6) The experiment permitted by the central government to open new sectors and industries to FDI can be carried out in the coastal region and in the central and western regions simultaneously. The provincial capital cities of the central and western regions can carry out experiments to open commerce, foreign trade and tourist agency to FDI. FDI in the provincial capital cities, border cities, cities along the Yangzi River, ETDZs, state high and new technological development zones and Shaanxi Yangling

agricultural development zone of the central and western regions will be granted the same preferential policies. Provincial authorities in the central and western regions will be empowered to authorize FDI worth up to US$30 million.

(7) Starting from 1 January 2000, FDI firms classified as an encouraged category located in the central and western regions can enjoy a 15 per cent enterprise income tax rate for three years after the expiry of the current preferential taxation policies. For enterprises which are at the same time regarded as technology advanced enterprises or export-oriented enterprises and whose export value of the year reaches more than 70 per cent of the total output value, enterprise income tax can be collected at a tax rate reduced by half, but the reduced tax rate should not be lower than 10 per cent.

(8) Foreign banks are encouraged to set up a representative office or set up a bank branch in the central and western regions.

(9) The central government has issued the Catalogue of Advantaged Industries for Foreign Investment in the Central-West Region.

Source: Office of the West Development Leading Group of the State Council (2000).

FDI has proved relatively successful in a number of aspects. First, the selective establishment of SEZs, beginning with a small number and gradually adding more, effectively gained nationwide support for the market-oriented economic reform drive. Second, the fast economic growth and development in SEZs and the coastal provinces not only provided the Chinese government with valuable experience in market-oriented economic reform, but also provided a clear demonstration to the inland areas. Third, the increasing economic ties between the coastal and the inland regions created significant benefits for both regions. However, the increasing inequalities between the coastal and the inland regions, due partly to the implementation of the uneven regional development strategy for FDI, cannot be ignored. Therefore, it seems necessary for the Chinese government to offer more preferential policies to the inland areas to help them attract FDI. As mentioned above, the development of a strategy to open the areas alongside the borders, alongside the river and alongside the coast, and the implementation of the west development strategy, are clearly a demonstration of this effort. The emerging pattern is one in which the coast, the Yangzi Valley, and all the inland provincial capitals develop more quickly and act as channels for capital, technology, and information for their respective hinterlands, but they still rely largely on their hinterlands for labour, energy and materials. Thus, we will see a constant spread of the simulative effects of FDI through the expansion of industrial activities to additional regions of the country.

Increasing Openness to FDI after WTO Accession

In December 2001, after 15 years of extensive negotiations, China entered the WTO. China's accession to the WTO is widely regarded as a major milestone in the development of the Chinese economy as well as the multilateral trading system. China made extensive commitments to the WTO to bring its economy into harmony with the rules of the WTO.

In goods, China must progressively lower its tariffs and phase out nontariff measures. China's simple average tariff rate dropped from 42.9 per cent in 1992 to 15.3 per cent at the beginning of 2002, and further reduced to 9.8 per cent in 2010.

In services, China made substantial commitments to the WTO to reduce restrictions on trade in services. Among the WTO members, China made the most commitments in terms of the number of service sectors open to international trade and FDI. However, China is taking a step-by-step approach to implement its commitments. In most of the service sectors, especially in telecommunications, banking and insurance, wholesale and retail, storage and transportation, China will fulfil its commitments in three to five years after China's accession to the WTO.

In intellectual property rights, China agreed to fully implement the General Agreement on Trade-Related Aspects of Intellectual Property Rights (TRIPS) to provide intellectual property rights protection and enforcement.

In FDI, China committed to comprehensively implement the Agreement on Trade-Related Investment Measures (TRIMs) after entering into the WTO. In particular, China's main commitments relating to FDI include the following.[7]

General commitments

- China would treat domestically produced and imported products the same, apply non-discriminatory laws and policies to all enterprises in China, eliminate dual prices practice and remove differences in treatment accorded to goods produced for sale in China versus those produced for export.

- China would ensure that all SOEs make purchases and sales based solely on commercial considerations and that the enterprises of other WTO members would have an opportunity to compete for sales and to make purchases from the SOEs on non-discriminatory terms and conditions.
- The Chinese government would not impose, apply or enforce laws, regulations or measures relating to technology transfer that were inconsistent with WTO rules and agreements on investment and intellectual property rights.
- China pledged to apply pricing policies on a non-discriminatory basis and outlined steps it would take to make such policies transparent. In addition, China would not use pricing policies for the purposes of giving protection to domestic industries and services providers.
- China pledged to establish independent tribunals, contact points and procedures for prompt review of administrative decisions and measures relating to the implementation of China's WTO commitments.
- China would ensure that all taxes and tariffs are applied on the basis of non-discrimination, and that special tariff reductions and exemptions on imports would apply on most favoured nation (MFN) basis.
- China agreed to eliminate all export subsidies that were contingent on export performance or upon the use of domestic goods over imported goods.
- China would eliminate foreign exchange balancing and trade balancing requirements, and remove government rules on foreign investment requiring technology transfer, local content, research and development, and export performance requirements. In addition, government approval of investment and importation would not be conditional on performance requirements by government officials or subject to secondary conditions. Permission for investment, import licences, quotas and tariff-rate quotas (TRQs) would be granted without regard to the existence of competing Chinese domestic suppliers.
- China would gradually eliminate a variety of production restrictions on motor vehicles, raise the limit (over time) of motor vehicle investment that can be approved at the provincial level and remove the 50 per cent foreign equity limit for joint ventures upon accession.

- Provide full trading and distribution rights, including the ability to provide service auxiliary to distribution for foreign firms in China.
- Open service sectors, including distribution, value-added telecommunications, insurance, banking, securities and professional services (including legal, accountancy, taxation, management consultancy, architecture, engineering, urban planning, medical and dental, and computer-related services). China would expand (over various transitional periods) the scope of allowed services and gradually remove geographical restrictions on foreign service providers.
- Acceleration of liberalization time frame, expansion of permitted ownership, and increased market access for various service sectors.
- Lifting of joint-venture restrictions on large department stores and chain stores.

Specific sectoral commitments

Motor vehicle industry

- Allowing non-bank foreign financial institutions to provide automobile financing.
- Commitments regarding importation, distribution, sale, and maintenance and repair of automobiles.
- Freedom to determine product range within two years of accession.
- Reduction of red tape, as provincial authorities will be empowered to authorize investments in the sector worth up to US$150 million (currently US$30 million) four years after accession.
- Wholly foreign-owned enterprises will be allowed in engine manufacturing.
- Removal of additional restrictions on the operations of foreign auto joint ventures in China.

Telecommunications

- 49 per cent foreign ownership in the first year and 50 per cent in the second year of accession in value-added and paging service investment.
- 49 per cent foreign ownership in six years in international and domestic mobile service.
- Upon accession up to 25 per cent, within one year of accession up to 35 per cent and within three years of accession up to 49 per cent of foreign ownership in local mobile operators.

Insurance

- 50 per cent foreign ownership for life insurance on accession.
- 51 per cent foreign ownership for non-life insurance on accession and wholly foreign-owned subsidiaries in two years after accession.
- Reinsurance will be completely open upon accession.
- Grant of seven new licences (five life insurance and two non-life insurance).
- Additional two companies will be allowed to open in a second city.
- Insurance brokers: upon accession up to 50 per cent equity, majority control within three years and all restrictions will be removed within five years.
- Geographic restrictions until two years after accession.

Distribution and auxiliary service

- Over three years, distribution rights will be provided for rental and leasing, air courier, freight forwarding, storage and restricted sectors such as wholesale, transportation, maintenance and repair.
- All restrictions on provision of service auxiliary to distribution will be phased out over three to four years, such as warehousing, advertising, technical testing and analysis, and packing service.
- Large retailers (at least 20 000 square meters or more than 30 outlets) will no longer be limited to 50 per cent equity participation.

Tourism

- Hotel operators will be allowed to set up wholly foreign-owned hotels within four years after accession, and majority ownership possible upon accession.
- Capital requirements will be gradually reduced to parity with local firms upon accession, and minimum annual turnover required to qualify as foreign investor will be reduced by 20 per cent to US$40 million.

Audio-visual service

- 49 per cent foreign participation in joint ventures engaged in the distribution of video and sound recordings.
- Foreigners will be allowed to invest in movie theatres but with foreign investment up to 49 per cent only.

China has made substantial commitments to the WTO in reducing foreign investment barriers and in liberalizing its FDI regime, which will certainly provide great opportunities for foreign investors to invest and operate business in China. Therefore, China's accession to the WTO would have a positive impact on China's FDI policy regime, particularly in the aspects of national treatment and transparency. Meanwhile, it also would help China to improve competition policies, industrial policies and intellectual property rights protection and enforcement.

THE DEVELOPMENT OF CHINA'S FDI LAWS AND REGULATIONS

According to China's laws and regulations, foreign investors can choose three main forms to invest in China, namely, equity joint ventures, cooperative joint ventures and wholly foreign-owned enterprises. In the 1990s, some new forms of FDI were gradually allowed to be established in China, such as a limited company with foreign investment, foreign-invested holding companies and build-operate-transfer (BOT). Since 2003, foreign investment through cross-border mergers and acquisitions (M&As) has also been permitted in a limited fashion in China. During the past three decades, China's approach to the management of the types of FDI firms has passed from restriction and control to encouragement and regulation in three broad phases.

The First Phase: 1979 to 1989

The Equity Joint Venture Law issued in 1979 was China's first law permitting and governing the establishment and operations of foreign economic entities in its territory since 1949. The law contains only 15 articles and is more like a series of political declarations allowing the legal entry of FDI and providing a statutory basis for the establishment of equity joint ventures on Chinese territory. The Equity Joint Venture Law explicitly states that the establishment of an equity joint venture must be on the principle of equality and mutual benefit, and that all the activities of a joint venture must be governed by the laws, decrees and pertinent rules and regulations of the People's Republic of China. Although the Equity Joint Venture Law is fairly general, with a few basic principles, it does provide a fundamental guideline for the establishment, operation, management and termination of equity joint ventures.

To improve the shortcomings of the Equity Joint Venture Law and to accommodate the needs of foreign investors, in September 1983 the

Chinese government issued the Regulations for the Implementation of the Law of the People's Republic of China on Chinese-Foreign Equity Joint Ventures.[8] Compared with the Equity Joint Venture Law, the implementing regulations provided greater details on all aspects of equity joint venture operations. The adoption of the implementing regulations greatly improved the investment climate and increased the confidence of foreign investors.

The issue of the SEZ Regulations in 1980 not only announced the creation of the four SEZs but also permitted the establishment of wholly foreign-owned enterprises within them. As the SEZ Regulations state:

> in order to develop external economic cooperation and technical exchanges and promote the socialist modernization programme, in the special economic zones, foreign citizens, overseas Chinese, compatriots in Hong Kong and Macao and their companies and enterprises are encouraged to open factories or set up enterprises and other establishments with their own investment, and their interests shall be legally protected. (Chu, 1987, p. 79).

Unlike the equity joint ventures, which the Chinese government seemed to have greater confidence in dealing with and was willing to launch on a national scale, the wholly foreign-owned enterprises were a lot more problematic ideologically and politically. Therefore, wholly foreign-owned enterprises were only permitted in the SEZs in the initial stage of China's foreign investment drive. To allow wholly foreign-owned enterprises to operate in the areas beyond the SEZs, China first had to allow the coexistence of a private sector in its socialist economy. Following a long-lasting and vigorous debate,[9] finally in 1984 the Chinese government formally announced that the private sector is a supplementary part of socialist economy, and granted the private economy legal status. With this major policy shift, the first wholly foreign-owned enterprise outside the SEZs was set up in Shanghai by 3M Company of the USA in 1984 and commenced operation in 1985 (Chu, 1987). By the end of 1985, more than 120 wholly foreign-owned enterprises had been established (*Beijing Review*, 1986).

In 1986, two important legal documents were issued by the Chinese government. One was the Law of the People's Republic of China on Enterprises Operated Exclusively with Foreign Capital,[10] and the other was the Provisions of the State Council on the Encouragement of Foreign Investment.[11] The adoption of these two laws was an important step forward in the evolution of Chinese regulatory framework relating to FDI.

After a trial period, in April 1986 the Law of the People's Republic of China on Enterprises Operated Exclusively with Foreign Capital was passed at the Fourth Session of the Sixth National People's Congress. This law specifies that China permits foreign firms, other economic entities or individuals to set up enterprises exclusively with foreign capital in China and protects the lawful rights and interests of wholly foreign-owned enterprises.

The issue of the Foreign Enterprise Law was needed by both the foreign investors and the Chinese side. From the perspective of foreign investors, there are a lot of reasons for foreign investors to prefer to create wholly owned ventures over joint ventures. However, two are the most important. One is to maintain maximum operating independence from Chinese participation and, therefore, to have a high degree of control over financing, marketing, pricing, the production schedule, quality control, purchase of materials, technology employed, and even external relations of various subsidiaries. Another important reason is to access fully all corporate resources and technology from the parent company and to more effectively protect their technologies. This point is especially important when the foreign enterprises are in technology-intensive industries.

From the Chinese perspective, among the determining factors, there are also two most important reasons to allow the establishment of wholly foreign-owned enterprises. The first is to increase China's competitiveness in the world FDI market by providing foreign investors with more entry alternatives to invest in China. This is particularly important considering the growing initiatives of other developing countries, especially the East and South-East Asian economies, to attract FDI. The second important reason is to accelerate the introduction of new and high-technology products through local production by wholly foreign-owned enterprises. This is consistent with China's industrial and technological development strategy, since it can both enhance China's technological development and reduce foreign exchange expenditure through import substitution.

Following legal permission for the operation of wholly foreign-owned enterprises on a nationwide scale, another major policy move towards favouring FDI was taken by the Chinese government in order to attract more FDI inflows into its domestic economy. Like any developing country, China was well aware of the importance of adopting policies to attract and to control FDI properly. Incentives for FDI were mainly offered in the form of tax holidays, tax reductions and import tax exemption. However, the growing and sustainable competitiveness of neighbouring Asian economies for FDI, combined with their liberalization measures, was a real concern to China in its efforts to attract FDI. In order to improve the investment environment, to increase its competitiveness and to accommodate the interests of foreign investors, in October 1986 China issued the Provisions of the State Council on the Encouragement of Foreign Investment. The Encouragement Provisions were intended to improve the investment environment, facilitate the absorption of FDI, introduce advanced technology, improve product quality, expand exports in order to generate foreign exchange and develop the national economy. The Encouragement Provisions offered a series of incentives to FDI, of which the more important ones included: (1) encouraging foreign investors to set up equity joint ventures, cooperative joint ventures and wholly foreign-owned ventures within China's territory; (2) granting special preferences to 'export-oriented' and 'technologically advanced' FDI firms, including reduction of land use fees and certain subsidies to be paid to labour, preferential tax treatment, and priorities in obtaining water, electricity and other infrastructure services in short supply; (3) establishing a limited foreign currency exchange market for FDI firms and (4) guaranteeing the right of autonomy of FDI firms in management and production decision-making. The adoption of the Encouragement Provisions was a major effort by the Chinese government to encourage FDI by offering incentives. It also demonstrated increased willingness to make greater accommodation for FDI activities through regulatory means. In order to implement the Encouragement Provisions more effectively, the central government issued implementing regulations, and as a combined effort the local governments at provincial and municipal levels subsequently also issued similar regulations.

In 1988, nearly nine years after the issue of the Equity Joint Venture Law, the Law of the People's Republic of China on Chinese-Foreign Contractual Joint Ventures[12] was finally adopted.

The first phase was highlighted by the issues of the three laws governing FDI firms in China. The evolving changes from control towards encouragement have strongly demonstrated the Chinese government's commitment to the establishment of a more liberalized FDI regime.

The Second Phase: 1990 to 1999

In the early 1990s, the Chinese government further liberalized its FDI regime and amended and established a series of laws and regulations aiming to achieve a more rapid and healthy development of FDI inflows into China. In 1990, the Amendments to the Equity Joint Venture Law and the Wholly Foreign-Owned Enterprise Implementing Rules were adopted. For the Amendments to the Equity Joint Venture Law, two significant changes are worth mentioning. The first is the abolition of the stipulation that the chairman of the board of an equity joint venture should be appointed by Chinese investors, and the second is the provision of protection from nationalization. The Wholly Foreign-Owned Enterprise Implementing Rules, based on the principles of the Wholly

Foreign-Owned Enterprise Law, provide a complete legal structure to facilitate the actual performance of these enterprises.

China's efforts to establish a regulatory legal framework for FDI continued. As a result, a series of laws and regulations relating to FDI were adopted after 1991, including, for example, the Foreign Investment Enterprise and Foreign Enterprise Income Tax Law, the Copyright Law, the Software Protection Regulations, the Patent Law Amendments, the Trademark Law, the Regulatory Provisions of Foreign Banks, the Securities Exchange Law, the Banking Law and the Foreign Exchange Control Regulations.

In 1994, the Chinese government implemented measures to reduce the problem related to inward FDI: overvaluation. In general, about 70 per cent of FDI inflows into China are in the form of equipment and technology (UNCTAD, *World Investment Report*, 1995). To translate the amount of these investments into cash tends to overvalue the amount of FDI. The motives behind overvaluation include: a larger share of dividends for the foreign investors than for the Chinese partners, resulting from the higher equity share of foreign investors compared with their local partners; lower taxes arising from larger capital expenditures and depreciation credits; and more management control. Overvaluation reduces the potential contribution of FDI to the development of the Chinese economy. It lowers tax revenues for the government, as well as the share of revenues accruing to the local partners in joint ventures. To deal with the problem of overvaluation, the State Administration for Import and Export Inspection and the Ministry of Finance jointly promulgated the Measures on Administration of the Appraisal of Assets Invested by Foreign Businessmen[13] in March 1994 and began to monitor more closely the fulfilment of contractual commitments with respect to the actual value and quality of equipment in FDI projects.

At the end of 1993, the investment code in China went through a thorough overhaul. The Company Law of the People's Republic of China[14] came into effect on 1 July 1994. For the first time it provided a firm legal foundation for the establishment of both large and small companies within the framework of a socialist market economy. The Company Law did not do away altogether with the three forms of FDI firms discussed above. Instead it attempted to re-classify them under one of the two classes of companies: the limited liability company and the company limited by shares. The Company Law gives China not just a single unified platform for foreign enterprises, but also a means of integrating them with a domestic business environment which is itself changing rapidly from central planning to a market economy. Based on the Company Law, foreign joint ventures and wholly foreign-owned enterprises are all limited liability companies.

In January 1995, the Interim Provisions Concerning Some Issues on the Establishment of Companies Limited by Shares with Foreign Investment[15] was promulgated, which provided foreign investors with another investment vehicle. As a result, foreign companies were also allowed to establish foreign-invested holding companies – either as joint ventures or wholly foreign-owned enterprises – but in order to do so the foreign company must have a sound reputation in China and must meet some strict conditions. The permission to establish a holding company has provided many multinational companies with a structure through which to operate nationally and to coordinate and manage investment companies already established in China.

The second phase witnessed both a rapidly growing body of FDI laws and regulations and a further relaxation on the forms of foreign investment. In this period, China has made great improvements towards establishing a more consistent and systematic FDI regulatory framework.

The Third Phase: 2000 Onwards

In anticipation of China's entry to the WTO, the Chinese government amended the Wholly Foreign-owned Enterprise Law and the Contractual Joint Venture Law in 2000 and the Equity Joint Venture Law in 2001.[16] The amendments removed earlier restrictions in the areas of foreign exchange balance requirement, raw materials and equipment sourcing, mandatory export requirement, and reporting of business plans. These legislative amendments represent the first major step on the part of the Chinese government to honour its commitments under its pending WTO membership. The key amendments are listed below.

Abolition of foreign exchange balance requirement
Previously, FDI firms were required to balance their own foreign exchange income and expenses. Pursuant to the earlier requirements, where an FDI firm desired to make payments or remittances in foreign currency outside of China, these had to be made from the company's own foreign exchange funds. The foreign exchange balancing requirement has now been deleted from the law. Foreign direct investment firms can now purchase foreign currency from commercial banks under the new legal regime, subject to the satisfaction of the relevant foreign exchange control rules.

Equal access to domestic and overseas suppliers
Foreign direct investment firms were required under previous laws to give priority to domestic suppliers when sourcing their raw materials and equipment. The new amendments permit free sourcing of raw materials,

fuel, components, and so on from either China's domestic market or from overseas, without priority requirements favouring domestic suppliers.

Removal of mandatory export requirement

Previously, the Wholly Foreign-Owned Enterprise Law required FDI firms to export at least 70 per cent of their production, except where special exemptions were granted, such as for advanced technology contributions. Mandatory export requirements were also imposed on joint ventures, in order to support the earlier foreign exchange balance requirement. Under the newly adopted amendments, mandatory export requirements were removed. China will encourage the use of advanced technology and the export of products, but each FDI firm shall be free to allocate sales of its products to either China's domestic or export market.

Abolition of business plan filing

Previously, FDI firms were required to file the production and business plan with the relevant government authority. The newly adopted amendments repeal this requirement, as the current focus for government control is on macroeconomic matters, rather than the operations of individual enterprises.

In 2005, China fundamentally amended the Company Law. The new Company Law,[17] which came into effect on 1 January 2006, is a significant reform of the old Company Law. The old Company Law had been criticized for various deficiencies, especially in terms of corporate governance. The new Company Law simplifies company establishment requirements and statutorily expands the rights of shareholders in China's companies. In particular, the new Company Law has the following improvements with respect to corporate governance: greater protection of shareholders by allowing shareholder derivative suits; shareholders' dissolution of the company by petitioning the court; protection of minority shareholders in limited liability companies; cumulative voting by shareholders in a company limited by shares; introduction of independent directors; maintaining independence of auditors; and piercing the corporate veil.

The provisions of the new Company Law apply to FDI firms to the extent that they do not conflict with the statutes governing these investment vehicles, namely, equity joint venture, cooperative joint venture and wholly foreign-owned enterprises. Each of these forms of FDI firms is organized in China as a limited liability company. The statutes and associated regulations provide for specific and unique provisions concerning each of these three forms of FDI firms in China. Where the unique provisions do not apply, the provisions of the new Company Law apply.

The current global FDI flows have been dominated by cross-border M&As, particularly in the services sector. However, cross-border M&As in China have been very limited due to the tight restrictions imposed by the Chinese government. To fulfil its commitments to the WTO, further liberalize the FDI regime and attract more FDI, China issued the Interim Provisions on Mergers and Acquisitions of Domestic Enterprises by Foreign Investors[18] in 2003 (also referred to here as the Provisions). This is the first comprehensive set of regulations on cross-border M&As in China.

With a view to promoting and regulating foreign investors' investment in China, introducing advanced technologies and management experience from abroad, improving the utilization of foreign investment, rationalizing the allocation of resources, ensuring employment and safeguarding fair competition and China's economic security, after a three-year trial period of the Interim Provisions on M&As, on 8 August 2006, six ministries of China jointly issued the Provisions on Mergers and Acquisitions of Domestic Enterprises by Foreign Investors[19] which took effect on 8 September 2006. The Provisions establish new rules for foreign investors acquiring interests in China's domestic companies.

The Provisions apply to any M&As by foreign investors, including foreign companies, foreign-invested investment companies registered in China, and foreign-invested enterprises (collectively referred to as *foreign investors*), of domestically registered companies, including limited liability companies, companies limited by shares, state-owned enterprises, private companies and foreign-invested enterprises (collectively referred to as *domestic companies*).

The Provisions define that a merger or acquisition of a domestic enterprise by foreign investors (or M&A transaction) could mean either an equity acquisition or an asset acquisition. An equity acquisition is defined as the acquisition by foreign investors of equity interest in a domestic company or the subscription by foreign investors of new equity in a domestic company, resulting in the conversion of such a domestic company to an FDI firm. An asset acquisition is defined as including both the establishment of an FDI firm by foreign investors with the purpose of using the FDI firm to acquire and operate assets purchased from domestic companies, and the direct acquisition of assets from domestic companies by foreign investors who then use those assets for establishing an FDI firm.

The Provisions represent a further opening towards cross-border M&As in line with standard international practice in that they allow for the first time the acquisition of equity interests held by shareholders of a Chinese domestic company by payment of equity interests held by shareholders of an overseas company or new shares issued by an overseas company. The Provisions increase corporate transparency by requiring parties to a cross-border acquisition to disclose whether or not they are affiliated with each other and, if they are under the common control of the same entity, to provide additional information regarding the purpose of the acquisition and whether the appraisal results conform to fair market value. The Provisions make specific and detailed provision for the use of special purpose vehicle (SPV) overseas by Chinese domestic firms making acquisitions in China – an important addition in view of the generally unrecorded but widespread practice of 'round-tripping' by Chinese companies seeking to benefit from incentives offered to foreign investors. The Provisions also establish interim anti-monopoly review procedures to protect market competitiveness and stability until the anti-monopoly law is promulgated.

On the other hand, the Provisions add a new screening requirement on cross-border M&A transactions in which the foreign investor obtains controlling rights of a domestic enterprise if the acquisition (1) involves a major industry, (2) has or may have an impact on national economic security or (3) may result in the transfer of famous trademarks or traditional Chinese brands. The lack of definition of terms including 'major industry', 'impact' on 'national economic security', 'famous' trademarks and 'traditional' Chinese brands appears to render the new screening requirement less than wholly transparent. The creation of a new layer of screening is in addition to the examination and approval process based on the Catalogues for Guidance of Foreign Investment Industries. It does not appear consistent with the repeatedly expressed intention of the Chinese authorities to streamline FDI approval procedures.

Although there are differences of opinion on whether the Provisions actually encourage or restrict foreign investment, there are positive indications that the legal environment for inward cross-border M&As in China is becoming more flexible (for example, use of shares as consideration) and settled (for example, more detailed approval procedures have been introduced).

After more than ten years of debate and drafting, China enacted its first ever Anti-Monopoly Law[20] in 2007, commencing operation on 1 August 2008. Article 1 of this law states that it was enacted for the purpose of preventing and prohibiting monopolistic activities, protecting fair market competition, promoting efficiency of economic operation, protecting the legitimate rights and interests of consumers and social public interests, and promoting the healthy development of a socialist market economy. The law sets out various rules regarding the regulation or prohibition of monopoly agreements, including resale price maintenance, price fixing, and anti-competitive supply and market practices. Various agreements can be exempted from the prohibition of monopoly agreements, including those that relate to technology development, cost reduction and resources preservation. Undoubtedly, the Anti-Monopoly Law will have significant implications on FDI in China, especially for FDI through cross-border M&As.

The Anti-Monopoly Law itself does not distinguish between foreign and domestic businesses. However, until July 2009, foreign investors were also subject to pre-merger notification and competition review under the Provisions on M&As. In order to ensure that the Provisions on M&As agree with the Anti-Monopoly Law and the Provisions of the State Council on Thresholds for Declaration of Concentrations of Undertakings, the Chinese government made some revisions on the Provisions on M&As and the new Provisions on Mergers and Acquisitions of Domestic Enterprises by Foreign Investors[21] take effect in July 2009. The new Provisions on M&As conform its pre-merger notification and review provisions to the Anti-Monopoly Law, so that foreign buyers would be subject to only one competition notification and review requirement, under the Anti-Monopoly Law.

According to the Anti-Monopoly Law, if a market concentration reaches the threshold of declaration, a declaration must be lodged in advance with the Anti-Monopoly Authority under the State Council. Cross-border M&As are regarded as one method of increasing concentration and should be certainly regulated. The new Provisions on M&As add one article to regulate the same standard and requirement as the Anti-Monopoly Law in order to keep the consistency across different laws and regulations. Meanwhile, some little changes of words and expressions have been made in order to avoid controversy and misunderstanding. The modification in the new Provisions on M&As ultimately ensures the general terms' accurate use in different laws and regulations.

The evolution of China's FDI laws and regulations in the third phase has been marked by the rapid development of a systematic regulatory framework to facilitate and to regulate FDI. Two characteristics of the third phase distinguish it from the first and the second phases. First, emphasis has been placed on the creation and development of a more consistent and systematic regulatory framework. Second, more efforts have been made to create and amend the legislation to conform with international rules and requirements for FDI.

INDUSTRIAL POLICIES FOR FDI

China has comprehensive industrial polices to guide FDI into the targeted industries in accordance with China's economic and industrial development strategy. In June 1995, China issued the Interim Provisions on Guiding Foreign Investment and the Catalogue for the Guidance of Foreign Investment Industries (hereafter referred to as the Catalogue). This is the first time China has used laws and regulations to guide FDI. The interim provisions were formulated in order to provide guidance for FDI towards sectors which suit China's national economic and social development plan, and protect the lawful rights and interests of foreign investors in accordance with relevant state laws governing FDI and the requirements of state industrial policy. As a general industrial policy, the Catalogue is a long-standing tool of Chinese authority to reflect their decisions and approach towards FDI in various industries at different stages of Chinese economic development. Foreign investors first consult with the most updated Catalogue to confirm the entry possibility and mode of investment vehicle in the industries in which they intend to invest.

To suit the development of FDI and fulfil China's commitments to the WTO in trade and investment liberalization, in February 2002, China issued the Provisions on Guiding the Orientation of Foreign Investment.[22] The provisions classify FDI into 'encouraged', 'permitted', 'restricted' and 'prohibited' categories. Foreign direct investment in encouraged industries is normally eligible for various incentives and investors are also permitted to establish wholly foreign-owned enterprises, equity joint ventures or cooperative joint ventures. In the event that any industries are not listed in the Catalogue, unless otherwise forbidden by other applicable laws and regulations, FDI is generally permitted and the investment may take vehicles of wholly foreign-owned enterprise, equity joint venture or cooperative joint venture with no restriction on Chinese or foreign partner being the majority shareholder. Foreign direct investment in restricted industries is subject to strict governmental examination and approval case by case and the investment vehicle is possibly limited to equity joint ventures or cooperative joint ventures under which Chinese partners hold majority interests in some cases. Foreign direct investment in prohibited industries by any foreign investors is not allowed at all.

According to the provisions, China encourages both a greater geographic dispersion of FDI inflows within China and more FDI inflows into the targeted economic sectors and industries, such as agriculture, resource exploitation, infrastructure, and environmentally friendly, export-oriented and high-technology industries. To accommodate the implementation of the provisions, China amended the Catalogue for the Guidance of Foreign Investment Industries in March 2002[23] and November 2004.[24]

In addition to the national industrial catalogue on guiding FDI, China issued and implemented a series of regional and sectoral industrial catalogues to guide FDI. For example, to implement the west development strategy, encourage FDI inflows into the central and western regions, and accelerate economic development in the central and western regions, China issued the Catalogue of Priority Industries for Foreign Investment in the Central-West Region in June 2000, which was subsequently amended in July 2004 and December 2008.[25] To encourage FDI in high-technology industry, to accelerate the pace in introducing advanced technologies from abroad, to strengthen abilities of internal assimilation and independent innovation, and to further improve the quality and level of FDI, China issued the Catalogue of Encouraged Hi-tech Products for Foreign Investment in June 2003,[26] which was further amended in December 2006.[27]

In November 2007, China's National Development and Reform Commission and Ministry of Commerce jointly revised and promulgated the Catalogue for the Guidance of Foreign Investment Industries (Amended in 2007),[28] which replaced its 2004 version and took effect on 1 December 2007.

Compared with its 2004 version, the 2007 Catalogue has increased the total entries from 370 to 478. Most importantly, the 'encouraged' entries were expanded dramatically, which implies that China is acting to further encourage FDI. Among the encouraged entries, most changes have been made to the manufacturing sector, in which the encouraged lists in the 2007 Catalogue were increased from 191 to 282. However, this increase in the encouraged lists in the manufacturing sector resulted from the break-down of the sector into more detailed industries rather than a significant broadening of scope of the sector.

In addition to the above expansion of quantity of the entries, dramatic changes were made to the contents of the 2007 Catalogue. The 2007 Catalogue has been revised mainly in the following aspects.

Promotion of upgrade of industrial structure

According to the 11th Five-year Plan on Foreign Capital Utilization,[29] China will move from emphasizing the quantity of FDI to emphasizing the quality of FDI and upgrade its industrial structure, inducting foreign capital to those industries with high value-added. It was also clarified that items under the restricted category in the Catalogue for Guidance for Industrial Structure Adjustment[30] also applies to FDI.

In order to eliminate less productive production capacity, under the 2007 Catalogue, encouragement for FDI in manufacturing sector has been shifted from traditional manufacturing industries in which domestic enterprises have already mastered necessary technologies and have strong production capacity to new high-technology, high-end equipment manufacturing, new materials production, infrastructure and modern agriculture. In order to encourage development of high-technology industry, 522 types of products in the Catalogue of Encouraged Hi-tech Products for Foreign Investment (2006) have been added into the 2007 Catalogue as encouraged items, accounting for 88 per cent of the products in the Hi-tech Products Catalogue. In line with China's commitment to the WTO, in addition to reducing restricted and prohibited items in the service sectors, the 2007 Catalogue has newly added service outsourcing and modern logistics and other service items into the encouraged category. In order to avoid the continued overheating of the real estate market and also in line with the Opinions on Regulating Access to and Administration of Foreign Investment in Real Estate Market,[31] under the 2007 Catalogue, FDI in general residences are no longer encouraged and FDI in the real estate secondary market exchange, intermediaries and brokerages are restricted.

Protection to environment and conservation of resources

China's economic growth suffered a great deal from its former extensive development practices of high input, high consumption of resources and heavy pollution but low efficiency, under which large quantities of resources and energy were wasted and the environment seriously damaged. Having woken up to this adverse effect, China has recently called for harmonious development between society and nature and conservation of resources for the next generation.

In response to the call for harmonious development, the 2007 Catalogue encourages FDI in the development of recycling, clean production, renewable energy, ecological environmental protection and comprehensive utilization of resources. Some relevant items satisfying these purposes have been added to the 2007 Catalogue in the encouraged category. Foreign direct investment is no longer encouraged for the exploration of important mineral resources which are rare in China or non-renewable. Further, FDI with high energy consumption, heavy resources consumption and high pollution is restricted or prohibited. Also, FDI is not allowed for exploration for some important non-renewable mineral resources.

Adjustment in export-oriented policy

In view of China's growing trade surplus and fast-expanding reserves of foreign currency, and in order to balance trade, especially to promote imports of high technologies and high-technology equipment, a general provision that FDI devoted to exporting 100 per cent of its products in the encouraged category was removed from the 2007 Catalogue. The message is that China will curb export processing growth and protect its important strategic resources. However, whether such a policy can really be success-fully implemented at the local level remains an open question since this has implications for local government revenue.

Promotion of coordinated regional development
In parallel with the strategies of developing western regions, boosting the rise of central regions and rejuvenating the old industrial bases in north-eastern regions, the general provision 'apply only to the central and western regions' was removed from items under the encouraged category in the 2007 Catalogue. Accordingly, the priority industries and characteristic industries in central and western regions, and old industrial bases in north-eastern regions which need to be encouraged for investment will be added to the Catalogue of Priority Industries for Foreign Investment in the Central-West Region in the future revision to the Central-Western Region Catalogue.

Protection of national economic and spiritual security
In order to protect national economic and spiritual security, China takes a prudent attitude towards the liberalization of certain strategic and sensi-tive industries. Appropriate adjustments have been made to the relevant items under the 2007 Catalogue for balance between domestic develop-ment and opening to the outside world. Under the 2007 Catalogue, many encouraged items for FDI are still limited to cooperative joint ventures or equity joint ventures, especially the survey and exploration of important mineral resources which is limited to joint venture or Sino-foreign coop-eration, and is restricted or even prohibited. Foreign direct investment in the survey and exploration of tungsten, molybdenum, tin, antimony and fluorite was previously restricted, but is completely forbidden now. Many restricted items are limited to joint venture rather than wholly foreign-owned enterprise and the Chinese partner must hold the control-ling interest in the joint venture. Participation in the publishing and media industry is still prohibited. In recognition of the Internet as an alterna-tive publishing medium, various Internet-based businesses, such as news websites, web-streaming audio-visual services, e-commerce and culture-related websites, have been added into the prohibited category in the 2007 Catalogue.

In summary, the changes to the Catalogue reflect China's continued effort to attract FDI in accordance with its economic, regional and indus-trial development strategies. Under the 2007 Catalogue, FDI in traditional manufacturing sectors and export-oriented projects will no longer be encouraged. Instead, FDI in high technology, new materials production, high-end equipment, modern agriculture and high-end services, such as modern logistics, have been newly encouraged. Projects associated with heavy pollution or high resources consumption, and exploration of important non-renewable mineral resources will be forbidden. However, some environmentally friendly and energy-saving projects will be more welcome. In order to balance the regional development, FDI in central-western regions and north-eastern old industrial bases will also be encouraged. For national economic and spiritual security, some strategic and sensitive industries, such as Internet-based services, are forbidden for FDI. These changes demonstrate that China is serious about upgrading its industrial structure through utilizing foreign capital in order to achieve sound and healthy economic development.

FOREIGN EXCHANGE MANAGEMENT RELATING TO FDI

After 1949, China created a foreign exchange control regime, aiming to maintain balanced international revenue and expenditure. However, the adoption of the open door policy in general and the introduction of FDI in particular have posed challenges to this regime and led to gradual changes to China's foreign exchange management from a tight control system to a more liberalized regime.

Under China's foreign exchange control regime, FDI firms are required to keep a balance between their foreign exchange receipts and expenditures. In practice, the regulations are implemented through requiring FDI firms to open a *renminbi* (RMB) deposit account and a separate foreign exchange deposit account with either the Bank of China or another bank approved by the State Administration for Exchange Control. All foreign exchange receipts and disbursements must flow through the foreign exchange account. Because the RMB is not convertible into foreign exchange, this rule effectively requires FDI firms to generate all foreign exchange needed for the remittance of dividends, expenditures and other distributions. Although the Chinese government recognizes that the foreign exchange balance is a critical operating issue for most FDI firms in China, there are several basic reasons why the Chinese government adopted such a foreign exchange management policy towards FDI firms at the risk of jeopardizing the effectiveness of its fiscal incentives offered to FDI firms. The first reason seems to be very obvious, that the Chinese government wants to protect its foreign exchange reserves. The second reason is to encourage FDI firms to export their products and further to help improve China's overall trade balance. The third reason is to promote localization of FDI firms so as to speed up the transfer of technology and upgrade China's manufacturing capabilities. With these basic reasons behind China's foreign exchange policy for FDI firms, it was not surprising that little assistance to FDI firms to meet this constraint was available from the Chinese government prior to 1986.[32]

A lack of ability to convert RMB profits to foreign currency for repatriation made foreign investors increasingly worry about their prospects of doing business in China. This also gradually became a major concern for the Chinese government and led to the adoption of the Foreign Exchange Balance Provisions[33] and the Encouragement Provisions in 1986 to facilitate FDI firms mainly in their efforts to solve the foreign exchange problems. The two provisions offered the following options to help FDI firms to balance their foreign exchange accounts (Liu et al., 1993).

Domestic sales of sophisticated products
This option is designed to provide temporary relief for FDI firms with limited foreign exchange by allowing them to sell sophisticated products produced by advanced or key technology provided by the foreign partners on the domestic market. This option is applied on a product-by-product basis. Therefore, the viability of the option depends on the sophistication of the technology provided by the foreign partner and the availability of a potential buyer of the products on the domestic market.

Foreign exchange adjustment
This option provides the opportunity to a foreign investor who establishes two or more ventures in China to adjust foreign exchange accounts through balancing the surplus in one venture with the deficit in another. The feasibility of this option depends largely on the agreement of all parties, particularly when the joint ventures involve different Chinese partners. Adjustment could be arranged either as a swap, in which case these ventures are actually buying and selling foreign exchange at a rate on which they agree, or as a parallel loan, without charging interest from each other.

Reinvestment of RMB profits
This option allows foreign investors to reinvest their RMB profits in Chinese domestic enterprises as an equity owner with a plan to begin or expand export production. Foreign exchange earned from such exports is allowed to be distributed to these RMB investors for repatriation. However, the effectiveness of this option largely depends on the export performance of the invested enterprises.

Export domestic products
This option allows FDI firms to purchase domestic products and sell them abroad. However, the resale of domestic goods that are subject to export quotas, under central administration and require an export licence is not allowed unless special approval is granted by the Ministry of Foreign Trade and Economic Cooperation. The purpose of this option is to enable foreign investors to use their existing distribution networks in the international market to solve a temporary foreign exchange problem. Therefore, a limit is set on the approved quantity of domestic products to be purchased for export by FDI firms within the amount needed for the shortfall in its operation for the year plus a necessary amount for profit repatriation.

Government assistance
The Foreign Exchange Balance Provisions state that direct assistance by means of foreign exchange allocation is the responsibility of the jurisdiction that granted the original approval of a given project. However, this option is subject to two preconditions. First, the government is only responsible for a foreign exchange imbalance that is obviously not the direct result of a venture's failure to fulfil its contractual obligations for exports and the generation of foreign exchange. Second, the government will consider direct assistance only when it is necessary. As a result, although this option provides the FDI firms with the possibility of government direct assistance, the feasibility of that assistance depends almost entirely on government decisions and sometimes on the particular circumstances.

Mortgage RMB on foreign exchange
This option provides the foreign investors with the opportunity to obtain a RMB loan from the Bank of China and other banks designated by the People's Bank of China for working capital or for investment in fixed assets through depositing an equivalent value of foreign exchange as security. By adopting this option, foreign exchange that may have been converted into RMB can be kept by the FDI firms for other purposes.

Import substitution
This option allows FDI firms to sell import substitutes on the domestic market to solve their foreign exchange problems. According to the Import Substitution Measures, a product which may be confirmed as an import substitute must meet the following conditions: (1) the product is equipped with advanced technology needed by the country, and the producer is

facing temporary difficulties in balancing its foreign exchange account in the initial period of operation in the process of increasing the local content of its product; (2) the relevant product must be one that is presently imported and will continue to be imported by the central or local governments; (3) the specifications, performance and delivery time of the product, and the technical and training services that are offered, must meet the requirements of the domestic purchaser. Furthermore, the product must reach international quality standards. Because of these requirements, it is very clear that only technologically advanced FDI firms are eligible to apply for import substitution status.

Foreign exchange swaps
Undoubtedly, the above options have greatly improved the situation of foreign exchange management of FDI firms. However, balancing foreign exchange will continue to be a problem until the RMB becomes convertible. A significant move made in this direction was the establishment of foreign exchange swap centres. The first foreign exchange swap centre was established in Shenzhen in 1985. In 1992 the first national level foreign exchange swap market was established in Beijing. Foreign direct investment firms were first allowed to participate in transactions on the foreign exchange swap centres in late 1986 following the issue of the Encouragement Provisions. Since then the foreign exchange swap markets have become the major and more direct resort of FDI firms to balance their foreign exchange accounts. As a result, foreign exchange balancing has become a much less important issue for FDI firms.

Evidently, the reform of China's foreign exchange management moved towards a more liberalized regime in general and towards a greater facilitation of FDI firms in particular. Beginning in 1994, China conducted a new round of foreign exchange management reform. Three major changes are worth mentioning. First, China for the first time since 1949 abolished the official exchange rate and adopted a unified market floating exchange rate published daily by the central bank based on the previous closing rate in a foreign exchange market participated in by designated Chinese banks and foreign banks doing business in China. Second is the establishment of a foreign exchange market for financial institutions which is expected to provide and stabilize the market exchange rate, improve liquidity and help eliminate the black market. Third is the abolition of the foreign exchange quota retention system.

Obviously, the single exchange rate system, a stable foreign exchange market, and a relatively efficient arrangement of foreign exchange demand

and supply through the market mechanism will have a strong and positive impact on the process of RMB convertibility. As a result, in December 1996, the Chinese government announced that it would adopt International Monetary Fund (IMF) Article 8, removing all remaining restrictions on foreign exchange transactions three years ahead of its original target. As the first step, RMB became convertible on current account in December 1996. This includes all payments for international goods and services trade, repayments of loans and profit remittance. It also binds China not to introduce discriminatory currency practices or multiple currencies in the future. This is an important step which will improve the authorities' ability to use indirect monetary policy instruments to adjust external balance and stabilize the RMB. It will also greatly assist China's international traders and foreign investors.

However, FDI firms in China were still required to balance their foreign exchange receipts and expenditures till early 2000, even though they could participate in the foreign exchange swap markets to balance their foreign exchange accounts. In 2000 and 2001, with the amendments of the joint venture laws and the wholly foreign-owned enterprise law, the requirements on FDI firms to balance their own foreign exchange accounts were finally eliminated.

TAX POLICIES FOR FDI

Since the early 1980s' initial offer of tax incentives to FDI firms in the SEZs and open coastal cities, China has extensively but selectively used tax incentives as 'economic levers' to guide FDI into its designated regions, economic sectors and industries.

From 1979 to 1983, the initial tax concessions offered to foreign investors were mainly reflected in three tax laws, namely the Equity Joint Venture Income Tax Law,[34] the Foreign Enterprise Income Tax Law[35] and the Industrial and Commercial Tax Provisions.[36]

The initial tax concessions offered in the Equity Joint Venture Income Tax Law[37] included tax holidays for newly established joint ventures that were scheduled to operate for a period of ten years or more, including a total tax exemption for the first two years commencing from the first profit-making year and a 50 per cent reduction for the three subsequent years. There was an additional 15 to 30 per cent reduction in income tax for an additional ten years for certain types of joint ventures in remote and poor areas; and a refund of 40 per cent of the income tax paid on the reinvested funds for any joint venture partner that reinvested its share of profits for a period of at least five consecutive years. Also included were the authorization of a local tax exemption or reduction when local governments found this appropriate, and loss carry-forward was allowed to be taken into account in determining the first profit-making year and in calculating taxable incomes.

The tax incentives included in the Foreign Enterprise Income Tax Law[38] were mainly: a tax exemption for the first profit-making year and a 50 per cent reduction in the tax for the following two years for enterprises engaged in agriculture, forestry, animal husbandry, and other low-profit operations, including deep-pit mining operations; an additional tax reduction of 15 per cent to 30 per cent, if approved by the Ministry of Finance, for an additional period of ten years; the authorization of tax exemption or reduction of local taxes, when the local government found appropriate, for enterprises having an annual income of less than 1 million yuan; and loss carry-forward was also allowed for a maximum of five years.

The tax concessions offered in the Industrial and Commercial Tax Provisions mainly were exemptions for the importation of machinery, equipment, spare parts, and materials by offshore oil exploration and extraction joint operations between Chinese and foreign companies for their own business use.

In 1984, with the extension of the special policies for FDI from the SEZs to the 14 coastal cities, the Chinese government issued the SEZs and the Coastal Cities Tax Reduction and Exemption Regulations.[39] The regulations offered further tax concessions to foreign investors. The primary objective of the 1984 tax regulations was to attract more FDI inflows into China and, at the same time, to facilitate the implementation of the uneven regional development strategy through tax incentives to affect the location decision of foreign investors and, therefore, to influence the spatial distribution of FDI inflows into China.

In 1986, further tax incentives were offered to the technologically advanced and export-oriented FDI firms under the Encouragement Provisions. For example, technologically advanced FDI firms and export-oriented FDI firms (if it exports 70 per cent or more of its annual products) were offered 50 per cent further income tax reduction for three years after the expiration of the initial period allowed for reduction and exemption. Obviously, the aim of the Chinese government was to incorporate the tax incentives with its regional economic development and industrial development strategies. This reflected the government's growing concern over the relationship between FDI inflows into some economic sectors and industries and the overall goals of national economic and technological development.

With the implementation of the Encouragement Provisions in 1986, and particularly with the adoption of the coastal development strategy in

1988, attracting FDI through offering tax incentives became very popular throughout China. From 1987 to 1990, local governments competed with each other to offer tax incentives for attracting FDI. In most cases, local governments extended the period and added categories under which FDI firms were entitled to various tax concessions for business income tax. Some local governments also offered unauthorized concessions in industrial and commercial tax and, particularly, they granted more tax exemptions and reductions for Taiwanese investment and increased the income tax refund on reinvestment. However, the 'tax concession war' proved to be ineffective in influencing foreign investors' location decisions. Conversely, it created an impression in the minds of foreign investors that China had unstable and inconsistent tax policies, which was detrimental to the Chinese government's persistent efforts to create a sound tax climate. As a result, the State Administration of Taxation had to order the local governments to delete or to revise all tax provisions not mandated by national legislation, in order to provide a consistent and sound tax climate for FDI (Wei, 1994).

In July 1991, China adopted the Foreign Investment Enterprise and Foreign Enterprise Income Tax Law[40] and its implementing rules.[41] This law has many significant features. First, it offers tax incentives to the manufacturing sector in general, and to infrastructure and agriculture in particular. Second, the law for the first time ensures that all the tax incentives apply to all FDI firms, regardless of their form, as long as they are in the designated industries or areas and satisfy other requirements. Third, in order to prevent FDI firms from transfer pricing, the standards of 'fair market price' and 'regular business practices' are employed to curb tax evasions through transfer pricing. Fourth, the law grants income tax exemption to all FDI firms, which effectively puts all the FDI firms on a level playing field as compared to the previous provisions in which only the FDI firms in the SEZs and ETDZs were granted such tax concessions.

At the beginning of 1994, China fundamentally changed its old taxation system and adopted a new taxation system. The new taxation system, which includes value-added tax, consumption tax, business tax and individual income tax, took effect on 1 January 1994 and applies both to domestic firms and to FDI firms. For example, the business income tax rate is 33 per cent and value-added tax rate is 17 per cent both for domestic firms and FDI firms. At the same time, China decided to gradually reduce the preferential treatments for FDI firms in order to establish a level playing field for domestic firms and FDI firms. However, because of the Asian financial crisis that occurred during 1997 to 1999, the preferential treatments for FDI firms including tax incentives were maintained till China introduced the new taxation system and unified the tax rates for domestic firms and FDI firms in 2008.

Table 2.1   National business income tax rate incentives for FDI firms

FDI firms	National Business Income Tax Rate
1. Productive FDI firms located in SEZs and ETDZs	15%
2. Productive FDI firms located in the old urban areas of the cities in the coastal economically opened areas, SEZs and ETDZs	24%
3. Productive FDI firms located in the old urban areas of the cities in the coastal economically opened areas, SEZs and ETDZs, but engaged in projects with technology-intensive and knowledge-intensive investment over US$30 million with a low profit margin, and energy, transportation and port construction	15%
4. Joint ventures engaged in port construction	15%
5. Wholly foreign-owned banks and joint-venture banks located in SEZs and government-permitted areas with investment over US$10 million scheduled to operate ten years or more	15%
6. Productive FDI firms and FDI firms located in Shanghai Pudong New ETDZ engaged in development and construction of airport, ports, railway, energy and transportation	15%
7. High and new technology FDI firms located in government-designated national high and new technology development zones and in Beijing New Technology Development Zone (TDZ)	15%
8. FDI firms engaged in business activities classified as encouraged categories	15%

Source: Wang (1997).

From the early 1980s, China has extensively but selectively used tax incentives to guide FDI into its designated regions, economic sectors and industries. The main features of China's tax incentives to FDI are summarized in Tables 2.1 to 2.3.

From the tables we can see that China's tax incentive policy for FDI firms has two key features. First, the tax incentives offered in the SEZs and ETDZs located in the open cities are much more favourable than in other open regions. Second, the tax incentives are more favourable for technologically advanced and export-oriented FDI firms. However, the question is how effective are these tax incentives in attracting FDI?

Table 2.2   National business income tax exemption and reduction for FDI firms

FDI firms	National Business Income Tax Exemption and Reduction
1. Productive FDI firms scheduled to operate for ten years or more	Commencing from the first profit-making year, two years exemption plus three years 50% reduction
2. Joint-venture FDI firms engaged in port construction scheduled to operate for 15 years or more	Commencing from the first profit-making year, five years exemption plus five years 50% reduction
3. FDI firms located in Hainan SEZ engaged in infrastructure construction of airport, ports, railway, highway, power station, coal mine, water conservancy, and in agricultural development and production scheduled to operate for 15 years or more	Commencing from the first profit-making year, five years exemption plus five years 50% reduction
4. FDI firms located in Shanghai Pudong New ETDZ engaged in the construction of airport, ports, railway and power station scheduled to operate for 15 years or more	Commencing from the first profit-making year, five years exemption plus five years 50% reduction
5. FDI firms located in SEZs engaged in service industries with investment over US$5 million scheduled to operate for ten years or more	Commencing from the first profit-making year, one year exemption plus two years 50% reduction
6. Wholly foreign-owned banks and joint-venture banks located in SEZs and government-permitted areas with investment over US$10 million scheduled to operate for ten years or more	Commencing from the first profit-making year, one year exemption plus two years 50% reduction
7. High and new technology joint-venture FDI firms located in government-designated national high and new TDZs scheduled to operate for ten years or more	Commencing from the first profit-making year, two years exemption
8. Export-oriented FDI firms if they export 70% or more of their annual products after the expiration of the initial period allowed for exemption and reduction	Further 50% reduction after the expiration of the initial period allowed for exemption and reduction
9. Technologically advanced FDI firms if they still are classified as technologically advanced enterprises after the expiration of the initial period allowed for exemption and reduction	Further three years 50% reduction after the expiration of the initial period allowed for exemption and reduction
10. FDI firms engaged in agriculture, forestry, and animal husbandry, or located in economically less developed and remote areas	Further ten years 15% to 30% reduction after the expiration of the initial period allowed for exemption and reduction

Source: Wang (1997).

Table 2.3   Other tax incentives for FDI firms

FDI firms	Other tax incentives
1. FDI firms engaged in the industries and projects classified as encouraged and restricted B categories	Tariff free and value-added tax exemption for imported equipment and technology
2. FDI firms engaged in the industries and projects classified as encouraged categories	Local business income tax exemption and reduction possible
3. Technologically advanced and export-oriented FDI firms and FDI firms located in Hainan SEZ engaged in the projects of infrastructure construction or agricultural development	100% refund for income tax paid on the reinvested portion if reinvestment allows an operational period of no less than five years
4. All FDI firms	40% refund for income tax paid on the reinvested portion if reinvestment allows an operational period of no less than five years
5. All FDI firms and foreign investors	No restriction on profits remittance and capital repatriation. Foreign investors are granted tax exemption for profits repatriation

Sources: Wang (1997); Foreign Investment Administration of the Ministry of Foreign Trade and Economic Cooperation (1998).

Admittedly, these tax incentives in general have had a positive impact on attracting FDI inflows into China. However, some tax incentives are more effective than others, some have more impact on one group of investors than on another, and some are in fact ineffective.

First, the tax incentives granted to technologically advanced and exported-oriented enterprises, and the tax concessions offered to FDI firms engaged in low-profit operations or located in remote and poor areas, are undoubtedly rational from the perspective of China's needs to introduce advanced technology, to expand international exports and to encourage the inflows of capital and technology into the targeted regions and sectors.

Second, the tax refund on reinvestment has a large influence on decisions by foreign investors to reinvest their profits, particularly when such profits are distributed in RMB terms.

Third, the tax incentive package of the two years' exemption plus three years 50 per cent reduction on income tax to joint ventures operating for at least ten years has a stronger impact on cheap labour-seeking, export-oriented FDI than on market-seeking or strategic-seeking FDI. The cheap labour-seeking FDI, because its primary goal is to reduce production costs and to make profits as soon as possible, has a strong short-term profit motive that can be induced by tax exemptions or reductions. As a result, the tax incentive package has a greater impact on the initial investment decisions of the cheap labour-seeking, export-oriented FDI. In contrast, market-seeking FDI and strategic-seeking FDI in general have a long-term profit expectation which can barely be influenced by short-term tax holidays. Their initial investment decisions are mainly determined by the host country's overall investment climate and their own global expansion strategy. Therefore, the tax incentive package has little impact on the initial investment decisions, and has no influence on the length of operations of the market-seeking FDI and the strategic-seeking FDI once they have made their investments in China.

Fourth, the tax incentive package offered in the form of tax holidays has greater impact on investors from Hong Kong, Macao, Taiwan, and other East and South-East Asian economies (mainly the overseas Chinese investors) than on investors from developed countries. The overseas Chinese investors are usually modestly capitalized and possess middle-level technology mainly for labour-intensive activities. These are more easily motivated by low labour cost and short-term profits. Therefore, the favourable tax concessions plus low labour costs and the advantages of cultural and geographical proximity with China have a greater impact on the initial investment decisions of the overseas Chinese investors to start or shift their operations into China. Unlike the overseas Chinese investors, most of the investors from the developed countries are large MNEs. These generally have advanced technology, superior technical capabilities, larger-scale operations and greater geographical diversification. Their initial investment decisions are usually determined by the overall investment environment of host countries, the long-term profit expectations and their own strategic global business expansion. For example, Guisinger and Associates (1985) in their empirical studies of investment incentives influencing FDI location decisions revealed that, for US and Japanese computer companies, investment (FDI) is accomplished for quite basic economic or strategic reasons: for example, to lower costs of production or distribution, to better serve existing markets and to achieve better international diversification possibilities. Investment analyses in the typical computer company do not even consider incentives until what are thought to be more fundamental decision elements are completely satisfied. Only then will the effects of financial incentives be calculated. Therefore, in general, the developed country investors are inelastic to short-term tax concessions. As a result, the tax incentive package has less effect on the initial investment decisions of the investors from developed countries, particularly the large MNEs, as compared to the overseas Chinese investors.

Fifth, the exemptions and reductions of the local income tax should be a location determinant affecting foreign investors' location decisions when they make their investments in China. However, since almost all of the provinces competed with each other to attract FDI by offering local income tax exemptions and reductions, this tax incentive turned out to be ineffective because it produced no specific location difference for the foreign investors in terms of local tax concessions. In fact, the competition among provinces in offering tax incentives to foreign investors created a situation which is well known as a 'prisoner's dilemma'. Guisinger and Associates (1985) pointed out that in the market for foreign investment, a prisoner's dilemma arises among countries when one country's increase in incentives is matched by increased incentives from a competitor. A point will be reached when the incentive levels stabilize and no country will be better off: unchanged relative incentives will produce the same market share as before. Indeed, both countries may be worse off because income is transferred to firms with no gain in market share.

Finally, let us examine the effectiveness of these tax incentives on FDI in China from the aspect of different taxation systems adopted by source countries. There are two taxation systems prevailing in the world. One is the 'territorial taxation system' and the other is the 'global taxation system'. Under the territorial system, a citizen or subsidiary earning income abroad needs to pay tax only to the host country governments, in other words, the home country government does not tax the income of its citizen or subsidiaries abroad. Under the global system, the home country government does tax the income of its citizen or subsidiaries but grants a tax credit for taxes paid to host country governments. A complication of the effect of tax incentives on FDI arises under the tax credit system.

According to the global taxation system, subsidiaries of foreign firms pay income taxes to the host country governments based on the tax laws of the host countries. However, when they repatriate income to their parent companies, they are liable to taxation at the home country's rate, with a credit for any taxes paid to the host country governments. In the normal practice of the credit system, only taxes actually paid to the host country governments are allowed to be credited by the home country government. This raises the problem that when a host country offers tax concessions, a foreign subsidiary is effectively prevented from benefiting from these tax incentives under the tax credit system. The taxes exempted in the host country would not go to the foreign subsidiary, but rather to the home country government. The result is that not only the tax concessions are ineffective on the investment decisions of the foreign investors from the countries with a tax credit system, but also the host country governments lose the tax revenues which would be paid to them if they had not offered the tax concessions.

Since China has offered substantial tax exemptions and tax reductions to FDI firms, and also because some of China's major foreign investors are subject to the global taxation with tax credit system, such as the USA, Japan and the UK, to avoid such an ineffective result, China has successfully negotiated a 'tax-sparing' provision into tax treaties with its FDI source countries that allows a credit for taxes spared by China's tax concessions against the home country's tax levied on income. However, the USA consistently refuses to include a tax-sparing provision in its tax treaties with any country. The traditional justification for the USA to adhere to this policy is the principle of capital export neutrality, since the tax-sparing credit may favour certain foreign investment over domestic investment. Based on this tax policy, the USA's overseas investors have to pay a certain amount of the tax forgone by their host countries. This has put the USA's subsidiaries in a disadvantageous position and effectively reduced their competitiveness compared to FDI firms from source countries that recognize the tax-sparing credit. In addition, this tax policy will create an incentive to defer profit repatriation and, in the case of China, to take the advantage of the tax refund on reinvestment funds to reinvest their profits in China. In general, the tax incentives offered by the Chinese government in the form of tax exemptions and tax reductions have virtually no effect on the investment decisions of the USA's investors.[42]

On 16 March 2007 Chinese lawmakers passed the much talked about Enterprise Income Tax Law,[43] unifying the tax rates for foreign and domestic enterprises. The new tax rate for both domestic and foreign enterprises will be 25 per cent. The law took effect on 1 January 2008. The new law has unified the two existing tax codes; one for domestic firms, the other for FDI firms, into one and represents a fundamental change in China's tax policy. Many of the tax incentives and tax holidays that existed in the old code for foreign investors have been changed or eliminated.

Undoubtedly, the new corporate income tax law and the unification of the tax rate will certainly and substantially reduce the incentive for FDI round-tripping. However, what are the impacts of the new tax law on domestic firms and FDI firms and on FDI inflows into China?

Although the current nominal income tax rate is set at 33 per cent, the actual average income tax burden on China's domestic firms is 25 per cent (Xinhua News Agency, 2007). So, the new tax law on average will not reduce the actual tax burden of domestic firms.

The current actual income tax burden on FDI firms is 15 per cent (Xinhua News Agency, 2007). On average, the new income tax law will increase the tax burden of FDI firms by 10 percentage points. It seems that the new tax law would have a negative impact on FDI firms, especially in

the short term, on small-scale, labour-intensive, quick profit earning enterprises from developing countries and economies.

However, we would argue that China's proposed unified corporate
income tax rate of 25 per cent for domestic firms and FDI firms will have
little effect on foreign investment in China, especially on large MNEs.

First, the average corporate income tax rate for the world's 159 countries and regions who levy corporate income tax is 28.6 per cent, and the
average corporate income tax rate for China's 18 neighbouring countries
and regions is 26.7 per cent (Xinhua News Agency, 2007). China's proposed unified tax rate of 25 per cent is below the average rate of corporate
income tax around the world. So, China's corporate income tax rate is
quite competitive for attracting foreign and domestic investment, and
therefore, there is little reason to believe that the new tax law will have a
major effect on foreign investment.

Second, numerous surveys of international investors have shown that
tax incentives are not the most influential factor for multinationals in
selecting investment locations. Foreign investors are of course interested
in tax rates, but more important are such factors as the broad investment
climate, including the domestic market, the cost and availability of labour,
basic infrastructure, and economic and political stability.

Third, China's overall investment environment is quite competitive,
with relatively efficient public services, good infrastructure, a large and
fast-growing domestic market, abundant and well-educated human
resources, low labour costs, and macroeconomic and political stability,
making China one of the most attractive locations for FDI. According to
the '2005 Foreign Direct Investment Confidence Index' (A.T. Kearney,
2007), in 2005 China was the most attractive FDI location in the world.
China has maintained its lead in the index for the fourth consecutive
year.[44] Once again, China is the top FDI location for first-time investors,
with more than half (55 per cent) of investors expected to make first-time
investments there in the next three years. One in five FDI dollars for
first-time investments will be committed to the Chinese market. China
has successfully overcome the perceived risk associated with first-time
market entry, which is typically the biggest barrier to generating new
FDI.

Fourth, the new tax law still has preferential stipulations. According
to the tax law, China will continue to offer tax incentives to investment in
projects concerning environmental protection, agricultural development,
water conservation, energy saving, production safety, high-technology
development and public welfare undertakings. High-technology enterprises can still enjoy a 15 per cent income tax rate, and small and medium-
sized enterprises with slim profits are only required to pay income tax at

20 per cent. Certain tax breaks will also be granted to enterprises in SEZs and less-developed western areas of the country.

Fifth, the new tax law also provides a five-year transitional period to offset the impact on foreign companies. The income tax rate will be gradually increased to 25 per cent during this period, and old foreign enterprises can still enjoy tax breaks within a regulated time limit as before.

Therefore, the new tax law will bring China's tax laws more in line with international standards. It is a fulfilment of its commitment to the WTO for equal treatment to domestic and overseas investors. The change in the tax law not only proves that the Chinese government is determined to continue its reform and opening up policies, and work hard to improve investment conditions, but also will help to create a more consistent tax climate for the operations of FDI firms.

On 18 October 2010, the State Council issued the Notice on Unification of City Maintenance and Construction Tax and Education Surcharge for Domestic Enterprises, Foreign Invested Enterprises, and Foreign Individuals.[45] Foreign direct investment firms and foreign individuals were exempt from city maintenance and construction tax and education surcharge – such taxes only apply to domestic enterprises and Chinese nationals. Starting from 1 December 2010, China began levying the city maintenance and construction tax as well as the education surcharge on FDI firms and foreign individuals, symbolizing the end of 'super national treatment' offered to FDI firms and marking the beginning of a fully unified national tax system for domestic and foreign companies (*People's Daily Online*, 2010b). China's move to unify the tax system is consistent with relevant WTO provisions and shows that the country is gradually moving towards common international rules.

CONCLUSION

During the past three decades, China's change of attitude from restricting to passively attracting and to actively selecting inward FDI has been fully reflected by the evolution of its FDI policies, laws and regulations. In all the policy aspects relating to FDI as we discussed in the above sections, the Chinese government has been taking a positive but gradual reform approach. In general this reform process relating to FDI has proved relatively successful. As the following discussion shows, this has been reflected in the quality of the evolving foreign investment environment and the rapid growth of FDI inflows into China.

In this chapter we have systematically examined the evolution and the main features of China's inward FDI policies, laws and regulations implemented since 1979. The terms and conditions made explicit by these policies, laws and regulations lay down the basic legislative and institutional framework for FDI in China. As we pointed out in the beginning of this chapter, to study FDI in China, one must have a good knowledge and understanding of the evolving changes of China's legal framework and policies towards FDI. The analysis in this chapter provides a policy guideline for the following chapters of this study. We now turn to the analysis of specific questions of FDI in China.

NOTES

1. For a detailed discussion of the political implications of China's foreign trade and FDI reforms, see Shirk (1994).
2. The four modernizations are the modernization of agriculture, industry, science and technology, and national defence, which were raised in the Fourth National People's Congress in January 1975.
3. The statement was made by Deng Xiaoping when he met with the Italian journalist Oriana Fallaci on 20 and 23 August 1980.
4. Profits dropped from 24.3 per cent in 1966 to only 16.4 per cent in 1978 (Chen, 1982).
5. The Law of the People's Republic of China on Joint Ventures Using Chinese and Foreign Investment (8 July 1979), available at http://www.novexcn.com/equity_jv_chin_foreign.html (accessed 29 November 2010).
6. The 14 coastal cities are Dalian, Qinhuangdao, Tianjin, Yantai, Qingdao, Lianyungang, Nantong, Shanghai, Ningbo, Wenzhou, Fuzhou, Guangzhou, Zhanjiang and Beihai.
7. These commitments are summarized from the US–China WTO agreement, the EU–China WTO agreement and China's commitments to the WTO Working Party.
8. Regulations for the Implementation of the Law of the People's Republic of China on Chinese-Foreign Equity Joint Ventures (20 September 1983), available at http://www.fdi.gov.cn/pub/FDI_EN/Laws/law_en_info.jsp?docid=51012 (accessed 29 November 2010).
9. During 1983 and 1984, several policy investigation teams were sent out by the central government to selected provinces. I was twice sent to Liaoning province, where the private economy developed very quickly, especially in the rural areas, to investigate the situation, development, and social and economic effects of the private economy, in order to provide first hand material and policy suggestions to the central government to make policies for the private economy.
10. The Law of the People's Republic of China on Enterprises Operated Exclusively with Foreign Capital (12 April 1986), available at http://www.danmex.org/html-en/china-laws-details.php?news_id=18 (accessed 30 November 2010).
11. The Provisions of the State Council on the Encouragement of Foreign Investment (11 October 1986), available at http://www.fdi.gov.cn/pub/FDI_EN/Laws/law_en_info.jsp?docid=50999 (accessed 29 November 2010).
12. Law of the People's Republic of China on Chinese-Foreign Contractual Joint Ventures (13 April 1988), available at http://www.novexcn.com/chin_for_contact_jv.html (accessed 29 November 2010).
13. Measures on Administration of the Appraisal of Assets Invested by Foreign Businessmen (18 March 1994), available at http://www.fdi.gov.cn/pub/FDI_EN/Laws/law_en_info.jsp?docid=63328 (accessed 29 November 2010).
14. The Company Law of the People's Republic of China (29 December 1993), available at http://www.lawinfochina.com/law/display.asp?id=641 (accessed 29 November 2010).

15. Interim Provisions Concerning Some Issues on the Establishment of Companies Limited by Shares with Foreign Investment (10 January 1995), available at http://www.fdi.gov.cn/pub/FDI_EN/Laws/law_en_info.jsp?docid=51118 (accessed 29 November 2010).

16. Law of the People's Republic of China on Foreign-capital Enterprises (revised 31 October 2000), available at http://www.fdi.gov.cn/pub/FDI_EN/Laws/law_en_info.jsp?docid=51034 (accessed 29 November 2010).
    Law of the People's Republic of China on Chinese-Foreign Contractual Joint Ventures (revised 31 October 2000), available at http://www.fdi.gov.cn/pub/FDI_EN/Laws/law_en_info.jsp?docid=51032 (accessed 29 November 2010).
    Law of the People's Republic of China on Chinese-Foreign Equity Joint Ventures (revised 15 March 2001), available at http://www.fdi.gov.cn/pub/FDI_EN/Laws/law_en_info.jsp?docid=51033 (accessed 29 November 2010).

17. The Company Law of the People's Republic of China (revised 27 October 2005), available at http://www.fdi.gov.cn/pub/FDI_EN/Laws/law_en_info.jsp?docid=50878 (accessed 29 November 2010).

18. Interim Provisions on Mergers and Acquisitions of Domestic Enterprises by Foreign Investors (7 March 2003), available at http://www.fdi.gov.cn/pub/FDI_EN/Laws/law_en_info.jsp?docid=51173 (accessed 29 November 2010).

19. Provisions on Mergers and Acquisitions of Domestic Enterprises by Foreign Investors (revised 8 August 2006), available at http://www.fdi.gov.cn/pub/FDI_EN/Laws/law_en_info.jsp?docid=66925 (accessed 29 November 2010).

20. Anti-Monopoly Law of the People's Republic of China (30 August 2007), available at http://www.fdi.gov.cn/pub/FDI_EN/Laws/law_en_info.jsp?docid=85714 (accessed 29 November 2010).

21. Provisions on M&As of Domestic Enterprises by Foreign Investors (revised 22 June 2009), available at http://www.fdi.gov.cn/pub/FDI_EN/Laws/law_en_info.jsp?docid=108906 (accessed 29 November 2010).

22. Provisions on Guiding the Orientation of Foreign Investment (11 February 2002), available at http://www.fdi.gov.cn/pub/FDI_EN/Laws/law_en_info.jsp?docid=51267 (accessed 29 November 2010).

23. Catalogue for the Guidance of Foreign Investment Industries (Amended 11 March 2002), available at http://www.fdi.gov.cn/pub/FDI_EN/Laws/law_en_info.jsp?docid=51272 (accessed 29 November 2010).

24. Catalogue for the Guidance of Foreign Investment Industries (Amended 30 November 2004), available at http://www.fdi.gov.cn/pub/FDI_EN/Laws/law_en_info.jsp?docid=87902 (accessed 29 November 2010).

25. Catalogue of Priority Industries for Foreign Investment in the Central-West Region (Amended 23 December 2008), available at http://www.fdi.gov.cn/pub/FDI_EN/Laws/law_en_info.jsp?docid=101064 (accessed 29 November 2010).

26. Catalogue of Encouraged Hi-tech Products for Foreign Investment (2 June 2003), available at http://www.fdi.gov.cn/pub/FDI_EN/Laws/law_en_info.jsp?docid=51273 (accessed 29 November 2010).

27. Catalogue of Encouraged Hi-tech Products for Foreign Investment (revised 31 December 2006) [in Chinese], available at http://www.bjmbc.gov.cn/web2/fcsArticleDetail.jsp?article_id=11723920890001 (accessed 29 November 2010).

28. Catalogue for the Guidance of Foreign Investment Industries (Amended 31 October 2007), available at http://www.fdi.gov.cn/pub/FDI_EN/Laws/law_en_info.jsp?docid=87372 (accessed 29 November 2010).

29. The 11th Five-year Plan on Foreign Capital Utilization (10 November 2006), available at http://www.fdi.gov.cn/pub/FDI_EN/Laws/GeneralLawsandRegulations/MinisterialRulings/P020061220577529212555.pdf (accessed 29 November 2010).

30. Catalogue for Guidance for Industrial Structure Adjustment (2007 version), [In Chinese], available at http://www.conch.cn//news_file/20081936297349.pdf (accessed 29 November 2010).

31.   Opinions on Regulating Access to and Administration of Foreign Investment in Real Estate Market (11 July 2006), available at http://www.fdi.gov.cn/pub/FDI_EN/Laws/law_en_info.jsp?docid=65464 (accessed 29 November 2010).

32.   The Chinese government did give some foreign exchange assistance to some of the top-priority, high-profile FDI firms, such as Shanghai Volkswagen and Beijing Jeep Corporation, to keep them going without having to shut down. However, it did not have enough resources and provided little alternatives to assist other FDI firms which were also facing a foreign exchange crisis in their operations.

33.   Provisions of the State Council Concerning the Balance of Foreign Exchange Income and Expenditure of Chinese-Foreign Equity Joint Ventures (15 January 1986), available at http://www.fdi.gov.cn/pub/FDI_EN/Laws/law_en_info.jsp?docid=51859 (accessed 29 November 2010).

34.   Income Tax Law of the People's Republic of China on Chinese-Foreign Equity Joint Ventures (10 September 1980), available at http://www.fdi.gov.cn/pub/FDI_EN/Laws/law_en_info.jsp?docid=75805 (accessed 29 November 2010).

35.   The Income Tax Law of the People's Republic of China Concerning Foreign Enterprises (13 December 1981), available at http://www.novexcn.com/income_tax_law.html (accessed 29 November 2010).

36.   Provisions of the General Administration of Customs and the Ministry of Finance Concerning the Levy and Exemption of Customs Duties and Consolidated Industrial and Commercial Tax on Imports and Exports for the Chinese-Foreign Cooperative Exploitation of Offshore Oil (1 April 1982), available at http://www.fdi.gov.cn/pub/FDI_EN/Laws/law_en_info.jsp?docid=89216 (accessed 29 November 2010).

37.   The Equity Joint Venture Income Tax Law also applied to cooperative joint ventures created as a legal entity.

38.   The Foreign Enterprise Income Tax Law also applied to wholly foreign-owned enterprises and the foreign partners in the cooperative joint ventures in which each partner retains its identity in joint operations.

39.   Provisional Regulations Promulgated by the State Council of the People's Republic of China on Reduction and Exemption of Enterprise Income Tax and Consolidated Industrial and Commercial Tax for 14 Coastal Port Cities, as well as the Four Special Economic Zones and Hainan Island (15 November 1984), available at http://www.novexcn.com/red_exem_comm_ent_tax_sez.html (accessed 29 November 2010).

40.   Income Tax Law of the People's Republic of China on Enterprises with Foreign Investment and Foreign Enterprises (9 April 1991), available at http://www.fdi.gov.cn/pub/FDI_EN/Laws/law_en_info.jsp?docid=51522 (accessed 29 November 2010).

41.   Rules for the Implementation of the Income Tax Law of the People's Republic of China on Enterprises with Foreign Investment and Foreign Enterprises (30 June 1991), available at http://www.fdi.gov.cn/pub/FDI_EN/Laws/law_en_info.jsp?docid=51518 (accessed 29 November 2010).

42.   However, if the USA's subsidiaries do not repatriate their profits to their parent companies located in the USA and, instead, reinvest the profits in China or send the profits to another subsidiary located in a third country, the tax incentives in the form of exemptions and reductions are still effective to their investment decisions.

43.   Enterprise Income Tax Law of the People's Republic of China (16 March 2007), available at http://www.fdi.gov.cn/pub/FDI_EN/Laws/law_en_info.jsp?docid=76240 (accessed 29 November 2010).

44.   According to the '2010 Foreign Direct Investment Confidence Index' (A.T. Kearney, 2010), China remains the top-ranked destination by foreign investors, a title it has held since 2002.

45.   Notice on Unification of City Maintenance and Construction Tax and Education Surcharge for Domestic Enterprises, Foreign Invested Enterprises, and Foreign Individuals (18 October 2010), [in Chinese], available at http://www.chinatax.gov.cn/n8136506/n8136593/n8137537/n8138502/9938060.html (accessed 2 December 2010).

PART I

Location Determinants

3. Location determinants of FDI and China's performance in attracting FDI inflows

INTRODUCTION

During the past three decades, China has attracted a huge amount of FDI inflows. By the end of 2009, China had attracted a total of US$934 billion FDI inflows,[1] making it the largest FDI recipient in the developing world. As a result, China's share both in the world total FDI inflows and in the total FDI inflows into developing countries has increased dramatically from 2 per cent and 11 per cent in the 1980s to around 7 per cent and 25 per cent in the 1990s and 2000s respectively. China's success in attracting FDI into its domestic economy has caused concerns in many other developing countries that China has attracted excessive FDI inflows into its domestic economy and that the huge amount of FDI inflows into China may represent a diversion of world FDI away from them.

However, China is large, and large countries normally receive a large amount of FDI inflows. Has China really received excessive FDI inflows from the world, based on its economic and geographical characteristics? To answer this question we have to investigate the location determinants affecting FDI inflows into developing countries and establish an empirical norm of the magnitude of aggregate FDI inflows from all source countries into a developing host country. Against the empirical norm, we can investigate the relative performance of China and other developing countries in attracting FDI inflows and answer whether or not China has attracted excessive FDI inflows relative to its potential.

Therefore, this chapter is designed to investigate and answer three key questions. First, what are the location determinants affecting FDI inflows into developing countries? Second, what is the relative performance of China in attracting FDI inflows as compared with its neighbouring Asian developing economies? Third, has China attracted excessive FDI inflows from the world?

The chapter is structured as follows. The next section provides a brief overview of FDI inflows into China from a global perspective. The third section sets out the problems which we will study in this chapter. The following section discusses the analytical framework and derives the basic model. The fifth section discusses a number of hypotheses concerning the location determinants affecting FDI inflows into developing countries. The subsequent section tests these hypotheses and gives the basic findings of the regression results. The seventh section investigates the relative performance of China and the East and South-East Asian developing economies in attracting FDI inflows by comparing their actual FDI inflows with the model's predictions. The final section summarizes the findings of this chapter and raises the questions which we will address in the next chapter.

CHINA'S FDI INFLOWS IN GLOBAL PERSPECTIVE

One of the most outstanding features of world FDI inflows during the 1990s and the 2000s was the considerable increase into developing countries. As shown in Figure 3.1, annual average FDI inflows into developing countries increased from US$26.43 billion in the late 1980s to US$124.45 billion in the 1990s and further to US$405.13 billion in the period of 2000 to 2009. As a result, the share of world FDI inflows going to developing countries nearly doubled from 16.31 per cent in the late 1980s to 31.74 per cent in the 1990s and further increased to 34.51 per cent in the period

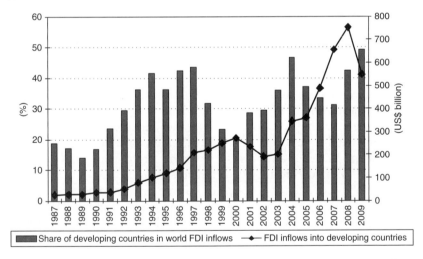

Sources: Compiled from United Nations Conference on Trade and Development (various issues), *World Investment Report*, New York and Geneva: United Nations Publication.

Figure 3.1   FDI inflows into developing countries (current US$)

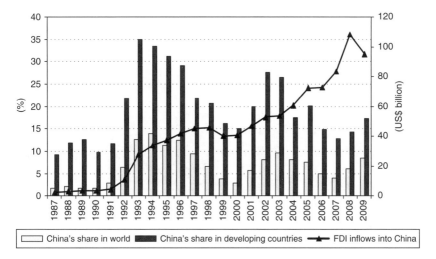

Note: Data for China include FDI inflows into the financial sector after 2005.

Sources: Compiled from United Nations Conference on Trade and Development (various issues), *World Investment Report*, New York and Geneva: United Nations Publication.

Figure 3.2 China's FDI inflows in global perspective (current US$)

of 2000 to 2009. In 2008, despite the decline of world FDI inflows caused by the global financial and economic crisis, FDI inflows into developing countries increased from US$655.89 billion in 2007 to US$752.61 billion in 2008, an increase of 14.75 per cent. In 2009, although FDI inflows into developing countries declined to US$548.29 billion, the share of developing countries in world FDI inflows increased to 49.21 per cent.

One of the major contributing factors to the large increase of FDI inflows into developing countries in the past two decades has been the large amount of FDI inflows into China. As shown in Figure 3.2, since the early 1990s and especially after China's entry into the WTO in 2001, FDI inflows into China have increased dramatically. Annual average FDI inflows into China increased from US$2.97 billion in the late 1980s to US$29.04 billion in the 1990s and further increased to US$68.64 billion during the period 2000 to 2009. As a result, China's shares in FDI inflows in the world and in developing countries have increased significantly. During the 1980s China's shares in FDI inflows in the world and in developing countries were around 2 per cent and 11 per cent respectively. However, in the 1990s China's shares increased dramatically, reaching 7.5 per cent and 23 per cent respectively. In the 2000s China's shares declined slightly due to the massive increase in world FDI inflows during the period 2004 to 2007.

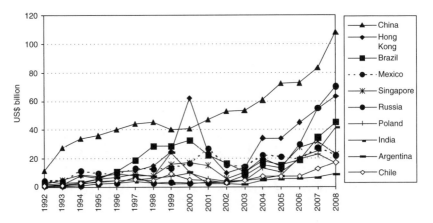

Note: Data for China include FDI inflows into financial sector after 2005.

Sources: Compiled from United Nations Conference on Trade and Development (various issues), *World Investment Report*, New York and Geneva: United Nations Publication.

Figure 3.3   FDI inflows into the top 10 developing economies (current US$)

However, during the period from 2000 to 2009, China still accounted for 6 per cent of total world FDI inflows and 17 per cent of total FDI inflows into developing countries. China's performance in attracting FDI inflows was particularly significant in 2008; when the world FDI inflows declined by 16 per cent, in contrast FDI inflows into China increased by 30 per cent. In 2009, FDI inflows into China declined to US$95 billion,[2] decreasing by 12 per cent. However, compared with the 37 per cent drop of global FDI inflows in 2009, FDI inflows into China were still very resilient.

Among the developing countries, China's performance in attracting FDI inflows has been the most outstanding. Figure 3.3 presents annual FDI inflows into the top ten developing countries and economies receiving FDI inflows. As the figure shows, since 1992 (except in 2000) FDI inflows into China have far exceeded FDI inflows into other developing countries and economies. With the exception of Hong Kong and Russia, whose FDI inflows have increased dramatically since 2005, the gap between China and other developing countries and economies in annual FDI inflows has grown significantly since 2001. As a result, during the period from 1992 to 2008, as shown in Figure 3.4, China attracted a total of US$826 billion FDI inflows (at 2000 US dollar prices), making China the largest FDI recipient among the developing countries and economies.

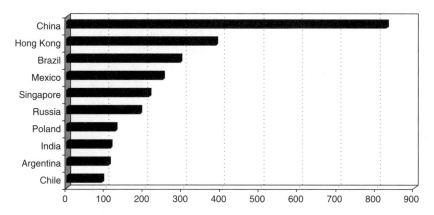

Note: Data for China include FDI inflows into the financial sector after 2005.

Sources: Compiled from United Nations Conference on Trade and Development (various issues), *World Investment Report*, New York and Geneva: United Nations Publication.

Figure 3.4 Total FDI inflows into the top 10 developing economies, 1992–2008 (2000 US$, billions)

Undoubtedly, China has been very successful in attracting FDI inflows, particularly after its WTO accession. However, China's success has caused concerns in other developing countries that China has attracted excessive FDI inflows from the world and, as a result, China has crowded out FDI inflows into their economies. Theoretically we cannot determine a priori whether China has attracted excessive FDI inflows from the world relative to its potential. To answer this question we have to investigate the location determinants affecting FDI inflows into developing countries and establish an empirical norm of the magnitude of FDI inflows from all source countries into a developing host country. Against the empirical norm, we can investigate the relative performance of China in attracting FDI inflows and answer the question whether China has attracted excessive FDI inflows relative to its potential. It is thus important to examine this issue empirically.

THE PROBLEM

The above analysis raises the questions of why there are differences in the magnitude of FDI inflows among developing countries and what location factors affect FDI inflows into developing countries? In order to analyse these issues, we may describe the magnitude of the developing country distribution of FDI inflows as the entries in the cells of a matrix. The matrix [FDI$_{ij}$] has its typical element FDI$_{ij}$ which is the FDI inflows from source country i into developing host country j.

$$[FDI_{ij}] = \begin{bmatrix} FDI_{11} & FDI_{12} & FDI_{13} & \cdots & FDI_{1N} \\ FDI_{21} & FDI_{22} & FDI_{23} & \cdots & FDI_{2N} \\ \cdots & \cdots & \cdots & \cdots & \cdots \\ FDI_{M1} & FDI_{M2} & FDI_{M3} & \cdots & FDI_{MN} \end{bmatrix}$$

$$[FDI_{*j}] = \begin{bmatrix} FDI_{*1} & FDI_{*2} & FDI_{*3} & \cdots & FDI_{*N} \end{bmatrix}$$

If we array the developing host countries along the columns and array the source countries along the rows, then summing down rows for each column, we get a row vector [FDI$_{*j}$] with its typical element FDI$_{*j}$. This represents the total FDI inflows from all source countries into developing host country j, and is the dependent variable which we will study in this chapter.

Our analysis asks the questions: what location factors determine the magnitude of a typical element FDI$_{*j}$ which is the total FDI inflows from all source countries into developing host country j, and what is the relative performance of China and other developing host countries in attracting FDI inflows? In order to answer these questions we first seek the determinants affecting the magnitudes of FDI inflows among developing countries, and then examine the difference between actual FDI inflows and the model's predictions for China and other developing host countries in order to compare the relative performance of China in attracting FDI inflows with that of its neighbouring East and South-East Asian developing countries and economies.

As we discussed in Chapter 1, in the FDI literature the determinants of FDI can be classified into two groups: source-side factors and host-side factors. According to Dunning's OLI paradigm, the source-side factors are ownership advantages and the internalization advantages and the host-side factors are location advantages. Empirically, both sets of determinants have been tested by scholars taking the two sets of determinants either together or separately (Dunning, 1993; Dunning and Lundan, 2008). Some empirical studies of host-side factors, for example, Scaperlanda and Mauer (1969), Lim (1983), Torrisi (1985), Hultman and McGee (1988), Coughlin et al. (1991), Wheeler and Mody (1992), Zhang (1994), Wei (1995, 1996a), Chen (1996), Broadman and Sun (1997), Chen (1997b, 2003, 2010b), Bevan and Estrin (2000), Chantasasawat et al. (2004), Janicki and Wunnava (2004), Eichengreen and Tong (2005),

Mercereau (2005), Zhou and Lall (2005), Buckley et al. (2007), Cravino et al. (2007), Kang and Lee (2007), Kaynak et al. (2007), Vogiatzoglou (2007, 2008), Wang et al. (2007), Amiti and Javorcik (2008), Resmini and Siedschlag (2008), Uttama and Peridy (2009) and Choong and Lam (2010), have shown that given the ownership advantages of the source countries' enterprises and the incentives for them to internalize the use of their ownership advantages, the location determinants of host countries, such as market size, economic growth, labour costs, trade barriers, infrastructure, distance, government policy and political stability, are very important in affecting the distribution of FDI inflows into host countries.

Using the same methodology, this study will focus upon the host-side factors to explore the location determinants of FDI inflows into developing countries. The following section will introduce the framework of analysis and derive the basic model.

FRAMEWORK OF ANALYSIS AND THE MODEL

In introducing the problems that we address, we assert the usefulness of a 'modified' gravity model. This section provides a description of the model, its theoretical underpinning, and its possible modifications.

The phrase 'gravity model' is drawn from the concept of gravitational attraction over space. In its unmodified form, the gravity concept postulates that an attracting force of interaction between two areas is created by the population masses of the two areas while a friction or resistance to interaction is caused by the intervening space over which the interaction must take place. The magnitude or strength of the gravitational attraction between two areas varies directly with some function of the size of the two areas and inversely with some function of the distance between them.

The basic idea underlying the gravity model is that interaction between two areas is a function of the concentration of relevant variables in the two areas, and of the distance between them. The gravity model has been extensively used by economists in studies of international trade flows.[3] Tinbergen (1962) pioneered the use of the gravity model in the study of the levels of bilateral trade flows. Linnemann (1966) elaborated the Tinbergen model and his results implicitly suggested that the relative distance is important in the determination of trade levels. Leamer (1974) used the framework laid out in his earlier work with Stern to test the adequacy of traditional trade theory, alongside more recent theory which stresses the importance of scale economies. Some economists also used the gravity model in studies of regional trade blocs, regional trade bias and home country trade bias.[4]

The theoretical validity of the gravity model has been examined by Niedercorn and Bechdolt (1969) within the framework of utility theory. More recently, Deardorff (1995) demonstrated that the gravity model is compatible with the neoclassical models, and he also found that what matters for bilateral trade volume is not just the absolute distance between the two countries, but their geographic positions relative to all other countries in the world. The gravity model has also been derived in an imperfect competition/differentiated product framework.[5]

More recently, Anderson and van Wincoop (2003) argued that estimated gravity equations do not have a theoretical foundation. This implies both that estimation suffers from omitted variables bias and that comparative statics analysis is unfounded. They therefore derived the theoretical gravity equation based on the utility function. The key implication of the theoretical gravity equation is that trade between regions, after controlling for size, is determined by *relative* trade barriers. Trade between two regions depends on the bilateral barrier between them relative to average trade barriers that both regions face with all their trading partners (multilateral resistance). Its key emphasis is on the need to consider the resistances to trade flows not just in the bilateral market under consideration, but relative to the multilateral resistance to all markets.

Apart from being extensively used in studies of trade flows, the gravity model has also been used in studies of FDI flows, including, for example, Coughlin et al. (1991), Wei (1995, 1996a), Chen (1997b, 2003, 2010b), Bevan and Estrin (2000), Chantasasawat et al. (2004), Janicki and Wunnava (2004), Zhang (1994), Eichengreen and Tong (2005), Mercereau (2005), Zhou and Lall (2005), Cravino et al. (2007), Wang et al. (2007) and Resmini and Siedschlag (2008).

As elaborated by Dunning's OLI explanation of FDI, many factors influence the flows of FDI. Since these factors are located in different areas, the general argument for the use of the gravity model in line with the OLI framework is that each factor may be categorized as a source country factor (the ownership advantages and internalization advantages), a host country factor (the location advantages) or a linkage factor (the distance and other bilateral factors). Source country factors reflect the capacity of a source country to conduct FDI in all possible host countries, while host country factors are characteristics of the overall attractiveness of a host country to attract and locate FDI inflows from all source countries. Linkage factors take account of the relationships between a particular pair of source country and host country, or a host country/a source country and all the other countries in the world.

We refer to our model as 'modified' gravity model because first we use a large range of factors in the model, and second, we use an improved linkage factor – remoteness – as a resistance factor affecting FDI flows. The remoteness factor is an index of a weighted average distance of a country to all the other countries in the world. The biggest advantage in using remoteness instead of the absolute distance as the distance factor is that first it takes account of a country's geographic position relative to the rest of the world. Second, because we examine the location determinants of FDI inflows from all source countries into developing host countries, remoteness provides us with a comparable distance factor for each of the developing host countries relative to all the other countries in the world.

In this study, in presenting the specified determinants of the country distribution of FDI inflows from all source countries into developing host countries, we shall therefore classify the determinants as source country variables, host country variables and linkage variables.

Based on the spirit of the gravity model and the discussion of the framework of analysis, the fundamental model used in this study can be written as:

$$FDI_{ij} = f(X_i, X_j, R_{ij}) \qquad (3.1)$$

$$i = 1, 2, 3, \ldots I$$

$$j = 1, 2, 3, \ldots J$$

where:

FDI_{ij} = the magnitude of FDI inflows from source country i into host country j
X_i = source country variables
X_j = host country variables
R_{ij} = linkage variables

As regard to the functional form of equation (3.1), we consider the use of the linear and log-linear forms.

First, the linear form of equation (3.1) can be written as:

$$FDI_{ij} = \alpha_0 + \alpha_1 X_i + \alpha_2 X_j + \alpha_3 R_{ij} \qquad (3.2)$$

Since our interest is in examining the location determinants of FDI inflows from all source countries into developing host countries, in order to obtain the host country aggregate equation $FDI_{\cdot j}$, the aggregate FDI inflows from all source countries into a developing host country j, we use the identity:

$$FDI_{*j} = \sum_{i=1}^{I} FDI_{ij} \qquad (3.3)$$

Substituting (3.2) for (3.3):

$$FDI_{*j} = \sum_{i=1}^{I} (\alpha_0 + \alpha_1 X_i + \alpha_2 X_j + \alpha_3 R_{ij})$$

$$= I\alpha_0 + \alpha_1 \sum_{i-1}^{I} X_i + I\alpha_2 X_j + \alpha_3 \sum_{i=1}^{I} R_{ij}$$

$$= I\alpha_0 + \alpha_1 X_* + I\alpha_2 X_j + \alpha_3 R_{*j} \qquad (3.4)$$

Since a source country i's variables X_i, which measure the overall outward investment potential of source country i, are determined by its own technological and economic development levels, the key feature of these variables is that they are common to all outward FDI of source country i and are independent from factors in the destination countries. Therefore, the aggregate source country variables X_* become a constant for each of the host countries, although a constant that changes over time. In the actual implementation, we use the world total FDI outflows (WFDIOUT) of all source countries to capture the effects of source country variables X_*. As a result, we have the following equation:

$$FDI_{*j} = \beta_0 + \beta_1 X_* + \beta_2 X_j + \beta_3 R_{*j} \qquad (3.5)$$

where:

$\beta_0 = I\alpha_0$
$\beta_1 = \alpha_1$
$\beta_2 = I\alpha_2$
$\beta_3 = \alpha_3$

Thus the equation for FDI_{*j} is a function of aggregate source country variables, host country variables and linkage variables. It states that, given the aggregate source country variables (source-side factors), the host country variables (host-side factors) and the linkage variables are the only things that matter to determine the distribution of FDI inflows from all source countries into each of the host countries. Therefore, we call equation (3.5) the host country aggregate FDI equation.

As is usual in the use of a gravity model in studies of international trade flows, we also adopt the log-linear form as the basic functional form to connect the magnitude of FDI inflows from all source countries to host country j to the relevant explanatory variables (aggregate source country variables, host country variables and linkage variables). Therefore, equation (3.5) can be rewritten in log-linear form as:

$$\ln FDI_{*j} = \beta_0 + \beta_1 \ln X_* + \beta_2 \ln X_j + \beta_3 \ln R_{*j} \qquad (3.6)$$

where

FDI_{*j} = the magnitude of total FDI inflows from all source countries into host country j
X_* = aggregate source country variables
X_j = host economy variables
R_{*j} = linkage variables

Thus based on the gravity model, we have derived the basic equation. In equation (3.6) the estimated coefficients of the $\ln X_*$, the $\ln X_j$ and the $\ln R_{*j}$ variables will be elasticities.

Equation (3.6) is the form of a modified gravity model used to explain the magnitude of FDI inflows from all source countries into a host country j. In fact, almost all empirical studies of location determinants of FDI inflows or stocks have used the functional form of this modified gravity model without systematically conducting the derivation of the model. Since our interest is to investigate the location determinants of FDI inflows into developing countries, and in particular into China, equation (3.6) is the fundamental equation in this study. The following section describes the location determinants and establish the independent variables.

THE HYPOTHESES

As shown in many studies, the location factors determining FDI inflows into developing countries are mainly market size, economic growth, per capita income, labour costs adjusted for productivity, resource endowments, political stability and investment incentives offered by the host country governments.[6] In the following sections we examine those location factors which we consider play an important role in determining the magnitude of FDI inflows into developing host countries.

Market Size of Developing Host Countries

In previous studies, the argument for the importance of market size as a location factor in the determination of the inflows of FDI is primarily based on the theory of economies of scale. It argues that larger economies can provide more opportunities to realize and explore economies of scale, to realize the specialization of productive factors and to absorb more efficiently the technology which the foreign investors desire to introduce. However, the significance of this argument is debatable in open economies. This is because in the open economies, enterprises and industries can realize and explore economies of scale through international markets instead of only relying on the domestic market. Therefore, the importance of market size as a location factor in the determination of FDI inflows should be discussed within the situation of open economies.

There are three basic arguments for the importance of the market size as a location factor in attracting FDI inflows even within open economies. First, for domestic market-oriented FDI and especially FDI in the services sector, domestic market size is a very important determinant affecting the investment location decision. This kind of FDI in the world total FDI inflows and in the FDI inflows into developing countries has increased rapidly since the mid-1990s. Second, for export-oriented FDI, as is the general case of most FDI projects in developing countries, particularly in East and South-East Asian economies, domestic market size can still be important because larger economies can provide more opportunities for industries and enterprises to benefit from external economies of scale and spillover effects. This is especially important for high-technology industries and those industries which have a relatively high requirement for well-trained skilled and semi-skilled labourers. Third, larger economies not only can sustain more economic activities but also can provide more opportunities for economic diversification. This is very important for strategic-seeking, conglomeration and diversification FDI.

The above discussion leads us to expect that the magnitude of FDI inflows will be greater the larger is the market size of the developing host country. The measure of market size used in this study is the gross domestic product of the developing host country, denoted by GDP. The expected influence of this variable on the magnitude of FDI inflows is positive.

The Degree of Development of Developing Host Countries

The degree of development of developing host countries is expected to be another important location determinant affecting FDI inflows. First, the supply of domestic entrepreneurship is generally assumed to be positively related to the degree of development of the country. Second, in general a country's education level is positively related to its level of economic and social development. Therefore, countries with a higher degree of development usually possess more human capital endowments and higher quality of labour forces. These are very important for attracting FDI inflows, particularly for FDI taking the form of joint ventures with local partners and for FDI with high technology and a high requirement for skilled labourers. Third, a higher degree of development also implies better conditions in local infrastructure, which is fundamental for attracting FDI inflows. Finally, a higher degree of development also implies a higher purchasing power of the host country's consumers. This is a very important determinant for market-oriented FDI. In this study the per capita GDP, denoted by PGDP, is used as a measure of degree of development of developing host countries. We expect that the influence of PGDP on the magnitude of FDI inflows into developing countries is positive.

Economic Growth in Developing Host Countries

A high rate of economic growth is an indicator of development potential, which is expected to be an important location determinant affecting FDI inflows. First, the higher level of economic growth represents a better overall economic condition of the host countries, which is very conducive to foreign investors. Second, a higher level of economic growth is an indicator of increasingly improved conditions in local infrastructure, which is fundamental for attracting FDI inflows. Third, a higher level of economic growth also implies a fast expansion of the market size, a rapid rise in domestic demand, and a growing purchasing power of the host country's consumers, which is a very important determinant of market-oriented FDI. Clearly, markets that are expected to grow faster will tend to attract higher levels of inward FDI. Therefore, the hypothesis is that there is a positive relationship between inward FDI and economic growth in the developing host economy. In this study, the real GDP growth rate, denoted by GR, is used as the comprehensive measure of development potential in the developing host countries under study.

Factor Costs in Developing Host Countries

In the FDI literature, the most important factor cost in the determination of FDI flows is the wage rate, especially when FDI is export oriented. Therefore, we take the relevant factor cost in the decision to locate FDI in the host country as that of labour costs. In particular, we expect lower labour costs to include higher levels of FDI inflows, especially for export-oriented FDI. However, we argue that a lower wage rate may also be accompanied by lower productivity, and thus the efficiency wage may not be low. Therefore, the best measure of labour costs should be the 'efficiency wage' rather than the absolute wage rate. Following this argument, in this study we use the efficiency wage as a measure of labour costs in each developing host country. The efficiency wage may be directly measured as:

$$EW_j = \frac{W_j}{\Pi_j}$$

where EW_j is the average efficiency wage in developing host country j, W_j is the absolute wage rate in developing host country j, and Π_j is the average productivity of labour in developing host country j. The efficiency wage as a measure of labour costs has the advantage of being unit free. It is expected to be negatively related to the level of FDI inflows.

There are two major problems involved in the international comparison of wage rates and labour productivity. One is the different price levels in different countries, and the other is the different exchange rates, especially in the context of the developing countries. To avoid these problems, in this study we use the total labour earnings as a percentage of the total value-added in each developing country as the corresponding measure of efficiency wage.[7] In fact, according to our above definition for the efficiency wage, the measure of the total labour earnings as a percentage of the total value-added is exactly the average efficiency wage in the developing host countries.[8] In this study, we expect the efficiency wage to be negatively related to the level of FDI inflows into developing countries.

Country Risk (Country Credit Rating)

Studies of FDI in developing countries have put particular emphasis on indicators of economic and political risk (such as Lucas, 1993; Singh and Jun, 1995). Country risk comprises three main elements: macroeconomic stability, for example economic growth, inflation and exchange rate risk; institutional stability, such as policies towards FDI, tax regimes, the transparency of legal regulations, intellectual property protection and the scale of corruption; and political stability, ranging from indicators of political freedom to measures of surveillance and revolutions. While there are a variety of ways in which country risk can be approximated for empirical studies, a common approach relies on country credit ratings, which provides information actually available to firms at the time of their investment decision.

Country credit ratings are developed by Institutional Investors, who have published credit ratings twice a year since 1979 to assess the credit-worthiness of about 150 countries, based on a survey of some 100 international bankers' perception of creditworthiness, including economic, financial and socio-political stability criteria. The resulting score scales from zero (very high chance of default) to 100 (least chance of default). Participants' responses are adjusted according to their institutions' assets, with heavier weights on those institutions with worldwide exposure and sophisticated country-analysis systems. This study uses the credit rating of the host country to measure the investor's perception of country specific risk. The hypothesis is that the lower the country risk (the higher the country credit rating) the higher the level of FDI inflows will be. The country credit rating, denoted as CDR, is compiled from various issues of *Institutional Investor* magazine.

Quality of Human Resources in Developing Host Countries

For developing countries, one of the biggest advantages is the abundance of human resource endowments, which is the primary target of FDI seeking cheap labour. However, as we discussed above, it is not low absolute wages that matter, but low efficiency wages derived from high labour productivity. Thus, it is those developing countries which have put great efforts in investing in and developing human capital that will tend to attract more FDI. In this study, we use the adult literacy rate as the indicator of the overall quality of human resources in developing countries. We expect the adult literacy rate, the proxy for the quality of human resources, denoted as READ, to be positively related to the inflows of FDI into developing countries.

Remoteness of Developing Host Countries

The use of remoteness instead of the absolute distance as the distance factor is mainly for two reasons. First, in this study since our interest lies in analysing the location determinants of aggregate FDI inflows from all source countries into developing host countries, remoteness as a linkage variable provides us with a standardized distance factor for each of the developing host countries with respect to all other countries in the world. Second, as Deardorff (1995) pointed out, what matters for bilateral export volumes is not just the absolute distance between the two countries, but their geographic position relative to all other countries. Though this point is derived from trade flows, we can argue that its basic principle is also valid in examining FDI flows. Our basic argument here is that in terms of the distance factor what matters for the magnitude of aggregate FDI inflows from all source countries into a developing host country is the developing host country's geographic position relative to the rest of the world.

The rationale for including the distance factor – remoteness – as one of the location determinants in affecting FDI inflows into developing host countries is that, first, remoteness is directly related to the level of transport costs. Therefore, on the one hand, we expect that remoteness has a positive effect on FDI inflows if the nature of FDI is domestic-market oriented and FDI and trade are substitutes. On the other hand, we expect that remoteness has a negative effect on FDI inflows if the nature of FDI is export oriented. Second, remoteness is also closely related to the level of transaction costs in terms of information gathering and familiarity with local market conditions. Therefore, we expect remoteness to have a negative effect on FDI inflows. At this aggregate level of study of FDI inflows from all source countries into developing host countries, we expect that remoteness has a net negative effect on FDI inflows. This argument rests on the importance of transaction costs for FDI inflows.

In this study we define a host country j's remoteness, denoted as RMT, as the weighted average distance to all the other countries in the world, and the weight is the share of country i's GDP in the world total GDP. The following formula expresses host country j's remoteness.

$$RMT_j = \sum_{i=1}^{I} w_i D_{ij}$$

where:

$$w_i = \frac{Y_i}{Y_w}$$

Y_i = country i's GDP
Y_w = world GDP
D_{ij} = direct distance between country i to country j.

According to the above definition, remoteness is a measure of the relative closeness of a country to the world economic centre. We expect that the closer a country is to 'the world economic centre' the higher the level of FDI inflows into that country will be.

In this study we chose 45 countries and economies as the 'other' countries in the world to calculate the weighted average distance of a given developing host country.[9] In fact, when we take a country's GDP share as the weight to calculate the weighted average distance of a given developing host country, it is not necessary to use all countries in the world in the calculation since most of the small countries' GDP shares in the world total GDP are very small and will make very little difference to the calculation of the weighted average distance of a given developing host country. The principle for choosing the countries in the calculation was based on their total outward FDI stock at the end of 2008. As long as a country's total outward FDI stock at the end of 2008 exceeded US$10 billion, it was chosen in the calculation. Thus we have 45 countries with combined total outward FDI stock of US$15 718 billion, accounting for 97 per cent of the world total outward FDI stock at the end of 2008. In addition their combined GDP shares were around 94 per cent of the world total GDP from 1991 to 2008.

The distance between country j and the other countries is the physical distance between their capital cities which is obtained from the Great Circle Calculator (at http://argray.com/dist/).

The Level of FDI Stock in Developing Host Countries

The level of FDI stock has been found to be an important explanatory factor of current FDI inflows in several previous studies, for example, Dobson (1993), Petri (1995) and Chen (1997b, 2003). Based on the results of the previous studies, we argue that the level of FDI stock may have certain demonstration effects on the investment location decision of foreign investors. Consequently, our hypothesis is that a higher level of FDI stock indicates an overall better investment environment in developing host countries, which may generate demonstration effects and induce higher levels of FDI inflows. We therefore expect that the level of FDI stock will have a positive effect on attracting FDI inflows. In this study, the level of FDI stock, denoted as FDIS, is calculated by adding the annual FDI inflows to the 1990 FDI stock of host countries at 1990 US dollar prices.

Openness of Developing Host Countries

The trade (exports plus imports) to GDP ratio is usually used as an indicator for the degree of openness of an economy. However, openness as a location factor may have a different effect on the inflows of different kinds of FDI. On the one hand, as usually argued by the 'protection jump' hypothesis, some kinds of FDI, for example some market-oriented FDI, are induced by high trade barriers. If this is the case, then openness would have a negative effect on the inflows of this kind of FDI. On the other hand, a higher degree of openness of an economy not only indicates more economic linkages and activities with the rest of the world, but also indicates a more open and liberalized economic and trade regime. As a result, it is expected to attract more FDI inflows, particularly the inflows of export-oriented FDI. In this study we expect that a developing country's openness, denoted as OPEN, has a positive effect on FDI inflows.

We have outlined above the host country factors that are expected to be the most important in the determination of the magnitude of FDI inflows into developing host countries. Other location factors, such as resource endowments, investment incentives and legal framework, are not tested in this study. This is mainly because of the data limitations and the difficulties in quantifying some of the variables. However, we acknowledge that these variables may have impacts on FDI flows even though we do not put them into our empirical tests. The following section presents the econometric analysis and the regression results.

THE EMPIRICAL MODEL AND VARIABLE SPECIFICATION

The research methodology is to use regression analysis to test the hypotheses set out above. The basic principle in choosing the samples of developing host countries is the data availability. We tried to choose as many samples as possible. However, because of data limitations we chose 50 developing countries and economies over 17 years from 1992 to 2008. The 50 developing countries and economies used in this study are: Botswana, Egypt, Kenya, Malawi, Mauritius, South Africa and Swaziland from Africa; Argentina, Bolivia, Brazil, Chile, Colombia, Costa Rica, El Salvador, Guatemala, Jamaica, Mexico, Nicaragua, Paraguay, Peru and Trinidad and Tobago from Latin America and the Caribbean; Azerbaijan, Bangladesh, China, Georgia, Hong Kong (China), India, Indonesia, Jordan, Kazakhstan, Malaysia, Pakistan, Philippines, Singapore, Sri Lanka, South Korea, Taiwan (China), Thailand, Turkey and Vietnam from Asia; Bulgaria, Croatia, Czech Republic, Estonia, Hungary, Poland, Romania, Russia, Slovakia and Slovenia from Central and Eastern Europe.

Using the basic equation (3.6) derived in this chapter and the hypotheses discussed above, to investigate the location determinants affecting FDI inflows into developing countries, we use the following empirical model:

$$\ln FDI_{*j,t} = \beta_0 + \beta_1 \ln WFDIOUT_{*,t} + \beta_2 \ln GDP_{j,t-k} + \beta_3 \ln PGDP_{j,t-k}$$

$$+ \beta_4 \ln GR_{j,t-k} + \beta_5 \ln EW_{j,t-k} + \beta_6 \ln CDR_{j,t-k} + \beta_7 \ln READ_{j,t-k}$$

$$+ \beta_8 \ln RMT_{j,t-k} + \beta_9 \ln FDIS_{j,t-k} + \beta_{10} \ln OPEN_{j,t-k} + v_j + \varepsilon_{j,t} \quad (3.7)$$

The dependent variable, denoted as $FDI_{*j,t}$, is the aggregate inflow of FDI from all source countries into developing host country j in year t. The value of FDI and the relevant following variables are measured at 1990 US dollar prices. There are ten independent variables. The independent variables – *GDP, PGDP, GR, EW, CDR, READ, RMT, FDIS* and *OPEN* – are hypothesized and defined in the above section. We include the world total FDI outflows (*WFDIOUT*) as an independent variable to control the aggregate supply-side effect of FDI on FDI inflows into developing host countries. The dependent and independent variables are summarized in Table 3.1.

The independent variables, except *WFDIOUT*, are lagged k years. This model assumes that the effect of the independent variables at time *t-k* appears only within period *t* and is fully completed within that period. The relationship shown in equation (3.7) is examined for $k=1$, the most likely appropriate lag. The independent variable *WFDIOUT*, which is world total FDI outflows, is determined by the source side factors and is independent from host countries' determinants, therefore, the current value ($k=0$) will be employed in the regression equation. The estimated coefficients of variables of $\ln WFDIOUT_{*,t}$, $\ln GDP_{j,t-k}$, $\ln PGDP_{j,t-k}$, $\ln GR_{j,t-k}$, $\ln EW_{j,t-k}$, $\ln CDR_{j,t-k}$, $\ln READ_{j,t-k}$, $\ln RMT_{j,t-k}$, $\ln FDIS_{j,t-k}$ and $\ln OPEN_{j,t-k}$ are elasticities.

REGRESSION RESULTS AND EXPLANATIONS

To conduct the econometric regression analysis, we applied linear regression with panel data method. The econometric regression analysis below uses a fixed-effects model, in order to eliminate the country-specific and time-invariant factors which may affect FDI inflows. The fixed-effects regression results of equation (3.7) are reported in Table 3.2 with the explanatory variables (except variable *WFDIOUT*) lagged one year ($k=1$) for the 50 developing host countries and economies for the period 1992 to 2008.

For Model 1, we include all the independent variables. We find that the variables *WFDIOUT, PGDP, GR, EW, RMT* and *READ* have the expected signs and the coefficients are statistically significant at the 1 per cent level. Variable *CDR* is positive and is statistically significant at the 5 per cent level. Variable *OPEN* is positive and the coefficient is statistically significant at the 10 per cent level. Variable *FDIS* is positive but the coefficient is not statistically significant. However, the coefficient of variable *GDP* not only has the wrong sign but also is not statistically significant.

Since there are ten independent variables in the regression, the wrong

Table 3.1   Variable list of the location determinants of FDI inflows into developing host countries

Variable name	Specification of variables	Sources
Dependent variable		
$FDI_{*j,t}$	Total FDI inflows from all source countries into developing host country j in year t. 1990 US$, millions	Various issues of United Nations Conference on Trade and Development, *World Investment Report*.
Independent variables		
$WFDIOUT_{*,t}$	World total FDI outflows in year t. 1990 US$, millions	Various issues of United Nations Conference on Trade and Development, *World Investment Report*.
$GDP_{j,t}$	Gross Domestic Product of developing host country j in year t. 1990 US$, millions	United Nations Statistical Division, National Accounts.
$PGDP_{j,t}$	Per capita GDP of developing host country j in year t. 1990 US$ per capita	Same as above.
$GR_{j,t}$	Annual real growth rate of GDP of developing host country j in year t. Percentage	Same as above.
$EW_{j,t}$	Efficiency wage of developing host country j in year t. Percentage	Calculated from International Labour Organization, LABORSTA Internet, and United Nations Statistical Division, National Accounts.
$CDR_{j,t}$	Credit rating of developing host country j in year t. Scale of zero to 100, with 100 representing the least chance of default or the best creditworthiness	Complied from various issues of *Institutional Investor*.
$READ_{j,t}$	Adult literacy rate of developing host country j in year t. Percentage	Calculated from United Nations Common Database (UNCDB).
$RMT_{j,t}$	Remoteness of developing host country j in year t. Index of weighted average distance to the rest of the world	Calculated from Great Circle Calculator and United Nations Statistical Division, National Accounts.
$FDIS_{j,t}$	Inward FDI stock of developing host country j in year t. 1990 US$, millions	Various issues of United Nations Conference on Trade and Development, *World Investment Report*.
$OPEN_{j,t}$	Total trade to GDP ratio of developing host country j in year t. Percentage	United Nations Statistical Division, National Accounts.

*Table 3.2   Regression results of location determinants affecting FDI
inflows into developing host countries and economies, 1992–
2008 (lag k=1), fixed-effects (dependent variable LFDI*_{•j,t}*)*

Variables	Model 1	Model 2	Model 3	Model 4	Model 5
Constant	46.19	–7.30	57.04	54.54	67.32
	(2.68)***	(–3.99)***	(3.31)***	(3.40)***	(4.11)***
LWFDIOUT	0.10	0.12	0.09	0.11	0.12
	(2.77)***	(2.99)***	(2.43)**	(3.20)***	(3.36)***
LGDP	–0.38	0.69	0.58		
	(–1.19)	(3.20)***	(2.52)**		
LPGDP	0.75	0.73		0.66	
	(5.50)***	(5.46)***		(5.42)***	
LGR	0.49	0.46	0.52	0.47	0.57
	(4.96)***	(4.67)***	(5.38)***	(4.81)***	(5.93)***
LEW	–1.21	–1.36	–1.21	–1.29	–1.13
	(–5.52)***	(–5.92)***	(–5.35)***	(–5.75)***	(–4.89)***
LCDR	0.53	0.91	0.89	0.80	
	(2.20)**	(3.86)***	(3.55)***	(3.47)***	
LRMT	–12.41		–13.99	–13.01	–16.33
	(–3.40)***		(–3.79)***	(–3.70)***	(–4.61)***
LFDIS	0.12				0.24
	(1.22)				(3.18)***
LREAD	2.17				1.60
	(3.28)***				(3.03)***
LOPEN	0.49		0.71	0.66	0.58
	(1.83)*		(3.02)***	(3.04)***	(2.10)**
Observations	646	646	646	646	646
Groups	50	50	50	50	50
R^2: within	0.52	0.50	0.50	0.52	0.50
between	0.07	0.73	0.21	0.11	0.10
overall	0.09	0.68	0.20	0.12	0.10
F-statistics	66.92***	96.55***	89.32***	89.16***	94.00***

Notes:
Standard errors are adjusted for heteroscedasticity and cluster effects on group.
t-statistics are in parentheses.
*   Statistically significant at 0.10 level (two-tail test).
**   Statistically significant at 0.05 level (two-tail test).
*** Statistically significant at 0.01 level (two-tail test).

sign and statistical insignificance of the variables *GDP* and *FDIS* might
be caused by the problem of high collinearity between variables *GDP*
and *FDIS* and the other independent variables. If this is the case, the
effect of variables *GDP* and *FDIS* on FDI inflows may be captured by

other variables, if we regress all of the independent variables in the same equation.

We examined the correlation coefficients between the independent variables. We found that there are collinearity problems among the independent variables. For example, the correlation coefficient between *GDP* and *FDIS* was 0.70, between *CDR* and *FDIS* was 0.59, and between *PGDP* and *READ* was 0.59 respectively. The relatively high correlation between those variables may be the cause of the insignificance of variables *GDP* and *FDIS* in the regression.

One way to solve the collinearity problem is to enter the variables which have high correlation into the regression equation separately. Therefore, we run another four separate regressions, Model 2, Model 3, Model 4 and Model 5, each with a different set of explanatory variables. The four models performed very well and all the independent variables have the expected signs and are statistically significant.

In line with our hypotheses and the regression results, we can now give some basic findings concerning the location determinants of FDI inflows into developing countries.

The market size (*GDP*) and the degree of development (*PGDP*) of the developing host country are positive and statistically significant location determinants affecting the magnitude of FDI inflows. The regression results, therefore, support the hypothesis that the larger and higher degree of development of an economy, the larger the magnitude of FDI inflows will be.

Market growth rate (*GR*) is a positive and statistically significant location determinant in affecting the magnitude of FDI inflows into developing host countries. The results demonstrate that the higher and faster the growth of an economy, the higher the level of FDI inflows will be.

Efficiency wage (*EW*), the proxy for labour costs, is a negative and statistically significant location determinant affecting the magnitude of FDI inflows into developing host countries. The results show that a higher efficiency wage in developing host countries deters FDI inflows. This indicates that FDI is responsive to the differences in efficiency wages across developing countries. It also reveals that taking advantage of developing countries' cheap labour is one of the main motives of foreign investors in developing countries.

In most other studies, as surveyed by Dunning (1993), the labour cost variables either have the wrong signs (positive) or are not statistically significant even though they have negative signs. Apart from the statistical problems, the main reason for the above results is the use of the absolute wage rates rather than the efficiency wage in these studies. A lower absolute wage rate may also be accompanied by lower productivity. Thus the efficiency wage may not be low. In other words, a higher absolute wage rate may be associated with higher productivity, thus the efficiency wage may not be high. Therefore, the analysis presented here shows that the best measure of labour costs should be the efficiency wage rather than the absolute wage rates.

Country credit rating (*CDR*) is found to exert a large influence on the magnitude of FDI inflows into developing countries. Economic, financial, institutional, social and political stabilities with high creditworthiness can be considered as one of the most influential tools to promote FDI inflows since it has a direct impact on the security and profitability of FDI projects.

Remoteness (*RMT*), the proxy for the relative distance of a developing country to the rest of the world, is a negative and statistically significant location determinant. The results show that the more 'remote' a developing host country is from the rest of the world, the smaller the magnitude of FDI inflows into that developing host country will be. The negative estimated coefficient of remoteness reveals an important point that transaction costs in terms of information gathering and familiarity with local market conditions are very important factors affecting the investment location decision of foreign investors.

The level of FDI stock (*FDIS*) is a positive and statistically significant factor affecting FDI inflows into developing host countries. The regression results show that a high level of existing FDI stock will attract more FDI inflows. This reveals the importance of the demonstration effect on the investment location decision of foreign investors.

The adult literacy rate (*READ*), the proxy for the quality of human resources, is a positive and statistically significant location determinant affecting the magnitude of FDI inflows into developing host countries. The results show that a higher adult literacy rate in developing host countries attracts higher FDI inflows. This indicates that FDI is not only responsive to the differences in labour costs but also is responsive to the differences in labour quality across developing countries.

Openness (*OPEN*) is a positive and statistically significant location determinant affecting the magnitude of FDI inflows into developing countries. The regression results indicate that the more open an economy is the more FDI inflows will go into that economy. Therefore, a more liberalized trade regime rather than imposing high trade barriers is important for developing countries to attract more FDI inflows to accelerate economic development.

Finally, the variable of world total FDI outflows (*WFDIOUT*) is positive and statistically significant. This signifies the impact of an overall supply-side effect on the inflows of FDI to developing countries.

To summarize, the main findings for the location determinants of FDI inflows into developing countries are countries with a larger market size, faster economic growth, higher per capita income, higher creditworthiness or lower country risk in terms of economic, financial, institutional, social and political stability, higher quality of human resources with higher adult literacy rates, a higher level of existing FDI stock and a more liberalized trade regime represented by the higher degree of openness attracted relatively more FDI inflows, while higher efficiency wages or lower labour productivity and greater remoteness from the rest of the world deterred FDI inflows during the period of analysis, 1992 to 2008.

HAS CHINA ATTRACTED EXCESSIVE FDI INFLOWS?

The statistical model in the above section has effectively established a norm of the magnitude of aggregate FDI inflows from all source countries into a developing host country. According to the model, the magnitude of aggregate FDI inflows from all source countries into developing host countries is a function of a developing host country's market size, economic growth, per capita income, efficiency wages, the credit rating, remoteness from the rest of the world, quality of human resources, existing FDI stock and the level of openness after controlling for the world total FDI outflows. Against the empirical norm, we can now examine the relative performance of China and to assess whether China has attracted excessive FDI inflows from the world.

To examine the relative performance of developing host countries in attracting FDI inflows, we define the relative performance of a developing host country in attracting FDI inflows as the percentage ratio of the difference between the actual FDI inflows and the FDI inflows predicted by the model. The calculation of the relative performance in attracting FDI inflows is based on the following equation:

$$RFDI_{*j,t} = ((AFDI_{*j,t} - PFDI_{*j,t})/PFDI_{*j,t}) * 100\% \qquad (3.8)$$

where:

$RFDI_{*j,t}$ = relative performance of host country j in attracting FDI inflows from all source countries in year t.

$AFDI_{*j,t}$ = actual FDI inflows from all source countries into host country j in year t.

$PFDI_{*j,t}$ = model predicted FDI inflows from all source countries into host country j in year t.

According to the equation, a positive figure for $RFDI_{*j,t}$ indicates that a developing host country's actual FDI inflows are more than the model's prediction, and the larger the figure the better the relative performance of that developing host country in attracting FDI inflows. In contrast, a negative figure for $RFDI_{*j,t,}$ indicates that a developing host country's actual FDI inflows are less than it could receive based on its location variables, and the smaller the figure the poorer the relative performance of that developing host country in attracting FDI inflows. If a developing host country's $RFDI_{*j,t,}$ is zero, then the amount of FDI inflows attracted by this developing host country is exactly equal to the amount of FDI that this developing host country should receive based on its location variables. In other words, this developing host country's relative performance in attracting FDI inflows is at the average of all developing host countries.

In this study, the calculation of the predicted FDI inflows is based on Model 2 in Table 3.2 because Model 2 has the highest overall explanatory power among the five models.

Let us first examine the aggregate relative performance of China in attracting FDI inflows for the last three decades. In aggregate, from 1982 to 2008, China attracted 5.88 per cent or US$38.77 billion (at 1990 US dollar prices) more FDI inflows than its potential based on its location variables. Therefore, although China is the largest FDI recipient among the developing countries, after controlling for its huge market size, increasing per capita income, fast economic growth, low labour costs, relatively well-educated human resources, and economic, financial, institutional, social and political stability, China's relative performance in attracting FDI inflows is at a level only moderately above its potential for the past three decades.

Compared to the East and South-East Asian developing economies, as shown in Table 3.3, from 1992 to 2008, China attracted 7.56 per cent or US$47.36 billion (at 1990 US dollar prices) more FDI inflows than its potential based on its location variables. As a result, China's relative performance in attracting FDI inflows was much better than that of Taiwan, South Korea and Singapore, similar to that of Hong Kong, Malaysia and Indonesia, but much lower than that of the Philippines, Vietnam and Thailand. Therefore, after controlling for its location variables, China's relative performance in attracting FDI inflows is at the average of its neighbouring Asian developing economies during 1992 to 2008.

Table 3.3   Aggregate relative performance of East and South-East Asian developing economies in attracting FDI inflows, 1992–2008

Economy	Relative performance in attracting FDI inflows (%)	Difference between actual and predicted FDI inflows (1990 US$ billions)
Philippines	360.85	15.93
Vietnam	324.44	23.17
Thailand	169.59	39.67
Indonesia	16.74	5.69
Malaysia	9.68	5.81
Hong Kong	8.37	24.39
China	7.56	47.36
Singapore	−20.93	−46.22
South Korea	−75.87	−180.65
Taiwan	−85.98	−220.57

Source: Author's calculation, using Model 2 of Table 3.2.

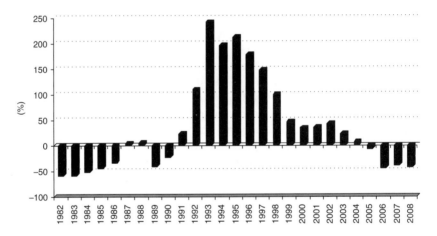

Source: Author's calculation, using Model 2 of Table 3.2.

Figure 3.5   China's annual relative performance in attracting FDI inflows, 1982–2008

From a dynamic point of view, as shown in Figure 3.5, China's relative performance in attracting FDI inflows fluctuated during the 1980s and 1990s. China attracted less FDI inflows than its potential during 1982 to 1986 but more between 1987 and 1988. However, from 1989 to 1990 China received less FDI inflows than it might have received.[10] Starting from 1992, FDI inflows into China surged at an unprecedented pace, mainly owing to a series of market-opening policies in the early 1990s. As a result, China received more FDI inflows than its potential from 1992 to 2000, but the relative performance fell during 1997 to 2000, mainly because of the Asian financial crisis. After China's accession into the WTO, China's relative performance was moderately above its potential during 2001 to 2004. However, since 2005 China's relative performance has been below its potential, especially in 2007 and 2008, mainly due to the current global financial crisis.

The above analysis reveals that in aggregate China's relative performance in attracting FDI inflows was at a level only moderately above its potential and at the average level of the East and South-East Asian developing economies. Therefore, despite the fact that China is the largest FDI recipient among the developing countries and has attracted a large amount of FDI inflows in absolute dollars, China has received only its fair share of global FDI inflows, or at most marginally more than its potential for the last three decades.

CONCLUSION

What are the location determinants of FDI inflows into developing countries? What is the relative performance of China in attracting FDI inflows for the last three decades? And has China attracted excessive FDI inflows from the world? This chapter has offered answers to these questions by using an econometric regression analysis to test the hypotheses based on the location advantages of the OLI framework explaining FDI and has, therefore, established an empirical norm of the magnitude of aggregate FDI inflows from all source countries into a developing host country. The study has provided the following main findings.

First, the empirical study of the distribution of FDI inflows into developing countries by focusing on the host country location factors has demonstrated that, given the ownership advantages and the internalization advantages of the source countries, the location advantages of host countries are very important in determining the distribution of the magnitude of FDI inflows among developing host countries.

Second, for the location determinants of FDI inflows into developing countries, the regression results provided strong support for the acceptance of our hypotheses. The main findings are: countries with a larger market size, faster economic growth, higher per capita income, higher creditworthiness or lower country risk in terms of economic, financial, institutional, social and political stability, higher quality of human resources with higher adult literacy rates, a higher level of existing FDI stock and a more liberalized trade regime represented by the higher degree of openness attracted relatively more FDI inflows, while higher efficiency wages or lower labour productivity and greater remoteness from the rest of the world deterred FDI inflows.

Third, by using the statistical model as an empirical norm, our analysis of the relative performance of China and other East and South-East Asian developing economies in attracting FDI inflows shows that China's relative performance in attracting FDI inflows was at a level only moderately above its potential and was at the average among the East and South-East Asian developing economies. Therefore, despite the fact that China is the largest FDI recipient among the developing countries and has attracted a large amount of FDI inflows in absolute dollars, in terms of its huge market size, increasing per capita income, fast economic growth, low labour costs, good creditworthiness with economic, financial, institutional, social and political stability, China received only its fair share of FDI inflows from the world or at most marginally more than its potential for the past three decades.

However, even though China only received its fair share of FDI inflows from the world as revealed above, we still need to give answers to the concerns that China's participation in attracting FDI inflows might cause a diversion of world FDI away from other developing countries towards China. Has China crowded out FDI inflows into other developing countries? What is the impact of FDI inflows into China on FDI inflows into other developing countries in general and into the East and South-East Asian developing economies in particular? We investigate and answer these questions in the next chapter.

NOTES

1. Calculated at 2000 US dollar prices.
2. Including FDI inflows into the financial sector.
3. For an earlier survey of the use of gravity models in the analysis of trade flows, see Leamer and Stern (1970). For a recent discussion of the use of gravity models in the analysis of trade flows, see Drysdale and Garnaut (1994).
4. There are many such studies, including, for example, Wolf and Weinschrott (1973), Deardorff (1984), Frankel (1994), Wei and Frankel (1994), Helliwell and McCallum (1995), McCallum (1995), Helliwell (1996, 1997, 1998), Wei (1996b), Hillberry (1998, 2002), Anderson and Smith (1999a, 1999b), Head and Ries (2001), Hillberry and Hummels (2002), Anderson and van Wincoop (2003), Chen (2004) and Chen et al. (2008).
5. For more detailed discussion, see Anderson (1979), Helpman and Krugman (1985) and Bergstrand (1989).

6. For a comprehensive survey of the studies of the location factors in determining FDI inflows into developing countries, see Dunning (1993).
7. Total labour earnings are calculated as the wage rate multiplied by total employment. The data for wage rates and employment are from the International Labour Organization, LABORSTA Internet at http://laborsta.ilo.org/. The data of total value-added are from United Nations Statistical Division, National Accounts at http://unstats.un.org/unsd/snaama/dnllist.asp. The calculation is based on local currency and current prices.
8. The derivation of the average efficiency wage is as follows:

$$EW = W/\Pi = (Y/L)/(V/L) = Y/V$$

   where EW is efficiency wage, W is wage rate, Π is labour productivity, Y is total labour earnings, V is total value-added and L is total labour.
9. The 45 countries and economies are: Argentina, Australia, Austria, Belgium, Brazil, Canada, Chile, China, Colombia, Denmark, France, Finland, Germany, Greece, Hong Kong (China), Hungary, India, Indonesia, Ireland, Israel, Italy, Japan, Kuwait, Malaysia, Mexico, Netherlands, New Zealand, Norway, Poland, Portugal, Russia, Saudi Arabia, Singapore, South Africa, South Korea, Spain, Sweden, Switzerland, Taiwan (China), Thailand, Turkey, United Arab Emirates, the UK, the USA, Venezuela.
10. China's poor performance in attracting FDI inflows during 1989 to 1990 was largely due to foreign countries' reaction to the Tiananmen Square Incident.

4. The impact of China on FDI inflows into other developing countries

INTRODUCTION

Since the 1990s and especially after China's accession to the WTO in 2001, China has become one of the most favoured destinations for FDI. In 2008, FDI inflows into China reached US$92.4 billion. In 2009, despite the global economic recession, which severely affected world FDI flows, China still attracted US$90 billion FDI inflows. In 2010, FDI inflows into China reached a historical high of US$105.74 billion.

There are increasing concerns that China's FDI success has been excessive, thereby crowding out FDI inflows into other developing countries. In Chapter 3, we revealed that based on China's location variables, China received only its fair share of FDI inflows from the world, or at most marginally more than its potential, for the last three decades. However, many developing countries, especially several of China's neighbouring Asian developing economies, have raised their concerns that the emergence of China has not only diverted FDI away from them but has also attracted their own domestic investors to leave their economies, resulting in a continuous loss of manufacturing industries and jobs, and further weakening their economies.

A growing China can add to other countries' FDI inflows by creating more opportunities for production networking and by raising the demand for raw materials and resources. At the same time, the extremely low Chinese labour costs may lure MNEs away from other developing countries when the MNEs consider alternative locations for low-cost export platforms. Theoretically, competition for any resource flow may obviously occur when the resource in question is available in limited amounts. However, this 'zero-sum' hypothesis is difficult to justify in the case of FDI. For example, FDI inflows accounted for only 12.3 per cent of world gross fixed capital formation in 2008 (UNCTAD, *World Investment Report*, 2009), and additional FDI resources can be easily diverted from domestic resources and other international capital flows should investment opportunities arise.

Therefore, this chapter examines empirically the question of whether the success of China in attracting FDI inflows has diverted FDI away from, or been complementary to, FDI inflows into other developing countries in general and into other Asian developing economies in particular. The next section discusses the current literature on the effects of FDI inflows into China on FDI inflows into other developing countries. The subsequent section sets out the framework of analysis, the hypotheses, the empirical model and the variable specification. Following this is a presentation and discussion of the regression results, before some final conclusions are drawn.

EFFECTS OF CHINA ON FDI INFLOWS INTO OTHER DEVELOPING COUNTRIES – A LITERATURE REVIEW

During the past three decades, China has been very successful in attracting FDI inflows, particularly after its WTO accession. However, this success has caused increasing concerns that FDI into China has come at the expense of other developing countries, particularly its neighbouring Asian developing economies. There has been an increasing number of empirical studies focusing on the effects of FDI inflows into China on FDI inflows into other developing countries, including, for example, Chantasasawat et al. (2004), Eichengreen and Tong (2005), Mercereau (2005), Zhou and Lall (2005), Cravino et al. (2007), Wang et al. (2007), Resmini and Siedschlag (2008) and Chen (2010b). All these studies develop models to explain the determinants of FDI flows augmented with FDI inflows into China. However, they differ in the measurement of this variable and in the estimation techniques.

Chantasasawat et al. (2004) use data for eight Asian economies (Hong Kong, Taiwan, South Korea, Singapore, Malaysia, Philippines, Indonesia and Thailand) in addition to China over the period 1985 to 2001 and estimate equations for China's FDI inflows and other Asian economies' FDI inflows using two-stage least squares. They find that the level of China's FDI is positively related to the levels of these economies' inward FDI, although this 'China Effect' is generally not the most important determinant of inward FDI into these economies. Policy and institutional factors such as openness, corporate tax rates and the level of corruption tend to be more important. Zhou and Lall (2005) and Wang et al. (2007) estimate panel models to investigate the effect of FDI inflows into China on FDI inflows into Asian economies. They also find that, on average, FDI inflows into China have raised rather than diverted FDI inflows into neighbouring economies.

Mercereau (2005) also investigates the impact of China's emergence on FDI inflows into Asia, using data from 14 Asian economies from 1984 to 2002 and using a number of econometric methods, including OLS with fixed country effects, dynamic panels with a lagged endogenous variable, and instrumental variables. In contrast to the above studies, he does not find a positive relationship between China's FDI inflows and FDI inflows into other Asian economies. However, he does not find much evidence that China's success in attracting FDI has been at the expense of other economies in the region either, with the exception of Singapore and Myanmar. Low-wage economies, which compete with China for low-wage investment, do not appear to have been particularly affected by China's emergence. Low levels of education or scientific developments are not associated with increased crowding out by China either. Some economic fundamentals, such as healthy government balances and low inflation, help explain the allocation of FDI inflows among Asian economies.

Eichengreen and Tong (2005) employ a gravity model and show that the emergence of China as a leading FDI destination has encouraged FDI inflows into other Asian economies via supply-chain production linkages. However, they also find evidence suggesting that FDI inflows into China have diverted FDI inflows away from Europe. They explain this diversion effect by the negative impact of distance on supply-chain production linkages. In contrast, Resmini and Siedschlag (2008) estimate an augmented gravity model to analyse the effects of FDI inflows into China originating in OECD countries on FDI inflows into the EU and other countries over the period 1990 to 2004. Their results suggest that on average, other things being equal, FDI inflows into China have been complementary to FDI inflows into other host countries and into the EU as well. However, this complementary relationship is not constant across countries, but is instead weaker in Europe than outside it. These complementarities follow a decreasing trend over the analysed period of time.

Cravino et al. (2007) examine the effect of foreign capital stock in China on the Latin American and Caribbean countries and they find no evidence of FDI diversion from OECD countries, in particular from the USA, into China at the expense of the Latin American and Caribbean countries. While the growth of capital stocks in China originating from the OECD was faster than in Latin American and Caribbean countries over the period 1990 to 1997, this relative growth has slowed down since then.

Finally, Chen (2010b), using data for 12 Asian developing economies over the period 1992 to 2008, investigates the impact of FDI inflows into China on FDI inflows into other Asian developing economies. Chen finds that FDI inflows into China have a statistically significant positive impact on FDI inflows into other Asian developing economies. This complementary relationship between Chinese and Asian FDI inflows may be linked to the increased resource demand by a rapidly growing Chinese economy and the production-networking activities among the Asian economies.

The above empirical studies suggest that there is little to suggest that China's FDI success has crowded out FDI inflows into other countries. On the contrary, there is strong empirical evidence that, on average, FDI inflows into China have been complementary to FDI inflows into other host countries, especially into China's neighbouring Asian economies.

THE EMPIRICAL MODEL AND VARIABLE SPECIFICATION

This study uses the same analytical framework and the modified gravity model established and derived in Chapter 3 to investigate the impact of FDI inflows into China on FDI inflows into other developing countries.

Based on the OLI framework in explaining FDI and the modified gravity model, the fundamental model used here can be written as:

$$\ln FDI_{*j} = \beta_0 + \beta_1 \ln X_* + \beta_2 \ln X_j + \beta_3 \ln R_{*j} \qquad (4.1)$$

where

FDI_{*j} = the magnitude of total FDI inflows from all source countries into host economy j
X_* = aggregate source country variables
X_j = host country variables
R_{*j} = linkage variables

Equation (4.1) states that, given the aggregate source country variables (source-side factors), the host country variables (host-side factors) and the linkage variables are the only things that matter to determine the distribution of FDI inflows from all source countries into each of the host countries. We adopt the log-linear form as the basic functional form to connect the magnitude of FDI inflows from all source countries to developing host country j to the relevant explanatory variables (the aggregate source country variables, the host country variables and the linkage variables).

For the aggregate source country variables X_*, using the same reasoning as in Chapter 3, we use the world total FDI outflows (*WFDIOUT*) of all source countries to capture the supply-side effects of FDI on FDI inflows into developing host countries.

For the host country variables and the linkage variables, we have hypothesized, defined and tested the location determinants affecting FDI inflows into developing countries in Chapter 3. Therefore, we will not repeat the hypotheses here. The empirical study in Chapter 3 reveals that the location factors determining FDI inflows into developing countries are market size, per capital income, real rate of economic growth, labour costs adjusted for productivity, country risk, remoteness from the rest of the world, existing level of FDI stock, quality of human resources and openness of an economy.

In this study, to avoid the high multi-collinearity problem revealed in Chapter 3, we drop the variables of *GDP*, *READ* and *FDIS* in the empirical regression. We argue that the effects of *GDP*, *READ* and *FDIS* on FDI inflows into developing countries can be captured by the variables of per capita income (*PGDP*) and real rate of economic growth (*GR*). First, a higher level of per capita income and economic growth implies a higher level of economic development, better overall economic conditions of the host economies, and better conditions in local infrastructure, which are fundamental for attracting FDI inflows. Second, a country's education level and the supply of domestic entrepreneurship are positively related to its level of economic growth and development. Therefore, countries with a higher degree of economic development usually possess more human capital endowments and a higher-quality labour force. These are very important for attracting FDI inflows, particularly for FDI with high technology and a high requirement for skilled labourers. Finally, a higher level of per capita income and economic growth also implies a fast expansion of the market size, a rapid rise in domestic demand, and a growing purchasing power of the host country's consumers, which is a very important determinant for market-oriented FDI. Clearly, markets that have higher per capita income and grow faster will attract higher levels of inward FDI.

Therefore, in this study the host country location variables include: per capita income (*PGDP*), real rate of economic growth (*GR*), labour costs (*EW*), country risk (*CDR*), remoteness (*RMT*) and openness (*OPEN*).

To investigate the effects of FDI inflows into China on FDI inflows into other developing countries, we add FDI inflows from all source countries into China, denoted as *FDICHN*, as an independent variable.

There are at least two aspects that need to be considered here. First, in examining in which low-wage export platform to locate, MNEs may choose between investing in China versus investing in another developing country. In this case, the MNEs will study the whole host of factors that would make a country desirable as a site for low-cost production. Investing in China will then reduce the FDI inflows into another developing country. The sign of *FDICHN*, according to this argument, is negative. We call this the 'investment-diversion effect'.

The second aspect is the production and resource linkages between a growing China and the other developing countries. In manufacturing, this takes the form of further specialization and growing fragmentation of the production processes. An investor sets up factories in both China and another developing country to take advantage of their respective competitiveness in distinct stages of the production process. Components and parts are then traded among China and other developing countries. An increase in FDI inflows into China is then positively related to an increase in FDI inflows into other developing countries. A different but complementary argument is that as China grows, its market size increases and its demand for minerals and resources also rises. Subsequently, MNEs rush into China to produce in China and to sell in China. At the same time, other MNEs also invest in other developing countries to extract minerals and resources to export to China. This line of reasoning leads to the prediction that the sign of *FDICHN* will be positive. We call this the 'investment-creation effect'. Theoretically we cannot determine a priori the net effect of investment creation and investment diversion for China. It is thus important to examine this issue empirically.

Based on the above discussion, to investigate the China effect on FDI inflows into other developing countries, we use the following empirical model:

$$\ln FDI_{*j,t} = \beta_0 + \beta_1 \ln WFDIOUT_t + \beta_2 \ln FDICHN_{*,t}$$

$$+ \beta_3 \ln FDICHN_{*,t-1} + \beta_4 \ln PGDP_{j,t-k} + \beta_5 \ln GR_{j,t-k} + \beta_6 \ln EW_{j,t-k}$$

$$+ \beta_7 \ln CDR_{j,t-k} + \beta_8 \ln RMT_{j,t-k} + \beta_9 \ln OPEN_{j,t-k} + v_j + \varepsilon_{j,t} \quad (4.2)$$

The dependent variable, denoted as $FDI_{*j,t}$, is the aggregate inflow of FDI from all source countries into developing host country j in year t. The value of FDI, and all the relevant following variables, is measured at 1990 US dollar prices. The independent variables *PGDP*, *GR*, *EW*, *CDR*, *RMT* and *OPEN* are discussed and defined in Chapter 3.

For the variable of total FDI inflows into China (*FDICHN*), to deal with the possible simultaneity problem between FDI inflows into China and FDI inflows into other developing countries, both the current year value of total FDI inflows into China ($FDICHN_{*,t}$) and the one-year lagged value of total FDI inflows into China ($FDICHN_{*,t-1}$) are tested in the empirical regressions. However, in the actual practice we enter the two variables into the regression equation separately to avoid the high collinearity problem between them.

We include the world total FDI outflows (*WFDIOUT*) as an independent variable to control the aggregate supply-side effect of FDI on FDI inflows into developing host countries.

The independent variables, excluding *WFDIOUT* and *FDICHN*, are lagged k years. This model assumes that the effect of the independent variables at time *t-k* appears only within period t and is fully completed within that period. The relationship shown in equation (4.2) will be examined for *k*=1, the most likely appropriate lag. The independent variable *WFDIOUT*, which is world total FDI outflows, is determined by the source-side factors and is independent from host country determinants, therefore, the current year value (*k*=0) will be employed in the regression equation. The estimated coefficients of ln*WFDIOUT*, ln*FDICHN*, ln*PGDP*, ln*GR*, ln*EW*, ln*CDR*, ln*RMT* and ln*OPEN* variables are elasticities. The econometric regression analysis below uses panel data and a fixed effects model, in order to eliminate the country-specific and time-invariant factors which may affect FDI inflows.

CHINA EFFECT ON FDI INFLOWS INTO DEVELOPING COUNTRIES

In this empirical study, there are 49 developing countries and economies in the sample and the time period is from 1992 to 2008. The 49 developing countries and economies are Botswana, Egypt, Kenya, Malawi, Mauritius, South Africa and Swaziland from Africa; Argentina, Bolivia, Brazil, Chile, Colombia, Costa Rica, El Salvador, Guatemala, Jamaica, Mexico, Nicaragua, Paraguay, Peru and Trinidad and Tobago from Latin America and the Caribbean; Azerbaijan, Bangladesh, Georgia, Hong Kong (China), India, Indonesia, Jordan, Kazakhstan, Malaysia, Pakistan, Philippines, Singapore, Sri Lanka, South Korea, Taiwan (China), Thailand, Turkey and Vietnam from Asia; Bulgaria, Croatia, Czech Republic, Estonia, Hungary, Poland, Romania, Russia, Slovakia and Slovenia from Central and Eastern Europe.

The fixed-effects regression results with the current year value of FDI inflows into China ($FDICHN_{*,t}$) are reported in Model 1 of Table 4.1. The model performs very well and all the independent variables have the expected signs and are statistically significant.

As a robustness check, the regression is also run with the one-year lagged value of FDI inflows into China ($FDICHN_{*,t-1}$). The regression results remain very similar to those with the current year value of FDI inflows into China and are reported in Model 2 of Table 4.1. The model performs very well and all the independent variables have the expected signs and are statistically significant.

Table 4.1   *Regression results of the effects of FDI inflows into China on FDI inflows into developing countries, 1992–2008 (lag k=1), fixed-effects (dependent variable $LFDI_{*j, t}$)*

Variables	Model 1	Model 2
Constant	55.16	64.29
	(3.41)***	(4.03)***
$LWFDIOUT_t$	0.09	0.07
	(2.44)**	(1.95)*
$LFDICHN_{*,t}$	0.28	
	(2.55)***	
$LFDICHN_{*,t-1}$		0.20
		(2.91)***
$LPGDP_{j,t-k}$	0.70	0.72
	(5.67)***	(5.87)***
$LGR_{j,t-k}$	0.45	0.46
	(4.60)***	(4.79)***
$LEW_{j,t-k}$	−1.21	−1.20
	(−5.25)***	(5.23)***
$LCDR_{j,t-k}$	0.47	0.50
	(1.91)*	(2.13)**
$LRMT_{j,t-k}$	−13.67	−15.56
	(−3.85)***	(−4.44)***
$LOPEN_{j,t-k}$	0.69	0.68
	(3.04)***	(3.03)***
Observations	629	629
Groups	49	49
R^2: within	0.53	0.53
between	0.10	0.10
overall	0.11	0.10
F-statistics	85.15***	84.33***

Notes:
Standard errors are adjusted for heteroscedasticity and clustering on group.
t-statistics are in parentheses.
*   Statistically significant at 0.10 level (two-tail test).
**   Statistically significant at 0.05 level (two-tail test).
***   Statistically significant at 0.01 level (two-tail test).

Our main variable of interest, *FDICHN*, is positive and highly significant in both regressions. A 10 per cent increase in the FDI inflows into China would raise FDI inflows into the developing countries by about 2 to 2.8 per cent. Despite considerable concerns that an increase in FDI inflows into China is at the expense of other developing countries, the regression results suggest that those countries can actually benefit from it. This implies that a growing China attracts more FDI inflows and at the same time can add to other developing countries' FDI inflows by creating more opportunities for production networking and by raising the demand for raw materials and resources.

As for the location variables, the regression results provide strong support for the hypotheses. The market size and the degree of development ($PGDP$) of the developing host country are positive and statistically significant location determinants affecting the magnitude of FDI inflows. The regression results, therefore, support the hypothesis that the larger and higher degree of development of an economy, the larger the magnitude of FDI inflows will be.

The market growth rate (GR) is a positive and statistically significant location determinant in affecting the magnitude of FDI inflows into developing countries, with the results implying that the higher and faster the growth of an economy, the higher the level of FDI inflows will be.

A host country's efficiency wage (EW), the proxy for labour cost, is a negative statistically significant determinant of the magnitude of FDI inflows that a country receives. This indicates that FDI is responsive to differences in efficiency wages across developing countries. It also reveals that taking advantage of developing countries' cheap labour is one of the main motives for foreign investors in developing countries.

A country's credit rating (CDR) is found to be a positive and statistically significant factor in influencing the magnitude of FDI inflows into developing countries. Economic, financial, institutional, social and political stabilities with high creditworthiness can be considered as one of the most influential tools to promote FDI since it has a direct impact on the security and profitability of FDI projects.

A developing country's remoteness (RMT), the proxy for the relative distance of a developing country to the rest of the world, is a negative and statistically significant location determinant. The results show that the more 'remote' a developing host country is from the rest of the world, the smaller the magnitude of FDI inflows into that developing host country will be. The negative estimated coefficient of remoteness reveals an important point that transaction costs in terms of information gathering and familiarity with local market conditions are very important factors affecting the investment location decision of foreign investors.

A developing country's openness ($OPEN$) is a positive and statistically significant location determinant affecting the magnitude of FDI inflows. The regression results indicate that the more open an economy the more FDI inflows will go into that economy. Therefore, a more liberalized trade regime rather than imposing high trade barriers is important for developing countries to attract more FDI inflows to accelerate economic development.

Finally, the variable of world total FDI outflows (*WFDIOUT*) is positive and statistically significant. This signifies the impact of an overall supply-side effect on the inflows of FDI to developing countries.

It is interesting to note that, although FDI inflows into China have a positive and statistically significant effect on FDI inflows into other developing countries, the China effect is not the most important factor determining FDI inflows into these developing countries. The empirical regression results suggest that, all else being equal, the marginal effect of the host countries' location variables on FDI inflows into their economies is much larger than the China effect. The marginal effect of the economic growth rate and country credit rating is two times, per capita income and economic openness is three times and efficiency wage is five times as large as that of the China effect, respectively.

CHINA EFFECT ON FDI INFLOWS INTO ASIAN DEVELOPING ECONOMIES

In the above empirical study with a large sample of developing countries, we find that there is a positive relationship between FDI inflows into China and FDI inflows into other developing countries. This implies that, on average, FDI inflows into China have been complementary to FDI inflows into other developing countries. However, several of China's neighbouring Asian developing economies have increasingly raised their concerns that the emergence of China has not only diverted FDI away from them but has also attracted their own domestic investors to leave their economies, resulting in a continuous loss of manufacturing industries and jobs, and further weakening their economies. Has China really crowded out FDI inflows into its neighbouring Asian developing economies? It is important to examine this issue empirically.

In this empirical study, the sample includes 18 Asian developing economies and the time period is from 1992 to 2008. The 18 economies are Azerbaijan, Bangladesh, Georgia, Hong Kong (China), India, Indonesia, Jordan, Kazakhstan, Malaysia, Pakistan, Philippines, Singapore, Sri Lanka, South Korea, Taiwan (China), Thailand, Turkey and Vietnam.

The fixed-effects regression results are reported in Model 1 and Model 2 of Table 4.2. The models perform very well and all the independent variables have the expected signs and are statistically significant.

As a robustness check, the regression is also run without the five Central Asian developing economies: Azerbaijan, Georgia, Jordan, Kazakhstan and Turkey. The regression results remain very similar to those with the five Central Asian developing economies in the sample and are reported

Table 4.2   *Regression results of the effects of FDI inflows into China on FDI inflows into Asian developing economies, 1992–2008 (lag k=1), fixed-effects (dependent variable LFDI*$_{*j,\,t}$*)*

Variables	Model 1	Model 2	Model 3	Model 4
Constant	38.93	56.59	78.86	97.05
	(1.46)	(2.31)**	(2.70)***	(3.70)***
LWFDIOUT$_t$	0.18	0.17	0.14	0.11
	(2.90)***	(2.58)***	(2.48)**	1.80)*
LFDICHN$_{*,t}$	0.31		0.33	
	(1.87)*		(1.86)*	
LFDICHN$_{*,t-1}$		0.17		0.28
		(1.76)*		(2.60)***
LGR$_{j,t-k}$	0.59	0.60	0.49	0.54
	(3.91)***	(3.96)***	(2.36)**	(2.60)***
LEW$_{j,t-k}$	−0.76	−0.76	−0.98	−0.91
	(−2.19)**	(−2.18)**	(−2.41)**	(−2.21)**
LCDR$_{j,t-k}$	1.61	1.62	1.58	1.45
	(2.49)**	(2.53)**	(1.98)**	(1.83)*
LRMT$_{j,t-k}$	−10.50	−14.16	−18.04	−21.80
	(−1.85)*	(−2.72)***	(−2.96)***	(−3.99)***
LOPEN$_{j,t-k}$	0.91	0.92		
	(2.75)***	(2.74)***		
Observations	243	243	187	187
Groups	18	18	13	13
R^2: within	0.55	0.55	0.55	0.56
between	0.03	0.00	0.02	0.01
overall	0.11	0.04	0.07	0.03
F-statistics	47.95***	48.85***	35.22***	36.69***

Notes:
Standard errors are adjusted for heteroscedasticity and cluster effects on group.
t-statistics are in parentheses.
*   Statistically significant at 0.10 level (two-tail test).
**   Statistically significant at 0.05 level (two-tail test).
***   Statistically significant at 0.01 level (two-tail test).

in Model 3 and Model 4 of Table 4.2.[1] The models perform very well and all the independent variables have the expected signs and are statistically significant.

Our main variable of interest, *FDICHN*, is positive and statistically significant in all the regressions, although the significance levels are lower than those in the large sample developing country regressions in the above section. A 10 per cent increase in the FDI inflows into China would raise FDI inflows into the Asian developing economies by about 2 to 3 per cent, which is similar to the results of the large sample developing country

Table 4.3   China's imports of raw materials from Asian economies (US$ million)

	1995	2000	2005	2008
All 12 Asian economies				
Animal, vegetable fats (HS 15)	954 (36)	804 (67)	2131 (64)	7092 (63)
Mineral products (HS 25, 26, 27)	2958 (41)	5614 (23)	16433 (18)	43072 (17)
Wood products (HS 47, 48)	1367 (43)	2684 (40)	2386 (23)	2495 (15)
Textile materials (HS 52, 54, 55)	5290 (53)	5893 (62)	5932 (42)	5830 (43)
Indonesia				
Animal, vegetable fats (HS 15)	70 (3)	245 (21)	749 (23)	2482 (22)
Mineral products (HS 25, 26, 27)	766 (11)	1104 (5)	2282 (2.5)	5269 (2)
Wood products (HS 47, 48)	180 (6)	928 (14)	893 (8)	1068 (7)
Malaysia				
Animal, vegetable fats (HS 15)	732 (28)	471 (39)	1271 (38)	4084 (36)
Singapore				
Mineral products (HS 27)	1123 (24)	852 (4)	2206 (3)	4325 (3)
South Korea				
Mineral products (HS 27)	398 (8)	2016 (10)	3506 (6)	9945 (6)
Taiwan				
Textile materials (HS 54)	1046 (31)	1268 (35)	1359 (36)	1120 (31)
Thailand				
Mineral products (HS 27)	7.6 (0.2)	383 (2)	806 (1)	1803 (1)
India				
Mineral products (HS 26)	153 (8)	373 (12)	5509 (21)	14314 (17)
Textile materials (HS 52)	24 (1)	186 (7)	275 (4)	1130 (15)
Pakistan				
Textile materials (HS 52)	173 (5)	398 (14)	581 (8)	599 (8)

Notes:
The 12 Asian economies include Bangladesh, Hong Kong, India, Indonesia, Malaysia, Pakistan, Philippines, Singapore, South Korea, Sri Lanka, Taiwan and Thailand.
Figures in parentheses are shares in China's total imports of the commodities.
HS 15: Animal, vegetable fats and oils, cleavage products, and so on.
HS 25: Salt, sulphur, earth, stone, plaster, lime and cement.
HS 26: Ores, slag and ash.
HS 27: Mineral fuels, oils, distillation products, and so on.
HS 47: Pulp of wood, fibrous cellulosic material, waste, and so on.
HS 48: Paper and paperboard, articles of pulp, paper and board.
HS 52: Cotton.
HS 54: Manmade filaments.
HS 55: Manmade staple fibres.

Source: Author's calculation. Data are from the United Nations Statistics Division, Commodity Trade Statistics Database, COMTRADE.

regressions. Therefore, despite increasing concerns that an increase in FDI inflows into China is at the expense of other Asian developing economies, the regression results suggest that those economies can actually benefit from it.

This may be linked to the increased resource demand by a rapidly growing Chinese economy and the production-networking activities among the Asian economies. As Table 4.3 shows, Asian economies have become increasingly important suppliers of China's growing demand for raw materials. In some resources, the Asian economies are the major suppliers to China, for example, Indonesia and Malaysia in animal, vegetable fats and oils; Taiwan, India and Pakistan in textile materials; and India, Indonesia and South Korea in mineral products. Therefore, China's fast economic growth associated with high demand for raw materials could generate great opportunities for MNEs to conduct resource-based FDI in Asian economies.

The evidence of production networking among China and other Asian economies can be found in the substantial two-way trade of intermediate and final goods in the same industries among those economies. Many of the Asian economies, particularly those in East and South-East Asia, are heavily involved in vertical specialization, particularly in the industries of electric and electronics equipment (HS 85). As shown in Table 4.4, the value and shares of two-way trade in the electric and electronic equipment industries between China and Asian economies have been substantial. The economic ties of mutual dependence among them have been deepening rapidly since the 1990s. The significance of the China effect in the level of FDI inflows into Asian economies may reflect such interdependence.

It is impossible to ascertain from the above regression results whether the China effect is driven primarily by resource demand or by production networking – this remains a topic for further research. However, the central result still holds: an increase in FDI inflows into China is positively and significantly related to FDI inflows into other Asian economies, or in other words, in recent decades the investment-creation effect has dominated the investment-diversion effect, so Chinese and Asian FDI inflows are complementary.

As for the location variables, the regression results show that the market growth rate (*GR*), efficiency wage (*EW*), country credit rating (*CDR*), remoteness (*RMT*) and openness (*OPEN*) are very important determinants in affecting FDI inflows into Asian developing economies. This implies that the Asian developing economies, particularly the East and South-East Asian developing economies, are the most attractive locations for export-oriented FDI. The variable of world total FDI outflows

Table 4.4   Two-way trade between China and Asian economies in electric and electronic equipment industries (HS 85)

	Exports to China (US$ million)	Share in total exports to China (%)	Imports from China (US$ million)	Share in total imports from China (%)
Hong Kong				
1995	1957	22.78	5736	15.94
2000	3203	33.97	10507	23.60
2005	4478	36.63	43029	34.57
2008	4153	32.15	80225	42.06
Malaysia				
1995	202	9.75	190	14.83
2000	2097	38.27	927	36.14
2005	12664	63.03	2641	24.90
2008	17226	53.66	4938	23.02
Philippines				
1995	10	3.62	84	8.16
2000	860	51.28	438	29.92
2005	9146	71.06	1482	31.61
2008	14353	73.59	2386	26.13
Singapore				
1995	499	14.69	548	15.66
2000	1457	28.79	1745	30.29
2005	6370	38.57	6653	40.00
2008	6443	31.94	9763	30.22
South Korea				
1995	1103	10.72	473	7.07
2000	5089	21.93	1942	17.20
2005	25774	33.55	8241	23.47
2008	37648	33.57	18426	24.92
Taiwan				
1995	2005	13.56	485	15.66
2000	6413	25.15	1088	21.59
2005	28877	38.67	4887	29.53
2008	41507	40.17	7637	29.52
Thailand				
1995	53	3.29	113	6.45
2000	816	18.63	416	18.55
2005	3706	26.49	1695	21.68
2008	5976	23.29	2962	18.95

Source: Author's calculation. Data are from the United Nations Statistics Division, Commodity Trade Statistics Database, COMTRADE.

(*WFDIOUT*) is positive and statistically significant. This signifies the impact of an overall supply-side effect on the inflows of FDI to Asian developing economies.

Again, it is interesting to note that, although FDI inflows into China have a positive and statistically significant effect on FDI inflows into other Asian developing economies, the China effect is not the most important factor determining FDI inflows into these Asian developing economies. Similar to the regression results of the large sample developing countries, the empirical regression results here suggest that, all else being equal, the marginal effect of the Asian developing economies' location variables on FDI inflows into their economies is much larger than the China effect.

IMPLICATIONS FOR FUTURE FDI INFLOWS INTO CHINA AND ASIAN ECONOMIES

Above we discussed the finding that the positive impact of the China effect on FDI inflows into Asian economies may be linked to the increased resource demand by a rapidly growing Chinese economy and the production-networking activities among the Asian economies. These two channels generating the positive China effect on FDI inflows into the Asian economies, especially into the ASEAN, are expected to be strengthened in the future.

First, with the creation and implementation of the ASEAN-China Free Trade Area (ACFTA) on 1 January 2010, the economic relationship between ASEAN and China has entered a new era. The ACFTA covers agreements on trade in goods and services and investment, which will accelerate and intensify the economic integration and result in a rapid development and expansion in trade and investment between ASEAN and China. Apart from the ACFTA, China has bilateral free trade agreements with a number of Asian economies, including Pakistan, Thailand, Singapore, Hong Kong and Macao, and is proposing to negotiate bilateral free trade agreements with India, South Korea and Taiwan. The reduction and elimination of barriers in trade and investment not only will lead to an expansion of trade and investment among China and other Asian economies, but also will create investment opportunities for third parties to invest in China and in other Asian economies in order to get into and take advantage of the enlarged Asian free trade areas.

Second, one of the major driving forces behind the economic integration of the Asian economy is the fast growth of the Chinese economy. China's economic growth and strong investment expansion is energizing the region and is providing the Asian economies with an expanding and diversified market. The fast growth of the Chinese economy will have a huge impact on the Asian economies. On the one hand, as China's economy grows, it will increase demand for consumer goods as the income of the Chinese people increases. On the other hand, the fast-growing Chinese economy will also increase demand for resources and raw materials to meet its fast expansion of production. Both will generate great opportunities not only for Asian economies to increase exports to the Chinese market, but also for MNEs to invest in Asian economies to produce goods and extract resources to supply the Chinese market.

Third, with the fast and deep integration among the Chinese and other Asian economies, the production-networking activities, particularly in vertical specialization, will intensify with each of the economies specializing in the production in which it has a comparative advantage. Currently, China and Asian economies have already developed substantial two-way trade in the electric and electronic equipment industries. In the years ahead, with the upgrading and restructuring of the industrial structures in China and Asian economies, we expect that the two-way trade among China and other Asian economies will expand into other industries, for example in automobile industries and machinery and equipment industries. This structural change and upgrading of industries in China and other Asian economies will provide huge opportunities for MNEs to invest in China and other Asian economies based on their comparative advantages and competitiveness.

Fourth, with rapid economic growth, a high rate of capital accumulation and a huge amount of foreign reserves, China has gradually become an increasingly important supplier of outward FDI. During the period 2004 to 2008, China's outward FDI increased from US$5.5 billion to US$55.9 billion, an increase of over nine times. Most of China's outward FDI flowed into Asian economies, accounting for 71.38 per cent of China's total outward FDI stock at the end of 2008. With rapid economic growth, in the next two decades we will witness a rapid increase in FDI outflows from China. On the one hand, China will accelerate industrial restructuring and industrial upgrading. Some labour-intensive manufacturing activities and industries will gradually lose competitiveness due to a combined result of increasing labour costs and shrinking labour forces as the population ages. As a result, these labour-intensive industries will move out of China and invest in other economies, mainly in other Asian developing economies. On the other hand, China's fast economic growth will cause a huge and growing demand for resources and raw materials. To meet this demand, China will increase investment overseas to expand and secure the supply of resources and raw materials. Asian economies with rich resource endowments would be the primary destinations for China's outward investment. Therefore, China will become a more and more important investor for Asian economies.

Overall, the relationship between China and Asian economies in terms of FDI would be complementary to each other in the next one or two decades. A growing China will attract more FDI inflows, on the one hand, and it will also create more opportunities for Asian economies to attract FDI inflows.

CONCLUSION

The vast volume of FDI inflows into China in the last three decades has been a source of celebration for some, and of concern for others. Has China really crowded out FDI inflows into other developing countries in general and into Asian developing economies in particular or has it been more of a win-win story? This chapter has built on an extensive literature seeking to answer this question by conducting an empirical analysis to test the hypotheses based on the location advantages of the OLI explanation of FDI. The three main findings can be summarized as follows.

First, for the location determinants of FDI inflows into developing countries, the regression results provide strong support for the acceptance of the hypotheses. The main findings are that countries with higher per capita income and a higher level of economic development, faster economic growth, higher creditworthiness or lower country risk in terms of economic, financial, institutional, social and political stability, and a higher level of economic openness, attracted relatively more FDI inflows, while higher efficiency wages or lower labour productivity and greater remoteness from the rest of the world deterred FDI inflows during the period of analysis, 1992 to 2008.

Second, the regression results have shown that FDI inflows into China have a statistically significant positive effect on FDI inflows into other developing countries. This positive and complementary effect of FDI inflows into China on FDI inflows into other developing countries and especially into Asian developing economies may be linked to the increased resource demand by a growing China and the production-networking activities among the developing countries and particularly among Asian developing economies. While the results did not allow the relative strength of these two linkages to be determined, it is likely that this positive China effect stems from a combination of both, leading to the central result that this effect is about investment creation, not investment diversion. This complementarity implies that much of the concern about Chinese FDI has been unfounded.

Third, although FDI inflows into China are positive and statistically significant to FDI inflows into other developing countries, the China effect is not the most important factor determining FDI inflows into the developing countries. The empirical regression results suggest that, all else being equal, the marginal effect of the host countries' location variables on FDI inflows into their economies is much larger than the China effect. Host countries' location variables, such as larger markets and a higher level of economic development, fast economic growth, lower labour costs accompanied with higher labour productivity, lower country risk with economic, financial, institutional, social and political stability, a higher degree of economic openness, and being relatively closer to the rest of the world play the fundamental role in attracting FDI inflows.

In the next two decades, China's economic growth and strong investment expansion will energize the Asia-Pacific region and will provide both the Asia-Pacific economies and other countries with an expanding and diversified integrated Asia-Pacific market. Overall, with the fast and deep integration among the Chinese and other Asian economies, the positive China effect on FDI inflows into other developing countries and particularly into the Asian developing economies will continue.

In Chapter 3 and this chapter our analysis has been focused on the location determinants affecting FDI inflows at the country level. However, since China is large, with considerable regional differences, it is necessary to examine the situation of FDI distribution within China. In the next chapter, using the same analytical method developed in Chapter 3, we analyse FDI inflows into China at the provincial level in order to examine the provincial characteristics and the FDI location decision within China.

NOTE

1. The variable *OPEN* is dropped from the regression.

5. Provincial characteristics and the FDI location decision within China

INTRODUCTION

In the previous chapters, we have examined the evolving changes of China's FDI policies and the growth pattern of FDI inflows into China during the past three decades. We find that the gradual liberalization of FDI policies since 1979 and the government's commitment for further opening up after China's accession to the WTO have greatly improved the investment environment in China. Foreign direct investment inflows into China have increased rapidly since the early 1990s and especially after China's accession to the WTO in 2001.

However, in terms of regional distribution, FDI inflows into China's provinces vary greatly. As a result, the provincial distribution of FDI inflows into China has been very uneven, with the eastern region provinces accounting for nearly 90 per cent of the total. This raises the questions of what are the causes of the uneven provincial distribution of FDI inflows into China, what provincial characteristics determine the FDI location decisions within China, and what is the relative attractiveness for FDI of China's 31 mainland provinces given their specific provincial characteristics? This chapter aims to investigate and answer these questions.

Using the same analytical framework as was established in Chapter 3, we argue for a set of source countries, the provincial differences in FDI inflows from the world are determined by the differences in location factors of each individual province. Consequently, at this level of analysis we take each individual province as the basic potential destination for hosting FDI inflows from all source countries in the world in order to find out what provincial location factors determine the provincial distribution of FDI inflows. This topic is particularly interesting in light of the increasing efforts of each individual province to attract FDI inflows to boost local economic development.

This chapter is structured as follows. The next section examines the regional and provincial differences in the distribution of FDI inflows during 1983 to 2008. The third section discusses the hypotheses of provincial location factors affecting the FDI location decision of foreign investors. In the subsequent section we conduct the empirical tests for the hypotheses. The fifth section analyses the relative attractiveness to FDI inflows among China's 31 mainland provinces. The final section summarizes the basic findings.

PROVINCIAL DISTRIBUTION OF FDI INFLOWS

As a nation, China has been successful in attracting FDI inflows. However, China is a large country with tremendous differences among its regions and provinces. Therefore, it is interesting and important to analyse the regional and provincial distribution of FDI inflows into China.

To facilitate the analysis of the regional and provincial distribution of FDI inflows into China, following the commonly used method of regional division in China and according to the economic development levels and the geographical locations of provinces, we group China's 31 mainland provinces into three regions, namely, the eastern region, the central region and the western region.[1] The reason for the division into regions is primarily for comparing the regional differences and dynamic changes in attracting FDI inflows.

Since 1979 China has attracted a total of US$934 billion FDI inflows (at 2000 US dollar prices). Here, we are interested in finding out who are the major recipients among China's three regions and 31 provinces. By the end of 2008, FDI in China was overwhelmingly concentrated in the eastern region, which accounted for 86.26 per cent of the total accumulative FDI inflows, while the central region and western region accounted for only 9.16 per cent and 4.58 per cent of the total respectively.

Table 5.1 presents the accumulative FDI inflows into China's three regions and 31 provinces in the period of 1983 to 2005 and three subperiods of 1983 to 1991, 1992 to 2001 and 2002 to 2005.[2]

In the period from 1983 to 2005, among the eastern region provinces, Guangdong has been the largest recipient, accounting for 25.28 per cent of the total accumulative FDI inflows, followed by Jiangsu (14.41 per cent), Shanghai (8.94 per cent), Shandong (8.44 per cent), Fujian (7.99 per cent), Liaoning (5.06 per cent), Zhejiang (5.01 per cent), Beijing (4.25 per cent) and Tianjin (3.62 per cent). Hebei and Hainan received smaller FDI inflows than other provinces in the eastern region. They attracted 1.72 per cent and 1.42 per cent of the total accumulative FDI inflows respectively.

Among the central region provinces, Hubei, Hunan, Jiangxi and Henan are the major recipients, accounting for 2.11 per cent, 1.70 per cent, 1.39 per cent and 1.10 per cent of the total accumulative FDI inflows,

Table 5.1   Accumulative FDI inflows into China's provinces, 1983–2005
(2000 US$, millions)

Province	1983–1991		1992–2001		2002–2005		1983–2005	
	Inflows	Share (%)	Inflows	Share (%)	Inflows	Share (%)	Inflows	Share (%)
Eastern Region	24014	89.07	330692	85.76	181234	86.82	535940	86.26
Beijing	2355	8.74	14852	3.85	9173	4.39	26380	4.25
Tianjin	679	2.52	15506	4.02	6684	3.20	22870	3.68
Hebei	253	0.94	7666	1.99	2753	1.32	10672	1.72
Liaoning	1328	4.93	17207	4.46	12904	6.18	31438	5.06
Shanghai	1967	7.30	32638	8.46	20939	10.03	55545	8.94
Jiangsu	1008	3.74	52227	13.54	36283	17.38	89519	14.41
Zhejiang	434	1.61	13679	3.55	17476	8.37	31589	5.01
Fujian	2109	7.49	37892	9.83	9706	4.65	49617	7.99
Shandong	1053	3.91	25403	6.59	25972	12.44	52428	8.44
Guangdong	12306	45.64	106422	27.60	38309	18.35	157037	25.28
Hainan	612	2.27	7200	1.87	1035	0.50	8846	1.42
Central Region	1326	4.92	34920	9.06	20656	9.90	56902	9.16
Shanxi	37	0.14	1797	0.47	573	0.27	2407	0.39
Jilin	136	0.50	3411	0.88	884	0.42	4430	0.71
Heilongjiang	286	1.06	4152	1.08	1312	0.63	5750	0.93
Anhui	135	0.50	3485	0.90	1581	0.76	5202	0.84
Jiangxi	101	0.37	3199	0.83	5334	2.56	8634	1.39
Henan	248	0.92	4820	1.25	1739	0.83	6807	1.10
Hubei	224	0.83	7793	2.02	5103	2.44	13120	2.11
Hunan	158	0.59	6263	1.62	4130	1.98	10551	1.70
Western Region	1620	6.01	19990	5.18	6853	3.28	28462	4.58
Inner Mongolia	55	0.21	733	0.19	799	0.38	1588	0.26
Guangxi	395	1.46	6957	1.80	1396	0.67	8748	1.41
Chongqing	76	0.28	2810	0.73	858	0.41	3744	0.60
Sichuan	279	1.03	3774	0.98	1791	0.86	5844	0.94
Guizhou	91	0.34	431	0.11	167	0.08	689	0.11
Yunnan	51	0.19	1064	0.28	469	0.22	1583	0.25
Tibet	0.04	0.00	0	0.00	0.47	0.00	0.51	0.00
Shaanxi	554	2.06	3129	0.81	955	0.46	4639	0.75
Gansu	33	0.12	537	0.14	131	0.06	701	0.11
Qinghai	5	0.02	53	0.01	73	0.04	131	0.02
Ningxia	3	0.01	148	0.04	136	0.07	287	0.05
Xinjiang	77	0.29	353	0.09	77	0.04	507	0.08
Regional Total	26960	100.00	385602	100.00	208743	100.00	621304	100.00

Note: Data for provincial FDI inflows are not available after 2005.

Sources: National Bureau of Statistics of China (various issues), *China Statistical Yearbook*, Beijing: China Statistics Press; Ministry of Commerce of China (various issues), *China Foreign Investment Report*, Beijing: MOFCOM.

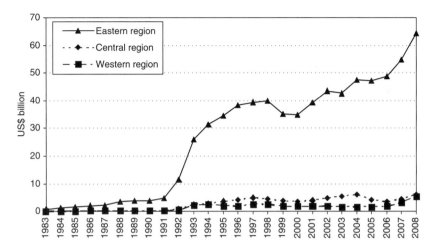

Sources: Calculated from National Bureau of Statistics of China (various issues), *China Statistical Yearbook*, Beijing: China Statistics Press; Ministry of Commerce of China (various issues), *China Foreign Investment Report*, Beijing: MOFCOM.

Figure 5.1   FDI inflows into China by region (2000 US$)

respectively. However, the other provinces in the central region each attracted less than 1 per cent of the total.

For the western region provinces, apart from Guangxi, whose share is 1.41 per cent, no other individual province has attracted more than 1 per cent of the total accumulative FDI inflows into China.

Figure 5.1 presents the annual FDI inflows into China by region during the period 1983 to 2008. As Figure 5.1 and Table 5.1 show, in the sub-period 1983 to 1991, FDI inflows into China were at a low level but increased steadily. In the initial stage of this period, FDI inflows were overwhelmingly concentrated in the four SEZs in Guangdong and Fujian provinces,[3] and the two municipalities of Beijing and Shanghai. With the development of overall economic reform, from 1984 to 1991 China gradually opened more and more areas to foreign investment. This included the opening up of the 14 coastal cities across ten provinces[4] and Hainan Island in 1984, the three 'development triangles' – the Yangzi River Delta, the Pearl River Delta and the Min Nan Delta – in 1985, the Shanghai Pudong New ETDZ and the entire coastal areas in 1988. As a result, FDI inflows into China continued to increase during the period from 1984 to 1991. However, because of the biased regional open policies, FDI inflows into China were overwhelmingly concentrated in the eastern region. As a result, the eastern region attracted US$24 billion, accounting for 89.07

per cent of the total FDI inflows, while the central region and the western region attracted US$1.3 billion, accounting for 4.92 per cent and US$1.6 billion, accounting for 6.01 per cent of the total respectively.

From the early 1990s, the Chinese government moved the implementation of the open policies for FDI towards a more level playing field throughout China. This major policy move was especially enhanced by Deng Xiaoping's call for deeper, faster and wider economic reform and liberalization in early 1992. The Chinese government then adopted and implemented a series of new policies and regulations to encourage FDI inflows. The results were astounding. FDI inflows into China surged dramatically and gradually spread from the initial concentrated areas to other provinces. Increasingly the most important areas for hosting FDI became the Yangzi River Delta region including Jiangsu, Shanghai, and Zhejiang and the Bohai Gulf including Shandong, Hebei, Tianjin, and Liaoning. Several provinces, such as Jiangxi, Hubei, Hunan and Henan in the central region, and Guangxi, Sichuan and Shaanxi in the western region, also witnessed relatively large increases in FDI inflows since 1992. Therefore, FDI inflows since the early 1990s have diffused from the initially concentrated southern coastal areas towards the south-eastern and eastern coastal areas as well as towards inland areas. However, owing to the negative impact of the Asian financial crisis, FDI inflows into China slowed down after 1998 and even declined in 1999 and 2000, before a moderate recovery in 2001. In this sub-period between 1992 and 2001, FDI inflows into all three regions increased. However, because of the much faster growth in FDI inflows in the eastern region than that in the central region and particularly in the western region, the gap between the eastern region and the central and western regions in terms of the absolute magnitude of annual FDI inflows has actually widened since the 1990s. As a result, the eastern region attracted US$331 billion FDI inflows, accounting for 85.76 per cent of the total, while the central region attracted US$35 billion FDI inflows (9.06 per cent), and the west region attracted US$20 billion FDI inflows (5.18 per cent).

After its accession to the WTO, with the implementation of the WTO commitments and broader and deeper liberalization in trade and investment, FDI inflows into China increased rapidly and continued to concentrate in the eastern region. FDI inflows into the eastern region increased from US$39.39 billion in 2001 to US$64.44 billion in 2008 (2000 US dollar prices). In contrast, during the same period, FDI inflows into both the central region and the western region increased only slightly by 2008. In the sub-period from 2002 to 2008, the eastern region attracted US$349.24 billion FDI inflows, accounting for 87.06 per cent of the total accumulative FDI inflows. The central region attracted US$34.68 billion (8.65 per cent), while the western region attracted US$17.23 billion (4.30 per cent).

In general, this description of the regional and provincial distribution of FDI has clearly revealed the uneven distribution of FDI in China. This raises the questions of what are the location determinants affecting FDI distribution across provinces in China and why has FDI been mainly concentrated in the eastern region provinces? The following sections will examine and answer these questions.

LOCATION DETERMINANTS OF FDI DISTRIBUTION WITHIN CHINA – THE HYPOTHESES

Building on the FDI literature, our general hypothesis is that facing the same set of source countries in the world, the provincial differences in FDI inflows are caused by the differences in location factors of each province. Therefore, in line with the hypotheses on the location determinants of FDI inflows into developing countries in Chapter 3, we take the following five groups of location factors as important in determining the magnitude of FDI inflows into each of China's host provinces.

1. Economic Factors

The economic factors include market size, level of economic development, growth rate of economy, labour costs and productivity, openness of economy to the outside world, and past performance in attracting FDI inflows.

Market size of the host province
The provincial market size is a very important indicator of the overall capacity of the economic activities of a host province. We expect the level of economic activities to be greater the larger the market of the host province. Consequently, we may hypothesize that the level of FDI inflows will be greater, the larger the market of the host province. Numerous studies of FDI location determinants have suggested that larger economies attract more FDI because there is more potential market demand. However, one point needs to be justified with respect to using provincial market size as a location factor determining the provincial distribution of FDI inflows within China. We argue that the provincial market size can be justified as important for both export-oriented FDI and FDI aimed at serving the domestic market. This is because larger economies can provide more opportunities for industries and enterprises to benefit from external economies of scale and spillover effects. In these circumstances, the influence of

provincial market size will still be positive on the inward FDI to host provinces. In addition, taking into account the increasing importance of FDI in service sectors, local market size is a very important location determinant. The measure of market size used in this study is the gross domestic product of the host province, denoted by GDP.

The level of economic development of the host province

The level of economic development is a comprehensive economic and social indicator of a province. A higher economic development level not only indicates good overall economic performance and higher purchasing power but also implies higher productivity associated with relatively good labour quality and advanced technology, better local infrastructure, and a better overall investment environment. Since the economic development levels of China's provinces are very different, we expect that the provincial economic development level has a positive impact on the provincial distribution of FDI inflows into China. In this study per capita GDP of the host province, denoted as PGDP, is used as a proxy for the provincial economic development level.

Economic growth rate of the host province

A high rate of economic growth is an indicator of development potential. Clearly markets that are expected to grow faster will tend to attract higher levels of inward FDI. Therefore, the hypothesis is that there is a positive relationship between inward FDI and economic growth in the host province. In this study, the real growth rate, denoted by GR, is used as the measure of economic growth in the host province.

Labour costs and productivity in the host province

In accordance with the argument for the use of efficiency wage in Chapter 3, we use the efficiency wage as a measure of labour costs in each of the host provinces. The expected impact of a high efficiency wage on FDI inflows into each of the host provinces is negative. The efficiency wage is measured as:

$$EW_j = \frac{W_j}{\Pi_j}$$

where EW_j is the average efficiency wage in host province j, W_j is the average wage rate of all employees in host province j, and Π_j is the overall labour productivity in host province j. The provincial overall labour productivity is measured as total value-added (approximated by GDP) over total employees in each province.

Openness of provinces to the outside world

The level of openness of a province indicates the intensity of economic interactions between that province and the rest of the world. A higher level of openness represents a higher level of international exposure of an economy. International business through trade generally sets the foundations for inward FDI and the international production that serves to substitute for or complement trade (UNCTAD, *World Investment Report*, 2002). In this study, we use two indicators for the openness of an economy. One is the trade to GDP ratio (TGDP) and the other is the export to GDP ratio (EGDP). We expect the level of provincial openness to have a positive impact on FDI inflows.

The level of accumulated FDI

Following the same argument in Chapter 3, we expect the level of provincial accumulated FDI stock to have a positive effect on attracting FDI inflows. The accumulated FDI, denoted as FDIS, is the FDI inflows accumulated since 1983 of each host province at 2000 US dollar prices.

2.   Infrastructure and Energy Supply

Intensity of transport infrastructure in the host province

The standard and intensity of transport infrastructure in each host province might be another important consideration for foreign investors. Consequently, we assume that more highways, more railways and more interior transport waterways, adjusted for the size of the host province, are positively related to FDI inflows. The proxy for the intensity of transport infrastructure used in this study is the ratio of the sum of the length of highways, railways and interior transport waterways divided by the size of the corresponding host province, denoted as TI. The unit of the intensity of transport infrastructure is kilometres per 100 square kilometres of the host province land area.

Provision of telecommunications in the host province

Another important infrastructure variable concerned by the foreign investors might be the provision of telecommunications in host provinces. Higher standard and availability of telecommunications services will save time and reduce the costs of communication and information gathering, thus facilitating business activities. Therefore, we expect the provision of telecommunications to be positively related to the levels of FDI inflows into host provinces. The provision of telecommunications, denoted as TELCOM, is measured as the number of telephone sets per 100 persons in each province.

Energy supply of the host province
Energy supply is an important input for many production activities. Therefore, it is expected that energy supply will have a positive link to FDI inflows, particularly for manufacturing and efficiency-seeking FDI. In this study, we use electricity production, denoted as EL, as a proxy for energy supply. It is measured by kWh per capita.

3.   Human Resource Endowment and Labour Quality

Labour quality in the host province
Since labour quality is directly related to labour productivity, it may be another important labour market variable affecting foreign investors' location decision. In this study we use two measures for labour quality. One is the percentage of literacy of the population aged 15 years or older, and another is the percentage of the population enrolled as university students. We expect the literacy rate, denoted as READ, and the university students enrolment rate, denoted as UNI, to be positively related to the levels of FDI inflows into each province.

4.   Geographical Location

China is a large country with a wide geographical distribution of provinces. Therefore, the geographical location might also be an important factor affecting FDI inflows. As we mentioned earlier, based on geographical location, China's 31 mainland provinces can be grouped into three regional groups, namely, the eastern coast region, the central region and the western region. Among the three regions, the eastern coast region is the most economically developed and is closer to the outside world. Therefore, we use a dummy variable, denoted as COAST, to test the impact of geographical location on FDI inflows. We give a value of one for the 12 provinces along the coastal line and a value of zero for other provinces.[5] We expect this dummy variable to have a positive impact on FDI inflows.

5.   Policy Factors

Since China adopted the open door policy three decades ago, increasing numbers of cities and areas have been gradually opened up to attract FDI and an evolving series of policies towards FDI have been implemented. Have these policies had any significant impact on the provincial distribution of FDI inflows? In this chapter we do not intend to test all of the policies during the entire period. However, among the FDI policies we do want to test are the impact of SEZ policies, the uneven regional open policies and the trade and investment liberalization policies implemented since the 1990s.

The unevenness regional open policies for FDI arose from the establishment of the four SEZs in 1979, the opening up of 14 coastal cities in 1984, and then the expansion of open policies to the 11 coastal provinces in 1988. Not until the early 1990s has the Chinese government gradually moved towards a more nationwide implementation of open policies for FDI. Therefore, two dummy variables, denoted as *SEZ* and *ROP*, for the SEZ policy and the regional open policy, are used to test their impact on the inflows of FDI into each province. For the dummy variable *SEZ*, we give a value of one for Guangdong, Fujian, Hainan and Shanghai, and a value of zero for other provinces. For the dummy variable *ROP*, we give a value of one for the 12 eastern region provinces from 1986 to 2005, a value of zero from 1986 to 1991 and a value of one from 1992 to 2005 for other provinces.

Since the early 1990s, to accelerate economic reform and also to gain accession to the WTO, China has embarked upon large-scale trade and investment liberalization. A series of policies towards trade and investment liberalization have been adopted and implemented. To test the impact of these trade and investment liberalization policies on FDI inflows, we use a dummy variable, denoted as *TIL*. We give a value of zero for the years from 1986 to 1991 and a value of one for the years from 1992 to 2005 for all provinces.

LOCATION DETERMINANTS OF FDI DISTRIBUTION WITHIN CHINA – AN EMPIRICAL ANALYSIS

In this section we conduct an empirical analysis of the location determinants of the provincial distribution of FDI inflows within China.

Variable Specification and the Model

The relationship between the inflows of FDI and the location variables in China's provinces is investigated over time and across provinces. Thirty provinces from 1986 to 2005 are included.[6] In this study, the dependent variable, denoted as $FDI_{*j,t}$, is the aggregate inflow of FDI from all source countries into China's host province j in year t. The value of FDI is at 2000 US dollar prices. There are 16 independent variables which are summarized in Table 5.2.

Table 5.2   Variable list of the location determinants of FDI inflows into China's provinces

Variable name	Specification of variables	Expected impact on FDI inflows
Dependent variable		
$FDI_{*j,t}$	Aggregate FDI inflows from all source countries into province j in year t. 2000 US\$, millions	
Independent variables		
$GDP_{j,t}$	Gross domestic product of province j in year t. Million yuan at 2000 prices	Positive
$PGDP_{j,t}$	Per capita GDP of province j in year t. Yuan per capita at 2000 prices	Positive
$GR_{j,t}$	Real growth rate of GDP of province j in year t	Positive
$EW_{j,t}$	Efficiency wage of province j in year t	Negative
$TGDP_{j,t}$	Total trade to GDP ratio of province j in year t	Positive
$EGDP_{j,t}$	Export to GDP ratio of province j in year t	Positive
$FDIS_{j,t}$	Accumulated FDI stocks of province j in the end of year t. 2000 US\$, million	Positive
$TI_{j,t}$	Transport intensity index of province j in year t. Kilometres per 100 square kilometres	Positive
$TELCOM_{j,t}$	Provision of telecommunications of province j in year t. Number of telephone sets per 100 persons	Positive
$EL_{j,t}$	Provision of electricity supply of province j in year t. kWh per capita	Positive
$UNI_{j,t}$	University students enrolment rate of population of province j in year t	Positive
$READ_{j,t}$	Literacy rates of population aged 15 years or older of province j in year t	Positive
$COAST_j$	Geographical location dummy variable. One for the 12 provinces located along the coastline, and zero for other provinces	Positive
SEZ_j	SEZ dummy variable. One for Guangdong, Fujian, Hainan and Shanghai, and zero for other provinces	Positive
$ROP_{j,t}$	Regional open policy dummy variable. One for the 12 coastal economically opened provinces. Zero from 1986 to 1991 and one from 1992 to 2005 for other provinces	Positive
TIL_t	Trade and investment liberalization policy dummy variable. Zero for the years 1986 to 1991 and one for the years 1992 to 2005 for all provinces	Positive

Note: All of the variables are calculated from National Bureau of Statistics of China (various issues), *China Statistical Yearbook*, Beijing: China Statistics Press.

We establish the following equation to test the location determinants of provincial distribution of FDI inflows into China:

$$\ln FDI_{*j,t} = \beta_0 + \beta_1 \ln GDP_{j,t-k} + \beta_2 \ln PGDP_{j,t-k} + \beta_3 \ln GR_{j,t-k}$$

$$+ \beta_4 \ln EW_{j,t-k} + \beta_5 \ln TGDP_{j,t-k} + \beta_6 \ln EGDP_{j,t-k} + \beta_7 \ln FDIS_{j,t-k}$$

$$+ \beta_8 \ln TI_{j,t-k} + \beta_9 \ln TELCOM_{j,t-k} + \beta_{10} \ln EL_{j,t-k} + \beta_{11} \ln UNI_{j,t-k}$$

$$+ \beta_{12} \ln READ_{j,t-k} + \beta_{13} COAST_j + \beta_{14} SEZ_j + \beta_{15} ROP_{j,t}$$

$$+ \beta_{16} TIL_t + v_j + \varepsilon_{j,t} \tag{5.1}$$

The independent variables, except for the dummy variables, are lagged k years. This model assumes that the effect of the independent variables at time $t - k$ appears only within period t and is fully completed within that period. The relationship shown in the above equation will be examined for $k = 1$, the most likely appropriate lag.

Regression Results and Explanations

We estimate equation (5.1) under random-effects panel regression in order that we do not preclude the use of key fixed effect indicators which we wish to identify separately. The most obvious of these are the geographical location variable (*COAST*), and the policy dummy variables. The regression results of the random-effects model are reported in Table 5.3.

Since there are 16 independent variables, before we run the regression, we conducted a correlation test for the independent variables. We found that the correlation coefficients between some of the independent variables were very high. The high correlation between these independent variables may incur high multi-collinearity problems if we enter all the independent variables into the same regression equation. Therefore, we have run five separate regressions each with a different set of explanatory variables. The five models performed very well. All regressions have relatively high explanatory power and all of the independent variables have the expected signs and are statistically significant.

The regression results show that the provincial differences in FDI inflows can be explained by the differences in provincial location factors. The provincial market size (*GDP*), the level of economic development (*PGDP*), the real growth rate of provincial economy (*GR*), the trade and export to GDP ratios (*TGDP* and *EGDP*), the level of accumulated FDI stock (*FDIS*), the intensity of transport infrastructure (*TI*), the provision

Table 5.3　Regression results of location determinants affecting FDI inflows into China's provinces, 1986–2005 (lag k=1), random-effects (dependent variable LFDI$_{*j,t}$*)*

Variables	Model 1	Model 2	Model 3	Model 4	Model 5
Constant	−6.30	−23.80	−4.27	−8.88	0.54
	(−6.19)***	(−4.93)***	(−4.63)***	(−11.19)***	(0.62)
LGDP	0.53	1.26			
	(5.62)***	(9.05)***			
LPGDP			0.59		
			(3.80)***		
LGR				0.14	0.15
				(2.18)**	(2.10)**
LEW	−0.56	−1.02	−1.03	−1.37	−2.09
	(−4.33)***	(−4.78)***	(−4.24)***	(−4.76)***	(−6.91)***
LTGDP	0.15				
	(1.78)*				
LEGDP			0.20	0.38	
			(1.85)*	(2.82)***	
LFDIS	0.30				
	(5.37)***				
LTI	0.38		0.56	1.15	1.27
	(3.94)***		(2.27)**	(6.08)***	(5.84)***
LTELCOM		0.14			
		(2.03)**			
LEL				1.27	
				(10.42)***	
LREAD		2.92			
		(2.83)***			
LUNI					0.77
					(7.22)***
COAST	0.49	0.66			
	(3.47)***	(2.92)***			
SEZ	0.37	1.15	0.49	0.74	1.10
	(2.32)**	(5.01)***	(2.11)**	(1.87)*	(3.03)***
ROP	0.42		0.45		
	(2.71)***		(2.92)***		
TIL	0.82		1.72		
	(5.42)***		(13.03)***		
Observations	581	586	581	541	543
Groups	30	30	30	30	30
R^2: overall	0.88	0.76	0.70	0.52	0.55
Wald Chi2	2321.37***	796.46***	1617.44***	444.51***	352.37***

Table 5.3 (continued)

of telecommunications (*TELCOM*), the energy supply (*EL*), the university students enrolment rate (*UNI*), and the provincial literacy rates – the proxy for labour quality – are positive and statistically significant location determinants of the provincial distribution of FDI. The provincial efficiency wage (*EW*), the proxy for labour costs adjusted for productivity, is negative and statistically significant as a location determinant affecting FDI inflows.

The geographical location (*COAST*), the SEZ policies (*SEZ*), and the regional differentiation in the timing of implementing the open policies (*ROP*) for FDI, have had a strong impact on the provincial distribution of FDI inflows into China. This indicates that, apart from the economic factors, the huge FDI inflows into the eastern region provinces were enhanced by the geographical location advantage, the special policies to the SEZs, and the implementation of the uneven regional open policies for FDI during the 1980s and the early 1990s. The gradual but obvious diffusion of FDI inflows into the inland provinces after 1992 is also partially due to the nationwide implementation of open policies for FDI since the early 1990s.

The implementation of trade and investment liberalization policies (*TIL*) since the early 1990s and particularly after China's entry into the WTO in 2001 had a strong positive effect on attracting FDI inflows into China across all provinces. Therefore, the sharp increase in the inflows of FDI into China since 1992 and after 2001 could be explained partially by the major policy changes in favour of FDI in the early 1990s, and the continued trade and investment liberalization during the 1990s and the early 2000s.

INWARD FDI ATTRACTIVENESS INDEX OF CHINA'S PROVINCES

With the empirical test results, we can construct the inward FDI attractiveness index for China's provinces by using the provincial location factors affecting FDI inflows. We adopt the same method used by UNCTAD

(*World Investment Report*, 2002) to construct the provincial inward FDI attractiveness index.[7] The provincial inward FDI attractiveness index is the average of the scores on 16 variables (including four dummy variables – *COAST*, *SEZ*, *ROP* and *TIL*) for each province. The score for each variable, except dummy variables, is derived using the following formula:

$$\text{Score} = (V_i - V_{min})/(V_{max} - V_{min})$$

where

V_i = the value of a variable for the province i
V_{min} = the lowest value of the variable among the provinces
V_{max} = the highest value of the variable among the provinces

According to the above formula, the province with the lowest value is given a variable score of zero and the province with the highest value is given a variable score of one. For dummy variables, the province with the value of zero is given a score of zero and the province with the value of one is given a score of one.

The variables used in the calculation of the provincial inward FDI attractiveness index include: provincial GDP, per capita GDP, real economic growth rate, cost adjusted productivity (which is the inverse of efficiency wage), trade to GDP ratio, export to GDP ratio, accumulated FDI stock, provision of transportation infrastructure, provision of tele-communications, electricity supply, university students enrolment ratio of population, literacy ratio of population, and four dummy variables including the location dummy variable *COAST*, the SEZ policy dummy variable *SEZ*, the regional open policy dummy variable *ROP*, and the trade and investment liberalization dummy variable *TIL*.

The provincial inward FDI attractiveness index is calculated for three periods: 1985 to 1990, 1991 to 2000 and 2001 to 2008, reported in Table 5.4. The provincial inward FDI attractiveness index reveals interesting results.

First, the index values among China's 31 mainland provinces differ greatly and are consistent with the provincial distribution of FDI inflows into China.

Second, Shanghai, Guangdong, Beijing and Tianjin have continuously been the top four provinces with the highest index values, while Tibet, Guizhou, Gansu, Yunnan and Qinghai have been the bottom five provinces with the lowest index values.

Third, based on the inward FDI attractiveness index values, the top ten provinces in the three periods are all located in the eastern region, while

Table 5.4   *Provincial FDI attractiveness index (minimum = 0,*
                maximum = 1)

Province	1985–1990		1991–2000		2001–2008	
	Value	Rank	Value	Rank	Value	Rank
Eastern region	0.4541	1	0.5469	1	0.5697	1
Beijing	0.5498	3	0.6152	3	0.6147	4
Tianjin	0.4763	4	0.5631	4	0.6364	3
Hebei	0.3227	11	0.3969	11	0.4057	11
Liaoning	0.4405	5	0.4683	8	0.4688	9
Shanghai	0.6396	2	0.8102	1	0.8139	1
Jiangsu	0.3939	7	0.5077	6	0.5961	5
Zhejiang	0.3613	10	0.4768	7	0.5374	6
Fujian	0.4360	6	0.5563	5	0.5321	7
Shandong	0.3622	9	0.4475	9	0.4964	8
Guangdong	0.6400	1	0.7280	2	0.7505	2
Hainan	0.3725	8	0.4456	10	0.4143	10
Central region	0.1738	2	0.2974	2	0.3150	2
Shanxi	0.1607	20	0.2869	18	0.3742	13
Jilin	0.2040	14	0.3102	15	0.3431	14
Heilongjiang	0.2044	13	0.3404	12	0.3165	20
Anhui	0.1421	25	0.2643	21	0.2689	25
Jiangxi	0.1443	24	0.2623	22	0.2880	23
Henan	0.1649	18	0.3011	16	0.3189	19
Hubei	0.1997	15	0.3283	13	0.3240	17
Hunan	0.1701	17	0.2858	19	0.2863	24
Western region	0.1402	3	0.2420	3	0.2805	3
Inner Mongolia	0.1549	22	0.2733	20	0.3891	12
Guangxi	0.2865	12	0.3233	14	0.3305	15
Chongqing	na		na		0.2894	22
Sichuan	0.1561	21	0.2612	23	0.2648	27
Guizhou	0.0896	29	0.1960	29	0.2322	30
Yunnan	0.1376	26	0.2296	26	0.2352	29
Tibet	0.0171	30	0.1502	30	0.1598	31
Shaanxi	0.1615	19	0.2572	25	0.3220	18
Gansu	0.0965	28	0.2074	28	0.2384	28
Qinghai	0.1212	27	0.2104	27	0.2686	26
Ningxia	0.1464	23	0.2590	24	0.3289	16
Xinjiang	0.1743	16	0.2942	17	0.3073	21

Note: na = not available.

Source: Author's calculation.

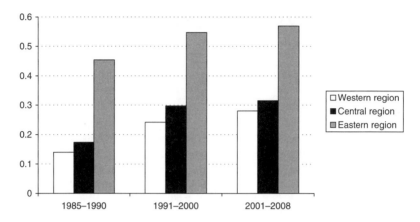

Source: Author's calculation.

Figure 5.2   Inward FDI attractiveness index by region

in the same periods, for the bottom ten provinces two are located in the central region and eight are located in the western region. As a result, the eastern region has the highest index values, which are around 100 per cent higher and 150 per cent higher than those in the central and western regions respectively.

Fourth, over the period from the mid-1980s to 2008, the values of the provincial inward FDI attractiveness index have been increasing for all three regions and provinces, indicating the continued improvement in the investment environment for FDI across China for the past three decades (see Figure 5.2). Among the provinces, the largest improvements in the ranks of inward FDI attractiveness index are for Jiangsu and Zhejiang in the eastern region, Shanxi and Inner Mongolia in the central region, and Ningxia and Shaanxi in the western region, indicating a relatively faster improvement in the location factors in attracting FDI inflows in these provinces.

Finally, compared with the eastern region, although there have been some improvements in the investment environment for FDI, the central and particularly the western region still have very low attractiveness to FDI based on their location factors. The central and western regions are lagging 15 to 20 years behind the eastern region in terms of attractiveness for FDI. The inward FDI attractiveness index values are largely based on structural economic factors that tend to change slowly over time, therefore it is unrealistic to expect that the central region and particularly the western region will attract large FDI inflows in the near future.

CONCLUSION

This chapter has investigated empirically the provincial distribution of FDI inflows into China during the past three decades. We have found that associated with the huge amount of FDI inflows into China, the provincial distribution has been very uneven. As a group the eastern region provinces received the overwhelming share while the central and western regions received only around 13 per cent of the total FDI inflows into China during the period 1983 to 2008. The causes of this uneven provincial distribution were then subjected to theoretical explanation and empirical investigation.

Using Dunning's OLI explanation of the causes of FDI by focusing on the location advantages, the empirical analysis of this chapter has shown that given the ownership advantages of source countries and the incentives for their MNEs to internalize their ownership advantages in order to reduce transaction costs, the location advantages or the location determinants of host provinces are crucial in attracting FDI inflows. In other words, facing the same set of source countries, provincial differences in the magnitude of FDI inflows received from the same set of source countries are determined by the differences in location advantages of host provinces. Therefore, the uneven provincial distribution of FDI inflows into China is caused by the differences in provincial characteristics and location factors of each individual province.

The empirical regression analysis provides strong support for the acceptance of the hypotheses set in this chapter. To summarize, the provinces with larger GDP, higher per capita income, higher rate of economic growth, higher level of openness represented by trade and export to GDP ratios, higher level of accumulated FDI stock, more intensive transport infrastructure, higher availabilities of telecommunications, higher level of electricity supply, higher level of labour quality approximated by literacy rates and represented by higher ratio of university students enrolment, and being located along the coast attracted relatively more FDI inflows. Meanwhile, higher labour costs and low productivity approximated by efficiency wages deterred FDI inflows. In addition, the SEZ policies and the regional differentiation in the timing of implementing the open policies for FDI had a strong impact on the provincial distribution of FDI inflows. Finally, the implementation of a series of trade and FDI liberalization policies in the 1990s and the early 2000s had a very strong positive effect on attracting FDI inflows into China across all provinces.

Based on the empirical analysis, we constructed the provincial inward FDI attractiveness index for China's 31 mainland provinces. The index results reveal that there are large differences among China's 31 mainland provinces in the attractiveness to FDI inflows. The most attractive provinces, according to the values of the inward FDI attractiveness index, are the eastern region provinces, particularly Shanghai, Guangdong, Beijing, Tianjin, Jiangsu, Fujian, Zhejiang and Shandong. Although there have been some improvements in the investment environment for FDI, the central region provinces and particularly the western region provinces are less attractive to FDI as compared to the eastern region provinces. As a result, the eastern region will continue to attract most of the FDI inflows into China and the situation of uneven regional distribution of FDI inflows into China will persist.

This chapter is an exploration of a topic that is of increasing importance to China in general and is of direct relevance to the economic development efforts of each individual province in particular. Two important implications for the provincial distribution of FDI in China can be drawn from this study. First, it is essential for each of the provinces to boost economic growth, to increase per capita income, to increase the interaction with the world economy, to enhance education and labour training, to raise labour productivity, and to improve basic infrastructure in order to attract more FDI inflows. Although this is not easy for all of the provinces, particularly for economically backward provinces in the western region, this is what is required in order to attract more FDI and to accelerate economic development. Second, since China launched the overall economic reform of late 1979, the economic growth rates of the eastern region provinces, which benefited from the regionally biased special policies, have been much faster than those of the inland and western less-developed provinces. This unbalanced economic growth between the coastal provinces and the inland and western provinces has led to uneven economic development and an increase in income gaps between them.

Although the open policies for FDI have been applied throughout China since 1992, the differences between the eastern region provinces and the central and western region provinces in the levels of economic development resulting from the unevenness of the implementation of regional open policies prior to this time cannot be overcome in the short term. All of these factors have had a very strong and direct impact on the location factors attracting FDI inflows. Therefore, if China wanted to help the economic development of inland provinces, particularly the less developed areas in the western region, it could: (1) shift the preferential policies for FDI from regional priority to industrial priority, namely to encourage those FDI projects engaged in technologically advanced, infrastructure-based, transportation, communication, agriculture, environmental protection, energy and raw materials, and modern service industries; (2) adjust its regional development strategy by offering special economic and industrial development policies to the central and western regions, and the launch of the west development strategy in 1998 is an important step in the right direction; and (3) encourage coastal areas to transfer managerial skills and technology accumulated and obtained from attracting and utilizing FDI to the inland regions in order to benefit more from FDI nationwide.

NOTES

1. The eastern region includes Beijing, Tianjin, Hebei, Liaoning, Shanghai, Jiangsu, Zhejiang, Fujian, Shandong, Guangdong and Hainan. The central region includes Shanxi, Jilin, Heilongjiang, Anhui, Jiangxi, Henan, Hubei and Hunan. The western region includes Inner Mongolia, Guangxi, Chongqing, Sichuan, Guizhou, Yunnan, Tibet, Shaanxi, Gansu, Qinghai, Ningxia and Xinjiang.
2. Data for provincial FDI inflows are not available after 2005.
3. Shenzhen, Zhuhai, and Shantou in Guangdong Province, and Xiamen in Fujian Province.
4. These ten coastal provinces include Liaoning, Tianjin, Hebei, Shandong, Shanghai, Jiangsu, Zhejiang, Fujian, Guangdong and Guangxi.
5. The 12 coastal provinces include Beijing, Tianjin, Hebei, Liaoning, Shanghai, Jiangsu, Zhejiang, Fujian, Shandong, Guangdong, Guangxi and Hainan.
6. Tibet is excluded from the test due to a lack of data.
7. UNCTAD named it the inward FDI potential index. However, I prefer to call it the inward FDI attractiveness index.

PART II

Investor Differences

6. Composition and investment intensity of source countries in China

INTRODUCTION

In the preceding chapters our studies of FDI in China have mainly focused on the analysis of location determinants of host countries and of host provinces of China. However, what is the composition of the source countries of FDI in China? Are there any differences in investment relations with China among source countries and what factors explain these differences? This chapter will discuss and answer these questions.

From the host country's point of view, a diversity of the sources of FDI can provide more opportunities for the host country to obtain and to absorb diversified information, technology, management skills and access to international markets, thus enhancing the gains to the host country's enterprises and economy. However, as we will see in the following section, one of the most prominent features of FDI in China is the overwhelming dominance of developing countries and economies. Comparing the two groups of developing and developed countries and economies, at the year end of 2008, investments from developing countries and economies accounted for 75.38 per cent of China's total inward FDI stock, while investments from developed countries accounted for only 24.62 per cent of the total.[1]

Why has China been so successful in attracting FDI inflows from developing countries and economies, especially from the Asian NIEs, but has been not very impressive in attracting FDI inflows from developed countries, especially from the Western European countries, even though they are the major investors for world FDI? In other words, what factors explain the investment relations between countries in the world? This chapter investigates and analyses these issues by using the concept of an investment intensity index. The investment intensity index reveals the relative importance of a country as a host for a source country's investment, compared with the rest of the world as a host for the same source country's investment.

This chapter is structured as follows. The next section presents an overview of the composition of FDI sources in China. The third section analyses the investment intensity of source countries in China. The following section puts forward some hypotheses and discusses the factors which are thought to be important in determining the investment intensity of source countries in China. The fifth section uses regression analysis to test the hypotheses, and the final section concludes the chapter.

THE COMPOSITION OF FDI SOURCES

Since 1979 more than 170 countries and economies have invested in China. We want to know who are the major investors? By the end of 2008, as shown in Table 6.1, FDI in China was overwhelmingly dominated by developing countries and economies, which accounted for 75.38 per cent of the total accumulative FDI inflows, while developed countries accounted for only 24.62 per cent of the total. Among the developing countries and economies, as a group the Asian NIEs[2] has been the largest investor, accounting for 56.64 per cent of the total. Within the Asian NIEs, Hong Kong has held the dominant position, accounting for 41.75 per cent of the total, followed by Taiwan (5.76 per cent), South Korea (4.74 per cent) and Singapore (4.39 per cent). The four ASEAN economies[3] accounted for 1.48 per cent of the total.

One notable feature is the large shares held by the tax-haven economies. Foreign direct investment inflows into China from the tax-haven economies increased dramatically in the 1990s and particularly in the 2000s. As a result, their combined share in total FDI inflows increased to 13.64 per cent by the end of 2008. The Virgin Islands took the dominant position, accounting for 9.78 per cent of the total, followed by the Cayman Islands (1.78 per cent) and Samoan Islands (1.30 per cent).

Among the developed countries, Japan and the USA are the most important investors in China, accounting for 7.78 per cent and 7.18 per cent of the total, while the combined share of the EU (15) was 7.19 per cent. Apart from the UK, Germany, Netherlands and France, whose shares are 1.89 per cent, 1.76 per cent, 1.06 per cent and 1.03 per cent respectively, no other individual developed country has contributed more than 1 per cent of the total accumulative FDI inflows into China.

Figure 6.1 presents the annual FDI inflows into China by developing and developed countries and economies during the period from 1983 to 2008. In the sub-period of 1983 to 1991, FDI inflows into China were at a low level but increased steadily. Developing countries and economies accounted for 66.75 per cent while developed countries accounted for 33.25 per cent of the total FDI inflows.

Table 6.1 Accumulative FDI inflows into China by developing and developed countries and economies, 1983–2008 (2000 US$)

	Year 1983–2008	
	US$ (million)	(%)
Developing countries & economies	620 925	75.38
NIEs	466 542	56.64
Hong Kong	343 888	41.75
Taiwan	47 423	5.76
South Korea	39 043	4.74
Singapore	36 188	4.39
ASEAN (4)	12 225	1.48
Malaysia	4721	0.57
Thailand	3241	0.39
Philippines	2453	0.30
Indonesia	1810	0.22
Tax-haven economies	112 372	13.64
Virgin Islands	80 521	9.78
Cayman Islands	14 693	1.78
Samoan Islands	10 733	1.30
Other developing countries	29 787	3.62
Developed countries	202 814	24.62
Japan	64 114	7.78
USA	59 172	7.18
EU (15)	59 262	7.19
UK	15 561	1.89
Germany	14 480	1.76
Netherlands	8715	1.06
France	8474	1.03
Italy	4254	0.52
Other developed countries	20 266	2.46
Canada	6118	0.74
Australia	5595	0.68
New Zealand	767	0.09
Total	823 739	100.00

Sources: National Bureau of Statistics of China (various issues), *China Statistical Yearbook*, Beijing: China Statistics Press; Ministry of Commerce of China, Invest in China, FDI Statistics.

Since 1992, there has been an unprecedented surge of FDI inflows into China. Both developing and developed countries and economies increased their investments in China, but the rate of increase for developing countries and economies was much higher than that of the developed countries from

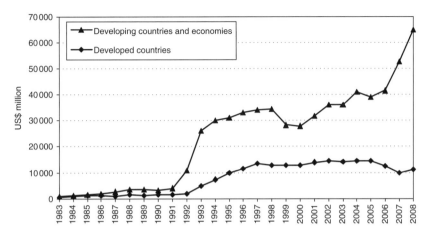

Sources: National Bureau of Statistics of China (various issues), *China Statistical Yearbook*, Beijing: China Statistics Press; Ministry of Commerce of China, Invest in China, FDI Statistics.

Figure 6.1   FDI inflows into China by developing and developed countries and economies (2000 US$, millions)

1992 to 1997. However, during 1997 to 2000, FDI inflows from developing countries and economies slowed down and declined, which was caused by the Asian financial crisis. In the same period, FDI inflows from developed countries were relatively stable. Despite the decline in 1997 to 2000, the share of developing countries and economies in total FDI inflows into China increased to 74.51 per cent while the share of developed countries declined to 25.49 per cent during the sub-period from 1992 to 2000.

After China's accession to the WTO in 2001, FDI inflows into China increased rapidly, almost entirely coming from developing countries and economies. FDI inflows from developing countries and economies increased from US$31.81 billion in 2001 to US$64.89 billion in 2008 (at 2000 US dollar prices). However, FDI inflows from developed countries only increased marginally during 2002 to 2005 and even declined during 2006 to 2008. As a result, the share of developed countries in total FDI inflows into China further declined to 23.41 per cent while the share of developing countries and economies increased to 76.59 per cent during the sub-period of 2001 to 2008.

Analysis of FDI in China by sources reveals great concentration in terms of the magnitudes invested by the source countries and economies. However, analysis of FDI sources in China requires caution. This is especially important in explaining the dominance of Hong Kong in China's

FDI and the large increase in FDI inflows from the tax-haven economies, because of the round-tripping issue.

Round-tripping involves the circular flow of capital out of China and the subsequent reinvestment of this 'foreign' capital in China for the purpose of benefiting from fiscal entitlements accorded to foreign investors. Because the funds originate in the host economy itself, round-tripping inflates actual FDI inflows. Studies such as the East Asia Analytical Unit (EAAU, 1995) and Lever-Tracy et al. (1996) suggest that a large volume of the FDI inflows from Hong Kong and Taiwan are due to round-tripping incentives. According to the UNCTAD (2007), a significant share of FDI inflows into China is round-tripping, mainly via Hong Kong and more recently and increasingly via some tax-haven economies – the Virgin Islands, Cayman Islands and Samoan Islands. Official estimates by the Chinese government are not available. One estimate made by Guonan Ma suggested that round-tripping inward FDI accounted for 25 per cent of China's FDI inflows in 1992[4] and the same figure was also estimated by Harrold and Lall (1993). However, Xiao (2004) estimated that the round-tripping FDI accounted for 40 per cent of China's total FDI inflows during 1994 to 2001.

Round-tripping typically involves three steps: (1) the accumulation of new capital in China, (2) the capital flight out of China, and (3) the round-tripping FDI back to China. Owing to the fast economic growth and a high level of saving, China has accumulated a large amount of new capital since the 1980s. However, a large part of the new capital has found its way abroad through mis-invoicing in international trade, smuggling, and other channels of capital flight since the people who are creating the new capital have strong incentives to diversify domestic risks and to seek better protection of property rights (Xiao, 2004). Some of this capital has stayed abroad waiting for opportunities to return to China. On average, the round-tripping FDI – the returning Chinese capital – is about 20 to 30 per cent of the total capital flight (Xiao, 2004). The accumulated capital flight then forms the base for sustained round-tripping FDI back home when the opportunities arise to make profits and create new capital at home.

Round-tripping is driven by a number of incentives. In the case of China, the main two incentives are preferential treatments offered to FDI and property rights protection. First, since the beginning of economic reform in 1978, the Chinese government has intensively and selectively applied a range of tax incentives, tariff concessions and preferential treatment to attract FDI flowing into the targeted areas and industries. The preferential treatment for FDI is the primary incentives for domestic firms to engage in round-tripping FDI. Second, China's property rights protection enforcement is weak. Many private enterprises operate in the environment of very restrictive regulations with loose property rights protection. So, the private sector has strong incentives to move their profits out of China and then move them back in the form of FDI when they see profit opportunities arise as the Chinese governments tend to give better protection of property rights to foreign investors. In addition, China's restrictive foreign exchange control regime and the less restrictive and more efficient financial services overseas both contribute to the incentives for FDI round-tripping.

Since its accession to the WTO, China has strengthened property rights protection, and at the same time reduced and eliminated much of the preferential treatment offered to FDI firms. In March 2007 China passed the new Enterprise Income Tax Law, unifying the corporate income tax rates for foreign and domestic enterprises at 25 per cent. The unification of the corporate income tax rate, the elimination of preferential treatment to FDI firms and improved property rights protection will reduce the incentives for FDI round-tripping.

Apart from round-tripping, another explanation for the rise of FDI inflows into China from the tax-haven economies is the 'transit' investment in China from other economies via the tax-haven economies in order to lower (or eliminate) their fiscal commitments. For example, the number of companies in Hong Kong that are incorporated in Bermuda and the Cayman Islands jumped by 5.2 times from 178 in 1990 to 924 in 2000 (Wu et al., 2002). As for Taiwan's companies, partly to take advantage of the tax regime in the tax-haven economies, but also to bypass Taiwan's government restrictions on investment in the mainland, after China, the Virgin Islands and the Cayman Islands rank second and third respectively as the biggest recipients of Taiwan's outward investment (Breslin, 2003). This suggests that FDI in China from Hong Kong and Taiwan is more significant than the official data suggest.

Therefore, when we interpret the composition of FDI sources in China, we should acknowledge the data problems such as these. However, since Hong Kong's investment is so dominant, even when we deduct 25 per cent (we assume that 25 per cent of Hong Kong's FDI in China is due to round-tripping) from Hong Kong's total FDI, it is still as high as 32 per cent of the adjusted total FDI stock in China, far ahead of any other investors. Therefore, despite the round-tripping problem, the general findings of FDI sources in China are still valid. The largest single investor in China is Hong Kong followed by Japan, the USA, Taiwan, South Korea and Singapore. As a group the Asian NIEs are the largest investor in China followed by the tax-haven economies, the EU (15) and the four ASEAN economies.

THE INVESTMENT INTENSITY OF SOURCE COUNTRIES IN CHINA

Why has China been so successful in attracting FDI inflows from developing countries and economies, especially from the Asian NIEs, but has been not very impressive in attracting FDI inflows from developed countries, especially from the Western European countries? In other words, what factors explain the investment relations between countries? One way to compare a country's relative importance for its source countries' investments is to calculate the source countries' investment intensity indexes. The concept of investment intensity originated from the concept of trade intensity. The trade intensity analysis was pioneered by Brown (1949) and developed and popularized by Kojima (1964). It uses an intensity of trade index which concentrates attention on variations in bilateral trade levels that result from differential resistances to bilateral trade flows. As Drysdale and Garnaut (1994) pointed out, because the trade intensity index is based on the aggregate level of countries' foreign trade, it is a crude index of relative resistances.

Based on the concept of trade intensity index, the investment intensity index can be calculated from the following equation:

$$III_{ij} = \left(\frac{\left(\frac{I_{ij}}{I_{*j}} \right)}{\left(\frac{I_{i*}}{I_{**}} \right)} \right) \times 100$$

where:

III_{ij} = investment intensity index of country i's investment in country j
I_{ij} = investment by country i in country j
I_{*j} = investment from the world in country j
I_{i*} = investment from country i in the world
I_{**} = total investment in the world.

The index measures the relative importance of country j as a host for country i's investment as compared to the rest of the world. It can be interpreted as a measure of the relative resistances to FDI flows between countries reflected by the variations in the investment intensity index. If the index is above 100 per cent, it indicates that country i's investment in country j is more than the amount of its share of investment in the world. This implies that the relative resistance to FDI flows between country i and country j is lower than those between country i and the rest of the world.

*Table 6.2   Investment intensity index of the major investors in China
(percentage)*

Economy	1992–1995	1996–2000	2001–2005	2006–2008	1992–2008
Hong Kong	882	1122	1135	1255	1145
Taiwan	1038	1084	724	475	881
South Korea	280	671	1601	691	833
Philippines	486	3114	1482	278	748
Thailand	510	1072	854	152	540
Singapore	253	734	365	494	476
Japan	98	241	195	111	168
Malaysia	85	269	259	79	149
Indonesia	192	866	129	71	148
New Zealand	7	49	na	133	86
Australia	54	147	207	41	83
USA	29	52	43	22	39
Germany	8	24	54	18	24
Canada	22	22	23	18	21
Italy	20	37	16	16	20
Netherlands	5	20	19	36	20
UK	15	18	18	12	16
Denmark	5	8	17	24	13
Austria	7	18	15	11	12
France	7	14	11	6	10
Switzerland	5	15	10	8	10
Finland	1	6	18	27	10
Sweden	3	9	8	11	9
Spain	4	2	4	6	4
Ireland	2	2	1	13	4
Portugal	1	3	4	4	4
Norway	2	7	2	3	3
Belgium	4	2	2	3	2

Note: na = not available.

Sources: Calculated from National Bureau of Statistics of China (various issues), *China Statistical Yearbook*, Beijing: China Statistics Press; United Nations Conference on Trade and Development (various issues), *World Investment Report*, New York and Geneva: United Nations Publication.

Table 6.2 reports the investment intensity indexes between China and its major investors. The table reveals two interesting findings. First, the investment intensity indexes of Hong Kong, Taiwan, Singapore, South Korea, Thailand, Malaysia, Indonesia and the Philippines are all over 100 per cent, indicating that China is more important as a host for these economies' investments as compared to the rest of the world. In contrast,

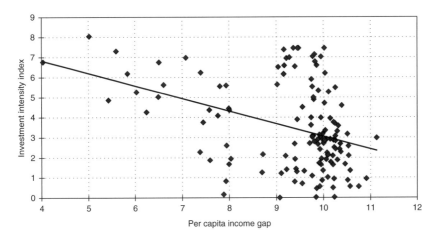

Sources: Calculated from National Bureau of Statistics of China (various issues), *China Statistical Yearbook*, Beijing: China Statistics Press; United Nations Conference on Trade and Development (various issues), *World Investment Report,* New York and Geneva: United Nations Publication; United Nations Statistical Division, National Accounts.

Figure 6.2   *The relationship between investment intensity and income gap of the major investors in China, 1992–2008 (logarithmic measure)*

with the exception of Japan, the investment intensity indexes are all below 100 per cent for the developed countries. However, among the developed countries, the investment intensity indexes of Japan, the USA, Australia and New Zealand are relatively high compared with those of the Western European countries, which may reflect the regional biases of these countries' investments in the Asia-Pacific region.

Second, the investment intensity indexes are higher for those investors in which the per capita income gaps between China and themselves are smaller. By contrast, the investment intensity indexes are lower for those investors in which the per capita income gaps between China and themselves are larger. The relationship between investment intensity and the per capita income gap is demonstrated in Figure 6.2.

THE DETERMINANTS OF INVESTMENT INTENSITY – THE HYPOTHESES

What factors explain the differences in the investment intensity indexes of source countries? We argue that the investment intensity index is affected by the economic proximity between countries. The economic proximity is a comprehensive conceptual measure of the overall similarities among countries. The factors affecting economic proximity mainly include the geographical distances and cultural differences (Braga and Bannister, 1994). Therefore, the factors affecting economic proximity also affect the investment intensity index.

There is apparent evidence that the bulk of world FDI flows is between countries with similar per capita incomes and similar relative factor endowments (Markusen, 1995), therefore, we also take the economic and technological gap among countries as one of the important factors affecting the investment intensity index.

Can these factors explain the differences of the investment intensity indexes of the source countries and economies in China? Based on the above discussion, we make the following hypotheses.

Hypothesis 1: The value of the investment intensity index of a source country in China is negatively related to the gap in economic and technological development levels between China and that source country.

Hypothesis 2: The value of the investment intensity index of a source country in China is positively related to the levels of economic proximity between China and that source country.

Based on hypothesis 1, the differences in per capita income between China and the source countries and economies are used as the proxy for the gap in economic and technological development levels. The difference in per capita income, denoted as DPGDP, is the per capita GDP difference at 1990 US dollar prices. The value of DPGDP is expected to be negatively related to the investment intensity index.

Based on hypothesis 2, the geographical distance between China andeach of the source countries and economies is used as a proxy for the transport and communication costs. The geographical distance, denoted as DIST, is expected to be negatively related to the investment intensity index. The distance between China and the source countries and economies is the physical distance between the capital cities which is obtained from the Great Circle Calculator (at http://argray. com/dist/).

The cultural difference between China and each of the source countries and economies is represented by the dummy variable *CCL*. We give a value of one for the economies in which the main culture and language are Chinese, including Hong Kong, Macao, Taiwan and Singapore, and zero

Table 6.3 *Variable list of the determinants of investment intensity index*
of source countries and economies in China

Variable name	Specification of variables	Sources and explanations
Dependent variable		
$III_{ij,t}$	Investment intensity index of source economy i in China (j) in time period t	Calculated from various issues of National Bureau of Statistics, *China Statistical Yearbook*; Ministry of Commerce of China, Invest in China, FDI Statistics; and various issues of UNCTAD, *World Investment Report*
Independent variables		
$DPGDP_{ij,t}$	Difference in per capita GDP between source economy i and China (j) in time period t. 1990 US$	Calculated from United Nations Statistical Division, National Accounts
$DIST_{ij}$	Geographic distance between the capital cities of source economy i and China (j)	Obtained from the Great Circle Calculator
CCL_i	Dummy variable for cultural difference	One for Hong Kong, Macao, Taiwan and Singapore, and zero for other source economies
$ESEA_i$	Dummy variable for East and South-East Asia region	One for Hong Kong, Macao, Taiwan, Singapore, South Korea, Malaysia, Indonesia, Philippines, Thailand and Japan, zero for other source economies
AP_i	Dummy variable for Asia-Pacific region	One for Hong Kong, Macao, Taiwan, Singapore, South Korea, Malaysia, Indonesia, Philippines, Thailand, Japan, Australia, New Zealand, Canada and the USA, zero for other source economies

for the other countries. The cultural difference is expected to be positively related to the investment intensity index.

Another two dummy variables, East and South-East Asia and the Asia-Pacific region, denoted as *ESEA* and *AP*, are used to test the regional effect on the investment intensity index. We give a value of one for the source countries and economies within these regions and zero otherwise.

The dependent and independent variables are summarized in Table 6.3.

EMPIRICAL ANALYSIS AND EXPLANATIONS

To test the above hypotheses relating to the explanatory variables for the investment intensity index of source countries in China, we use the following empirical model:

$$\ln III_{ij,t} = \beta_0 + \beta_1 \ln DPGDP_{ij,t} + \beta_2 \ln DIST_{ij} + \beta_3 CCL_i$$

$$+ \beta_4 ESEA_i + \beta_5 AP_i + v_i + \varepsilon_{i,t} \qquad (6.1)$$

The dependent variable, denoted as $III_{ij,t}$, is the investment intensity index of economy i in China (j) in time period t. The independent variables of *DPGDP, DIST, CCL, ESEA* and *AP* are hypothesized and defined in the above section.

In this empirical study, we choose 34 source countries and economies whose combined FDI accounted for 84 per cent of the total accumulated FDI inflows into China.[5] The 34 countries and economies are: Argentina, Australia, Austria, Belgium, Brazil, Canada, Denmark, Finland, France, Germany, Greece, Hong Kong (China), Indonesia, Ireland, Italy, Japan, Luxembourg, Macao (China), Malaysia, the Netherlands, New Zealand, Norway, Philippines, Portugal, Singapore, South Africa, South Korea, Spain, Sweden, Switzerland, Taiwan (China), Thailand, the UK and the USA.

In order to reduce annual fluctuations in the investment intensity index, we use the average investment intensity index of four periods, 1992 to 1995, 1996 to 2000, 2001 to 2005 and 2006 to 2008. Therefore, we have a panel dataset of 34 source countries and economies over four time periods ($t = 1, 2, 3$ and 4), containing 136 observations.

We first estimate equation (6.1) by using the pooled OLS regression. The regression results are reported in Table 6.4. The regression performed very well. All of the independent variables have the expected signs and are statistically significant.

For a robustness check, we also estimate equation (6.1) under random-effects panel regression in order that we do not preclude the use of key fixed effect indicators which we wish to identify separately. The most obvious of these are the distance variable (*DIST*) – the proxy for the transport and communication costs; and the cultural and language variable (*CCL*) – the proxy for the cultural difference between China and each of the source countries and economies; and the regional dummy variables – *ESEA* and *AP* – which may have an important bearing on the investment intensity of source countries and economies in China. The regression results of the random-effects model are reported in Table 6.5. The model performed

Table 6.4   Pooled OLS regression results of the determinants of investment intensity of source countries and economies in China, 1992–2008

Variables	Model 1	Model 2
Constant	11.36	4.58
	(15.44)***	(4.86)***
LnDPGDP	–0.61	–0.19
	(–7.89)***	(–2.03)**
LnDIST	–0.62	–0.16
	(–13.05)***	(–6.11)***
CCL		0.72
		(2.45)**
ESEA		1.42
		(4.01)***
AP		1.70
		(6.73)***
R²	0.55	0.78
Observations	136	136
F-statistics	127.21***	265.42***

Notes:
Standard errors are adjusted for White's heteroscedasticity.
t-statistics are in parentheses.
**   Statistically significant at 0.05 level (two-tail test).
***   Statistically significant at 0.01 level (two-tail test).

very well and all of the independent variables have the expected signs and are statistically significant. For our dataset, the random-effects model produces essentially the same estimates as the pooled OLS regression.

We now interpret the regression results. In general, the per capita income gap between China and the source countries and economies has a negative impact on the investment intensity index. This implies that FDI flows are negatively related to the differences in the economic and technological development levels between countries. This result is consistent with the findings obtained by Markusen (1995) and Caves (1996) that the bulk of FDI is between countries with similar per capita incomes and similar relative factor endowments. This has partially explained the low levels of investment of the developed countries in China.

The distance between China and the source countries and economies, the proxy of transport and communication costs, is an important constraining factor affecting the investment intensities of source countries and economies in China. By contrast, the common Chinese culture and language and the existence of overseas Chinese relations have a positive impact on the investment intensities of source countries and economies in

Table 6.5   Random-effects model regression results of the determinants of investment intensity of source countries and economies in China, 1992–2008

Variables	Model 1	Model 2
Constant	11.28	5.00
	(8.48)***	(3.73)***
LnDPGDP	−0.60	−0.23
	(−4.33)***	(−1.76)*
LnDIST	−0.62	−0.17
	(−10.22)***	(−4.24)***
CCL		0.79
		(1.87)*
ESEA		1.31
		(2.62)***
AP		1.71
		(4.69)***
Observations	136	136
Groups	34	34
R^2: overall	0.55	0.78
Wald Chi2	545.66***	5123.77***

Notes:
Standard errors are adjusted for White's heteroscedasticity and clustering on group.
t-statistics are in parentheses.
*   Statistically significant at 0.10 level (two-tail test).
**   Statistically significant at 0.05 level (two-tail test).
***   Statistically significant at 0.01 level (two-tail test).

China. Thus our results support for Caves (1996) view that languages and cultures shared between countries reduce MNEs' transaction costs and the bulk of foreign investments go where the transactional and information-cost disadvantages are least.

The positive East and South-East Asia and Asia-Pacific regional dummies show that the countries and economies within these regions invested more in China than the countries outside these regions. This implies that the countries tend to invest more in the region where they are situated. This result is also consistent with other studies, such as see Caves (1996). Also, Braga and Bannister (1994) found that the investment intensities among East Asian economies significantly increased during the 1980s. The result has also partially explained the relatively higher investment intensities in China for Japan, the USA, Australia and New Zealand as compared to other developed countries, especially the Western European countries.

In general, the regressions provide strong support for our hypotheses set out above. The investment intensities in China of the source countries and economies are negatively related to the gap of the economic and technological development levels and positively related to the levels of economic proximity between China and the source countries and economies.

With the regression results we can now give some explanations for the differences of investment intensities and provide some implications for future investment in China by the major investors.

Since the Asian NIEs' investments, particularly Hong Kong's investment, have been the largest part of the story of FDI in China, it is worth looking at the Asian NIEs' investments in a little more detail. The remarkable intensities of the Asian NIEs' investments in China are well explained by the factors of the gap of economic and technological development levels and the levels of economic proximity between China and the Asian NIEs.

First, it is generally agreed that the economic and technological development level of the Asian NIEs is above that of China but lower than that of the developed countries. In the last four decades the Asian NIEs have been developing their economies relatively faster than other developing countries. This has led to both a rapid accumulation of human and physical capital and a rapid rise in real wages in the Asian NIEs' economies. The changes in resource endowments of production factors have led to a rapid development in economic restructuring and technological upgrading in the Asian NIEs. Consequently, many labour-intensive industries have lost competitiveness, and investment abroad was seen as a means of utilizing accumulated managerial expertise, technical expertise and the established export markets by these industries. Coincidently, China with an abundant labour supply has a comparative advantage in labour-intensive activities. The labour-intensive production technology and the well-established international export markets of the Asian NIEs are well suited to what China needs to realize its comparative advantages and to promote its international exports. Therefore, China is a good location for the Asian NIE investors to explore overseas investment opportunities.

The second factor was the close proximity of Hong Kong, Taiwan, and to a less extent Singapore and South Korea to China. The common Chinese culture, language and close geographical distance greatly reduced the costs of doing business in China for these investors.

The rapid increase and the high investment intensities in China from ASEAN economies (Thailand, the Philippines, Malaysia and Indonesia) in the 1990s and the 2000s resembled the early pattern of the Asian NIEs' investments in most aspects. In general, the changing domestic economic structures, the extensive Chinese business networks,[6] and the close geographical location have led to and facilitated the companies of ASEAN economies to venture into China.

China – having relatively abundant labour resources and a comparative advantage in labour-intensive activities – is an attractive location for developing-country investors to explore overseas investment opportunities, particularly for export-oriented FDI. Since its accession to the WTO, China has, on the one hand, reduced trade and investment barriers and improved the investment environment, while on the other, its export markets have been greatly enlarged as WTO member countries – particularly developed countries – have opened domestic markets for China's exports. Therefore, there are great incentives for developing-country investors to increase FDI in China in general and to increase export-oriented FDI in particular. It is expected that China will remain an important host country for investments from developing countries and economies well into the future.

Investments from developed countries are somewhat different from that of the Asian NIEs and other developing countries. This is because, first, the economic and technological gap between the developed countries and China is relatively large and the transfer of technology is hampered, to a certain extent, by the appropriateness of the technology. Second, the firms of developed countries usually possess more advanced technology and production techniques. Since the legal framework for protecting intellectual property rights in China is relatively weak, the firms from the developed countries possessing advanced technology and production techniques are reluctant to invest in China. Third, the developed countries, especially the Western European countries are generally not in close proximity to China, therefore, the costs for their firms to do business in China are relatively high. Fourth, the service sector in developed countries is advanced and has recorded the highest growth rates in global FDI flows over the last three decades. However, most of China's service sectors were closed to FDI before its 2001 accession to the WTO. Fifth, the large MNEs are the main carriers of FDI from developed countries and cross-border M&As are the increasingly important means by which they carry out FDI. However, cross-border M&As transactions by foreign investors in China have only been allowed in an experimental fashion in recent years.

All of these factors have negative impacts on the investment decision of the developed-country investors. Consequently, the magnitudes and the intensities of investment from developed countries in China are very low compared with their total investments in the world. However, compared with other developed countries especially the Western European economies, the intensities of investments in China from Japan, the USA, Australia and New Zealand are relatively high. This reveals the regional investment bias of these countries towards the Asia-Pacific region.

The current composition of FDI sources in China needs to be diversified if China wants to benefit more from FDI. The diversification of FDI sources is not only necessary for China to attract more FDI, but it is also very important for it to attract high quality FDI. In general, enterprises from developed countries with high technological and innovative capabilities have advantages in high technology, product differentiation, managerial and entrepreneurial skills, and knowledge-based intangible assets. Host countries with larger market size, faster economic growth and higher income will attract more market-oriented FDI. China's huge domestic market, fast growth and rising income are very attractive to market-oriented FDI from developed countries. Therefore, China has a great potential to attract FDI from the developed countries. However, to realize its potential, China should fulfil its commitments to the WTO in trade and investment liberalization, particularly in strengthening the intellectual property rights protection, opening more service sectors to FDI, and relaxing restrictions in cross-border M&As.

CONCLUSION

In this study we analysed the difference of investment intensity and tested the determinants affecting the variations of the investment intensity indexes of the source countries and economies in China. The investment intensity index measures the investment relations between China and its source countries and economies by comparing the relative importance of China as a host for the source countries' and economies' investments as compared to the rest of the world as hosts for these countries' and economies' investments. The investment intensity index provides a very useful method in analysing the resistance factors influencing the investment flows between countries. The study reveals several main findings.

First, the investment intensity index of the source countries and economies in China varies enormously. However, comparing the two groups of the developed countries, and the developing countries and economies, the investment intensity indexes of the developing countries and economies are all above 100 per cent and are much higher than those of the developed countries. This implies that China is more important as a host for the developing countries' and economies' investments than for the developed countries' investments.

Second, what factors explain the differences of the investment intensities of the major investors in China? The regression analyses provide strong support for our hypotheses that the investment intensity is positively related to the levels of economic proximity and negatively related to the gap in economic and technological development levels between China and the source countries and economies. In general, the economic and technological development gaps and the levels of economic proximity are important factors affecting FDI flows between countries.

Third, on the one hand, since the economic proximity is positively related to the investment intensity between countries, the high economic proximity between China and the East and South-East Asian economies, particularly Hong Kong and Taiwan, implies that China will remain a very important host country for the investments from these economies. On the other hand, with the sustained and fast economic growth in China, combined with the huge inflows of FDI and technology into its domestic economy, the economic and technological development gaps between China and the developed countries will tend to be reduced. As a result, China will become a more important host country for FDI from the developed countries in the near future. However, to realize its potential, China should fulfil its commitments to the WTO in trade and investment liberalization, particularly in strengthening the intellectual property rights protection, opening more service sectors to FDI and relaxing restrictions in cross-border M&As.

This chapter has revealed the overwhelming dominance of developing countries' and economies' investment in China, analysed the differences in investment relations between China and its major investors, and explained the determinants affecting the variations of the investment intensity indexes of the source countries and economies in China. However, several questions still need to be answered; in particular: are there differences between the major investors in their investment behaviour in terms of investment pattern, mode of entry, export propensity, capital intensity and labour productivity? We analyse these issues in the next chapter.

NOTES

1. The calculation is based on 2000 US dollar prices.
2. The Asian NIEs include Hong Kong, Singapore, South Korea and Taiwan.
3. The four ASEAN economies include Indonesia, Malaysia, Philippines and Thailand.
4. In the conference entitled 'China Update 2007' held in The Australian National University in 2007, Dr Guonan Ma informed the author that he estimated in 1993 that the round-tripping FDI accounted for 25 per cent of China's total FDI inflows in 1992.
5. The tax-haven economies of the Virgin Islands, the Cayman Islands and the Samoan Islands, are excluded from the sample, because of the 'transit' investment issue discussed in the previous section.
6. For more detailed analysis on overseas Chinese business networks see EAAU (1995).

7. FDI in manufacturing and comparison of overseas Chinese affiliates and foreign country affiliates

INTRODUCTION

In Chapter 6 we identified the major investors in China. In terms of the single investors, Hong Kong is the largest investor, followed by Japan, the USA, Taiwan, South Korea and Singapore. As a group the overseas Chinese investors, namely Hong Kong, Macao and Taiwan, have been the largest group of investors, accounting for 49.29 per cent of the total FDI inflows into China during 1983 to 2008,[1] followed by the other developing country investors, accounting for 26.09 per cent, and the developed country investors, accounting for 24.62 per cent of the total.

The diversity of FDI sources in China provides a valuable case study of the differences between the major investors. To facilitate the study, we classify the major investors in China into two groups. One group is the overseas Chinese investors and the other is the foreign country investors. Do these two groups of investors differ in their investment and production behaviour? Although there is a growing body of studies on FDI in China, owing to the constraint of data availability, there has been a lack of studies on the comparison of the investment and production behaviour between the two groups of investors. This chapter intends to explore this issue by using some available data.

To compare the investment and production behaviour between the overseas Chinese investors and the foreign country investors, we confine our analysis to the manufacturing sector for two main reasons. First, the manufacturing sector is the largest FDI recipient among all the economic sectors in China. Between 1997 and 2008, the manufacturing sector attracted 62.72 per cent of the total accumulative FDI inflows into China. Second, the data required for the analysis of the two groups of investors are available in the manufacturing sector for the period from 2000 to 2003. With these data we analyse the characteristics of FDI firms in the manufacturing sector in general, and explore and compare the differences in investment and production behaviour between the overseas Chinese investors and the foreign country investors in the manufacturing sector in particular.

We argue that due to the ownership advantages resulting from the differences in economic and technological development levels, the overseas Chinese affiliates (OCAs) and the foreign country affiliates (FCAs) should exhibit differences in their investment and production behaviour. This study investigates the differences, in terms of investment pattern, mode of entry, export propensity, capital intensity and labour productivity, between the overseas Chinese affiliates and the foreign country affiliates in the manufacturing sector in China.

The chapter is structured as follows. The next section discusses the features of the sectoral distribution of FDI inflows into China. The third section analyses the structural changes of FDI in the manufacturing sector. The characteristics of the overseas Chinese affiliates and the foreign country affiliates in the manufacturing sector are compared in the fourth section. The final section concludes the chapter.

SECTORAL DISTRIBUTION OF FDI INFLOWS

At the end of 2008, the sectoral distribution of FDI in China was characterized by a high concentration in the manufacturing sector. The manufacturing sector attracted 62.72 per cent, the service sector attracted 34.74 per cent, while the primary sector attracted only 2.54 per cent of the total accumulative FDI inflows into China between 1997 and 2008.[2]

China's manufacturing sector is very competitive in attracting FDI. Studies (Chen, 2002; McKibben and Wilcoxen, 1998; UNCTAD, *World Investment Report*, 2000; Walmsley and Hertel, 2001) of the impacts of China's accession to the WTO predicted that after the accession to the WTO, China's labour-intensive manufacturing industries, especially the textiles and clothing industries, would grow rapidly, led by the large expansion of exports as a result of the reduction of import tariffs and the elimination of import quotas from the developed countries on the imports of China's labour-intensive manufactured goods. The introduction of foreign capital, technology and advanced equipment to upgrade labour-intensive industries would accelerate this process. China's labour-intensive industries are quite competitive, with abundant and well-educated human resources and low labour costs, making it one of the most attractive locations for export-oriented FDI. Therefore, FDI will continue to flow into China's labour-intensive industries, particularly for export-oriented FDI.

Over the past three decades, FDI inflows into China's manufacturing sector have gradually shifted from being heavily concentrated in labour-intensive industries, which is mainly export-oriented FDI, towards more investments in capital-intensive industries and technology-intensive industries, which are mainly domestic-market oriented FDI. The changing industrial structure of FDI from the high concentration in labour-intensive industries towards more investments in capital-intensive and technology-intensive industries is an indication that FDI inflows have been increasingly targeting China's huge domestic market. As China maintains high economic growth and increases per capita income, its domestic market demand provides good opportunities for market-oriented FDI. Therefore, market-oriented manufacturing FDI inflows into China will continue into the future.

Around 60 per cent of global FDI is in the service sector, but in China the proportion is quite different, with the Chinese service sector attracting a notably smaller share of the country's total FDI. This is largely owing to the relatively small size of the service sector in China compared to the rest of the world. China's service sector accounts for around 40 per cent of GDP, compared to around 70 per cent in developed countries and 60 per cent in mid-income countries. The relative underdevelopment of China's service sector could represent a serious bottleneck in the overall development of China's national economy.

There are many reasons for the slow development of China's service sector. The two main reasons are the closed nature of the sector and the monopolistic structure. Before China's accession to the WTO, China's service sector had been relatively closed to foreign direct participation. The closed nature of the service sector to foreign competition has effectively protected the state monopolies. At present, China's many service industries are still monopolized by SOEs, especially in the industries of telecommunications and public utilities.

Opening the service sector has been one of the most important issues in the bilateral negotiations of China's accession to the WTO. China made substantial WTO commitments to open its service sector to international trade and FDI. However, China takes a step-by-step approach to implement its commitments. In most service industries, especially in telecommunications, banking and insurance, wholesale and retail, storage and transportation, China aimed to fulfil its commitments in three to five years after its WTO accession. As a result, as Figure 7.1 shows, since China's accession to the WTO in 2001, although the manufacturing sector continued to receive large FDI inflows, the growth rate of FDI inflows into the manufacturing sector slowed down since 2004. By contrast, FDI flows into the service sector have risen rapidly since 2006. By 2008, the share of FDI in the service sector increased to 44 per cent, while the share of FDI

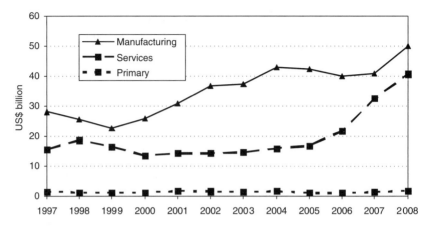

Sources: National Bureau of Statistics of China (various issues), *China Statistical Yearbook*, Beijing: China Statistics Press; Ministry of Commerce of China, Invest in China, FDI Statistics.

Figure 7.1 FDI inflows into China by sector (current US$)

in the manufacturing sector declined to 54 per cent. With further and full implementation of its WTO commitments, China will attract more FDI into its service sector.

Foreign direct investment inflows into China's primary sector have been low but relatively stable at around 2.5 per cent. This is not surprising given the declining share of the agricultural sector in China's national economy and the rapid decline of the overall comparative advantage in agricultural production in China (Chen, 2006). The low level of FDI flows into China's primary sector has been due to institutional and policy factors more than economic factors. China's agricultural land tenure system and the traditional small-scale family-based agricultural production pattern have limited the inflows of agricultural FDI which favour large-scale production and advanced technology. Therefore, China would not attract a large amount of FDI into its agricultural sector without changing its land tenure system and reforming the traditional small-scale family-based farming pattern. China's FDI policies for the mining industries are relatively restricted. According to its Catalogue for the Guidance of Foreign Investment Industries (Amended in 2007), with the exception of the coal (excluding special coal), petroleum, natural gas, iron ore and manganese mining industries, most mining industries are either restricted or prohibited from receiving FDI. Therefore, unless China liberalizes its FDI policies for the mining industries, there would not be a big rise in FDI in its mining industries.

CHANGING PATTERN OF FDI FIRMS IN THE MANUFACTURING SECTOR

As shown in the above section, FDI in China has been overwhelmingly directed to the manufacturing sector. Consequently, FDI firms have become a major part of China's manufacturing sector. In 2008, FDI firms made up 19.32 per cent of manufacturing enterprises, held 32.10 per cent of manufacturing assets, employed 32.97 per cent of the manufacturing labour force and contributed 32.86 per cent of manufacturing output value.

During the past three decades and especially after China's accession to the WTO, FDI firms in the manufacturing sector have undergone both rapid expansion and structural changes.

Rapid Expansion of FDI Firms in Manufacturing

As Table 7.1 shows, during the period from 2001 to 2008, FDI firms in manufacturing expanded dramatically. The total assets of FDI firms grew from 2513 billion yuan in 2001 to 8182 billion yuan in 2008, an increase of 226 per cent. This compares to domestic firms whose total assets increased by 131 per cent during the same period. Therefore, the growth of FDI firms was 1.7 times higher than the growth of domestic firms.

Among the three industry groups of manufacturing, from 2001 to 2008, the growth in total assets of FDI firms was the highest in the capital-intensive sector,[3] increasing by 313 per cent, which was closely followed by

Table 7.1 Total assets of FDI firms and domestic firms in manufacturing by sector (billion yuan at 2000 prices)

Sector	2001	2008	Change (%)
FDI firms			
Labour intensive	996	2546	156
Capital intensive	620	2560	313
Technology intensive	897	3077	243
Total	2513	8182	226
Domestic firms			
Labour intensive	2210	4989	126
Capital intensive	3514	8099	130
Technology intensive	1786	4223	136
Total	7510	17311	131

Sources: Calculated from National Bureau of Statistics of China (various issues), *China Statistical Yearbook*, Beijing: China Statistics Press.

*Table 7.2   Total assets of FDI firms in manufacturing by industries
             (billion yuan at 2000 prices)*

Industry	2001	2008	Change (%)
FDI firms			
Food processing	73	243	233
Food manufacturing	69	165	139
Beverage manufacturing	77	180	133
Tobacco processing	1.8	0.8	–57
Textiles	134	337	152
Clothing and other fibre products	83	207	148
Leather and fur products	53	130	146
Timber processing	27	50	84
Furniture manufacturing	19	70	271
Paper and paper products	96	269	181
Printing	39	66	70
Cultural, educational and sports goods	34	77	130
Petroleum refining and coking	41	145	256
Chemical materials and products	155	614	297
Medical and pharmaceutical products	58	166	188
Chemical fibres	33	93	181
Rubber products	44	119	171
Plastic products	104	241	131
Non-metal mineral products	129	326	153
Ferrous metal smelting	50	319	534
Non-ferrous metal smelting	31	184	498
Metal products	111	257	131
General machinery	103	436	324
Special purpose machinery	46	293	539
Transport equipment	213	936	339
Electrical machinery and equipment	175	569	225
Electronics and telecommunications equipment	478	1484	210
Instruments and meters	37	129	246
Total	2513	8182	226

Sources: Calculated from National Bureau of Statistics of China (various issues), *China
Statistical Yearbook*, Beijing: China Statistics Press.

that of FDI firms in the technology-intensive sector,[4] up by 243 per cent.
Foreign direct investment firms in the labour-intensive sector[5] also had a
large expansion and their total assets increased by 156 per cent.

Among the industries, as shown in Table 7.2, from 2001 to 2008, the
expansion of FDI firms was more significant in the following ten indus-

*Table 7.3　Employment in FDI firms and domestic firms in manufacturing
by sector (million workers)*

Sector	2001	2008	Change (%)
FDI firms			
Labour intensive	5.41	12.61	133.12
Capital intensive	0.99	3.06	209.52
Technology intensive	2.65	9.77	268.14
Total	9.05	25.45	181.06
Domestic firms			
Labour intensive	15.92	24.78	55.68
Capital intensive	11.12	13.98	25.66
Technology intensive	8.06	12.97	60.83
Total	35.11	51.73	47.35

Sources:　Calculated from National Bureau of Statistics of China (various issues), *China Statistical Yearbook*, Beijing: China Statistics Press.

tries: food processing, furniture manufacturing, petroleum refining and coking, chemical materials and products, ferrous metal smelting, non-ferrous metal smelting, general machinery, special machinery, transport equipment, and instruments and meters, which had an above average rate of increase in total assets. It is interesting to note that in these industries, only two are labour-intensive industries (food processing and furniture manufacturing) and the other eight are capital-intensive and technology-intensive industries.

In developing countries, where capital is relatively scarce but labour is abundant, foreign companies can be a major source of employment. Apart from directly creating employment, FDI also indirectly affects employment by raising the growth of the economy and demand for goods from other firms. Research conducted by the International Labour Organization (ILO) suggests that the indirect employment effects associated with FDI may be as important, if not more important, than the direct effects (Dunning, 1993).

Together with the rapid expansion in total assets, FDI firms also substantially increased employment in manufacturing. As Table 7.3 shows, the total number of workers employed by FDI firms increased from 9.05 million in 2001 to 25.45 million in 2008, or 181.06 per cent. The increase in employment by domestic firms was only 47.35 per cent during the same period. As a result, by the end of 2008, the share of the labour force employed by FDI firms in the manufacturing sector had increased from 20.49 per cent in 2001 to 32.97 per cent in 2008.

The increase in employment by FDI firms has been fastest in the technology-intensive sector, increasing 268.14 per cent during the period from 2001 to 2008. Foreign direct investment firms in the capital-intensive sector also increased employment dramatically, by 209.52 per cent during the same period. As a result, by the end of 2008, 42.97 per cent of the labour force in the technology-intensive sector and 33.72 per cent of the labour force in the labour-intensive sector were employed by FDI firms.

Foreign direct investment firms have made significant contributions to employment in the following industries. As shown in Table 7.4, by the end of 2008 the share of the labour force employed by FDI firms was as follows: 73.79 per cent in electronics equipment, 66.95 per cent in culture and sports goods, 59.02 per cent in leather, 49.93 per cent in clothing, 49.52 per cent in instruments, 45.75 per cent in furniture, 45.72 per cent in other manufacturing, 43.03 per cent in plastic and 40.22 per cent in electrical machinery.

Increasing Importance of FDI Firms in Manufacturing

Foreign direct investment firms have become increasingly important in China's manufacturing sector owing both to the large magnitude and rapid growth in investment. As shown in Table 7.5, in terms of total assets, the share of FDI firms in the manufacturing sector has increased from 18.93 per cent in 1995 to 25.07 per cent in 2001, and further to 32.10 per cent in 2008. In other words, one-third of the total assets of China's manufacturing sector were held by FDI firms in 2008.

Among the three industry groups of manufacturing, FDI firms in the technology-intensive sector gained a greater share than FDI firms in the labour-intensive and capital-intensive sectors in manufacturing. By 2008, as shown in Table 7.5 and Figure 7.2, the share of FDI firms in the technology-intensive sector reached 42.15 per cent, increasing 8.71 percentage points as compared to that in 2001. The share of FDI firms in the labour-intensive sector increased to 33.79 per cent in 2008, rising by 2.72 percentage points from 2001. The share of FDI firms in the capital-intensive sector is still relatively low compared with those in the technology-intensive and labour-intensive sectors; however, it increased to 24.01 per cent in 2008, rising by 9.01 percentage points since 2001.

Following this rapid growth, FDI firms in some industries have gained dominant or significant positions in the manufacturing sector as measured by their share of total assets in their respective industries. As shown in Table 7.6, by the end of 2008, in the industries of leather and fur products (54.52 per cent), cultural, educational and sports goods (61.36 per cent), and electronics and telecommunication equipment (69.55 per cent), FDI firms had gained the dominant position. In the industries of clothing and other fibre products

Table 7.4   Employment in FDI firms in manufacturing by industries (million workers)

Industry	2001	2008	Change (%)	Shares in that industry's total in 2008 (%)
FDI firms				
Food processing	0.30	0.66	121.19	20.94
Food manufacturing	0.22	0.47	114.40	30.64
Beverage manufacturing	0.16	0.30	81.67	26.13
Tobacco processing	0.003	0.002	−28.57	1.01
Textiles	0.69	1.61	134.09	24.71
Clothing and other fibre products	1.11	2.29	105.80	49.93
Leather and fur products	0.78	1.61	107.05	59.02
Timber processing	0.12	0.20	69.14	15.11
Furniture manufacturing	0.12	0.48	290.91	45.75
Paper and paper products	0.18	0.40	124.52	26.04
Printing	0.10	0.23	125.80	28.49
Cultural, educational and sports goods	0.41	0.89	115.13	66.95
Petroleum refining and coking	0.02	0.09	423.35	10.16
Chemical materials and products	0.26	0.64	147.11	14.82
Medical and pharmaceutical products	0.12	0.32	156.21	21.07
Chemical fibres	0.06	0.09	59.69	20.84
Rubber products	0.16	0.38	146.87	39.36
Plastic products	0.44	1.10	147.58	43.03
Non-metal mineral products	0.38	0.76	97.23	15.14
Ferrous metal smelting	0.08	0.28	236.01	8.93
Non-ferrous metal smelting	0.06	0.24	297.86	13.02
Metal products	0.41	0.98	138.37	29.83
General machinery	0.28	0.99	250.62	20.11
Special purpose machinery	0.14	0.77	446.96	24.81
Transport equipment	0.33	1.33	297.69	28.03
Electrical machinery and equipment	0.63	2.12	236.30	40.22
Electronics and telecommunications equipment	1.12	5.00	345.76	73.79
Instruments and meters	0.36	0.58	62.37	49.52
Total	9.05	25.45	181.06	32.97

Sources: Calculated from National Bureau of Statistics of China (various issues), *China Statistical Yearbook*, Beijing: China Statistics Press.

*Table 7.5   Shares of FDI firms in manufacturing by total assets by sector
             (%)*

Sector	1995	2001	2008
Labour intensive	25.19	31.07	33.79
Capital intensive	10.75	15.00	24.01
Technology intensive	22.04	33.44	42.15
Total	18.93	25.07	32.10

Sources: Calculated from National Bureau of Statistics of China (various issues), *China
Statistical Yearbook*, Beijing: China Statistics Press.

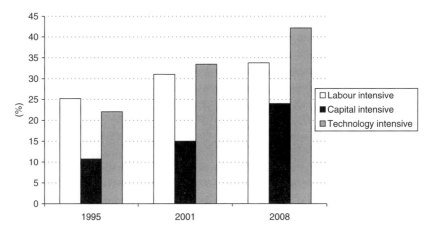

Source: Calculated from National Bureau of Statistics of China (various issues), *China
Statistical Yearbook*, Beijing: China Statistica Press.

*Figure 7.2   Share of FDI firms in the manufacturing sector (by total
              assets)*

(46.34 per cent), furniture manufacturing (46.13 per cent), paper and paper
products (45.69 per cent), rubber products (45.50 per cent), plastic products
(43.43 per cent), and instruments and meters (42.86 per cent), the shares of
FDI firms have risen to between 40 to 50 per cent of the industries' total assets.

Changes in the Structure of FDI Firms in Manufacturing

Empirical studies have revealed that MNEs, relative to indigenous firms,
are more likely to concentrate their activities in sectors in which the

Table 7.6   Shares of FDI firms in manufacturing by total assets by industries (%)

Industry	1995	2001	2008
Food processing	20.50	23.42	28.01
Food manufacturing	32.19	38.50	39.79
Beverage manufacturing	25.31	27.24	38.43
Tobacco processing	0.95	0.72	0.22
Textiles	18.81	21.68	27.80
Clothing and other fibre products	47.91	43.92	46.34
Leather and fur products	46.45	52.75	54.52
Timber processing	31.42	36.11	23.15
Furniture manufacturing	35.46	48.08	46.13
Paper and paper products	19.89	35.49	45.69
Printing	21.74	34.80	31.50
Cultural, educational and sports goods	42.93	61.30	61.36
Petroleum refining and coking	1.64	10.35	15.66
Chemical materials and products	12.58	17.16	28.18
Medical and pharmaceutical products	19.49	17.69	26.70
Chemical fibres	15.06	21.73	35.09
Rubber products	25.08	37.84	45.50
Plastic products	37.11	46.12	43.43
Non-metal mineral products	16.40	20.52	23.03
Ferrous metal smelting	4.59	5.16	11.49
Non-ferrous metal smelting	11.30	9.72	16.45
Metal products	29.35	40.66	33.94
General machinery	13.34	20.56	28.39
Special purpose machinery	8.21	13.84	27.38
Transport equipment	20.09	24.14	38.06
Electrical machinery and equipment	22.44	30.53	34.76
Electronics and telecommunications equipment	44.49	56.68	69.55
Instruments and meters	23.87	34.76	42.86
Total	18.93	25.07	32.10

Sources: Calculated from National Bureau of Statistics of China (various issues), *China Statistical Yearbook*, Beijing: China Statistics Press.

revealed comparative advantage index is greater than 1, or is increasing over time (Dunning, 1993). In other words, FDI firms tend to invest in the industries in which the country has a comparative advantage or the country's comparative advantage is increasing.

For developing countries, because they have a comparative advantage in labour-intensive activities, FDI flows into those countries are mainly aimed to make use of the local comparative advantage of cheap labour

*Table 7.7   Industrial structure of FDI firms in manufacturing by total
assets by sector (%)*

Sector	1995	2001	2008
Labour intensive	50.91	39.63	31.11
Capital intensive	21.71	24.67	31.28
Technology intensive	27.38	35.71	37.61
Total	100.00	100.00	100.00

Sources: Calculated from National Bureau of Statistics of China (various issues), *China
Statistical Yearbook*, Beijing: China Statistics Press.

and, therefore, FDI will usually concentrate in labour-intensive sector. In
the case of China, in the early stage of FDI flows into manufacturing, FDI
firms were overwhelmingly concentrated in the labour-intensive sector. By
the end of 1995, as shown in Table 7.7, in terms of the total assets of FDI
firms in manufacturing, 50.91 per cent were in the labour-intensive sector,
while only 21.71 per cent and 27.38 per cent were in the capital-intensive
and technology-intensive sectors.

With its fast economic growth, high level of capital accumulation, large
improvement in human capital development and technology progress,
China's comparative advantage has changed rapidly. Though China
still has a strong comparative advantage in labour-intensive activities
owing to its huge population and abundant labour supply, China has
greatly improved its comparative advantage in both capital-intensive
and technology-intensive activities. As a result, FDI flows into China's
manufacturing sector have gradually shifted from a high level of concentration in labour-intensive sector towards increasing investment in capital-
intensive and technology-intensive sectors.

As Table 7.7 shows, by the end of 2001 the structure of FDI firms in
the manufacturing sector had changed. In terms of the total assets of FDI
firms, the share of the labour-intensive sector had fallen to 39.63 per cent,
while the shares of the capital-intensive and technology-intensive sectors
had risen to 24.67 per cent and 35.71 per cent, respectively.

After China's accession to the WTO, the pattern of FDI in China's
manufacturing sector has altered significantly. Although a large amount
of FDI has still flowed into the labour-intensive sector, the share of the
labour-intensive sector in the total assets of FDI firms has continued to
fall, while the shares of the capital-intensive and technology-intensive
sectors in the total assets of FDI firms have been increasing. By the end
of 2008, as shown in Table 7.7 and Figure 7.3, the investment structure of

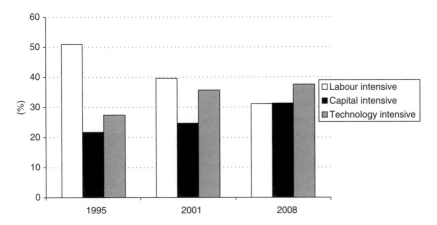

Sources: Calculated from National Bureau of Statistics of China (various issues), *China Statistical Yearbook*, Beijing: China Statistics Press.

Figure 7.3 Structural changes of FDI firms in manufacturing (by total assets)

FDI firms in China's manufacturing sector has changed fundamentally. The technology-intensive sector has become the largest recipient of FDI, and the capital-intensive sector has also surpassed the labour-intensive sector in FDI receipts. In terms of the total assets of FDI firms, the shares of the technology-intensive sector and capital-intensive sector have increased to 37.61 per cent and 31.28 per cent, respectively, while the share of the labour-intensive sector has fallen to 31.11 per cent.

As shown in Table 7.8, by 2008 the electronics and telecommunication equipment industry attracted the largest amount of FDI, accounting for 18.13 per cent of the total assets of FDI firms, followed by transport equipment (11.44 per cent), chemical materials and products (7.50 per cent), electrical machinery and equipment (6.96 per cent), general machinery (5.33 per cent), and the textile industry (4.11 per cent). Together these six industries held 53.47 per cent of the total assets of FDI firms. It is worth noting that, the top five industries are all capital-intensive and technology-intensive industries.

This analysis has revealed three important characteristics of FDI inflows into the manufacturing sector during the last three decades and particularly after China's accession to the WTO.

First, FDI inflows into the manufacturing sector increased dramatically. The growth rate of investment in total assets of FDI firms was 1.7 times higher than that of domestic firms.

*Table 7.8   Industrial structure of FDI firms in manufacturing by total
assets by industries (%)*

Industry	1995	2001	2008
Food processing	4.64	2.90	2.97
Food manufacturing	3.34	2.75	2.01
Beverage manufacturing	3.73	3.08	2.21
Tobacco processing	0.10	0.07	0.01
Textiles	8.76	5.32	4.11
Clothing and other fibre products	5.11	3.32	2.53
Leather and fur products	3.41	2.10	1.59
Timber processing	1.32	1.09	0.61
Furniture manufacturing	0.78	0.76	0.86
Paper and paper products	2.25	3.81	3.28
Printing	1.16	1.54	0.80
Cultural, educational and sports goods	1.35	1.34	0.94
Petroleum refining and coking	0.27	1.62	1.77
Chemical materials and products	5.48	6.15	7.50
Medical and pharmaceutical products	2.34	2.30	2.03
Chemical fibres	1.60	1.32	1.14
Rubber products	1.62	1.74	1.45
Plastic products	4.14	4.14	2.94
Non-metal mineral products	6.68	5.12	3.99
Ferrous metal smelting	2.58	2.00	3.90
Non-ferrous metal smelting	1.64	1.22	2.24
Metal products	4.87	4.43	3.14
General machinery	4.11	4.10	5.33
Special purpose machinery	1.81	1.82	3.58
Transport equipment	7.77	8.48	11.44
Electrical machinery and equipment	6.16	6.98	6.96
Electronics/telecommunications equipment	11.51	19.03	18.13
Instruments and meters	1.46	1.48	1.58
Total	100.00	100.00	100.00

Sources: Calculated from National Bureau of Statistics of China (various issues), *China
Statistical Yearbook*, Beijing: China Statistics Press.

Second, although FDI inflows into all three groups of manufacturing
industries increased dramatically, the growth rate of FDI inflows into the
technology-intensive sector and capital-intensive sector was much higher
than that of FDI inflows into the labour-intensive sector.

Third, FDI inflows into the manufacturing sector have gradually
changed the investment structure, shifting from a high level of concentra-

tion in the labour-intensive sector towards increasing investment in the technology-intensive and capital-intensive sectors.

COMPARISON OF THE OVERSEAS CHINESE AFFILIATES AND THE FOREIGN COUNTRY AFFILIATES

Foreign direct investment firms in China's manufacturing sector can be broadly divided into two major groups, namely, the overseas Chinese affiliates and the foreign country affiliates. The overseas Chinese affiliates are enterprises funded by investors from Hong Kong, Macao and Taiwan. Among the overseas Chinse investors, Hong Kong is the largest investor, followed by Taiwan and Macao. The foreign country affiliates are enterprises funded by investors from foreign countries. Among the foreign country investors, developed countries, such as Japan, the USA and the EU, are the most important investors, followed by other developed country investors and the developing country investors.

In this section, we analyse the differences between the overseas Chinese affiliates and the foreign country affiliates in terms of the pattern of investment, the modes of entry, the market orientation, the capital intensity and the labour productivity in manufacturing in China.

The Investment Patterns

To analyse the investment patterns of the overseas Chinese affiliates and the foreign country affiliates in manufacturing we use the data from the National Annual Enterprise Census conducted by the National Bureau of Statistics of China (NBS). The census covers the population of all SOEs and non-state-owned enterprises with individual annual sales values above 5 million yuan in the manufacturing sector across all provinces (except for Taiwan). The data available to the author cover the period from 2000 to 2003. The total number of firms covered varies from 134 130 in 2000 to 169 810 in 2003.

The dataset provides information for the overseas Chinese affiliates and the foreign country affiliates in 29 manufacturing industries. With the data we analyse and answer two main questions. First, does the investment pattern of the overseas Chinese affiliates differ as compared with that of the foreign country affiliates? Second, what are the main differences in the investment patterns in the manufacturing sector between the overseas Chinese affiliates and the foreign country affiliates?

Table 7.9 presents the total assets, the industrial structure and the

Table 7.9 Total assets, industry share and industry composition of the foreign country affiliates and the overseas Chinese affiliates in China's manufacturing sector, 2003

Industry	Total assets (billion yuan)		Industrial share (%)		Percentage composition in that industry (%)	
	FCAs	OCAs	FCAs	OCAs	FCAs	OCAs
Food and feed processing	78.4	37.0	3.71	2.56	67.94	37.06
Food manufacturing	49.9	35.0	2.36	2.42	58.76	41.24
Beverage manufacturing	54.1	40.1	2.56	2.77	57.43	42.57
Tobacco processing	0.6	1.3	0.03	0.09	29.81	70.19
Textiles	68.4	117.7	3.24	8.13	36.75	63.25
Clothing and other fibre products	42.5	61.9	2.01	4.28	40.71	59.29
Leather and fur products	28.6	43.1	1.35	2.98	39.89	60.11
Timber processing	13.6	14.9	0.65	1.03	47.76	52.24
Furniture manufacturing	13.1	17.6	0.62	1.22	42.57	57.43
Paper and paper products	72.3	42.7	3.43	2.95	62.87	37.13
Printing	12.9	32.2	0.61	2.22	28.60	71.40
Cultural, education and sports goods	13.6	31.2	0.64	2.15	30.36	69.64
Petroleum refining and coking	16.7	31.6	0.79	2.18	34.60	65.40
Chemical materials and products	139.2	69.0	6.59	4.77	66.86	33.14
Medical and pharmaceutical products	46.5	28.2	2.20	1.95	62.24	37.76
Chemical fibres	13.0	21.7	0.62	1.50	37.52	62.48
Rubber products	39.6	20.0	1.88	1.38	66.49	33.51
Plastic products	55.4	82.1	2.62	5.67	40.29	59.71
Non-metal mineral products	75.0	71.5	3.55	4.94	51.19	48.81
Ferrous metal smelting and pressing	37.1	52.2	1.76	3.61	41.57	58.43
Non-ferrous metal smelting and pressing	20.8	24.5	0.99	1.69	46.01	53.99
Metal products	57.2	61.7	2.71	4.26	48.11	51.89
General machinery	108.2	42.5	5.13	2.94	71.80	28.20
Special purpose machinery	46.3	29.9	2.19	2.07	60.76	39.24
Transport equipment	299.4	53.2	14.18	3.67	84.91	15.09
Electrical machinery and equipment	135.0	99.1	6.40	6.84	57.67	42.33
Electronics and telecom-munications equipment	513.0	238.2	24.30	16.45	68.29	31.71

Table 7.9 (continued)

Industry	Total assets (billion yuan)		Industrial share (%)		Percentage composition in that industry (%)	
	FCAs	OCAs	FCAs	OCAs	FCAs	OCAs
Instruments and meters	46.7	23.6	2.21	1.63	66.42	33.58
Others	13.7	24.1	0.65	1.67	36.22	63.78
By sector						
Labour intensive	616.0	690.2	29.18	47.67	47.16	52.84
Capital intensive	599.2	296.1	28.38	20.45	66.92	33.08
Technology intensive	895.7	461.5	42.43	31.88	66.00	34.00
Total	2110.9	1447.8	100.00	100.00	59.32	40.68

Sources: Author's calculation based on the National Bureau of Statistics of China, National Annual Enterprise Census.

industrial composition of the overseas Chinese affiliates and the foreign country affiliates by manufacturing industries at the end of 2003.

How does the investment pattern of the overseas Chinese affiliates compare with that of the foreign country affiliates? From Table 7.9 we can see that there are clear differences in the industrial structure between the overseas Chinese affiliates and the foreign country affiliates.

First, in the manufacturing sector, we look at the five largest recipients of FDI from the two groups of investors. Table 7.10 shows the composition of this investment in those five recipients. The table indicates that for the overseas Chinese investors, three out of the five largest industries are labour-intensive industries, in contrast, for the foreign country investors, all of the five largest industries are capital-intensive and technology-intensive industries. This comparison reveals that the patterns of investment in China's manufacturing sector by the overseas Chinese investors are relatively more concentrated in the labour-intensive sector, while those of the foreign country investors are relatively biased to the capital-intensive and technology-intensive sectors.

Second, we examine the industrial structure of the three industry groups of manufacturing of the overseas Chinese affiliates and the foreign country affiliates. As Figure 7.4 illustrates, for the overseas Chinese affiliates, 47.67 per cent of investment was in the labour-intensive sector, 20.45 per cent in the capital-intensive sector and 31.88 per cent in the technology-intensive sector. For the foreign country affiliates, investments were 29.18 per cent in the labour-intensive sector, 28.38 per cent in the capital-intensive sector

Table 7.10   Composition of the five largest manufacturing industries by the overseas Chinese affiliates and the foreign country affiliates, 2003

	Composition of the five largest manufacturing industries (%)				
OCAs	Electronics and telecommunications equipment (16.45)	Textiles (8.13)	Electrical machinery (6.84)	Plastic products (5.67)	Non-metal mineral products (4.94)
FCAs	Electronics and telecommunications equipment (24.30)	Transport equipment (14.18)	Chemical materials and products (6.59)	Electrical machinery (6.39)	General machinery (5.13)

Sources: Author's calculation based on the National Bureau of Statistics of China, National Annual Enterprise Census.

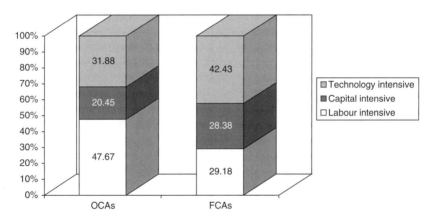

Sources: Author's calculation based on the National Bureau of Statistics of China, National Annual Enterprise Census.

Figure 7.4   Industrial structure of OCAs and FCAs in manufacturing (end 2003)

and 42.43 per cent in the technology-intensive sector. In other words, more than 70 per cent of the total investments in China's manufacturing from the foreign country affiliates were in the capital-intensive and technology-intensive sectors, and nearly half (48 per cent) of the total investments in

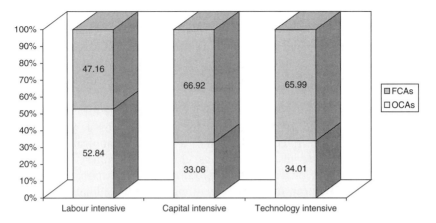

Sources: Author's calculation based on the National Bureau of Statistics of China, National Annual Enterprise Census.

Figure 7.5   Composition of OCAs and FCAs in manufacturing by sector (end 2003)

China's manufacturing from the overseas Chinese affiliates were in the labour-intensive sector.

Third, we compare the industrial composition of the two groups of investors in the three industry groups of manufacturing as shown in Figure 7.5. It is clear that the overseas Chinese investors accounted for the majority shares of investments only in the labour-intensive sector, while the foreign country investors dominated the shares of investments in both the capital-intensive and technology-intensive sectors.

As shown in Table 7.9 above, investments in China's manufacturing sector from the overseas Chinese investors were mainly concentrated in the labour-intensive sector, and had a dominant position in textiles, clothing, leather, non-metal mineral products, plastic products, cultural and sports goods, and metal products. This is not surprising. On the one hand, they have fully developed labour-intensive industries at home and well-established international export markets for the labour-intensive products. On the other hand, they are losing their comparative advantages in the labour-intensive end of the industry as they are upgrading their industrial structures at home. Consequently, many labour-intensive industries have lost competitiveness, and investment abroad is seen as a means of utilizing accumulated managerial, technical expertise and the established export markets by these industries. Coincidently, China with its abundant labour supply has a comparative advantage in labour-intensive activities. The labour-intensive production technology and the well-established international export markets of the overseas Chinese investors are well suited to what China needs to realize its comparative advantages and to promote its international exports. Therefore, China is a good location for the overseas Chinese investors to explore overseas investment opportunities.

Investments in China's manufacturing sector from the foreign country investors are biased to the capital-intensive and technology-intensive sectors, and concentrated in electronics and telecommunication equipment, chemical materials and products, electrical machinery and equipment, medical and pharmaceutical products, and transport equipment industries. The concentration of the foreign country affiliates in these capital-intensive and technology-intensive industries reflects the advanced technology and the specific ownership advantages possessed by the firms of the developed foreign country investors, since they have the most superior technology in these industries in the world. Investments from the foreign country investors are also relatively important in food processing, food manufacturing, and beverage manufacturing industries. This is mainly attributed to the large investments in these industries by Singapore, South Korea and Thailand.

Finally, let us examine the patterns of investment in China's manufacturing sector of the overseas Chinese investors and the foreign country investors by using the relative sector investment intensity indexes. The index measures the relative importance of sector j as a host for investor i's investment as compared to all manufacturing sectors. If the index is above 100 per cent, it indicates that investor i's investment in sector j is more than the amount of its share of investment in all manufacturing sectors.

The relative sector investment intensity is defined as follows:

$$SII_{ij} = \left(\frac{\left(\dfrac{I_{ij}}{I_{i*}} \right)}{\left(\dfrac{I_{*j}}{I_{**}} \right)} \right) \times 100$$

where:

SII_{ij} = relative sector investment intensity of investor i in sector j
I_{ij} = investment from investor i in sector j
I_{i*} = investment from investor i in all manufacturing sectors
I_{*j} = investment from all investors in sector j
I_{**} = investment from all investors in all manufacturing sectors.

Table 7.11   *Relative sector investment intensity of the overseas Chinese affiliates and the foreign country affiliates in manufacturing (%)*

Sector	2001		2002		2003	
	OCAs	FCAs	OCAs	FCAs	OCAs	FCAs
Labour intensive	129.84	77.56	127.51	79.34	129.87	79.51
Capital intensive	80.67	114.53	89.43	107.94	81.30	112.82
Technology intensive	79.20	115.64	77.69	116.76	83.58	111.26

Sources: Author's calculation based on the National Bureau of Statistics of China, National Annual Enterprise Census.

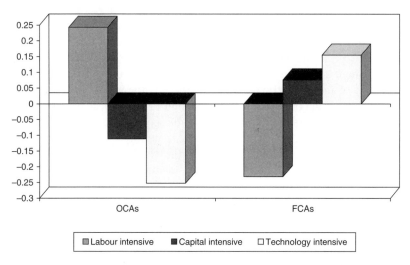

Sources: Author's calculation based on the National Bureau of Statistics of China, National Annual Enterprise Census.

Figure 7.6   *Relative sector investment intensity of OCAs and FCAs in 2002 (logarithmic measure)*

Table 7.11 presents the relative sector investment intensity of the overseas Chinese investors and the foreign country investors in the three industry groups of manufacturing for the years of 2001, 2002 and 2003.

Figure 7.6 is the logarithmic measures of the relative sector investment intensity of the overseas Chinese investors and the foreign country investors in 2002. The logarithmic transformation is defined as:

$$LSII_{ij} = \ln (SII_{ij})$$

where $LSII_{ij}$ is the logarithmic measure of the relative sector investment intensity of investor i in sector j.

The differences in investment pattern between the overseas Chinese investors and the foreign country investors is more apparent as revealed by the relative sector investment intensity indexes in the three industry groups of manufacturing. As illustrated in Table 7.11 and Figure 7.6, for the overseas Chinese affiliates the relative sector investment intensity is above 100 only for the labour-intensive sector, while for the foreign country affiliates the relative sector investment intensity is above 100 for both the capital-intensive and technology-intensive sectors.

The revealed differences in the investment patterns between the overseas Chinese investors and the foreign country investors in China's manufacturing sector imply several points. First, as a country climbs the 'ladder' of economic and technological development, the pattern of outward investment of source countries and economies changes from labour-intensive sector to capital-intensive and technology-intensive sectors, indicating the investment sequence as source countries and economies change their proportion of factor endowments and their economic and technological structures. Second, compared with the foreign country investors, the overseas Chinese investors are at a lower level of economic and technological development, therefore their investments are mainly concentrated in the labour-intensive sector. In contrast, for the foreign country investors, because they are more economically and technologically advanced and have comparative advantages in both physical capital- and human capital-intensive activities, their investment pattern is biased towards the capital-intensive and technology-intensive sectors. Third, since the investments from the overseas Chinese investors are mainly in the labour-intensive sector, in which China has comparative advantages, while the investments from the foreign country investors are mainly in the capital-intensive and technology-intensive sectors, in which China has comparative disadvantages, we would expect that the overseas Chinese investments are more export-oriented as compared with the foreign country investments.

Type of Entry

Foreign direct investment in China can take mainly three forms of entry, namely, contractual joint ventures, equity joint ventures and wholly owned enterprises.

To compare the types of entry of the two groups of investors, our concern here is to compare the investment choice between joint ventures and wholly owned enterprises of the overseas Chinese investors and the foreign country investors.

Table 7.12   Shares of wholly owned enterprises of the overseas Chinese affiliates and the foreign country affiliates in manufacturing (%)

Sector	2000		2003	
	OCAs	FCAs	OCAs	FCAs
Labour intensive	50.56	42.28	62.43	55.68
Capital intensive*	57.53	45.04	64.47	60.16
Technology intensive	61.09	51.12	69.46	67.89
All manufacturing	54.25	46.18	64.68	61.96

Note: * Excluding non-ferrous metal smelting and pressing industry and transport equipment industry, in which policy restrictions on setting up wholly owned enterprises are significant.

Sources: Author's calculation based on the National Bureau of Statistics of China, National Annual Enterprise Census.

Do the two groups of investors differ in the investment choice between joint ventures and wholly owned enterprises? Table 7.12 shows the shares of wholly owned enterprises by the two groups of investors and by the three industry groups of manufacturing in 2000 and 2003. The calculation is based on the registered capital in wholly owned enterprises as a percentage of the total registered capital of the overseas Chinese affiliates and the foreign country affiliates respectively.

First, during the period from 2000 to 2003, the shares of wholly owned enterprises increased for both the overseas Chinese affiliates and the foreign country affiliates, indicating that the two groups of investors have been increasingly choosing wholly owned enterprises as the main entry mode to invest in China. This implies both a more liberalizing FDI regime in China and an increase in technology inflows brought in by FDI firms.

Second, for both the overseas Chinese affiliates and the foreign country affiliates the shares of wholly owned enterprises are lowest for the labour-intensive sector, higher in the capital-intensive sector and highest in the technology-intensive sector. In other words, the more capital intensive and the higher the technology content an enterprise is, the more likely it is to be wholly owned.

The above finding provides strong evidence to support the theoretical prediction that the more the high-technology intensity of the intangible assets, the more important it is for the MNEs to protect such assets, and the more likely it is for the MNEs to set up wholly owned enterprises rather than to enter into joint ventures with local partners. Blomstrom and Zejan (1991) in their studies on joint ventures find that MNEs are less likely to seek a foreign partner when they value their firms' intangible assets as important. According to Morck and Yeung (1991), a firm's intangible assets are roughly equivalent to the firm's market value less the value of tangible assets such as plant and equipment. These assets can generally be characterized as 'knowledge capital' ranging from proprietary product or process know-how to reputations and trademarks (Markusen, 1995). Since these knowledge-based intangible assets involve very high transaction costs due to market failures and are most likely to produce spillover effects and externalities owing to their nature as public goods, the MNEs are most likely to set up wholly owned enterprises rather than entering into joint ventures whenever they value the costs of protecting their new and high-technology and proprietary products more highly than the benefits gained from entering into joint ventures.

We would expect that MNEs in different industries are likely to possess different specific intangible assets. It is reasonable to assume that MNEs in the capital-intensive and technology-intensive sectors possess more new and high-technological intangible assets than MNEs in the labour-intensive sector. That being the case, it is not very difficult to explain why the shares of wholly owned enterprises in China's manufacturing are higher in capital-intensive and technology-intensive sectors than those in the labour-intensive sector for both the overseas Chinese investors and the foreign country investors.

Third, comparing the two groups of investors, the shares of wholly owned enterprises of the overseas Chinese affiliates are higher in each of the three industry groups of manufacturing than those of the foreign country affiliates. On average the overseas Chinese investors have a higher propensity to set up wholly owned enterprises than the foreign country investors.

This funding is very interesting because based on the theoretical prediction we would expect that MNEs from different source countries are likely to possess different specific intangible assets. It is reasonable to assume that MNEs from developed source countries possess more new and high-technological intangible assets than MNEs from developing source countries. Therefore, it is expected that the shares of wholly owned enterprises are higher for developed countries' affiliates than for developing countries' affiliates. But how can we explain the relatively lower shares of wholly owned enterprises of the foreign country affiliates as compared to the overseas Chinese affiliates in China's manufacturing?

To answer this question, we have to understand the factors and rationale behind the investors' choice between entering into joint ventures with local partners versus setting up wholly owned enterprises. The biggest advantage of entering into joint ventures for the MNEs is to reduce the costs of doing business abroad. This is especially important for the MNEs when they enter a new and unfamiliar foreign market. However, entering into joint ventures also incurs various transaction costs, especially when the MNEs possess more advanced and high-technology intensive intangible assets. Therefore, the choice of MNEs between entering into joint ventures and setting up wholly owned enterprises depends on the valuation and judgment of each of the individual MNEs on the benefits and costs between the two modes of entry.

As discussed in Chapter 6, Hong Kong, Macao and Taiwan are, relatively, in close proximity to mainland China. The common Chinese culture and language and close geographical distance greatly reduce the costs of doing business in China for the overseas Chinese investors. In general, they would judge the costs of protecting their intangible assets to be higher than the benefits provided by the local Chinese partners when entering into joint ventures. In other words, they would value the benefits higher than the costs in setting up wholly owned enterprises. As a result, the overseas Chinese investors are most likely to choose setting up wholly owned enterprises than entering into joint ventures when they make investment decisions.

By contrast, foreign countries in general, and the developed countries in particular, especially the Western European countries, are not in close proximity to China. The differences in culture and language and the large geographical distance greatly increase the costs of doing business in China for the foreign country investors. This directly affects the success or failure of a business. Therefore, understanding how to reduce the costs of doing business in China would be one of the most important considerations for the foreign country investors when they make the investment choice between entering into joint ventures with local Chinese partners and setting up wholly owned enterprises. Given the high costs of doing business in China compared to the overseas Chinese investors, the foreign country investors would value the benefits from the local Chinese partners to be higher than the costs of protecting their intangible assets in entering into joint ventures. In other words, the foreign country investors would judge the costs of doing business are higher than the benefits in setting up wholly owned enterprises. This is a rational choice given that the foreign country investors are not in close proximity to China and face high transaction costs to operate in China. However, this may also imply that foreign country investors might not bring the most advanced technology into China in order to reduce the costs of protecting their intangible assets.

Nonetheless, the data also reveal that the difference between the overseas Chinese affiliates and the foreign country affiliates in the propensity to set up wholly owned enterprises was reduced substantially between 2000

Table 7.13   Comparison of market orientation of the overseas Chinese
             affiliates, the foreign country affiliates and Chinese domestic
             enterprises in manufacturing (exports to sales ratio, %)

Type of enterprises	1995	2000	2003
OCAs	42.80	43.14	45.36
FCAs	35.95	39.86	40.72
DOEs	9.85	10.59	10.54

Sources: Author's calculation based on the National Bureau of Statistics of China,
National Annual Enterprise Census, and the Office of the Third National Industrial Census
(1997a, 1997b).

and 2003. On average, the difference was reduced from 8.07 percentage
points in 2000 to 2.72 percentage points in 2003. This trend is especially
significant in the technology-intensive sector, in which the difference was
reduced from 9.97 percentage points in 2000 to 1.57 percentage points in
2003. This implies that China's business environment has been improving
and the transaction costs of doing business in China for foreign country
investors have been greatly reduced. The increasing propensity of foreign
country investors to set up wholly owned enterprises also implies that
foreign country investors have increasingly brought more intangible assets
and advanced technology into China.

Market Orientation

In the above analyses we have found that investments in China's manufacturing from the overseas Chinese investors are mainly concentrated in the
labour-intensive sector and investments from the foreign country investors
are biased towards the capital-intensive and technology-intensive sectors.
Consequently, we have inferred that since China has a comparative advantage in labour-intensive manufacturing industries, therefore, the investments of the overseas Chinese investors as compared to the investments of
the foreign country investors are more export oriented.

Are the overseas Chinese affiliates more export oriented than the foreign
country affiliates? Table 7.13 shows the exports to sales ratios of the overseas Chinese affiliates, the foreign country affiliates and Chinese domestic
enterprises (DOEs) in 1995, 2000 and 2003.

The information presented in Table 7.13 confirms that the overseas
Chinese affiliates do have a higher exports to sales ratio than the foreign
country affiliates. This implies that the overseas Chinese affiliates are
mainly export oriented, which is consistent with their firm-specific owner-

ship advantages and their investment patterns in China as revealed in the previous section.

The relatively low exports to sales ratio of the foreign country affiliates does confirm that the developed countries have invested in China mainly for the purpose of targeting the Chinese domestic market. This is also consistent with their firm-specific ownership advantages and their investment patterns in China. However, we have to point out that although the exports to sales ratio of the overseas Chinese affiliates is higher than that of the foreign country affiliates, it is not as high as expected. This is mainly because among the foreign country affiliates the developing country affiliates, for example, from ASEAN economies are more export oriented, which may tend to pull up the exports to sales ratio of the foreign country affiliates. Therefore, the exports to sales ratio of the developed countries affiliates would be lower if we separated the developing countries' affiliates from the foreign country affiliates. Unfortunately, data availability prevents us from doing so.

It is also interesting to note that both the overseas Chinese affiliates and the foreign country affiliates have a much higher propensity to export than Chinese domestic enterprises. During the period from 1995 to 2003, on average, the exports to sales ratio of Chinese domestic enterprises was only around 10 per cent, while the exports to sales ratios of both overseas Chinese affiliates and foreign country affiliates were above 40 per cent. This implies that using China as an export platform with low costs of production is one of the main motives for FDI in China.

Capital Intensity and Labour Productivity

According to theories about FDI, for a firm to invest overseas it must possess an ownership advantage that confers a degree of market power or cost advantage sufficient to offset the cost of producing abroad. This could be a product or production process to which other firms do not have access, or an intangible asset or capability such as technology, information, managerial, marketing and entrepreneurial skills, organizational systems or access to intermediate or final goods markets. Although the ownership advantages are firm specific, they are influenced and determined by the economic and technological development levels of source countries. In general, affiliates from developed countries possess more, and higher technology, ownership advantages than affiliates from developing countries. Therefore, we would expect that foreign country affiliates, compared with overseas Chinese affiliates, would be superior in terms of capital intensity and labour productivity.

Capital intensity refers to the degree to which capital is used as an input relative to labour in production. It is an important indicator measuring the technical level of the production process. In general, at given price levels of capital and labour, the higher the capital intensity the higher the technology content of the production. Therefore, at a given quality level (education and technical training) of labour, a high capital intensity is always associated with a high productivity of labour. The combination of the two production factors, or the capital to labour ratio, is mainly determined by the factor endowments, prices of the factors and the technical nature of the production process. Given the condition of factor endowments and the price levels of factors, the intensity of a factor used in the production process depends on the technical nature of the production process. Generally, a high-technology product would need more capital than a low technology product.

Are there differences between the overseas Chinese affiliates and the foreign country affiliates in terms of capital intensity and labour productivity? Table 7.14 presents the average size of the overseas Chinese affiliates, the foreign country affiliates and Chinese domestic enterprises in manufacturing in 2000 and 2003 both in terms of the value of total assets and the number of workers per enterprise, capital intensity and average labour productivity.

In order to further understand the difference between the two groups of investors, Table 7.15 compares their relative labour productivity. In each case a ratio equal to one implies that the labour productivity of the relevant enterprises is equal. Higher values imply a more productive enterprise and similarly lower values imply a less productive enterprise. In addition, we provide the indexes of the relative size of the enterprise in terms of both the total assets and employment levels, and the relative capital–labour ratio. The first step is to compare the foreign country affiliates with the overseas Chinese affiliates, and the second step is to compare the foreign country affiliates and the overseas Chinese affiliates with Chinese domestic enterprises.

As shown in Tables 7.14 and 7.15, there are differences between the foreign country affiliates and the overseas Chinese affiliates with respect to size, capital intensity and average labour productivity. On average, the foreign country affiliates were larger in size, had a higher capital–labour ratio and a higher average labour productivity than the overseas Chinese affiliates in China's manufacturing sector. The superiority of foreign country affiliates in each measure over the overseas Chinese affiliates presented an increasing trend in the period from 2000 to 2003.

In terms of the value of total assets, on average each foreign country affiliate had 110 million yuan in 2000 and 123 million yuan in 2003, which was 71 per cent and 78 per cent larger than the average size of the overseas

Table 7.14 *Size, capital intensity and labour productivity of the overseas Chinese affiliates, the foreign country affiliates and Chinese domestic enterprises (at 2000 prices)*

Type of enterprises and sectors	2000				2003			
	Size of enterprise (million yuan)	Scale of enterprise (workers)	Capital to labour ratio (yuan/worker)	Average labour productivity (yuan/worker)	Size of enterprise (million yuan)	Scale of enterprise (workers)	Capital to labour ratio (yuan/worker)	Average labour productivity (yuan/worker)
FCAs								
Labour intensive	62.53	276	226395	48443	62.38	297	210179	55491
Capital intensive	205.97	267	772104	118077	239.92	290	827813	222220
Technology intensive	159.85	347	460785	106907	195.24	400	462549	133043
Total	110.06	294	374391	76460	122.66	324	377538	103933
OCAs								
Labour intensive	49.17	304	161775	34668	50.92	338	150332	38611
Capital intensive	108.08	258	419223	72353	113.09	221	512331	111995
Technology intensive	85.31	325	262800	64213	96.48	392	246030	71449
Total	64.43	303	212986	45561	69.09	336	205517	53376
DOEs								
Labour intensive	34.34	260	132289	27421	35.43	226	157078	39620
Capital intensive	125.78	448	280904	43900	127.80	344	371144	78555
Technology intensive	66.82	335	199193	32201	69.19	261	265218	53931
Total	62.12	319	194829	33717	64.23	261	246352	54616

Sources: Author's calculation based on the National Bureau of Statistics of China, National Annual Enterprise Census.

Table 7.15 Comparison of size, capital intensity and labour productivity of the overseas Chinese affiliates, the foreign country affiliates and Chinese domestic enterprises

Type of enterprises and sectors	2000				2003			
	Size of enterprise (in terms of total assets)	Scale of enterprise (in terms of employment)	Capital to labour ratio	Average labour productivity	Size of enterprise (in terms of total assets)	Scale of enterprise (in terms of employment)	Capital to labour ratio	Average labour productivity
FCAs/OCAs								
Labour intensive	1.27	0.91	1.40	1.40	1.23	0.88	1.40	1.44
Capital intensive	1.91	1.03	1.84	1.63	2.12	1.31	1.62	1.98
Technology intensive	1.87	1.07	1.75	1.66	1.92	1.02	1.88	1.86
Total	1.71	0.97	1.76	1.68	1.78	0.96	1.84	1.95
FCAs/DOEs								
Labour intensive	1.82	1.06	1.71	1.77	1.76	1.31	1.34	1.40
Capital intensive	1.64	0.60	2.75	2.69	1.88	0.84	2.23	2.83
Technology intensive	2.39	1.04	2.31	3.32	2.68	1.53	1.74	2.47
Total	1.77	0.92	1.92	2.67	1.91	1.24	1.53	1.90
OCAs/DOEs								
Labour intensive	1.43	1.17	1.22	1.26	1.44	1.50	0.96	0.97
Capital intensive	0.86	0.58	1.49	1.65	0.88	0.64	1.38	1.43
Technology intensive	1.28	0.97	1.32	1.99	1.39	1.50	0.93	1.32
Total	1.04	0.95	1.09	1.35	1.08	1.29	0.83	0.98

Sources: Author's calculation based on the National Bureau of Statistics of China, National Annual Enterprise Census.

Chinese affiliates in 2000 and 2003 respectively. The difference in terms of size between the foreign country affiliates and the overseas Chinese affiliates was more significant in both the capital-intensive sector and the technology-intensive sector. This suggests that foreign country affiliates are more able than the overseas Chinese affiliates to capture economies of scale.

In terms of capital intensity, on average the capital to labour ratio in the foreign country affiliates was 76 per cent higher in 2000 and 84 per cent higher in 2003 than in the overseas Chinese affiliates. This implies that the foreign country affiliates use relatively more capital and less labour than the overseas Chinese affiliates in production. It also reveals that the foreign country affiliates adopt a more capital-intensive production method than the overseas Chinese affiliates in manufacturing. This superiority of the foreign country affiliates over the overseas Chinese affiliates is especially significant in the capital-intensive and technology-intensive sectors. The greater capital intensity in the foreign country affiliates can be accounted for primarily by a higher technology content embodied in the production process, since at a given factor price ratio, the nature of production technology is the primary determinant for the capital to labour ratio.

It is expected that, other things being equal, the larger average capital scale and a higher capital to labour ratio will lead to a higher labour productivity in the foreign country affiliates compared to the overseas Chinese affiliates. In fact, as Tables 7.14 and 7.15 show, the average labour productivity in the foreign country affiliates was 68 per cent higher in 2000 and 95 per cent higher in 2003 than in the overseas Chinese affiliates. The higher average labour productivity of foreign country affiliates over the overseas Chinese affiliates is more significant in the capital-intensive and technology-intensive sectors.

This analysis reveals that the foreign country affiliates and the overseas Chinese affiliates do have significant differences in terms of capital scale, capital intensity and average labour productivity. In general, the foreign country investors tend to adopt more capital-intensive technologies than the overseas Chinese investors. As revealed by the capital intensity and capital scale, the enterprises funded by the foreign country investors not only have higher capital to labour ratios but also are much larger than the enterprises funded by the overseas Chinese investors. As a result, the foreign country affiliates have higher average labour productivity than the overseas Chinese affiliates, especially in capital-intensive and technology-intensive sectors.

It is also interesting to compare the foreign country affiliates and the overseas Chinese affiliates with Chinese domestic enterprises. As Tables 7.14 and 7.15 show, in 2000 both the foreign country affiliates and the overseas Chinese affiliates were more capital intensive and had higher average labour productivity than Chinese domestic enterprises. For the foreign country affiliates, on average the capital to labour ratio was 92 per cent higher and the average labour productivity was 167 per cent higher than those of Chinese domestic enterprises. Although the differences between the overseas Chinese affiliates and Chinese domestic enterprises were not as dramatic as this, the overseas Chinese affiliates still had a 9 per cent higher capital to labour ratio and 35 per cent higher average labour productivity than Chinese domestic enterprises, respectively. These results are not surprising, since they confirm the generally accepted theoretical predictions that FDI firms, possessing firm-specific ownership advantages, are usually more productive than domestic enterprises.

However, analysing from a dynamic point of view, we find that the superiority of FDI firms over Chinese domestic enterprises has been declining over time. In terms of the capital intensity, during the period from 2000 to 2003, on average the capital to labour ratio of the foreign country affiliates increased only marginally by 0.84 per cent and of the overseas Chinese affiliates even declined by 3.51 per cent. By contrast, the capital to labour ratio of Chinese domestic enterprises increased dramatically by 26.45 per cent. As a result, the gap between FDI firms and Chinese domestic enterprises in terms of capital intensity has been reduced substantially. For the foreign country affiliates, although their capital to labour ratio was still higher than that of Chinese domestic enterprises, the margin has fallen from 92 per cent to 53 per cent. For the overseas Chinese affiliates, the capital to labour ratio has fallen below that of Chinese domestic enterprises in both the labour-intensive sector and technology-intensive sector. As a result, on average the capital to labour ratio of the overseas Chinese affiliates was 17 per cent lower than that of Chinese domestic enterprises in 2003.

The closing gap between FDI firms and Chinese domestic enterprises in terms of capital intensity could be attributed to a couple of factors. First, through enterprise reform and restructuring, Chinese domestic enterprises have improved their structure and production methods by increasing physical capital investment and reducing labour input. As Table 7.14 shows, the average number of workers employed by Chinese domestic enterprises decreased from 319 workers per enterprise in 2000 to 261 workers per enterprise in 2003, a fall of 18.18 per cent. Millions of workers were laid off by domestic enterprises through enterprise reform during the late 1990s and the early 2000s. Also there was a large increase in the number of domestic enterprises during the period 2000 to 2003. For example, the total number of domestic enterprises increased from 0.108 million in 2000 to 0.137 million in 2003, up 26.85 per cent, while the total employment of domestic enterprises increased only 3.33 per cent. These changes have dramatically increased the capital to labour ratio of Chinese domestic enterprises.

Second, as shown in Table 7.14, between 2000 and 2003, the average number of workers employed both by the foreign country affiliates and the overseas Chinese affiliates increased more than 10 per cent. The fast expansion in employment of FDI firms, especially in the labour-intensive sector and the technology-intensive sector, tends to slow down the growth or even reduce the capital to labour ratio of FDI firms. These changes indicate that through enterprise reform and competition, Chinese domestic enterprises have been catching up in terms of capital intensity with FDI firms, especially in the labour-intensive sector.

In terms of labour productivity, the superiority of FDI firms over Chinese domestic enterprises has been weakening. During the period from 2000 to 2003, labour productivity in the foreign country affiliates and in the overseas Chinese affiliates on average increased by 35.93 per cent and 17.15 per cent respectively, while labour productivity in Chinese domestic enterprises increased by 61.98 per cent. In other words, labour productivity in Chinese domestic enterprises increased 1.7 times and 3.6 times than in the foreign country affiliates and the overseas Chinese affiliates respectively. As a result, labour productivity in the foreign country affiliates was on average 90 per cent higher in 2003, dropping from 167 per cent higher in 2000, than that of Chinese domestic enterprises. Nonetheless, the superiority of the foreign country affiliates over Chinese domestic enterprises in terms of labour productivity was still significant. However, in 2003, labour productivity in the overseas Chinese affiliates on average had fallen 2 per cent below that in Chinese domestic enterprises. This was mainly driven by the labour-intensive sector, in which labour productivity in the overseas Chinese affiliates was 3 per cent lower than that in Chinese domestic enterprises in 2003. In the capital-intensive sector and technology-intensive sector, although labour productivity in the overseas Chinese affiliates was still 43 per cent and 32 per cent higher respectively than in Chinese domestic enterprises, the gap between the overseas Chinese affiliates and Chinese domestic enterprises had narrowed substantially.

The above analysis has revealed a couple of interesting findings. First, FDI firms on average have higher capital intensity (as measured by capital to labour ratio) than do Chinese domestic enterprises. However, the difference in capital intensity between FDI firms and Chinese domestic enterprises has been reduced particularly between the overseas Chinese affiliates and Chinese domestic enterprises and in the labour-intensive sector. Second, FDI firms on average have higher labour productivity than do Chinese domestic enterprises, especially in capital-intensive and technology-intensive sectors. However, the gap between FDI firms and

Chinese domestic enterprises in labour productivity has been closing especially in the labour-intensive sector in which the labour productivity of the overseas Chinese affiliates has fallen below that of Chinese domestic enterprises.

CONCLUSION

Foreign direct investment inflows into China have been overwhelmingly concentrated in the manufacturing sector. Between 1997 and 2008, the manufacturing sector attracted 62.72 per cent of the total accumulative FDI inflows into China. China's manufacturing sector is very competitive in attracting FDI inflows. China has been maintaining its position as the number one destination for manufacturing and assembly since the early 2000s. Therefore, China's manufacturing sector will continue to attract large FDI inflows.

With the rapid increase in FDI inflows into manufacturing, FDI firms in the manufacturing sector have also undergone some structural changes. The two most important changes are as follows.

First, the growth rate of FDI inflows into the technology-intensive sector and capital-intensive sector was much higher than for the labour-intensive sector. As a result, the relative importance of FDI firms in the technology-intensive sector has surpassed the relative importance of FDI firms in the labour-intensive sector in China's manufacturing industries. In 2008, FDI firms in the technology-intensive sector held 42.15 per cent of the sector's total assets, while FDI firms in the labour-intensive sector held 33.79 per cent of the sector's total assets.

Second, the investment pattern of FDI firms in manufacturing has been changing gradually, especially after China's entry into the WTO. Foreign direct investment inflows into manufacturing have shifted from being concentrated in the labour-intensive sector towards increasing investment in the technology-intensive sector and capital-intensive sector. As a result, the technology-intensive sector and capital-intensive sector have become more and more important to FDI, and by 2008 their combined share reached 68.89 per cent of the total assets of FDI firms in manufacturing.

The changing structure of FDI in the manufacturing sector might be influenced by the changing pattern in comparative advantage in China's economy. Through nearly 30 years of economic reform and fast economic growth, China's comparative advantage has changed gradually. Although China still has strong comparative advantage in labour-intensive activities, China has greatly increased its comparative advantages in capital-intensive and technology-intensive activities. As FDI firms tend to invest in the industries in which the host country has a comparative advantage or the host country's comparative advantage is increasing, it is expected that China's increasing comparative advantage in capital-intensive and technology-intensive activities will increasingly attract more and more FDI inflows into the technology-intensive and capital-intensive sectors.

Foreign direct investment firms in Chinese manufacturing can be divided into two groups of investors; namely, the overseas Chinese investors and the foreign country investors. In this chapter we analysed and compared the differences in investment and production behaviour between the overseas Chinese investors and the foreign country investors with respect to their investment patterns, types of entry, market orientation, capital intensity and average labour productivity. Several main findings are worth emphasizing.

First, between the two groups of investors, their investment patterns both in terms of the industrial structure and in terms of relative sector investment intensity in manufacturing are different. The overseas Chinese investors tend to invest more in the labour-intensive sector while the foreign country investors tend to invest more in the capital-intensive and technology-intensive sectors. This is clearly revealed by the relative sector investment intensity indexes. For the overseas Chinese investors, the relative sector investment intensity index is above 100 per cent only for the labour-intensive sector, indicating that this sector is more important a host for the overseas Chinese investors' investments than the capital-intensive sector and technology-intensive sector in Chinese manufacturing. By contrast, for the foreign country investors, the relative sector investment intensity indexes are above 100 per cent both for the capital-intensive and technology-intensive sectors, indicating that they are more important as host sectors for foreign country investors than the labour-intensive sector in Chinese manufacturing.

Second, in terms of the types of entry, the study finds that for both foreign country investors and the overseas Chinese investors the more technology intensive a sector is, it is more likely to be wholly owned. This is consistent with the theoretical predictions that the more the high-technology intensity of the intangible assets, the more important it is for the MNEs to protect such assets, and the more likely it is for the MNEs to set up wholly owned enterprises rather than to enter into joint ventures with local partners.

One interesting finding is that the overseas Chinese investors tend to have stronger incentives to secure control over the business than the foreign country investors. This is reflected by the higher propensity for overseas Chinese investors to set up wholly owned enterprises. It seems contradictory with the theoretical predictions that the foreign country investors possessing more intangible assets should have a higher propensity to set up wholly owned enterprises than the overseas Chinese investors. In fact, given the high transaction costs of doing business in China for the foreign country investors compared to the overseas Chinese investors, it is a rational choice for foreign country investors to enter into joint ventures with local Chinese partners in order to reduce the costs of doing business. However, this may imply that foreign country investors might not bring in the most advanced technologies in entering into joint ventures with local Chinese partners for the purpose of reducing the costs of protecting their intangible assets.

We also find that the shares of wholly owned enterprises for both the overseas Chinese affiliates and the foreign country affiliates have been increasing over time, indicating that the two groups of investors have been increasingly choosing wholly owned enterprises as the main entry mode to invest in China. As a result, the difference between these two groups in the propensity to set up wholly owned enterprises was reduced substantially between 2000 and 2003. This implies that China's business environment was improving and the transaction costs of doing business in China for FDI firms in general and for foreign country investors in particular were greatly reduced. The increasing propensity of foreign country investors to set up wholly owned enterprises also implies that foreign country investors have increasingly brought in more intangible assets and advanced technology into China.

Third, the overseas Chinese affiliates have a higher propensity to export than the foreign country affiliates. This is consistent with the revealed investment patterns of the two groups of investors. It is also interesting to note that both the overseas Chinese affiliates and the foreign country affiliates have a much higher propensity to export than Chinese domestic enterprises. This implies that using China as a low cost of production export platform is one of the main motives for FDI in China.

Fourth, the overseas Chinese investors in China tend to adopt more labour-intensive technologies than the foreign country investors. As revealed by the capital intensity and the scale of capital, the overseas Chinese affiliates not only have a lower capital to labour ratio but also are much smaller than the foreign country affiliates. As a result, the overseas Chinese affiliates have lower average labour productivity than the foreign country affiliates.

Fifth, the comparison between foreign country affiliates and the overseas Chinese affiliates with Chinese domestic enterprises also reveals some interesting findings. Foreign direct investment firms on average are more advanced and superior than Chinese domestic enterprises in terms of firm size, capital intensity and labour productivity. However, the relative superiority of FDI firms over Chinese domestic enterprises in capital intensity and labour productivity has been lessening. In the labour-intensive sector, both capital intensity and labour productivity of the overseas Chinese affiliates have fallen below those of Chinese domestic enterprises, though FDI firms still had relatively higher capital intensity and labour productivity in the capital-intensive sector and technology-intensive sector than the Chinese domestic enterprises. These changes indicate that through enterprise reform and competition, Chinese domestic enterprises have been catching up with FDI firms, especially in the labour-intensive sector.

Finally, through the analyses of Chapter 6 and this chapter, the Chinese case has offered valuable evidence on the differences among these groups of investors. The distinctive features of the overseas Chinese investments as compared to the foreign country investments are confirmed. The diversity of foreign investors suggests that there is considerable scope for China to introduce and absorb foreign capital, technology, and modern management skills in many industries from the world. The best way to encourage foreign firms to bring in advanced technologies is to maintain open and competitive markets, because competition forces firms to be more efficient. A more open investment regime, which is a crucial factor in attracting more foreign firms to invest, is also the best channel for encouraging such competition. Diversification of FDI sources is an important issue for China. Diversification will help make FDI inflows more sustainable and bring wider benefits. Therefore, it is vital for China to encourage competition from all sources and to make effective efforts to protect intellectual property rights.

In the preceding chapters, our analyses of FDI in China have focused on the location determinants, the performance of China in attracting FDI inflows, the impact of FDI inflows into China on FDI inflows into other developing countries, the provincial distribution of FDI inflows within China, the composition of FDI sources, and the differences of the major investors. However, what are the impacts of FDI on China's economy in terms of capital formation, employment creation, economic growth, productivity improvement and export promotion? We examine and answer these questions in the following chapters.

NOTES

1. The calculation is based on 2000 US dollar prices.
2. Data for actual FDI inflows by sectors are not available before 1997.

3. Capital-intensive sector includes tobacco processing, paper and paper products, petroleum refining and coking, chemical materials and products, chemical fibres, ferrous metal smelting, non-ferrous metal smelting, and transport equipment.
4. Technology-intensive sector includes medical and pharmaceutical products, general machinery, special purpose machinery, electrical machinery and equipment, electronics and telecommunications equipment, and instruments and meters.
5. Labour-intensive sector includes food processing, food manufacturing, beverage manufacturing, textiles, clothing and other fibre products, leather and fur products, timber processing, furniture manufacturing, printing, cultural, educational and sports goods, rubber products, plastic products, non-metal mineral products, metal products and others.

PART III

Economic Impacts

8. The contribution of FDI to China's economic growth

INTRODUCTION

China achieved an impressive economic growth with an annual average rate of around 10 per cent between 1978 and 2008, the highest in the world in that period. China's remarkable achievement in economic growth seems to owe much to the adoption of the overall market-oriented economic reform program launched three decades ago, in which actively encouraging inward FDI was one of the most important aspects. As we revealed in the previous chapters, the gradual liberalization of restrictions on FDI, and the government's commitment for further opening up, has greatly improved the investment environment. Foreign firms have been attracted by the huge domestic market and pool of relatively well-educated, low-cost labour, which has made China one of the most attractive destinations for FDI in the world. By the end of 2009, China had attracted a total of US$934 billion FDI inflows (at 2000 US dollar prices), making it the largest FDI recipient in the developing world.

The huge amount of FDI inflows have contributed greatly to China's economy in terms of capital formation, employment creation, expansion of exports, and economic growth. In 2008, FDI inflows accounted for 6 per cent of China's gross fixed capital formation, while FDI firms produced 33 per cent of industrial output value, employed 33 per cent of the manufacturing labour force, and created 55 per cent of China's total exports.

Considerable evidence on the positive effects of inward FDI on China's economy have been found in recent studies, including, for example, Kueh (1992), Chen et al. (1995), Lardy (1995), Wei (1996a), Pomfret (1997), Dees (1998), Henley et al. (1999), Buckley et al. (2002), Zhang (2006), Ran et al. (2007), Tang et al. (2008), Vu et al. (2008), Tuan et al. (2009) and Whalley and Xin (2010). However, systematic treatment of the role of FDI in China's economy and especially empirical analysis on the impact of FDI on China's economic growth through spillover effects have been limited and overlooked. Therefore, in this chapter we examine empirically the issues of the impact of FDI on China's economic growth, with a particular emphasis on the spillover effects. We first identify the possible channels through which FDI may affect China's economic growth. Then, using a panel dataset containing China's 30 provinces over the period from 1986 to 2005, we estimate an augmented growth model in which direct effects (for example, raising output and productivity) and spillover effects (for example diffusing technology and management skills) of FDI on China's economic growth are analysed.

This study makes two contributions to the existing literature on the impact of FDI on China's economic growth. The empirical specifications used in this study not only include direct effects of FDI as a capital input on economic growth, but also enable us to examine the spillover effects of FDI on China's economic growth.

The structure of the chapter is as follows. The next section presents an overview of the contributions of FDI to China's economy in terms of capital formation and employment creation. The third section discusses the literature on the impact of FDI on China's economic growth and raises the issues to be examined in this study. The following section sets out the framework of analysis and specifies the empirical model. The fifth section describes the variables and the data. The sixth section discusses the regression results and calculates the contribution of FDI to China's economic growth. The final section provides the conclusion.

THE CONTRIBUTIONS OF FDI TO CHINA'S ECONOMY

In the FDI literature, FDI is believed to have played some major roles in the development process of a host country's economy, via capital formation, the creation of employment opportunities, promotion of international trade, technology transfer and spillover effects to the domestic economy (Caves, 1996; Dunning, 1993; Markusen and Venables, 1999; UNCTAD, *World Investment Report*, 1999, 2004).[1] Over the past three decades, China has attracted huge amounts of FDI inflows and FDI firms have generated some important impacts on China's economy.

Capital Formation

How important FDI inflows have been in China's domestic capital formation? To answer this question we analyse the ratio of FDI inflows in China's domestic gross fixed capital formation and the share of FDI in China's total investment in fixed assets[2] for the period 1994 to 2008.[3]

Foreign direct investment has provided an important source of external finance to China's economic development. As shown in Figure 8.1, FDI

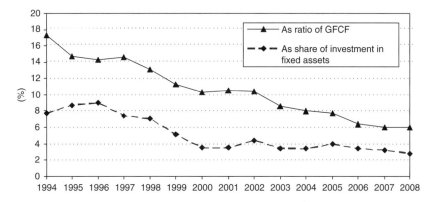

Note: GFCF = gross fixed capital formation.

Sources: Calculated from National Bureau of Statistics of China (various issues), *China Statistical Yearbook*, Beijing: China Statistics Press.

Figure 8.1 FDI inflows as ratio of GFCF and share of total investment in fixed assets in China, 1994–2008

inflows reached 17.3 per cent of China's domestic gross fixed capital formation in 1994. However, since then the ratio of FDI inflows in China's domestic gross fixed capital formation has declined, falling to 6 per cent in 2008. The main reason for this declining trend is the much higher growth rate of China's domestic gross fixed capital formation relative to that of FDI inflows into China. During the period 1994 to 2008, the annual growth rate of China's domestic gross fixed capital formation was 14.7 per cent, while that of FDI flows into China was 6.6 per cent.

The ratio of FDI inflows in China's domestic gross fixed capital formation may overestimate the real contribution of FDI to China's domestic capital formation. In fact, total FDI flows into China have not all been used in investment in fixed assets. There is evidence that investment in fixed assets made by FDI firms accounted for only a portion of the total FDI inflows into China each year. Foreign direct investment firms' investment in fixed assets accounted for around 80 per cent of the total FDI inflows into China in the late 1990s, and the figure for earlier years was much lower. The remainder (around 20 per cent) of FDI inflows may have been used by FDI firms as working capital and for inventory investment (Chen, 2002).

To evaluate the contribution of FDI to China's domestic capital formation, we use the share of FDI in China's total investment in fixed assets. As shown in Figure 8.1, the share reached a peak of 9 per cent in 1996. Since then it fell to around 3.5 per cent or less after 2000.

The above analysis suggests that FDI made an important contribution to China's domestic capital formation during the 1990s. However, since 2000, the role of FDI in China's domestic capital formation has been declining. Nevertheless, for a large and fast growing economy like China, with average annual GDP growth around 10 per cent for the past three decades, FDI has provided an important supplementary source of finance to its domestic capital formation.

Creation of Employment Opportunities

In developing countries, where capital is relatively scarce but labour is abundant, one of the most prominent contributions of FDI to the local economy is the creation of employment opportunities. In general, FDI has direct and indirect employment effects in a host country. The direct employment refers to the total number of people employed within the FDI firms. The indirect employment effects refer to the employment opportunities indirectly generated by FDI firms' activities in the host country. The indirect employment effects are difficult to measure, but country case studies conducted by the ILO show that the indirect employment effects associated with inward direct investment may be as, if not more, important than the direct effects (Dunning, 1993).

Because of the difficulties in measuring the indirect employment effects of FDI, we confine our analysis within the scope of the direct employment effect of FDI in China's manufacturing sector. Figure 8.2 shows FDI firms' employment in the manufacturing sector during 1995 to 2008 and indicates that FDI firms' manufacturing employment increased significantly after 2001. While they employed 6.05 million workers or 8.9 per cent of China's manufacturing employment in 1995, the figures had increased to 25.45 million workers or 32.97 per cent in 2008. In other words, by the end of 2008, FDI firms employed one-third of China's manufacturing labour force.

This analysis reveals that FDI has made great contributions to China's economy in terms of capital formation and employment creation. However, the impact of FDI on China's economic growth is yet to be established. Therefore, in the following sections, we investigate the impact of FDI on China's economic growth.

FDI AND ECONOMIC GROWTH

Theoretically, because FDI brings into the host country a package of capital, technology, production know-how, management skills, marketing skills and

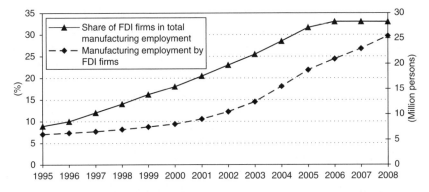

Sources: Data for 1995, 1999–2001, 2003, and 2005–2008 are calculated from National Bureau of Statistics of China (various issues), *China Statistical Yearbook*, Beijing: China Statistics Press. Data for the other years are estimated by the author.

Figure 8.2   FDI firms' manufacturing employment in China, 1995–2008

information, competition and so on (Dunning, 1977, 1993), it is expected that FDI can increase host countries' economic growth by a number of means. First, through capital accumulation in a recipient economy, FDI is expected to be growth enhancing by encouraging the incorporation of new inputs and technologies into the production function of a host economy. Second, FDI is believed to be a leading source of technology transfer and human capital augmentation in developing countries. Technological progress takes place through a process of capital deepening in the form of the introduction of new varieties of knowledge-based capital goods. It also proceeds via specific productivity-increasing labour training and skill acquisition promoted by MNEs. Third, through the knowledge spillovers such as learning by doing (demonstration effects), research and development, human resource movement, training courses, technical assistance and exposure to fierce competition, FDI improves the efficiency of local firms of host countries, thus increasing host countries' economic growth.

Development economists have long argued that countries pursuing externally oriented development strategies are more likely to achieve higher rates of economic growth than those that are internally focused. A number of studies have examined the relationship between inward FDI and economic growth in the developing host countries.[4] A generally accepted conclusion is that FDI has played a significant role in promoting economic growth in host countries because FDI represents the transmission to the host countries of a package of capital and intangible resources.

There has been an increasing body of literature on FDI in China and considerable evidence of the positive effects of inward FDI on China's economy have been found in recent years. For example, Chen et al. (1995) find that FDI has been positively associated with economic growth and the increase of total fixed investment in China. Wei (1996a) finds statistical evidence that FDI is positively associated with cross-city differences in growth rates in China. Dees (1998) finds evidence supporting the view that FDI affects China's growth through the diffusion of knowledge and ideas. Buckley et al. (2002) investigate for China the proposition that economic and technological conditions in a host country modify the relationship of inward FDI with growth. They find that FDI favours growth in the economically stronger provinces, and that the full benefits of FDI are realized when competition in local markets is at its strongest. Zhang (2006) finds that FDI seems to promote income growth and this positive growth effect seems to rise over time and to be stronger in the coastal than in the inland regions.

More recently, Vu et al. (2008), using sectoral FDI inflow data into China, evaluate the sector-specific impact of FDI on growth. The study finds that FDI has a statistically significant positive effect on economic growth, operating both directly and through its interaction with labour. The study also finds that the effects seem to be very different across economic sectors, with most of the beneficial impact concentrated in manufacturing industries. Tang et al. (2008) investigate the causal link between FDI, domestic investment and economic growth for the period 1988 to 2003. They find that rather than crowding out domestic investment, FDI is complementary with domestic investment. As a result, FDI has not only assisted in overcoming shortage of capital, it has also stimulated economic growth through complementing domestic investment in China. Tuan et al. (2009) investigate the role that inward FDI plays in the process of regional development and the channels through which economic growth would be affected by using city level (cities in the Yangzi River Delta and the Pearl River Delta) panel data estimations for the period since China's economic opening and reform. While the study finds that FDI exerted spillover effects and affected total factor productivity (TFP) growth of the recipients, major technology- and knowledge-related factors including R&D and human capital also played critical roles in TFP enhancement and regional growth. Whalley and Xin (2010) investigate the contribution of inward FDI to China's recent rapid economic growth using a two-stage growth accounting approach. After decomposing the Chinese economy into FDI and non-FDI sectors, the study results indicate that China's foreign-invested enterprises may have contributed over 40 per cent of China's economic growth in 2003 and 2004, and without this inward FDI, China's overall GDP growth rate could have been around 3.4 percentage points lower. These findings provide empirical evidence and support that FDI brings into the host countries a package of resources which promote economic growth.

In most of the previous studies on the impact of FDI on China's economic growth, FDI is treated as one of the factor inputs along with labour and domestic capital in the production function. This method captures the direct contribution of FDI as a capital input to the output growth and the increase in productivity due to the use of advanced technology by FDI firms in production. However, the indirect impact – the spillover effects – of FDI on China's economic growth is overlooked, which is expected to be one of the important contributions of FDI to host countries' economic growth.

Foreign direct investment may generate positive spillovers to host countries' economic growth through three channels. First, FDI can generate positive spillovers to domestic firms in improving productivity through the demonstration effect and competition, which may improve host countries' TFP, thus increasing host countries' economic growth. Second, FDI can generate vertical positive spillovers through strengthening domestic industrial linkages through the client and supplier networks, which will improve the productivity of domestic firms in the upstream and downstream industries, thus promoting host countries' economic growth. Third, FDI can generate positive spillovers through passing information to host countries about the international markets, the best business practice and the advance of technological innovation in the world, thus facilitating host countries to adjust to the changes in the world economy, increasing competitiveness of domestic firms in the world markets, and contributing to host countries' economic growth. Therefore, this study attempts to examine empirically the impact of the spillover effects of FDI on China's economic growth.

FRAMEWORK OF ANALYSIS AND THE EMPIRICAL MODEL

We estimate the impact of FDI on China's economic growth by specifying an aggregate production function as follows:

$$Y_{it} = A_{it}L_{it}^{\beta_1}DK_{it}^{\beta_2}FK_{it}^{\beta_3} \tag{8.1}$$

where

Y_{it} = the real gross domestic product (GDP) of province i in year t
L_{it} = total labour input of province i in year t

DK_{it} = domestic capital stock of province i in year t
FK_{it} = foreign capital stock of province i in year t
A_{it} = total factor productivity level of province i in year t.

In this specification, we divide China's economy into two sectors, the domestic sector and the FDI sector. FDI is treated as a separate factor of capital input in the aggregate production function. Therefore, equation (8.1) allows us to measure the direct contribution of FDI sector to China's economic growth both as a capital input to the output growth and the increase in TFP due to the use of advanced technology by FDI firms in production.

We are also interested in investigating whether FDI has spillover effects on economic growth through influencing the TFP A_{it}. Therefore, to investigate the spillover effects of FDI, we define the TFP A_{it} as the following:

$$A_{it} = B_{it}e^{\alpha SFK_{it}}$$

where A_{it} is the TFP level of province i in year t; B_{it} is the residual TFP level of province i in year t; and SFK_{it} is the presence of FDI in province i in year t; α is the spillover effects factor of FDI.

This specification permits the TFP A_{it} to be endogenously determined by the presence of FDI in province i in year t (SFK_{it}), and exogenously influenced by the residual TFP B_{it}, which includes the contribution of FDI sector to TFP due to the use of advanced technology by FDI firms in production. The variable of the presence of FDI in a province (SFK_{it}) represents the spillover effects of FDI on economic growth. The proposition is that the higher the presence of FDI, the higher the spillover effects of FDI on local economic growth.

Inserting the TFP A_{it} into the aggregate production function, by taking the natural logarithm of the production function and rearranging the items on the right-hand side, with the addition of a constant term (β_0) and an error term (ε_{it}), we obtain the following equation:

$$\text{Ln}\,Y_{it} = \beta_0 + \beta_1 \text{Ln}L_{it} + \beta_2 \text{Ln}DK_{it} + \beta_3 \text{Ln}FK_{it} + \beta_4 SFK_{it} + \varepsilon_{it} \quad (8.2)$$

One variable – human capital (HK) – has been suggested in recent growth models as a determinant of growth (for example, Barro and Sala-i-Martin, 1995; Levin and Raut, 1997). In particular, these models predict a positive impact of human capital on economic growth. Therefore, we incorporate the variable of human capital into the aggregate production function. Then the empirical regression model is expanded as the following:

$$\text{Ln } Y_{it} = \beta_0 + \beta_1 \text{Ln} L_{it} + \beta_2 \text{Ln} DK_{it} + \beta_3 \text{Ln} FK_{it} + \beta_4 SFK_{it} + \beta_5 HK_{it} + \varepsilon_{it}$$
$$(8.3)$$

where β_1 represents output elasticity of labour, β_2 is the marginal product of domestic capital stock and β_3 is the marginal product of foreign capital (FDI) stock. The spillover effects of FDI and the impact of human capital on economic growth are captured by the coefficients β_4 and β_5 respectively. In this specification, if β_4 is positive and statistically significant, then FDI has generated positive spillover effects to provincial economic growth.

Equation (8.3) is the form of an augmented production function model that we will use to estimate the impact of FDI on China's economic growth. This augmented production function model not only captures the direct contribution of FDI (as a factor of capital input) to economic growth, but also captures the spillover effects of FDI on economic growth. The following section will describe the variables and the data.

VARIABLE SPECIFICATION AND THE DATA

In most empirical studies, the presence of FDI is measured as the share of FDI stock in total capital stock or the ratio of FDI stock to output of an industry or region to capture the spillover effects of FDI on local economic growth. In this study, we use two measures of FDI presence to investigate the spillover effects of FDI on China's economic growth. One is the share of FDI stock in total capital stock of a province (SFK_{it}) and another is the ratio of FDI stock to provincial GDP ($RFDI_{it}$). The hypothesis is that provinces with a higher share of FDI stock in total capital stock or a higher ratio of FDI stock to GDP will have higher spillover effects from FDI to the local economy, thus promoting provincial economic growth.

In this study the human capital (HK_{it}) is measured as the ratio of the number of university students to total population of each province. We expect the human capital to be positively related to the economic growth of the host province.

The data for provincial gross domestic product (Y) and provincial total capital stock are from Wu (2009). Wu uses the conventional perpetual inventory method by employing the recently released national accounts figures to derive a capital stock series for China's 31 provinces and three economic sectors (that is, agriculture, manufacturing and services) for the period 1977 to 2006. This is one of the most comprehensive datasets of capital stock series for China's 31 provinces and three economic sectors.

The data for FDI stock (FK) is calculated in several steps. First, the US dollar value of annual FDI inflows are converted into RMB value by

Table 8.1   Variables of the impact of FDI on China's provincial economic growth

Variable Name	Specification of variables	Sources
Dependent variable		
Y_{it}	Gross domestic product of province i in year t. Billion yuan at 1978 prices	Wu (2009)
Independent variables		
L_{it}	Total number of employed persons of province i in year t. Million persons	Various issues of National Bureau of Statistics of China, *China Statistical Yearbook*
DK_{it}	Domestic capital stock of province i in year t. Billion yuan at 1978 prices	Calculated from Wu (2009) and various issues of National Bureau of Statistics of China, *China Statistical Yearbook*
FK_{it}	FDI stock of province i in year t. Billion yuan at 1978 prices	Calculated from various issues of National Bureau of Statistics of China, *China Statistical Yearbook*
SFK_{it}	Share of FDI stock in total capital stock of province i in year t. Percentage	Same as above
$RFDI_{it}$	Ratio of FDI stock to GDP of province i in year t. Percentage	Same as above
HK_{it}	Human capital of province i in year t measured as the ratio of the number of university students to total population. Percentage	Same as above

using the annual average official exchange rate. Second, the RMB value of annual FDI inflows are deflated into the real value at 1978 prices by using China's national consumer price index (CPI). Third, a 5 per cent depreciation rate is assumed for foreign capital (FDI). Finally, FDI stock is accumulated for each year-end measured as billion yuan at 1978 prices.

The domestic capital stock (DK) of each province is obtained by deducting the FDI stock (FK) from the total capital stock. Labour (L) is the total number of employed persons in each province measured as million persons.

The dependent and independent variables and the data sources are summarized in Table 8.1.

REGRESSION RESULTS AND EXPLANATIONS

We estimate equation (8.3) under fixed-effects panel regression in order to eliminate the province-specific and time-invariant factors which may affect economic growth. The data used in this study are a panel dataset at the provincial level, containing 30 China's provinces over the period 1986 to 2005.[5]

Since we have two measures for the spillover effects of FDI – the share of FDI stock in provincial total capital stock and the ratio of FDI stock to provincial GDP – we enter these two variables separately in the regression. The two models performed very well. All of the independent variables have the expected signs and are statistically significant at the 1 per cent level, and the models have high explanatory power. The fixed-effects regression results are reported in Table 8.2.

The regression results show that labour input (L) and domestic capital

Table 8.2   Regression results of production function of all provinces, 1986–2005, fixed-effects model (dependent variable LY_{it})

Variables	(1)	(2)
Constant	−0.9189	−1.0358
	(−4.31)***	(−4.20)***
LL	0.5131	0.5781
	(6.26)***	(5.91)***
LDK	0.6396	0.6290
	(25.51)***	(26.33)***
LFK	0.0542	0.0596
	(6.71)***	(7.88)***
SFK	0.0320	
	(9.57)***	
RFDI		0.0086
		(7.83)***
HK	0.2183	0.2302
	(9.53)***	(9.59)***
Observations	590	590
Groups	30	30
R² Overall	0.97	0.96
F-statistics	4248.23***	3970.95***

Notes:
Standard errors are adjusted for heteroscedasticity and clustering on group.
t-statistics are in parentheses.
*   Statistically significant at 0.10 level (two-tail test).
**   Statistically significant at 0.05 level (two-tail test).
***   Statistically significant at 0.01 level (two-tail test).

stock (*DK*) are positive and statistically significant at the 1 per cent level, indicating the significant contributions of labour and domestic capital inputs to provincial economic growth.

The variable of foreign capital stock (*FK*) is positive and statistically significant at the 1 per cent level in both models, which provides strong support that FDI as a factor of capital input directly contributes to provincial economic growth. The estimation results show that a 10 per cent increase in foreign capital stock will raise provincial GDP by about 0.55 to 0.60 per cent. This implies that provinces with higher FDI inflows, thus higher foreign capital stock, will have higher economic growth contributed directly by the increase in foreign capital input associated with high productivity of FDI firms.

For the two variables of the spillover effects of FDI – the share of FDI stock in total capital stock (*SFK*) and the ratio of FDI stock to GDP (*RFDI*) – both are positive and statistically significant at the 1 per cent level in the separate regressions. This is consistent with the hypothesis that FDI has positive spillover effects on provincial economic growth through increasing provincial TFP. Thus, the regression results have provided strong empirical evidence to support the hypotheses that FDI inflows into China together with a package of knowledge-based intangible resources and firm-specific ownership advantages have produced positive spillover effects on China's provincial economic growth. The coefficient of the share of FDI stock in total capital stock is 0.032. It means that, holding the labour and capital inputs and other variables constant, a 10 percentage point increase in the share of FDI stock in total capital stock will raise provincial GDP by 0.32 per cent. This implies that provinces with higher FDI inflows, thus higher share of FDI stock in total capital stock, will have higher spillover effects from FDI to the local economy, thus raising provincial economic growth.

The variable of human capital (*HK*) is positive and statistically significant at the 1 per cent level in both models, which provides empirical evidence that human capital contributes to economic growth. The coefficient of the human capital is 0.22, which means that a 10 percentage point increase in the ratio of university students to total population will raise provincial GDP by 2.2 per cent. This implies that provinces with better education and higher human capital will have higher economic growth.

The Impact of FDI on Economic Growth by Regions

China is a large country with enormous contrasts in geographical and economic conditions between provinces. The degree of economic development is substantially different across the provinces of China and the

Table 8.3   Economic and technological indicators by region

Economic and technological indicators	Eastern coastal region	Central and western region
Economic growth (year 1986–2005) (%)	12.80	10.48
Per capital GDP (year 2005)	5736	2273
Accumulative FDI inflows (end 2005)	530.55	83.49
Human capital (year 2005)	1.73	1.05
Level of R&D (year 2005)	7	1
Exports to GDP ratio (year 2005) (%)	41.73	6.89
Transportation intensity index (year 2005)	80	33
Level of telecommunications (year 2005)	91	47

Notes:
Per capita GDP is measured as yuan per person at 1978 constant prices.
Accumulative FDI inflows are measured as US$ billion calculated at current prices.
Human capital is measured as the ratio of university students to total population in each province.
The proxy for the level of R&D is the number of patent applications per 10 000 persons in each province.
The measure of the transportation intensity index is the ratio of the sum of the length of highways, railways and interior transport waterways divided by the land size of the corresponding province, measured as kilometres per 100 square kilometres.
The measure of the level of telecommunications is the number of telephone sets per 100 persons in each province.

Source: Calculated from National Bureau of Statistics of China (various issues), *China Statistical Yearbook*, Beijing: China Statistics Press.

geographical distribution of FDI is characterized by its concentration in the coastal areas. While an overall positive impact of FDI on economic growth is revealed in the above empirical analysis, China's large absolute size and economic diversity may mean that the impact of FDI on economic growth may be different between geographical and economic regions.

To investigate the impact of FDI on economic growth by region, we divide the full sample of 30 provinces into two sub-samples, namely the eastern coastal region provinces[6] and the central and western region provinces.[7] Between the two regions, as Table 8.3 shows, the eastern coastal region is more economically and technologically developed, more trade liberalized and open to the world economy, has better infrastructure and has attracted the overwhelming share of total accumulative FDI inflows into China.

To investigate the impact of FDI on economic growth by region, we also use equation (8.3) to conduct the empirical analysis. To eliminate the province-specific and time-invariant factors which may affect economic growth, we run the regression under fixed-effects model with panel data. The panel dataset for the eastern coastal region contains 11 provinces and

Table 8.4   Regression results of production function of the eastern coastal region provinces and the central and western region provinces, 1986–2005, fixed-effects model (dependent variable LY_{it})

Variables	Eastern coastal region	Central and western region
Constant	−0.7475	−0.6544
	(−1.93)*	(−3.03)***
LL	0.6498	0.2618
	(4.58)***	(3.22)***
LDK	0.5253	0.7312
	(11.10)***	(27.43)***
LFK	0.0765	0.0467
	(4.25)***	(5.51)***
SFK	0.0343	0.0242
	(8.93)***	(3.15)***
HK	0.2388	0.1980
	(8.02)***	(6.12)***
Observations	220	370
Groups	11	19
R² Overall	0.95	0.97
F-statistics	2546.80***	2839.76***

Notes:
Standard errors are adjusted for heteroscedasticity and clustering on group.
t-statistics are in parentheses.
*   Statistically significant at 0.10 level (two-tail test).
**   Statistically significant at 0.05 level (two-tail test).
***   Statistically significant at 0.01 level (two-tail test).

the panel dataset for the central and western region contains 19 provinces over the period 1986 to 2005. The fixed-effects regression results for the two models are reported in Table 8.4. Both models performed very well. All independent variables have the expected signs and are statistically significant at the 1 per cent level.

The regression results show that FDI has a positive and statistically significant impact on economic growth in both the eastern coastal region provinces and the central and western region provinces. This is consistent with the regression results of the full sample containing all provinces. However, the regression results do show that the coefficient of foreign capital stock (*FK*) is higher in the eastern coastal region, at 0.077, than that in the central and western region, which is 0.047. This implies that FDI has a larger direct contribution to economic growth in the eastern coastal region than in the central and western region. In particular, the coefficient of the FDI spillover effects variable – the share of foreign capital stock in total capital stock (*SFK*) – is 0.034 in the eastern coastal region while it is 0.024 in the central and western region, indicating that FDI has larger spillover effects to economic growth in the eastern coastal region than in the central and western region.

Referring to the differences in economic and technological conditions between the eastern coastal region provinces and the central and western region provinces and the regression results, we may argue that, given the level of FDI stock, provinces with higher human capital stock, higher levels of economic development (per capita GDP), higher levels of R&D activities, higher levels of infrastructure, and higher levels of economic interactions with the rest of the world, will facilitate and enhance the diffusion of spillovers of technology, production know-how and management skills from FDI to the local economy, and therefore will benefit more from FDI to promote provincial economic growth. Thus, this study provides empirical evidence to suggest that local economic and technology conditions, especially local absorptive capability, do matter in influencing the diffusion of spillovers from FDI to the local economy.

Calculating the Contribution of FDI to Economic Growth

The above sections show that FDI has a positive and statistically significant impact on China's economic growth both in terms of direct contribution as a factor of capital input and in terms of indirect contribution through spillover effects. However, how much does FDI contribute to China's economic growth? To answer this question, we use the empirically estimated coefficients of independent variables obtained from the above regressions and the growth accounting method to calculate the contribution of factors to China's economic growth. The statistical data for inputs and outputs are the provincial average for the period 1986 to 2005. The calculation is made for all provinces, the eastern coastal region provinces and the central and western region provinces. The calculation results are presented in Table 8.5.

First we examine the contribution of factors to economic growth for all provinces. During the period 1986 to 2005, the average annual GDP growth rate of all provinces was 11.77 per cent. As Table 8.5 shows, domestic capital made the largest contribution, at 7.41 percentage points; foreign capital was the second largest contributor, at 1.46 percentage points; labour contributed 1.09 percentage points; human capital contributed 0.012 percentage points; while foreign capital share – the spillover effects of FDI – contributed 0.007 percentage points to the economic growth rate. The calculations reveal that although the empirical regression results show a positive and statistically significant impact of the spillover effects of FDI on economic growth, the magnitude of the contribution

Table 8.5 Growth accounting: factor contribution to economic growth, 1986–2005

	GDP	L	DK	FK	SFK	HK	Residual TFP
All provinces							
Coefficient		0.5153	0.6369	0.0542	0.0320	0.2183	
Average annual growth (%)	11.7708	2.1270	11.5821	26.8537	0.2108	0.0537	
Contribution to growth rate (percentage points)		1.0914	7.4079	1.4555	0.0067	0.0117	1.7976
Share of contribution (%)		9.27	62.93	12.37	0.06	0.10	15.27
Eastern coastal region							
Coefficient		0.6498	0.5253	0.0765	0.0343	0.2388	
Average annual growth (%)	12.7957	1.5896	12.1916	27.7348	0.3056	0.0620	
Contribution to growth rate (percentage points)		1.0330	6.4042	2.1217	0.0105	0.0148	3.2115
Share of contribution (%)		8.07	50.05	16.58	0.08	0.12	25.10
Central and west region							
Coefficient		0.2618	0.7312	0.0467	0.0242	0.1980	
Average annual growth (%)	10.4751	1.7628	10.8110	29.4585	0.0731	0.0499	
Contribution to growth rate (percentage points)		0.4615	7.9050	1.3757	0.0018	0.0099	0.7212
Share of contribution (%)		4.41	75.47	13.13	0.02	0.09	6.88

Note: The unit for average annual growth of SFK and HK is one percentage point.

Source: Author's calculation.

from the spillover effects of FDI to China's economic growth was still very small. Therefore, we could not overstate the contribution from spillover effects of FDI to China's economic growth. However, the empirical analysis and calculation does reveal that FDI has made a significant contribution to China's economic growth. During the period from 1986 to 2005, FDI directly as a factor of capital input and indirectly through the spillover effects contributed 1.462 percentage points to China's average annual GDP growth, accounting for 12.43 per cent of China's average annual economic growth rate.

Comparing the two regions, during the period from 1986 to 2005, the average annual GDP growth rate was 12.80 per cent in the eastern coastal region and 10.48 per cent in the central and western region. In terms of the contribution of FDI to economic growth, foreign capital contributed 2.12 percentage points and the share of foreign capital – the spillover effects of FDI – contributed 0.01 percentage points to the economic growth rate in the eastern coastal region while they contributed 1.38 percentage points and 0.002 percentage points to the economic growth rate in the central and western region. It is apparent that FDI made a larger contribution to economic growth in the eastern coastal region than in the central and western region both in terms of the direct contribution as a factor of capital input and in terms of the indirect contribution through spillover effects to economic growth. As Table 8.5 shows, during the period 1986 to 2005, the direct and indirect contribution of FDI to economic growth accounted for 16.66 per cent of the average annual GDP growth rate in the eastern coastal region while it accounted for 13.15 per cent of the average annual GDP growth rate in the central and western region. This is clear evidence that the contribution of FDI to economic growth is different between China's regions. This suggests that the differences in economic and technological conditions between different regions of China might be important location factors influencing the impact of FDI on local economic growth.

Another interesting finding from Table 8.5 is that the residual TFP in the eastern coastal region is higher than that in the central and western region. During the period 1986 to 2005, the residual TFP contributed 3.21 percentage points to, and accounted for 25.10 per cent of, the average annual economic growth rate in the eastern coastal region, while in the central and western region the residual TFP only contributed 0.72 percentage points to, and accounted for, 6.88 per cent of the average annual economic growth rate. The higher residual TFP in the eastern coastal region is an indication that technology progress, human capital improvement, large amount of FDI inflows embodying a package of intangible knowledge-based resources, and spillover effects from FDI have contributed significantly to the economic growth in the eastern coastal region.

CONCLUSION

China achieved remarkable economic growth in the last three decades with an average annual growth rate around 10 per cent. At the same time, China has also attracted a huge amount of FDI inflows, totalling US$934 billion (at 2000 US dollar prices) at the end of 2009, making it the largest FDI recipient in the developing world. The huge amount of FDI inflows has made great contributions to China's economy in terms of capital formation, employment creation, export promotion, increasing competition, technology transfer and economic growth.

The main purpose of this study is to investigate empirically the contribution of FDI, with a special emphasis on whether FDI has generated the spillover effects on China's economic growth. Based on theoretical foundations, an augmented empirical growth model is specified and a panel dataset containing 30 China's provinces over the period from 1986 to 2005 is used under the fixed effects model. The study has provided the following main findings.

First, the regression results provide strong evidence that FDI contributes to China's economic growth both directly through increasing capital input and indirectly through positive spillover effects. This implies that provinces with higher FDI inflows, thus higher foreign capital stock and higher share of FDI stock in total capital stock, will have higher economic growth contributed directly by the increase in foreign capital input associated with high productivity of FDI firms and indirectly by the diffusion of technology spillovers from FDI to the local economy.

Second, the study finds that the impact of FDI on economic growth is different between China's regions. The regression results show that both the direct and indirect contributions of FDI to economic growth are higher in the eastern coastal region than those in the central and western region. Referring to the difference in economic and technology conditions between the regions and the regression results, the study suggests that, given the level of FDI stock, provinces with higher human capital stock, higher levels of economic development (per capita GDP), higher levels of R&D activities, higher levels of infrastructure, and higher levels of economic interactions with the rest of the world, will facilitate and enhance the diffusion of technology spillovers from FDI to the local economy, and therefore will benefit more from FDI to promote provincial economic growth. Thus, this study provides empirical evidence to suggest that local economic and technology conditions, especially local absorptive capability, do matter in influencing the diffusion of spillovers from FDI to the local economy.

Third, the study reveals that FDI has made a significant contribution to China's economic growth. During the period 1986 to 2005, of the 11.77 per cent average growth rate of China's real GDP, 1.46 percentage points came from direct and indirect contributions of FDI, which constituted 12.43 per cent of the total growth rate in that period. The study also reveals that both the direct and indirect contributions of FDI to China's economic growth have been larger in the eastern coastal region than in the central and western region. During the period 1986 to 2005, the direct and indirect contributions of FDI to economic growth were 64 per cent and 42 per cent higher in the eastern coastal region than in the central and western region, respectively.

Finally, the study finds that although the empirical regression results show a positive and statistically significant impact of the spillover effects of FDI on economic growth, the magnitude of the contribution from the spillover effects of FDI to China's economic growth was still very small. This implies that China still has a lot of benefits to gain from FDI. Therefore, apart from improving local economic and technology conditions to attract more FDI inflows, China should encourage contact, information exchange, production and technological cooperation, joint R&D activities, industrial linkages and competition between domestic firms and FDI firms, in order to enhance and accelerate the diffusion of positive spillovers from FDI to China's economy.

NOTES

1. We discuss the contribution of FDI to China's international trade expansion, the productivity spillovers and export spillovers of FDI to China's domestic firms in the following two chapters.
2. Gross fixed capital formation refers to the value of acquisitions less those disposals of fixed assets during a given period. Gross capital formation equals gross fixed capital formation plus changes in inventories. Total investment in fixed assets refers to the volume of activities in construction and purchases of fixed assets and related fees, expressed in monetary terms during the reference period of the whole country.
3. China unified its dual exchange rate system in 1994. As a result, the exchange rate of RMB to US dollar depreciated sharply from 5.76 yuan per US dollar in 1993 to 8.62 yuan per US dollar in 1994. For consistency, data before 1994 were excluded from the analysis.
4. For a literature survey, see de Mello (1997).
5. Tibet is excluded from the sample because of a lack of data.
6. The eastern coastal region provinces include Beijing, Tianjin, Hebei, Liaoning, Shanghai, Jiangsu, Zhejiang, Fujian, Shandong, Guangdong and Hainan.
7. The central and western region provinces include Shanxi, Inner Mongolia, Jilin, Heilongjiang, Anhui, Jiangxi, Henan, Hubei, Hunan, Guangxi, Chongqing, Sichuan, Guizhou, Yunnan, Shaanxi, Gansu, Qinghai, Ningxia and Xinjiang.

9. Spillover effects of FDI on China's domestic firms' productivity

INTRODUCTION

In the previous chapter, we revealed that the huge amount of FDI inflows into China has contributed positively to China's economy in terms of capital formation, employment creation and economic growth. However, we may still want to ask the question: what would be the impact of FDI on China's domestic firms' productivity through technology spillovers? The question is significant in a theoretical sense as it is hypothesized that FDI contributes positively to the host country's productivity growth through its technology spillovers to domestic firms (Dunning, 1993; Caves, 1996). The question is also significant in an empirical sense as evidence from both developed and developing countries varies in supporting the existence of positive externalities generated by FDI (Gorg and Greenaway, 2004).

The inconsistency between the theoretical prediction and what has been found and presented in many empirical studies with respect to the impact of FDI on domestic firms' productivity could be due to many factors, among which three stand out. First, it is not clear through which channels FDI exerts its spillovers. For example, it could occur through increased intra-industry competition, through sharing the common labour pool with domestic firms, or through forward and backward linkages with domestic firms. Second, there are a number of technical problems associated with specific estimation methods, such as endogeneity and selection bias, which may influence the empirical results. Third, it is generally assumed in literature that spillovers from FDI are consistent over time, across industries and regions, and furthermore independent of its industrial and regional penetration. This assumption may render some difficulties in the empirical studies as spillovers from FDI could be diverse in forms, time-variant and dependent on its industrial and regional variations.

Studies which examine the productivity spillovers of FDI in both developed and developing countries involve case studies (Javorcik, 2004; Moran, 2001), industry-level studies (Blomstrom, 1986; Caves, 1974b; Driffield, 2000) and firm-level studies (Girma and Wakelin, 2001; Haddad and Harrison, 1993; Haskel et al., 2007; Keller and Yeaple, 2003; Suyanto et al., 2009). Some of the key findings from these studies can be summarized as follows.

First, productivity spillovers of FDI in developed countries are much more significant than those in developing countries presumably due to the lack of absorptive capacity in the latter countries (Aitken and Harrison, 1999; Haddad and Harrison, 1993). Second, in the inter-industry setting, in particular in relation to backward linkage, productivity spillovers of FDI are more pronounced than those associated with the intra-industry setting (Javorcik, 2004). Third, the horizontal spillovers of FDI, namely, the intra-industry productivity spillovers of FDI, mainly resulted from local firms copying the technologies of foreign affiliates through observation or sharing the common intermediate goods and labour market (Campos and Kinoshita, 2002; Damijan et al., 2003). Fourth, the vertical spillovers of FDI are more likely to take place through backward or forward linkages, that is, through the contacts between domestic suppliers of intermediate inputs and their multinational clients (Lin and Saggi, 2005; Markusen and Venables, 1999; Rodriguez-Clare, 1996). Finally, attempts have been made to use the vertical spillovers of FDI to seek possible channels through which the horizontal spillovers of FDI may take place (Javorcik, 2004; Lipsey, 2006). They argue that if multinationals transfer technology to domestic suppliers in order to reduce input costs and increase input quality, the downstream domestic firms, even as the competitors of multinationals, can also benefit in improving their productivity. This point of view has been partly supported with Indonesian data (Blalock and Gertler, 2008).

Attempts to disentangle the different effects of FDI on domestic firms' productivity continue. There are a few areas in which further contributions could be made. First, it is useful to conduct studies of those large economies which have been the recipients of large quantities of FDI from diverse sources, such as China. Second, few studies have attempted to distinguish between the different spillovers of FDI on domestic firms' productivity resulting from simple increases in the penetration of FDI in a industry or a region. Studies in these areas will overcome the trans-temporal or trans-regional aggregation problem. Third, there are some econometric problems associated with the existing studies. They include the problem of selection bias due to firms' entry and exit and the problem of endogeneity resulting from some specific macroeconomic policies, firm-, industry- and region-specific and time-invariant factors which may affect both domestic firms' productivity and FDI inflows.

In this chapter, our study focuses on examining the horizontal technology spillovers of FDI on China's domestic firms' productivity by using the manufacturing firm-level panel data of China during the period 2000 to 2003. The study addresses two questions. First, are there horizontal productivity spillovers from FDI to China's domestic firms? Second, if so, how or through what channels are productivity spillovers of FDI transferred? Methodologically, we use the neighbourhood matching technique (Hahn et al., 2001; Imbens and Angrist, 1994) to adjust the selection bias by incorporating firm's entry and exit into the model estimation, and the first difference technique to deal with the endogeneity bias resulting from some specific macroeconomic policies, firm-, industry- and region-specific and time-invariant factors which may affect both domestic firms' productivity and FDI inflows.

This study makes three contributions to the existing literature concerning the technology spillovers of FDI. First, it is a systematic study of horizontal technology spillovers of FDI on the productivity of China's domestic firms by using the trans-temporal firm-level data. Second, this study adds value to the literature by considering the entry and exit of domestic firms due to the competition effect caused by the inflows of FDI. This consideration helps correct the underestimation of spillovers of FDI caused by domestic firms' self-selection. Third, this study attempts to use the non-linear specification to capture the changes in technology spillovers of FDI on the productivity of domestic firms taking into account changes over time in FDI penetration in manufacturing industries.

The chapter is structured as follows. The next section reviews the channels through which horizontal technology spillovers of FDI take place. The third section describes the firm-level panel data used for the estimation and defines the variables. The fourth section presents the estimation strategy and specifies the estimation equations. The penultimate section presents and discusses the estimation results. The final section concludes the chapter.

THE MECHANISM OF HORIZONTAL TECHNOLOGY SPILLOVERS OF FDI

According to the OLI framework explaining FDI (Dunning, 1993), FDI firms can compete locally with more informed domestic firms because they possess firm-specific ownership advantages, such as advanced technology and know-how, mature marketing and managerial skills, well-organized international distribution channels, coordinated relationships with suppliers and good reputation. Since both FDI firms and domestic firms can imitate each other in the same market, domestic firms are usually expected to obtain additional increases in productivity. This positive impact of foreign presence on domestic firms' productivity is called technology spillovers of FDI, and is expected to be an important channel through which developing countries can close the technology gap with developed countries.

According to previous studies, including, for example, Aitken and Harrison (1999), Lipsey (2002), Javorcik (2004), Blalock and Gertler (2008), there are three channels through which the horizontal technology spillovers of FDI firms can take place. The first channel originates from domestic firms' imitation of FDI firms, or through 'learning by doing'. This is because FDI firms' advantages in productivity have the characteristics of public goods, and therefore they are generally not tradable in the traditional goods market. As a result their value cannot be fully internalized. If domestic firms can copy production technologies of FDI firms operating in the local market through observing or learning their management skills through hiring workers trained by FDI firms and so on, they can achieve a rapid increase in their productivity (Rugman, 1986). The second channel originates from the increased competition effect caused by the presence of FDI firms in the domestic market. If FDI firms' entry leads to more competition in the host country market, domestic firms may be forced to improve their productivity by using their existing resources more efficiently or searching for new technologies (Aitken and Harrison, 1999; Blomstrom and Kokko, 1998). The third channel originates from the entry of FDI firms affecting both forward and backward industrial linkages of domestic firms' production with FDI firms. For example, FDI firms have incentives to make their local suppliers in upstream industries improve the quality of, and decrease the price of, intermediate goods by transferring technology and sharing with them technical know-how with respect to management and quality control. This will increase domestic firms' productivity in the upstream industry directly. It will also increase domestic firms' productivity in the same industry with FDI firms indirectly through benefiting from high quality and low price inputs (Blalock and Gertler, 2008).

Although the presence of FDI is expected to increase domestic firms' productivity from a theoretical perspective, most empirical studies have failed to provide sufficient evidence of the positive horizontal technology spillovers of FDI (Gorg and Greenaway, 2004). The inconsistency between FDI theory and the empirical results highlights that there may be factors that weaken the positive horizontal technology spillovers of FDI. First, since domestic firms and FDI firms are operating in the same industry, the increased competition gives FDI firms the incentive to prevent technology leakage and spillovers from taking place through resorting to formal protection of their intellectual property and trade secrecy, paying higher wages to reduce labour turnover, or locating in countries and industries where domestic firms have limited imitative capacities to begin with (Javorcik, 2004). Such an incentive would weaken the positive horizontal technology spillovers from FDI to domestic firms. Second, the presence of FDI firms can also generate some negative spillovers on domestic firms through 'market stealing' or crowding-out effect. Aitken and Harrison (1999) point out that the market-stealing effect is more likely to happen in the short run. This study argues that the market-stealing effect could be positively related to the degree of FDI penetration in a monopolistic competitive market. If so, the stealing effect could last longer. Intuitively, more FDI firms in the domestic market may draw more demand away from domestic firms competing in the same industry. If the negative competitive effect outweighs the positive 'learning by doing' effect, the aggregate spillovers of FDI could be negative.

This helps in part to explain the insignificance of the horizontal technology spillovers of FDI firms on domestic firms' productivity found in many empirical studies. However, there are further questions that remain unanswered. For example, how do the positive and negative spillovers of FDI within an industry interact with each other? Is there any way in which one could get hold of net positive horizontal technology spillovers from FDI resulting from such an interaction? The key is to find a mechanism through which one can compare the positive and negative horizontal technology spillovers of FDI. This mechanism, in our argument, is the degree of penetration or established market power of FDI in the domestic market.

To justify this argument, we assume that FDI firms enter the domestic market to maximize their profits and thus they have an incentive to establish market power through increasing their degree of penetration in the market. The assumption is reasonable because: (1) FDI firms usually have ownership advantages over domestic firms and it is relatively easy for them to establish market power; (2) it is more efficient for FDI firms to use their established market power to prevent technology leakage and other positive spillovers from taking place than resorting to formal legal protection of their interests; (3) FDI firms can exert their established market power to reduce competition by restricting free entry, thus increasing their profitability; and (4) the established market power of FDI firms can also help them to control the upstream and downstream firms so that they can extract more profits from low-cost and high-quality inputs.

Given that the degree of penetration of FDI firms (market power) in an industry of a host country is positively related with the negative spillovers of FDI, and negatively related with the positive spillovers of FDI, there would be a complex relationship between the degree of presence and the spillovers of FDI. More specifically, when the share of FDI firms in an industry is relatively low and they are yet to establish significant market power, it is more possible for the positive spillovers of FDI (including the 'learning by doing' effect and the competition effect) to dominate. However, when the share of FDI firms (the market power) in an industry increases, other things being equal, it is expected that the positive spillovers of FDI would decline along with the increase of the negative spillovers of FDI due to FDI firms' market power effects. When the negative spillovers outweigh the positive spillovers, domestic firms' productivity may be harmed by the increasing degree of presence of FDI firms in that industry.

If this postulation is correct, the standard model designs used in the literature to detect the horizontal spillovers of FDI firms could be modified. For example, most of the previously quoted studies measure horizontal spillovers by regressing, within a panel structure, some indicator of productivity of domestic firms against a linear indicator of 'presence' of FDI firms in the same industry. By looking at the average sign and statistical significance of this estimated coefficient, inferences are then made in these studies on the presence or absence of horizontal spillovers and their impact on the performance of domestic firms. However, if the real horizontal spillovers of FDI firms vary as the degree of penetration of FDI increases, the linear regression may suffer from some aggregation problems leading to a misleading conclusion.

In responding to these problems, this study uses a non-linear function to fit for the relationship between the horizontal presence of FDI and domestic firms' productivity, aiming to disentangle the interactions between the positive and negative marginal impact of FDI firms along with the variations in degree of penetration of FDI in the domestic market.

DATA AND VARIABLE DEFINITION

The data used in this study are from the National Annual Enterprise Census conducted by the National Bureau of Statistics of China (NBS). The census covers the population of all state-owned and non-state-owned enterprises with annual sales value above 5 million yuan in the manufacturing sector (China Industrial Classification Code: 13-42) across all regions (31 provinces and municipal cities excluding Taiwan) in China. These enterprises account for more than 95 per cent of total industrial output value in China. The sample is an unbalanced dataset at the firm level during the period 2000 to 2003. The number of firms covered in the sample varies from 134 130 in 2000 to 169 810 in 2003, and the change in the number of firms over time is caused by firms' natural entry and exit.

To distinguish between domestic firms and FDI firms, we use both firms' ownership type information from the China Enterprise Registration Code (CERC) and their capital composition: domestic firms are defined as the currently operating firms with the share of foreign registered capital less than 25 per cent of the total registered capital (or CERC 100-190) and FDI firms are defined as the current operating firms with the share of foreign registered capital more than or equal to 25 per cent of the total registered capital (or CERC 200-340).[1]

Based on these definitions, we choose domestic firms' output value (1990 prices) as the dependent variable. The real output value of domestic firms is defined as the total output value of firms, calculated by deflating the output value with the producer price index at the firm level with 1990 as the base year.

The independent variables include capital, labour, intermediate inputs, proxies for FDI spillovers, and some dummy variables to control for the regional-, industrial- and time-specific effects on productivity of domestic firms.

The variable of capital is defined as the value of fixed assets of a firm at the end of the year, deflated by using the price index for investment goods with 1990 as the base year.

In order to maintain time consistency in data as much as possible, the variable of labour is defined as the total labour which is carried through 2000 to 2002 and a variable of *Zai Gang* (registered or being listed) labour is used as a substitute for 2003 due to data availability. Although it is argued that there are a large amount of non-productive workers in Chinese domestic firms, the approximation by using *Zai Gang* workers to substitute for total labour is still reasonable since the correlation between the total labour and *Zai Gang* labour at the firm level in 2000 is above 95 per cent.

According to the NBS definition, the variable of intermediate goods is defined as firms' total output value minus value-added and plus net value-added tax, deflated by using the intermediate input deflator reported at the country level with 1990 as the base year.

The variable of horizontal spillovers of FDI is defined as the sum of foreign registered capital divided by total registered capital in each industry, denoted as *Horizontal$_{jt}$* which captures the degree of foreign capital participation (or foreign capital share) in the industry. *Horizontal$_{jt}$* is defined as:

$$Horizontal_{jt} = \left(\sum_{i \in j} ForeignCapital_{it} \right) \Big/ \left(\sum_{i \in j} TotalCapital_{it} \right) \quad (9.1)$$

To control the impact of FDI in downstream and upstream industries on domestic firms' productivity, following Javorcik (2004), we incorporate the proxies for backward and forward spillovers of FDI in the regressions.

The variable of backward spillovers is defined as:

$$Backward_{jt} = \sum_{k \neq j} \alpha_{jk} Horizontal_{kt} \qquad (9.2)$$

where α_{jk} is the proportion of industry j's output supplied to industry k, taken from China's 2002 input-output table at the two-digit level based on the International Standard Industrial Classification (ISIC) Code. The greater the foreign presence in industries supplied by industry j and the larger the share of intermediates supplied to industries with FDI presence, the higher the value of the variable.

The variable of forward spillovers is defined as:

$$Forward_{jt} = \sum_{m \neq j} \sigma_{jm} \left[\left[\sum_{i \in m} Horizontal_{mt} * (Y_{it} - EX_{it}) \right] \Big/ \left[\sum_{i \in m} (Y_{it} - EX_{it}) \right] \right]$$
$$(9.3)$$

where σ_{jm} is the share of inputs purchased by industry j from industry m in total inputs sourced by industry j, it is also taken from China's 2002 input-output table at the two-digit level based on the ISIC Code. Y_{it} is the total output of FDI firms at time t. As only intermediates sold in the domestic market are relevant to this study, goods produced by FDI firms for exports EX_{it} are excluded. The greater the foreign presence in industries sourced by industry j and the larger the share of intermediates sourced from industries with FDI presence, the higher the value of the variable.

We also include another variable – the ratio of the capital from Hong Kong and Taiwan to the capital from other foreign investors, denoted as $HKTWRatio_{jt}$, at the industry level to distinguish the different spillovers of Hong Kong and Taiwan investment from those of other foreign investment. The variable $HKTWRatio_{jt}$ is defined as:

$$HKTWRatio_{jt} = \left(\sum_{j \in i} CapitalShare\_HKTW_{it} \right) \Big/ \left(\sum_{j \in i} CapitalShare\_Other_{it} \right)$$
$$(9.4)$$

In addition, we control the regional-, industrial- and time-specific dummy variables which may affect domestic firms' productivity.

Table 9.1 presents some basic information of the sample for each year under study including the number, average output, average labour, capital, intermediate inputs of domestic firms, FDI firms and total firms,

Table 9.1   Summary statistics of China's domestic and FDI firms, 2000–2003

	lnY	lnL	lnK	lnM	FDI share	HKTW ratio	Number of firms
2000							
Total firms	9.516	4.950	7.629	9.226	0.290	0.827	134130
	(1.507)	(1.178)	(1.746)	(1.547)	(0.117)	(0.502)	
Domestic	9.370	4.916	7.510	9.078	–	–	108714
firms	(1.511)	(1.191)	(1.736)	(1.554)			
FDI firms	10.140	5.092	8.141	9.859	–	–	25416
	(1.320)	(1.114)	(1.692)	(1.348)			
2001							
Total firms	9.564	4.871	7.553	9.277	0.302	0.855	147690
	(1.465)	(1.154)	(1.753)	(1.493)	(0.116)	(0.503)	
Domestic	9.425	4.823	7.425	9.140	–	–	119113
firms	(1.462)	(1.160)	(1.738)	(1.489)			
FDI firms	10.144	5.073	8.085	9.849	–	–	28577
	(1.329)	(1.109)	(1.717)	(1.368)			
2002							
Total firms	9.694	4.857	7.552	9.408	0.310	0.781	154317
	(1.404)	(1.137)	(1.736)	(1.432)	(0.122)	(0.411)	
Domestic	9.569	4.797	7.423	9.283	–	–	123816
firms	(1.390)	(1.136)	(1.716)	(1.420)			
FDI firms	10.202	5.099	8.072	9.914	–	–	30501
	(1.345)	(1.108)	(1.719)	(1.372)			
2003							
Total firms	9.823	4.836	7.550	9.522	0.317	0.829	169810
	(1.380)	(1.121)	(1.715)	(1.427)	(0.127)	(0.519)	
Domestic	9.697	4.761	7.419	9.396	–	–	135355
firms	(1.357)	(1.108)	(1.689)	(1.408)			
FDI firms	10.321	5.127	8.062	10.018	–	–	34455
	(1.359)	(1.126)	(1.726)	(1.393)			

Notes: The figures reported in this table are based on the full sample. The numbers in parenthesis are standard errors.

Sources: Author's calculation based on the National Bureau of Statistics of China, National Annual Enterprise Census.

the share of foreign capital in total capital, and the ratio of the capital from Hong Kong and Taiwan to the capital from other foreign investors.

Table 9.2 presents the number of FDI firms and the shares of foreign capital in each industry. As the table shows, there are large variations in the shares of foreign capital participation across industries. In the

Table 9.2   Capital share and number of FDI firms by industries,
           2000–2003

Industry	2000	2001	2002	2003	Average
Food and feed processing	0.234	0.246	0.239	0.240	0.240
	1017	1154	1225	1377	1193
Food manufacturing	0.464	0.484	0.467	0.437	0.463
	765	823	876	951	854
Beverage manufacturing	0.360	0.374	0.375	0.387	0.374
	380	404	406	460	413
Tobacco processing	0.005	0.007	0.005	0.006	0.006
	4	4	4	6	5
Textiles	0.255	0.267	0.281	0.298	0.275
	2003	2274	2450	2812	2385
Clothing and other fibre products	0.406	0.413	0.414	0.441	0.419
	2705	2984	3203	3670	3141
Leather and fur products	0.466	0.481	0.486	0.532	0.491
	1153	1305	1423	1658	1385
Timber processing	0.295	0.315	0.318	0.299	0.307
	453	531	529	610	531
Furniture manufacturing	0.363	0.378	0.428	0.474	0.411
	399	436	479	548	466
Paper and paper products	0.373	0.361	0.362	0.360	0.364
	631	684	688	741	686
Printing	0.238	0.267	0.274	0.295	0.268
	442	488	504	556	498
Cultural, education and sports goods	0.627	0.609	0.621	0.669	0.632
	770	820	917	1131	910
Petroleum refining and coking	0.054	0.044	0.076	0.063	0.059
	112	89	121	92	104
Chemical materials and products	0.195	0.193	0.203	0.216	0.202
	1274	1502	1596	1850	1556
Medical and pharmaceutical products	0.191	0.174	0.185	0.182	0.183
	464	554	545	597	540
Chemical fibres	0.287	0.262	0.259	0.325	0.283
	164	154	162	181	165
Rubber products	0.390	0.388	0.422	0.422	0.405
	319	348	342	393	351
Plastic products	0.439	0.452	0.460	0.468	0.455
	1730	1914	2010	2194	1962
Non-metal mineral products	0.222	0.221	0.221	0.213	0.219
	1245	1402	1445	1553	1411
Ferrous metal smelting and pressing	0.052	0.044	0.053	0.063	0.053
	198	223	223	245	222

Table 9.2   (continued)

Industry	2000	2001	2002	2003	Average
Non-ferrous metal smelting	0.088	0.096	0.110	0.113	0.102
and pressing	213	188	222	309	233
Metal products	0.394	0.388	0.398	0.387	0.392
	1336	1525	1616	1756	1558
General machinery	0.228	0.243	0.248	0.260	0.245
	961	1093	1235	1592	1220
Special purpose machinery	0.128	0.175	0.150	0.166	0.155
	651	810	823	929	803
Transport equipment	0.215	0.221	0.213	0.220	0.217
	865	998	1103	1224	1048
Electrical machinery and	0.317	0.340	0.356	0.368	0.345
equipment	1578	1819	1963	2163	1881
Electronics and tele-	0.479	0.498	0.527	0.573	0.519
communication equipment	1927	2167	2352	2712	2290
Instruments and metres	0.423	0.427	0.429	0.468	0.437
	542	608	628	781	640
Others	0.458	0.468	0.524	0.463	0.478
	1115	1276	1411	1364	1292
All manufactures	0.290	0.302	0.310	0.317	0.305
	25416	28577	30501	34455	29737

Notes: The figures in first and second rows for each industry represent foreign capital share and number of observations respectively. The last column contains the averages of foreign capital share and observations over the four year period.

Sources: Author's calculation based on the National Bureau of Statistics of China, National Annual Enterprise Census.

cultural, education and sports goods, and electronics and telecommunication equipment industries, foreign capital has taken the dominant position, accounting for 63.2 per cent and 51.9 per cent of the industry's total capital respectively. In the following eight industries: food manufacturing; clothing and other fibre products; leather and fur products; furniture manufacturing; rubber products; plastic products; instruments and metres; and other manufacturing; foreign capital has accounted for over 40 per cent of each industry's total capital stock. In those industries where state-owned shares are relatively high, the share of foreign capital has been below 20 per cent, and some of them below 10 per cent, in each industry's total capital stock. They include tobacco processing; petroleum refining and coking; medical and pharmaceutical products; ferrous metal smelting and pressing; non-ferrous metal smelting and pressing; and special purpose machinery.

METHODOLOGY AND MODEL SPECIFICATION

To examine the spillovers of FDI on domestic firms' productivity, we use the following specification:[2]

$$\ln Y_{ijrt} = \beta_0 + \beta_1 \ln L_{ijrt} + \beta_2 \ln K_{ijrt} + \beta_3 \ln M_{ijrt}$$

$$+ \beta_4 Horizontal_{jt} + \beta_5 Horizontal_{jt}^2 + \beta_6 HKTWRatio_{jt}$$

$$+ \beta_7 Backward_{jt} + \beta_8 Forward_{jt}$$

$$+ \alpha_j + \alpha_r + \alpha_t + \varepsilon_{ijrt} \tag{9.5}$$

where Y_{ijrt} denotes the real output of domestic firm i operating in industry j and region r at time t, and L_{ijrt}, K_{ijrt} and M_{ijrt} denote the labour, capital and intermediate inputs in the production of domestic firms respectively. *Horizontal*$_{jt}$ measures the share of foreign presence in industry j at time t. *HKTWRatio*$_{jt}$ represents the relative share of the capital from Hong Kong and Taiwan to the capital from other foreign investors. *Backward*$_{ij}$ and *Forward*$_{ij}$ measure the backward and forward productivity spillovers generated by FDI presence in the downstream and upstream industries respectively. $\alpha_j = \Sigma_j \varpi_j d_j$ denotes the industry-specific effect, $\alpha_r = \Sigma_r \chi_r d_r$ denotes the regional-specific effect, and $\alpha_t = \Sigma_t \delta_t d_t$ denotes the time-specific effect. ε_{ijrt} captures the random errors.

The model described above can be estimated by using the pooled OLS with White's correction for heteroscedasticity (Javorcik, 2004). However, there are two econometric problems which need to be solved in estimating the model.

The first is the problem of selection bias that relates to firms' entry and exit. In previous studies, the samples used for examining the relationship between FDI presence and domestic firms' productivity are usually restricted to those firms with time-series observations (balanced panel). This is because allowing free entry and exit of firms (or using the unrestricted unbalanced panel data) may lead to disparity of the firms' productivity in distribution over time, given that the less productive domestic firms may choose to exit while more productive domestic firms may choose to enter the industry. The estimated coefficient of FDI in their regressions thus should actually be explained as the impact of FDI on surviving domestic firms' productivity from a comparative static aspect. This result is biased from the real impact of FDI on domestic firms' productivity since the exit and entry of domestic firms can also account for a large proportion of changes in domestic firms' productivity. In order

Table 9.3   Comparison among samples, 2000–2003

Sample items	Number of domestic firms			
	2000	2001	2002	2003
Domestic firms with free exit and entry	108 714	119 113	123 816	135 355
Domestic firms with matched exit and entry	80 236	76 603	78 061	89 039
Domestic firms with no exit and entry	49 658	49 658	49 658	49 658

Notes:
Domestic firms with free exit and entry are defined as the full sample. It is the same as reported in Table 9.1.
Domestic firms with matched exit and entry are defined as the firms surviving through any consecutive two years plus those matched firms between the exit and entry firms. This is the sample used in this study.
Domestic firms with no exit and entry are defined as the firms surviving through the whole four years.

Sources: Author's calculation based on the National Bureau of Statistics of China, National Annual Enterprise Census.

to deal with this problem, we extend our regressions with the balanced panel data plus the exit and entry of firms with similar productivity so as to capture the impact of FDI on domestic firms when there is no change in productivity of domestic firms over time due to their choice of exiting and entering. To do so, the neighbourhood matching technique (with the propensity score) is applied to sort out those domestic firms with same level of productivity between the exiting and entering groups at the 2-digit level for industries and in 31 regions.[3] Table 9.3 presents the comparison among the sample used in this study (domestic firms with matched exit and entry); the balanced sample (domestic firms with no exit and entry) and the unrestricted unbalanced sample (domestic firms with free exit and entry).

The second is the endogeneity problem that may exist between FDI inflows in the industry and those uncontrolled factors in the regression model as specified. There may be some firm-, industry-, region-specific and time-invariant factors, such as the macroeconomic situation, openness to trade and the level of infrastructure that may affect domestic firms' productivity and also be highly correlated to FDI inflows in each industry. These uncontrolled factors could lead to biased estimation on the impact of FDI on domestic firms' productivity when using the pooled OLS method if they are not well controlled. To deal with this problem, we use the first differential (FD) regression. Although this method suffers from losing a large number of observations and their related information, it is widely used to deal with the endogeneity problem.

The first differential regressions take the form:

$$d \ln Y_{ijrt} = \beta_0 + \beta_1 d \ln L_{ijrt} + \beta_2 d \ln K_{ijrt} + \beta_3 d \ln M_{ijrt}$$

$$+ \beta_4 dHorizontal_{jt} + \beta_5 dHorizontal_{jt}^2 + \beta_6 dHKTWRatio_{jt}$$

$$+ \beta_7 dBackward_{jt} + \beta_8 dForward_{jt}$$

$$+ \alpha_j + \alpha_r + \alpha_t + \varepsilon_{ijrt} \qquad (9.6)$$

Finally, the cluster effects are also considered through incorporating the assumption of random effects in each regression (Wooldridge, 2006).

ESTIMATION RESULTS AND INTERPRETATIONS

Table 9.4 reports the estimation results. Both the basic pooled OLS estimation and the FD estimation are conducted.

Since the FD estimation method deals with the problem of potential endogeneity, it produces unbiased and efficient estimates compared to the pooled OLS estimation. Therefore, our explanations of the regression results are based on the FD estimation.

The regression results show that labour, capital and intermediate inputs have the conventional signs and are statistically significant. However, the variables of backward and forward spillovers are not statistically significant (in the FD regression), which implies that there are no significant spillovers from FDI on China's domestic firms' productivity through backward and forward industrial linkages. In terms of investment from Hong Kong and Taiwan, the estimation results show that the overseas Chinese investment on average does not have higher spillovers on China's domestic firms' productivity than other foreign investment.

As to the variables of interest in this study, the horizontal FDI share and its square term, after controlling for different sources of FDI (HKTWRatio), backward and forward linkages of FDI, dummy variables of industry, region and time, we find that the estimated coefficient for the horizontal FDI share is positive and statistically significant and the coefficient for the square of horizontal FDI share is negative and statistically significant. It reveals that the horizontal impact of FDI on China's domestic firms' productivity follows an inverse U-shaped curve, confirming the

Table 9.4   Results from pooled OLS and FD regressions (domestic firms with matched exit and entry, dependent variable ln Y)

Variables	OLS	FD
Constant	0.827***	−0.008*
	(0.009)	(0.004)
ln$L$	0.042***	0.039***
	(0.001)	(0.001)
ln$K$	0.010***	0.008***
	(0.001)	(0.001)
ln$M$	0.910***	0.888***
	(0.001)	(0.002)
Horizontal	0.115***	0.124***
	(0.030)	(0.038)
Horizontal²	−0.191***	−0.185***
	(0.046)	(0.058)
HKTW Ratio	−0.005*	−0.002
	(0.002)	(0.002)
Backward	0.268*	−0.047
	(0.105)	(0.134)
Forward	−0.402**	0.068
	(0.143)	(0.195)
Adjusted R²	0.995	0.885
Observations	298 973	184 500

Notes:
All regressions are estimated using dummy variables to control 28 industries, 31 regions and year effects (for OLS regression, the reference group is the food production industry, Beijing, 2000, while for FD regression, the reference group is the food production industry, Beijing, 2000–2001).
*   Represents significant at 10 per cent level.
**   Represents significant at 5 per cent level.
***   Represents significant at 1 per cent level.
The numbers in parenthesis are standard errors.

existence of the non-linear relationship between the horizontal FDI share and domestic firms' productivity.

This finding suggests that the growing FDI presence in China can increase domestic firms' productivity, but the marginal positive spill-overs from foreign investment are declining as the horizontal FDI share increases in the same industry. This finding implies that the impact of the horizontal FDI presence on domestic firms' productivity does not follow a linear process. The existence of the non-linear relationship between the horizontal FDI share and domestic firms' productivity might explain the lack of significance of horizontal spillovers when being tested using the linear modelling technique.[4] An explanation of this finding is that when FDI initially enters an industry, it is more likely that it will produce a positive and significant impact on the productivity of domestic firms through exerting positive spillovers which impact on domestic firms. The spillovers effect, however, may decrease as the industrial share of foreign investment increases since FDI firms begin to 'steal' domestic firms' market share which is linked to firms' productivity. When the industrial share of foreign investment exceeds a critical threshold, the competition effect could become larger than the positive spillovers, and thereby the net effect of FDI on domestic firms' productivity could become negative. As a consequence, it is not surprising that the impact of the horizontal FDI presence on domestic firms' productivity may be ambiguous when it is tested on average using a linear functional form.

The estimated coefficients of the horizontal FDI share and its square term with the FD estimation are 0.124 and −0.185 and are statistically significant at the 1 per cent level. The estimation results indicate that a 1 percentage point increase in the FDI share may initially cause on average around a 0.124 per cent increase in productivity of domestic firms in the same industry, though the marginal impact is declining as FDI share increases. The turning point (the critical value), calculated by using the estimated coefficients,[5] of the industrial FDI share where the increasing positive spillovers of FDI could be peaking is around 34 per cent. In the period 2000 to 2003, the average industrial FDI share in terms of capital in China's manufacturing was 30 per cent. This implies that the positive horizontal spillovers of FDI on China's domestic firms' productivity were still increasing during the period of analysis, between 2000 and 2003.

CONCLUSION

Using the manufacturing firm-level data for China during the period 2000 to 2003, this study examines the horizontal spillovers of FDI on the productivity of domestic firms with the control of the inter-industry linkages between FDI presence and domestic firms, different sources of FDI from Hong Kong and Taiwan and from other foreign investors, and dummy variables of region, industry and time. After dealing with the selection bias from firms' exit and entry with the neighbourhood matching technique, and the endogeneity problem with first differencing technique, the study finds that FDI initially has significant positive spillovers on the productivity of domestic firms within the same industry in China's manufacturing sector. However, the marginal positive spillovers effect decreases as the share of FDI increases, and it even becomes negative when the share of FDI in an industry reaches a critical value (a turning point). The results also show that the share of FDI in China's manufacturing sector on average has not reached the turning point during the period of analysis, 2000 to 2003. This means that further increases in FDI would continue to benefit China's domestic manufacturing firms in terms of further improvement in their productivity. However, the study finds that FDI does not have significant spillover effects on China's domestic firms' productivity through backward and forward industrial linkages, and also finds that overseas Chinese investment on average does not have higher spillovers than FDI from other foreign investors on China's domestic firms' productivity.

These findings suggest that host countries could enlarge the positive spillovers of FDI and thereby foster domestic firms' productivity by encouraging domestic firms' learning by doing to increase their capacities for absorbing positive spillovers from FDI firms, strengthening industrial linkages between domestic firms and FDI firms, improving domestic capital and labour markets, leveling the playing field between domestic and FDI firms, and deepening the industrial reform with respect to firms' entry and exit.

NOTES

1. According to China's regulation, to be an FDI firm, the minimum share of foreign registered capital must be equal to or above 25 per cent of the total registered capital of the firm.
2. I would like to thank Dr Yu Sheng for the technical assistance with the regressions in this chapter.
3. For the details of neighbourhood matching technique please see Imbens and Angrist (1994) and Hahn et al. (2001). The related results are available from the author upon request.
4. Many previous empirical studies, such as Aitken and Harrison (1999), Javorcik (2004) and Blalock and Gertler (2008), found little learning-by-doing effects from direct foreign competitors in the same industry.
5. The calculation is based on the equation: $X^* = |\beta_1 / 2\beta_2|$, where X^* is the value of FDI share at the turning point, and β_1 and β_2 are the estimated coefficients of FDI share and FDI share square respectively.

10. Spillover effects of FDI on China's domestic firms' exports

INTRODUCTION

Since the early 1980s, China's exports have increased rapidly from US$20 billion in 1980 to US$1431 billion in 2008 with an annual growth rate of 17 per cent. Consequently, China has become the largest exporting nation in the world.

What are the sources of China's rapid export expansion since the early 1980s? Apart from the market-oriented economic reforms and trade liberalization particularly since the 1990s and after China's accession to the WTO in 2001, one of the main sources is the massive inflows of FDI associated with the fast export growth of FDI firms, whose export share in China's total exports increased from 0.05 per cent in 1980 to 55.25 per cent in 2008.

What, however, are the impacts of FDI on China's domestic firms' exports? This question is worthy of both theoretical analysis and empirical investigation because it is expected that export spillovers are one of the main benefits generated by FDI to host economies. This can not only help domestic firms improve productivity, promote specialization and increase exports, but also can help host countries improve resource allocation and play their comparative advantages in international trade since FDI tends to be in the sectors in which host countries have comparative advantages or the comparative advantages are increasing (Dunning, 1993). Therefore, this chapter aims to investigate empirically the impact of FDI on China's domestic firms' exports. We seek to answer the questions: what is the contribution of FDI to China's export expansion, and particularly, what is the impact of FDI on China's domestic firms' exports?

The chapter is arranged as follows. The next section presents the contribution of FDI to China's international trade expansion. The third section discusses the theoretical explanations of export spillovers of FDI on domestic firms' exports and presents the literature review. The fourth section documents the data sources and specifies the FDI variables, namely, the proxies for horizontal, backward and forward spillovers of FDI. The following section specifies the empirical model for the investigation of the spillover effects of FDI on domestic firms' exports. In particular, a Heckman two-step procedure regression has been combined with the first differencing regression technique to deal with the endogeneity problem associated with firms' fixed effects and the sample selection problem due to domestic firms' non-random selection between exporting and non-exporting behaviours. The sixth section discusses the estimation results. The final section makes the conclusion.

CONTRIBUTION OF FDI TO CHINA'S EXPORT EXPANSION

There is considerable evidence that FDI contributes to the growth of host countries' exports. In the case of China, the most prominent contribution of FDI perhaps is expanding China's exports. The direct way to measure the impact of FDI on China's export growth is to examine the trade performance of FDI firms. Table 10.1 presents FDI inflows into China and FDI firms' export performance from 1980 to 2008. With the rapid increase

Table 10.1   FDI firms' international trade performance, 1980–2008

Year	FDI inflows (US$ billion)	Value of FDI firms' trade (US$ billion)			FDI firms' trade as % of China's total trade		
		Total trade	Exports	Imports	Total trade	Exports	Imports
1980	0.44	0.04	0.01	0.03	0.11	0.05	0.17
1985	1.66	2.36	0.29	2.06	3.39	1.09	4.89
1990	3.49	20.12	7.81	12.31	17.43	12.58	23.07
1995	37.52	109.82	46.88	62.94	39.10	31.51	47.66
2000	40.72	236.71	119.44	117.27	49.91	47.93	52.10
2001	46.88	259.10	133.24	125.86	50.84	50.07	51.68
2002	52.74	330.24	169.99	160.25	53.20	52.21	54.29
2003	53.51	472.17	240.31	231.86	55.48	54.84	56.17
2004	60.63	663.18	338.61	324.57	57.44	57.07	57.83
2005	60.31	831.64	444.18	387.46	58.49	58.30	58.71
2006	62.97	1036.27	536.78	472.49	58.87	58.19	59.70
2007	74.77	1255.16	695.37	559.79	57.74	57.10	58.56
2008	92.40	1409.92	790.49	619.43	55.01	55.25	54.69

Sources: National Bureau of Statistics of China (various issues), *China Statistical Yearbook*, Beijing: China Statistics Press, and National Bureau of Statistics of China (various issues), *China Foreign Economic Statistical Yearbook*, Beijing: China Statistics Press.

in FDI inflows, FDI firms' exports increased spectacularly from US$0.01 billion in 1980 to US$119.44 billion in 2000 and further to US$790.49 billion in 2008, with an annual growth rate of 47.82 per cent. As a result, the importance of FDI firms in China's exports has increased dramatically from only 0.05 per cent in 1980 to 47.93 per cent in 2000 and further to 58.30 per cent in 2005, before falling slightly to 55.25 per cent in 2008. The rapid increase in FDI inflows and their export performance partly reflects China's policy in relation to FDI attraction deliberately biased towards export-oriented FDI. As a result, FDI firms have rapidly become a major exporter.

Foreign direct investment firms have played an even more important role in China's manufacturing exports. According to the National Annual Enterprise Census conducted by the NBS, during 2000 to 2003, on average, FDI firms' export propensity (exports to sales ratio) was 42 per cent, while that of domestic firms was only 10 per cent. Among the 29 manufacturing industries, in ten industries FDI firms' export propensities exceeded 50 per cent, including, for example, cultural, educational and sports goods (82 per cent); leather and fur products (73 per cent); furniture (71 per cent); other manufacturing (71 per cent); and instruments and metres (70 per cent).

In 18 industries, FDI firms have dominated the industries' exports. For example, the share of FDI firms' exports in the industry's total exports was 92 per cent in electronics and telecommunication equipment; 90 per cent in instruments and metres; 87 per cent in printing; 78 per cent in plastic products; 76 per cent in furniture; 75 per cent in paper and paper products; and 72 per cent in cultural, educational and sports goods. Overall, FDI firms accounted for 67 per cent of China's total manufacturing exports.

Clearly, FDI firms have made a significant contribution to China's export expansion during the last three decades. However, apart from the direct contribution, have FDI firms generated any export spillovers to China's domestic firms' export performance? This remains an empirical question.

EXPORT SPILLOVERS FROM FDI: THEORETICAL EXPLANATION AND EMPIRICAL EVIDENCE

Some empirical studies have investigated the relationship between FDI and China's international trade. For example, Chen (1997d, 1999), using a gravity model, investigated the impact of inward FDI stock on China's provincial trade and China's bilateral trade for the period from 1990 to 1993. The studies found that inward FDI stock has a positive impact both on China's provincial trade and on China's bilateral trade with its 101 trading partners. The explanation for this finding is that given the overwhelming dominance of developing source economies and their labour-intensive investment pattern, FDI in China is mainly export oriented and, therefore, has a positive impact on promoting China's international trade. Along this line, Lardy (1995), Tse et al. (1997) and Sun and Parikh (2001) also find a positive impact of FDI presence on China's export expansion.

Liu et al. (2001) used a gravity model with the panel data of bilateral trade for China and its 19 trading partners over the period from 1984 to 1998 to examine the causal relationship between FDI inflows into China and China's imports and exports. They found that the growth of China's imports from a country/region causes the growth of FDI inflows from that home country/region, which in turn causes the growth of exports from China to that home country/region. Later, Li (2003) used the panel data of bilateral trade and FDI flows for China and its 75 trading partners over the 1989 to 2000 period to confirm the mechanism in Liu et al. (2001). He found that inward FDI tends to have a larger predicted impact on China's imports than outward FDI, and this result is highly dependent on FDI's motivation and region-specific characteristics. Using the similar method but with a different dataset, Hu and Ma (1999) explored a more specific relationship between China's intra-industry trade with the rest of world and FDI inflows. They found that China's intra-industry trade is heavily driven by FDI inflows. Yu and Zhao (2008) investigated empirically the impacts of Japanese direct investment in China on Sino-Japanese bilateral trade. They found that Japanese direct investment in China has contributed not only to the increase of Chinese exports to Japan, but also to the increase of Chinese imports from Japan. The study suggests that the relations between Japanese direct investment in China and the bilateral trade are complementary.

The above empirical studies made some contributions in explaining the relationship between FDI inflows and the expansion of China's international trade. However, they did not explore how the entry of FDI firms may affect domestic firms' export behaviour.

Theoretically, FDI firms possessing specific ownership advantages bring into host countries a package of resources, which include not only capital but also technology, production know-how, management skills, marketing networks, information of international markets, and so on (Caves, 1996; Dunning, 1993). Therefore, FDI firms are expected to have positive export spillovers on domestic firms. Empirical studies focusing on investigating and evaluating export spillovers from FDI firms have not been explored widely (Gorg and Greenaway, 2004). However, although existing empirical studies have produced mixed results, some studies do find positive export spillovers of FDI firms on domestic firms' exports.

In summary, FDI firms can generate export spillovers to domestic firms through three main channels. First, FDI firms can reduce the export costs of domestic firms through knowledge spillovers (demonstration effects), thus encouraging domestic firms to engage and increase exports (Aitken, et al., 1997; Barrios et al. 2003; Greenaway et al. 2004; Kokko et al. 2001; Ruane and Sutherland 2005). Second, FDI firms can generate positive technology spillovers to domestic firms to increase domestic firms' productivity, which may improve domestic firms' competitiveness and increase domestic firms' exports (Barrios et al. 2003; Javorcik, 2004). Third, FDI firms can strengthen domestic industrial linkages through supplying and purchasing intermediate inputs, which not only will increase the productivity of domestic firms in the upstream and downstream industries but also will promote them to be involved in international production specialization, thus enhancing domestic firms' ability to export (Javorcik, 2004; Kneller and Pisu, 2007).

Empirical studies on export spillovers from FDI firms to domestic firms in China are very limited. For example, Zheng et al. (2004), using panel data at the regional level for the period from 1985 to 1999, examined the impact of FDI on the export performance of Chinese domestic firms. They found that FDI has some positive effects on domestic firms' export performance, but the influence is less than that on all firms (foreign and domestic). Ma (2006), using panel data at the provincial level for the 1993 to 2000 period, examined whether exports by multinational firms increase the probability of exporting by Chinese domestic firms. Ma found that FDI firms funded by the overseas Chinese investors do not increase the probability of exporting by local firms, while FDI firms from the OECD countries positively influence the export decision of local firms, particularly under processing trade. Cheung (2010), using panel data at the industry level for the period 1995 to 2006, investigated the impact of FDI via exports on the innovation performance of domestic firms in China's high-tech product industries. Cheung found that R&D activities of foreign-invested enterprises have positive spillovers on the innovation performance of domestic firms in the same industry through learning by doing or competition, thus promoting domestic firms' export performance. Buck et al. (2007), using firm-level panel data for the period 1998 to 2001, investigated export spillovers from FDI firms to Chinese domestic firms. By using a two-step modelling strategy, their estimations show that multinational firms in China positively affect local Chinese firms' exports. Sun (2009) used the pooled firm-level data to assess the impact of FDI on China's domestic firms' exports in the cultural, educational and sporting product manufacturing industry between 2000 and 2003. After dealing with the sample-selection bias, he found that there are some positive effects of FDI on domestic firms' exports in this industry though the impacts are asymmetric across regions and differ among types of firms.

The above empirical studies made some contributions in explaining the relationship between FDI inflows and domestic firms' exports. However, empirical arguments for and against the role of FDI in export spillovers in a country are still debated. This has been true not only of country- and industry-level studies, but also firm-level studies. Thus, a study of the impact of FDI on China's domestic firms' exports is very important not only because China has been the largest FDI recipient among the developing countries, but also because China has become the largest exporter in the world. Therefore, this study intends to explore how the entry of FDI firms may affect China's domestic firms' export behaviour. In particular, this chapter investigates and answers a number of questions. First, will FDI generate export spillovers on domestic firms' exports? Secondly, through which channel, horizontal or vertical, is FDI more likely to produce export spillovers on domestic firms' exports if there is any? Third, do different types of FDI, in terms of market orientation, have different export spillovers on domestic firms' exports?

DATA AND VARIABLE DEFINITION

We use the same dataset as in Chapter 9, which is the manufacturing firm-level data from the NBS National Annual Enterprise Census. The sample is an unbalanced dataset at the firm level during the period 2000 to 2003. In this study, to control for firms' entry and exit and their possible impact on the relationship between FDI and domestic firms' exports, we restrict the sample used for regressions to those domestic firms which appeared in at least two consecutive years (between 2000 and 2003) and use the neighbourhood matching technique to sort out unmatched domestic firms with the same exporting behaviour between each two consecutive years.[1] As a result, the sample used in this study contains 250 868 observations.

Using the same methodology employed in Chapter 9, we distinguish between domestic firms and FDI firms. We use domestic firms' average export propensity (export ratio) as the dependent variable. Domestic firms' average export propensity is defined as domestic firms' export revenue divided by their total sales revenue.

For the variables of FDI spillovers at the industry level, we follow Javorcik (2004) to account for both the relative importance of FDI in firms' capital stock and FDI firms' scale in the industry. Specifically, the variable for horizontal spillovers is defined as the weighted sum of foreign capital share, with the weight being each firm's share in the industry's output:

$$Horizontal_{jt} = \left(\sum_{i \in j} ForeignShare_{it} * Y_{it} \right) \Big/ \left(\sum_{i \in j} Y_{it} \right) \quad (10.1)$$

where $ForeignShare_{it}$ denotes the share of foreign registered capital in total registered capital in FDI firms at time t, and Y_{it} the total output of the same FDI firm at the same time. The value of this variable increases with the output of FDI firms and the share of foreign registered capital in these firms.

The variable of backward spillovers is defined as:

$$Backward_{jt} = \sum_{k \neq j} \alpha_{jk} Horizontal_{kt} \quad (10.2)$$

where α_{jk} is the proportion of industry j's output supplied to industry k, taken from China's 2002 input-output table at the two-digit level based on the ISIC Code. The greater the foreign presence in industries supplied by industry j and the larger the share of intermediates supplied to industries with FDI presence, the higher the value of the variable.

The variable of forward spillovers is defined as:

$$Forward_{jt} = \sum_{m \neq j} \varphi_{jm} \left[\left[\sum_{i \in m} ForeignShare_{it} * (Y_{it} - EX_{it}) \right] \Big/ \left[\sum_{i \in m} (Y_{it} - EX_{it}) \right] \right]$$
$$(10.3)$$

where φ_{jm} is the share of inputs purchased by industry j from industry m in total inputs sourced by industry j. It is also taken from China's 2002 input-output table at the two-digit level based on the ISIC Code. EX_{it} denotes the export value of FDI firm i at time t estimated with the output constant price. As only intermediates sold in the domestic market are relevant to this study, goods produced by FDI firms for exports EX_{it} are excluded. The greater the foreign presence in industries sourced by industry j and the larger the share of intermediates sourced from industries with FDI presence, the higher the value of the variable.

In addition to FDI variables, we control for some firm characteristics affecting domestic firms' export behaviour, including productivity, capital to labour ratio, R&D activities, operational scale, age and indirect foreign investment. For domestic firms' productivity, we use domestic firms' TFP as an approximation, which is estimated by using the semi-parametric regression method following Levinsohn and Petrin (2003). All value variables used for the productivity estimation are calculated at 2000 prices.

Domestic firms' exports are controlled in the estimation in order to deal with the possible reverse causality problem. The TFP is expected to have a positive impact on domestic firms' exports.

Domestic firms' capital to labour ratio is defined as the log of net value of fixed assets at 2000 prices divided by total number of employed workers. Given China's comparative advantage in labour-intensive activities, the capital to labour ratio is expected to have a negative impact on domestic firms' exports.

Domestic firms' R&D index is defined as the total revenue from new products divided by total revenue. Research and development activities can increase firms' competitiveness and therefore are expected to have a positive impact on domestic firms' exports.

Domestic firms' age is based on their establishment year. In our sample, domestic firms' average age is 12.4 years. Domestic firms' operational scale is a dummy variable, which takes a value of one if the domestic firm is classified as a large or medium sized firm, and zero if not. We have no pre-judgment of the impact of these two variables on domestic firms' exports.

Finally, indirect foreign investment is the foreign equity share in total registered capital of domestic firms ranging from zero to less than 25 per cent. This variable controls the direct impact of foreign capital on domestic firms' exports and is expected to be positive.

The descriptive statistics of domestic firms' basic information are presented in Table 10.2.

METHODOLOGY AND MODEL SPECIFICATION

To examine whether FDI may affect domestic firms' exports through either horizontal or vertical channels, we start with a model specification that regresses domestic firms' export propensity with respect to the horizontal, backward and forward FDI spillovers variables at the industry level, and other control variables at the firm level.[2]

$$\ln ExportRatio_{ijrt} = \beta_0 + \beta_1 Horizontal_{jt} + \beta_2 Backward_{jt} + \beta_3 Forward_{jt}$$

$$+ \beta_4 \ln TFP_{ijrt} + \beta_5 \ln (K/L)_{ijrt} + \beta_6 Open Year_{ijrt} + \beta_7 D\_Scale_{ijrt}$$

$$+ \beta_8 RnD_{ijrt} + \beta_9 IFI_{ijrt} + \sum \alpha_r D_r + \sum \alpha_j D_j + \sum \alpha_t D_t + u_{ijrt} \quad (10.4)$$

where $\ln ExportRatio_{ijrt}$ denotes the logarithm of export propensity of domestic firm i operating in industry j and region r at time t. $Horizontal_{jt}$ measures the export spillovers generated by FDI presence in the same

Table 10.2 Major economic indicators of domestic firms, 2000–2003

Economic indicators	2000		2001		2002		2003		Total	
	Non-exporting domestic firms	Exporting domestic firms	Non-exporting domestic firms	Exporting domestic firms	Non-exporting domestic firms	Exporting domestic firms	Non-exporting domestic firms	Exporting domestic firms	Non-exporting domestic firms	Exporting domestic firms
Number of observations	88645	19401	97374	21136	99451	23839	109553	26347	395023	90723
Average output value (10000 yuan)	26323 (88986)	116143 (638757)	28201 (103926)	117195 (693802)	31783 (135355)	123749 (764732)	35684 (135689)	141766 (975163)	30741 (118983)	125759 (792419)
Average number of employed workers (person)	234 (507)	765 (2671)	213 (504)	640 (2390)	206 (561)	579 (2091)	193 (439)	546 (2010)	210 (503)	623 (2277)
Net value of fixed assets (10000 yuan)	6868 (43102)	31888 (265715)	6845 (54193)	29766 (284308)	6965 (59056)	27252 (272385)	6649 (43801)	27441 (266796)	6826 (50507)	28884 (272210)
Average intermediate input value (10000 yuan)	20271 (70230)	89672 (496880)	21765 (84692)	91458 (553411)	24451 (109044)	95696 (604997)	27225 (107446)	108933 (766945)	23611 (95237)	97216 (624804)
Firms' productivity (lnTFP)	1.06 (0.83)	0.95 (0.76)	1.06 (0.81)	0.95 (0.75)	1.06 (0.81)	0.95 (0.75)	1.07 (0.84)	0.98 (0.81)	1.06 (0.82)	0.96 (0.77)
K/L ratio (10000 yuan/person)	27.2 (107.1)	25.0 (88.8)	29.5 (101.6)	24.7 (53.4)	29.7 (60.8)	24.6 (48.5)	30.7 (60.7)	25.1 (62.8)	29.4 (84.1)	24.9 (64.1)

Note: Numbers in brackets are standard deviations.

Sources: Author's calculation based on the National Bureau of Statistics of China, National Annual Enterprise Census.

industry j at time t, and *Backward*$_{jt}$ and *Forward*$_{jt}$ measure the export spillovers generated by FDI presence in the downstream and upstream industries respectively. Since all the three variables are estimated with the data on firm-level capital stock (registered capital), no lags of those variables are required to be included in equation (10.4). For the firm level control variables, $\ln TFP_{ijrt}$ denotes the logarithm of domestic firms' TFP (estimated by using the LP method as explained in the above section), which is used to control for the possible impact of productivity disparity across firms on their exporting behaviour (Melitz, 2003). The variable $\ln (K/L)_{ijrt}$ denotes the logarithm of capital to labour ratio at the firm level, which is used to control the impact of comparative advantage disparity across firms on their exporting behaviour. The variables *OpenYear*$_{ijrt}$, *D_Scale*$_{ijrt}$, *RnD*$_{ijrt}$ and *IFI*$_{ijrt}$ are the firms' open year, a dummy variable for firms' scale, R&D index representing domestic firms' innovation ability, and indirect foreign investment respectively. Finally, there are three groups of dummy variables, $\sum \alpha_r D_r$, $\sum \alpha_j D_j$ and $\sum \alpha_t D_t$, used to control for the regional, industrial and time specific effects, and u_{ijrt} is used to capture the random errors.

Before we run the regression, we have to solve two econometric problems. The first econometric problem is the endogeneity. It is believed that there are some unobserved time-invariant and firm-specific factors, such as firms' entrepreneurship, local transportation and communication facilities, government policies, and so on, which may be positively related to firms' export propensity, and the horizontal, upstream and downstream FDI presence. Without considering these factors, the pooled OLS regression may lead to biased estimation of the impacts of FDI on domestic firms' export behaviour. To deal with this problem, we adopt the FD regression technique to eliminate the unobserved time-invariant and firm-specific factors from the OLS regression and re-examine the impact of FDI on domestic firms' export behaviour. Thus, equation (10.4) can be re-arranged as:

$$d\ln ExportRatio_{ijrt} = \beta_0 + \beta_1 dHorizontal_{jt} + \beta_2 dBackward_{jt} + \beta_3 dForward_{jt}$$

$$+ \beta_4 d\ln TFP_{jrit} + \beta_5 d\ln (K/L)_{ijrt} + \beta_6 dOpenYear_{ijrt} + \beta_7 dD\_Scale_{ijrt}$$

$$+ \beta_8 dRnD_{ijrt} + \beta_9 dIFI_{ijrt} + \sum \alpha_r D_r + \sum \alpha_j D_j + \sum \alpha_t D_t + u_{ijrt} \quad (10.5)$$

The second econometric problem is the sample selection due to the truncated dependent variable because some domestic firms are not exporting. According to Melitz (2003), domestic firms choosing to export may usually incur additional sunk costs, which are related to marketing exploration. Thus, domestic firms with exporting ability will not enter the international market if the profits from exporting activities cannot compensate for their loss. In China's manufacturing industries between 2000 and 2003, on average two-thirds of domestic firms were not exporting. Since those non-exporting domestic firms (their exports were all equal to zero) with different abilities of exporting are not included in our regression, the impact of FDI on their ability of exporting cannot be estimated. Therefore, both the OLS and FD regressions may tend to underestimate the impact of FDI on domestic firms' export behaviour. To deal with this sample selection problem, we adopt the Heckman two-step procedure (Wooldridge, 2002) to include the non-exporting domestic firms in the regression. We first assume that domestic firms with similar characteristics may have similar exporting probability (though some of them may not export due to many other constraints), and then estimate the inversed *Mills* ratio to capture the probability of both exporting and non-exporting firms choosing to export. Thus, the impact of FDI on domestic firms' export behaviour can be estimated by regressing domestic exporting firms' export propensity with regards to the variables of FDI presence with the control of the *Mills* ratios. To fulfil this two-step procedure, a dummy variable representing whether domestic firms export or not in the base year (2000) – highly related to domestic firms' exporting choice but not related to their export propensity – is used in the first step to identify the two regressions. The above model can be summarized in equation (10.6).

$$d \ln ExportRatio_{ijrt} = \beta_0 + \beta_1 dHorizontal_{jt} + \beta_2 dBackward_{jt} + \beta_3 dForward_{jt}$$

$$+ \beta_4 d \ln TFP_{ijrt} + \beta_5 d \ln (K/L)_{ijrt} + \beta_7 dD\_Scale_{ijrt} + \beta_8 dRnD_{ijrt}$$

$$+ \beta_9 dIFI_{ijrt} + \gamma dMills_{ijrt} + \sum \alpha_t D_t + v_{ijrt} \qquad (10.6)$$

where $Mills_{ijrt}$ is the *Mills* ratio, which has been estimated from the first-step probit model:

$$P(y \, export_{ijrt} = 1 | export_{ijrt} > 0) = \theta_0 + \theta_1 dHorizontal_{jt} + \theta_2 dBackward_{jt}$$

$$+ \theta_3 dForward_{jt} + \lambda D\_Export_{ijr-t} + \theta_4 d \ln TFP_{ijrt} + \theta_5 d \ln (K/L)_{ijrt}$$

$$+ \theta_7 dD\_Scale_{ijrt} + \theta_8 dRnD_{ijrt} + \theta_9 dIFI_{ijrt} + \sum \phi_t D_t + v_{ijrt} \quad (10.7),$$

and D_Export_{ijr-t} is domestic firms' export status before year t used to identify the first-stage probit model for domestic firms' exports ($y \, export_{ijrt} = 0, 1$) (Christofides et al., 2003; Heckman, 1979; Wooldridge, 1995, 2002).

Equations (10.6) and (10.7) can provide consistent estimates on the impact of intra-industry and inter-industry FDI on domestic firms' export propensity, with the control of time-invariant and firm-specific factors and the truncated dependent variable problems.

EMPIRICAL RESULTS: THE IMPACT OF FDI ON DOMESTIC FIRMS' EXPORTS

The empirical estimation of the export spillovers of FDI firms on China's domestic firms' exports is conducted by regressing domestic firms' export propensity with horizontal, backward and forward spillovers variables of FDI and other control variables with the four-year dataset by using the specified models presented in the above section. The two-step Heckman procedure is applied to OLS and FD regressions. The estimation results are reported in Table 10.3 and Table 10.4.

The Impact of FDI on Domestic Firms' Export Propensity

We first use the pooled OLS method to conduct the regression with the adjustment for heteroscedasticity and the cluster effects. As shown in column (1) of Table 10.3, the estimated results show that FDI has no impact on domestic firms' export propensity. The estimated elasticities to the horizontal, backward and forward spillovers variables are all positive but not statistically significant even at the 10 per cent level. Most of the estimated coefficients of the control variables are consistent with our prediction.

The OLS estimates are biased due to endogeneity. As we discussed in the previous section, there are some unobserved time-invariant and firm-specific factors, such as firms' entrepreneurship, local transportation and communication facilities, government policies and so on, which may be related to firms' export propensity, and the horizontal, upstream and downstream FDI presence. To deal with this problem, we adopt the FD regression to eliminate the unobserved time-invariant and firms-specific characteristics from our estimation.

The estimation results with the FD regression (column (2) of Table 10.3) show that FDI has a positive impact on domestic firms' export propensity in the same industry. The elasticity of domestic firms' export propensity to the horizontal spillovers variable is 0.042 and significant at the 1 per cent level. The estimation results show that FDI has no significant impact on domestic firms' export propensity through backward and forward industrial linkages. The regression results imply that the export spillovers

*Table 10.3   Estimation results of the impact of FDI on domestic firms'
export propensity*

Variables	OLS (1)	FD (2)
ln*TFP*	−0.016***	0.004***
	(0.003)	(0.001)
ln (*K/L*)	−0.010***	−0.003***
	(0.002)	(0.001)
Open Year	0.103***	–
	(0.005)	–
D_Scale	0.126***	−0.023***
	(0.009)	(0.003)
RnD	−0.000	0.057***
	(0.000)	(0.007)
Inversed Mills Ratio	−0.229***	0.069***
	(0.011)	(0.007)
IFI	0.111***	0.102***
	(0.035)	(0.031)
Horizontal	0.009	0.042***
	(0.083)	(0.013)
Backward	0.055	0.011
	(0.634)	(0.028)
Forward	0.188	−0.019
	(0.487)	(0.076)
Constant	0.588***	0.004***
	(0.212)	(0.001)
Observations	52 713	23 562
R^2	0.489	0.017

Notes:
For concision, regional, industrial and time dummies are not reported, but they are
controlled and jointly significant in each regression.
*   Represents significant at 10 per cent level.
**   Represents significant at 5 per cent level.
***   Represents significant at 1 per cent level.
The numbers in parenthesis are standard errors.

of FDI firms to China's domestic firms' exports are mainly in the same
industry through demonstration effects.

For the control variables, domestic firms' export propensity is negatively
related to their capital–labour ratio and firms' operational scale, which
implies that domestic firms' exports are mainly relying on China's comparative advantage in labour-intensive manufacturing activities. Domestic
firms' export propensity is positively related to firms' productivity and R&D
activities, implying that FDI can also promote domestic firms' exports
through their positive productivity spillovers as revealed in Chapter 9.
Indirect foreign investment is a positive and statistically significant factor in

Table 10.4   Estimation results of the impact of non-exporting and high-exporting FDI firms on domestic firms' export propensity (FD regression)

Variables	Non-exporting FDI firms	High-exporting FDI firms
ln*TFP*	0.005***	0.004***
	(0.001)	(0.001)
ln (*K/L*)	−0.003***	−0.003***
	(0.001)	(0.001)
Open Year	−	−
	−	−
D_Scale	−0.023***	−0.023***
	(0.003)	(0.003)
RnD	0.057***	0.057***
	(0.007)	(0.007)
Inversed Mills Ratio	0.069***	0.069***
	(0.007)	(0.007)
IFI	0.101***	0.101***
	(0.031)	(0.031)
Horizontal	−0.110	0.248**
	(0.068)	(0.122)
Backward	0.308	0.797
	(0.198)	(0.655)
Forward	0.559*	1.874**
	(0.290)	(0.755)
Constant	0.003***	0.002***
	(0.001)	(0.001)
Observations	23 562	23 562
R^2	0.018	0.018

Notes:
For concision, regional, industrial and time dummies are not reported, but they are
controlled and jointly significant in each regression.
*   Represents significant at 10 per cent level.
**   Represents significant at 5 per cent level.
***   Represents significant at 1 per cent level.
The numbers in parenthesis are standard errors.

domestic firms' export propensity. Finally, the significant coefficient of the
Mills ratio suggests that the sample selection problem does matter for the
regression. So the adjustment with the Heckman selection is appropriate.

The Impact of FDI Firms' Market Orientation on Domestic Firms' Exports

One notable feature of FDI firms in China is the high propensity to export.
During the period from 2000 to 2003, the average export propensity
of FDI firms was 42 per cent and in ten industries out of the 29 manu-

facturing industries FDI firms' export propensity exceeded 50 per cent. Therefore, it is important to investigate whether FDI firms' own export behaviour may affect domestic firms' exports.

We group FDI firms into non-exporting FDI firms (the current export revenue is equal to zero) and high-exporting FDI firms (the export revenue is more than or equal to 50 per cent of the total sales revenue). Equations (10.1) to (10.3) are used to calculate the corresponding horizontal, backward and forward FDI spillovers variables for each group of these FDI firms. The estimation results are shown in Table 10.4.

The estimation results show that high-exporting FDI firms are more likely to generate positive export spillovers on domestic firms' export propensity in the same industry than non-exporting FDI firms. As shown in Table 10.4, the estimated coefficient of the horizontal FDI spillovers variable for the high-exporting FDI firms is 0.248 and significant at the 5 per cent level, while the estimated coefficient for the non-exporting FDI firms is −0.110 and not significant at the 10 per cent level. The regression results provide further evidence that the positive export spillovers to China's domestic firms' exports are mainly generated by high-exporting FDI firms in the same industry through demonstration effects.

The regression results provide some evidence of positive export spillovers on domestic firms' export propensity from high-exporting FDI firms and non-exporting FDI firms through forward industrial linkages. The estimated coefficient of the forward FDI spillovers variable for the high-exporting FDI firms is 1.874 and significant at the 5 per cent level and for the non-exporting FDI firms is 0.559 and significant at the 10 per cent level. The results suggest that FDI firms in the upstream industries can improve domestic firms' competitiveness, thus increasing domestic firms' exports by supplying intermediate inputs with good quality to downstream domestic firms.

However, the estimation results do not find significant evidence that FDI firms generate export spillovers to domestic firms through backward linkage. One possible explanation is that FDI firms, particularly high-exporting FDI firms, are highly engaged in processing trade in China. In 2006, Foreign direct investment firms accounted for 84 per cent and 85 per cent of China's total processing exports and imports respectively, and processing exports and imports accounted for 80 per cent and 58 per cent of FDI firms' total exports and imports respectively. Foreign direct investment firms purchase materials and intermediate inputs from overseas and sell their products to the international markets after processing and assembling in the special export-processing zones or duty-free zones specifically designed and created for export-oriented FDI firms. As a result, they have little backward linkage with domestic firms.

CONCLUSION

Using the firm-level census data of Chinese manufacturing industries for the period from 2000 to 2003, this chapter carries out a number of empirical regressions to investigate the impact of FDI on China's domestic firms' export performance. In searching for the export spillovers from FDI firms to domestic firms, we not only examined the horizontal impact but also investigated the impact through vertical industrial linkages between FDI firms and domestic firms. In addition, we examined the impact of different FDI firms, in terms of the market orientation, on domestic firms' exports.

After controlling for the impact of firm-specific characteristics of productivity, capital to labour ratio, R&D activities, scale, age and indirect foreign investment of domestic firms, and dealing with some econometric problems of endogeneity and sample selection, our empirical regressions reveal the following three findings.

First, the study finds that FDI firms have a positive impact on the export propensity of domestic firms in the same industry through demonstration effects, and this positive impact is mainly generated by high-exporting FDI firms.

Second, the study finds some evidence that FDI firms, in particular high-exporting FDI firms, have positive export spillovers to domestic firms in the downstream industries through forward industrial linkage, meaning that domestic firms can get intermediate inputs with good quality from upstream FDI firms. Thus, domestic firms can improve competitiveness and increase exports.

Third, the study does not find significant evidence that FDI firms, particularly high exporting FDI firms, generate export spillovers to domestic firms through backward industrial linkage. An explanation is that FDI firms, particularly high exporting FDI firms, are highly engaged in processing trade in China. Because they are concentrated in the special export-processing zones and the import duty-free zones specifically designed for export-oriented FDI firms and import almost all the materials and intermediate inputs from overseas and export the processed and assembled products abroad, they have very little backward industrial linkage with domestic firms. Therefore, these FDI firms generate no significant backward spillovers to domestic firms. This finding is consistent with the findings in Chapter 9, in which we do not find significant backward productivity spillovers from FDI firms to China's domestic firms.

This study attempts to use the firm-level data to examine the relationship between FDI and domestic firms' exports throughout the whole manufacturing industry in China. Two contributions are made to the previous literature. First, in addition to the intra-industry impact of FDI on domestic firms' exports through demonstration effects, our analysis points out that industrial linkages can be another important channel through which FDI can promote domestic firms' export activities. Second, we distinguish FDI firms by their different characteristics such as market orientation in order to reveal how different types of FDI firms may have different impacts on domestic firms' exports, which can help to provide some useful policy implications.

The results of this study raise a very important policy implication for the Chinese government's FDI policies. For the past three decades, the Chinese government's FDI policies have been deliberately biased towards attracting export-oriented FDI aiming to boost its exports. Undoubtedly, the export-oriented FDI policies have been very successful in terms of promoting China's export growth. As a result, China has become the largest exporting nation and the largest holder of foreign reserves in the world. However, China's domestic firms have benefited very little from the export-oriented FDI policies in terms of the positive export spillovers from the export-oriented FDI firms through backward industrial linkages. Therefore, the Chinese government should adjust its FDI policies to encourage FDI firms to engage in industrial linkages with domestic firms, so that domestic firms can benefit more from FDI inflows.

In 2007, the Chinese government issued the amended Catalogue for the Guidance of Foreign Investment Industries. The changes to the Catalogue reflect China's continued effort to attract FDI in accordance with China's economic, regional and industrial development strategies. Under the 2007 Catalogue, FDI in traditional manufacturing industries and export-oriented projects will no longer be encouraged, instead, FDI in new high technology, new materials production, high-end equipment, modern agriculture and high-end services, have been newly encouraged. These changes may improve the industrial linkages between FDI firms and domestic firms, help to upgrade China's industrial structure through utilizing foreign capital in order to benefit more from FDI inflows and achieve sound and healthy economic development.

NOTES

1. For the details of neighbourhood matching technique please see Imbens and Angrist (1994) and Hahn et al. (2001). The related results are available from the author upon request.
2. I would like to thank Dr Yu Sheng for the technical assistance with the regressions in this chapter.

11. Conclusion, policy implications and prospects

Foreign direct investment in China provides a valuable opportunity for both the theoretical study and empirical analysis of the issues involved when such investment occurs. This study, with respect to the main issues raised in Chapter 1, has analysed the location determinants, the investor differences and the economic impacts of FDI in China over the past three decades. The results obtained from this study have provided us with much insight into the general issues of FDI in developing countries. In particular, this study has extended our knowledge in three main ways: (1) greater understanding of the general causes of FDI from the aspect of the 'demand-side' factors by focusing on investigating the location determinants affecting inter-country and inter-province distributions of FDI; (2) better knowledge of the differences between the developing source countries and economies and the developed source countries in their investment relationships with China, and the distinctive features of the investments from the overseas Chinese investors as compared to those from the foreign country investors; and (3) further evidence of the impact of FDI on economic growth, the spillover effects of FDI on productivity, and exports of domestic firms in the case of FDI in China. This chapter summarizes the study, links the main findings of the different chapters, presents policy implications and discusses the prospects for FDI inflows into China.

SUMMARY OF THE STUDY

How has China changed from totally prohibiting FDI to becoming the largest FDI recipient among developing countries within a period of three decades? To understand China's change of attitude from restricting to encouraging inward FDI, as well as to provide a general policy background for this study, the study starts with an examination of the evolution of changes to China's FDI policies. In general, in all of the policy aspects relating to FDI, China has taken a positive but gradual reform approach. This has been demonstrated by the gradual shifts from the establishment of the four SEZs to the nationwide implementation of open policies for FDI, from granting permission for joint ventures to allowing wholly foreign-owned enterprises, from tight foreign exchange control to RMB convertibility on current account, from offering tax incentives to attract FDI to the application of national treatment, from attracting greenfield investments to allowing cross-border M&As and from encouraging FDI to designated industries to opening more and more industries especially service sectors to foreign investments. Despite the limitations, this reform process has proved both politically necessary and empirically successful. The gradual changes to China's FDI policies clearly indicate that China has continued to express a strong desire to stimulate and guide its economic development through promoting a more liberalized legal and policy environment to attract FDI and through further pursuing economic reform to establish a more market-oriented economy.

Since the early 1990s and especially after China's accession to the WTO, China has received a huge amount of FDI inflows, making it the largest FDI recipient among the developing countries. However, China is large, and large countries normally receive a large amount of FDI inflows. What factors affect the inter-country distribution of FDI inflows and has China really received excessive FDI inflows from the world compared to what it should have, based on its economic and geographical characteristics? According to Dunning's eclectic OLI paradigm, a host country's overall attractiveness to FDI is determined by the location advantages it possesses. Because resource endowments are not evenly distributed among countries and social and economic factors as well as government policies are also different among countries, the attractiveness of host countries to FDI varies. This implies that given the ownership advantages and the internalization advantages of the source countries the differences in location advantages of host countries are very important in determining the distribution of FDI inflows into host countries.

Against the theoretical background, Chapter 3 investigated the location determinants affecting FDI inflows into developing countries by using a modified gravity model and econometric regression analysis to test the hypotheses based on the location advantages of the theory of FDI. The regression results provide strong support for the acceptance of the hypotheses. The main findings are that countries with a larger market size, faster economic growth, higher per capita income, higher creditworthiness or lower country risk in terms of economic, financial, institutional, social and political stability, higher quality of human resources with higher adult literacy rates, a higher level of existing FDI stock and a more liberalized trade regime represented by the higher degree of openness, attract relatively more FDI inflows, while higher efficiency wages or lower labour productivity and greater remoteness from the rest of the world deter FDI inflows.

By using the statistical model as an empirical norm, the analysis of the relative performance of China and other East and South-East Asian developing economies in attracting FDI inflows offers no obvious evidence that China has attracted excessive FDI inflows. We find that China's relative performance in attracting FDI was at a level only moderately above its potential and was at the average among the East and South-East Asian developing economies. Therefore, although China is the largest FDI recipient among developing countries and attracted a large amount of FDI inflows in absolute dollars, allowing for its huge market size, increasing per capita income, fast economic growth, low labour costs, good creditworthiness and other economic and geographical characteristics, China received its expected share of FDI inflows from the world, or at most marginally more than its potential for the last three decades.

However, many developing countries, especially several of China's neighbouring Asian developing economies, have raised their concerns that the emergence of China has not only diverted FDI away from them but has also attracted their own domestic investors to leave their economies, resulting in a continuous loss of manufacturing industries and jobs, and further weakening their economies. Has China crowded out FDI inflows into other developing countries? Chapter 4, using the same analytical method developed in Chapter 3, investigated empirically the impact of FDI inflows into China on FDI inflows into other developing countries in general and into Asian developing economies in particular. The empirical regression results show that FDI inflows into China have a statistically significant positive effect on FDI inflows into other developing countries and into Asian developing economies. This positive and complementary effect of FDI inflows into China on FDI inflows into other developing countries and especially into Asian developing economies may be linked to the increased resource demand by a growing China and the production-networking activities among the developing countries, and particularly among Asian developing economies. While the results did not allow the relative strength of these two linkages to be determined, it is likely that this positive 'China effect' stems from a combination of both, leading to the central result that this effect is about investment creation, not investment diversion. These complementarities imply that much of the concern about China's inward FDI has been unfounded.

The study also reveals that, although FDI inflows into China are positive and statistically significant to FDI inflows into other developing countries, the China effect is not the most important factor determining FDI inflows into the developing countries. The empirical regression results suggest that, all else being equal, the marginal effect of the host countries' location variables on FDI inflows into their economies is much larger than the China effect. Host countries' location variables, such as a larger market and higher level of economic development, fast economic growth, lower labour costs accompanied with higher labour productivity, lower country risk with economic, financial, institutional, social and political stability, a higher degree of economic openness and being relatively closer to the rest of the world, all play a fundamental role in attracting FDI inflows.

As a nation, China has been very successful in attracting FDI inflows. However, in terms of regional distribution, FDI inflows into China's individual provinces differ greatly. As a result, the provincial distribution of FDI inflows into China has been very uneven, with the eastern region provinces accounting for nearly 90 per cent of the total. What are the causes of the uneven provincial distribution of FDI inflows into China and what provincial characteristics determine the FDI location decision within China? Using the same analytical method developed in Chapter 3, the importance of location advantages in determining the distribution of FDI inflows has also been confirmed by the empirical study of provincial distribution of FDI inflows into China in Chapter 5. The empirical analysis shows that facing the same set of source countries, provincial differences in the magnitude of FDI inflows are determined by the differences in location advantages of host provinces. Provinces with larger GDP, higher per capita income, higher rate of economic growth, higher level of openness represented by trade and export to GDP ratios, higher level of accumulated FDI stock, more intensive transport infrastructure, higher level of telecommunications, higher level of electricity supply, higher level of labour quality approximated by literacy rates and represented by higher ratio of university students enrolment, and being located along the coast all attracted relatively more FDI inflows, while higher labour costs and low productivity approximated by efficiency wages deterred FDI inflows. In addition, the SEZ policies and the regional differentiation in the timing of implementing the open policies for FDI had a strong impact on the provincial distribution of FDI inflows. Finally, the implementation of a series of trade and FDI liberalization policies in the 1990s and the early 2000s had a very strong positive effect on attracting FDI inflows into China across all provinces.

Since the economic reform began, the economic growth rates of the eastern region provinces, which benefited from the regionally biased open policies, have been much faster than those of the central and western region provinces. This unbalanced economic growth between the coastal provinces and the less-developed inland provinces has led to uneven economic development and an increase in income gaps between regions. The differences between the eastern region provinces and the central and western region provinces in the levels of economic development cannot be reduced in the near future. All of these factors have also had a very strong and direct impact on the location factors attracting FDI inflows.

Based on the empirical analysis, we constructed the provincial inward FDI attractiveness index for China's 31 mainland provinces. The index results reveal that there are large differences among China's 31 mainland provinces in the attractiveness to FDI inflows. The most attractive provinces, according to the values of the inward FDI attractiveness index, are the eastern region provinces, particularly Shanghai, Guangdong, Beijing, Tianjin, Jiangsu, Fujian, Zhejiang and Shandong. Although there have been some improvements in the investment environment for FDI, the central region provinces and particularly the western region provinces are less attractive to FDI as compared to the eastern region provinces. Because the inward FDI attractiveness index values are largely based on structural economic factors that tend to change slowly over time, it is unrealistic to expect that the central region and particularly the western region will attract large FDI inflows in the near future. As a result, the eastern region will continue to attract most of the FDI inflows into China and the situation of uneven regional distribution of FDI inflows into China will persist.

In terms of the sources of FDI in China, the most prominent feature is the overwhelming dominance of developing countries and economies, accounting for 75.38 per cent of the total FDI in China. More remarkably, the overseas Chinese investors from Hong Kong, Macao and Taiwan accounted for nearly half of the total FDI in China. Why do investments from developing countries and economies, especially the overseas Chinese investors, dominate FDI in China, and what factors explain the variations of investment intensity between China and its source countries and economies? Chapter 6 provided answers to these questions by analysing the difference of investment intensity of the source countries and economies, and testing the determinants affecting the variations of the investment intensity indexes of the source countries and economies in China.

The investment intensity index measures the relative importance of China as a host for the source countries' investments as compared to the rest of the world as hosts for these countries' investments. The investment intensity indexes of source countries in China vary enormously. However, comparing the two major groups of developing and developed source countries and economies, the study shows that the investment intensity indexes of the developing source countries and economies are not only all above 100 per cent, but also much higher than those of the developed source countries. This reveals that China is more important as a host for the developing source countries' and economies' investments than for the developed source countries' investments.

What factors explain the differences of the intensities of investments in China of the major investors? The regression analyses provided strong support for our two hypotheses. In general, the economic and technological development gaps and the levels of economic proximity are important factors affecting FDI flows between countries. Two implications can be drawn from the regression results. First, since the economic proximity is positively related to the investment intensity between countries, the high economic proximity between China and the East and South-East Asian economies, particularly Hong Kong and Taiwan, implies that China will remain a very important host for the investments from these economies. Second, with the sustained and fast economic growth in China, combined with the huge inflows of FDI and technology into its domestic economy, the economic and technological development gaps between China and the developed countries will tend to be reduced. As a result, China will become a more important host for FDI from developed source countries in the near future.

However, one important question still needs to be answered: are there differences in investment and production behaviour among the major investors in terms of investment pattern, mode of entry, export propensity, capital intensity and labour productivity? According to Dunning's OLI framework for FDI, the investment potential and investment patterns of enterprises are determined by the nature and extent of their possession of ownership advantages and the incentive to internalize the use of their ownership advantages. However, the creation and development of the ownership advantages of enterprises are closely related to their home countries' technological and innovative capabilities and overall economic development levels. Enterprises from developed source countries with high technological and innovative capabilities and a high overall economic development level will possess not only more ownership advantages in general but also more ownership advantages in the forms of high technology, product differentiation, managerial and entrepreneurial skills, and knowledge-based intangible assets in particular. By contrast, developing source countries have relatively lower technological and innovative capabilities and are at the mid-level of economic development, so the ownership advantages possessed by their enterprises are not only relatively less in general but also are more concentrated in the forms of labour-intensive production technology, standardized manufactured products and well-established export market networks.

The incentives for enterprises to internalize the use of their ownership advantages through FDI depend on the nature of the ownership advantages and the degree of imperfections in the markets for the ownership advantages they possess. Therefore, the more technology-intensive and the higher the imperfections of the markets, the stronger incentives for the enterprises to internalize the use of their ownership advantages through FDI and control operations. Since enterprises in the technology-intensive sector and the capital-intensive sector possess more high technology and knowledge-based intangible assets than enterprises in the labour-intensive sector, there is more incentives to set up wholly owned enterprises in the technology-intensive and capital-intensive sectors than in the labour-intensive sector. Similarly, since enterprises from the developed source countries possess greater more ownership advantages through technology-intensive and knowledge-based intangible assets than enterprises from the developing source countries, enterprises from developed source countries have greater incentives to internalize the use of their ownership advantages and a stronger tendency to secure control over the business than enterprises from the developing source countries.

Are these propositions valid for the major investors in their investments in China? Chapter 7 investigated and compared the investment and production behaviour in China's manufacturing sector between the overseas Chinese investors (from Hong Kong, Macao and Taiwan) and the foreign country investors (mainly from the OECD countries). It is argued that because of the differences in ownership advantages resulting from the differences in economic and technological development levels, the overseas Chinese investors and the foreign country investors should have differences in their investment and production behaviour. The study provides two main findings.

First, FDI inflows into China have been overwhelmingly concentrated in the manufacturing sector. By the end of 2008, the manufacturing sector had attracted nearly two-thirds of the total accumulative FDI inflows into China. With the rapid increase in FDI inflows into manufacturing, FDI firms in the manufacturing sector have also undergone some structural changes. Two are most important. First, the growth rate of FDI inflows into the technology-intensive sector and capital-intensive sector was much higher than that of FDI inflows into the labour-intensive sector. As a result, the relative importance of FDI firms in the technology-intensive sector has surpassed the relative importance of FDI firms in the labour-intensive sector in Chinese manufacturing. In 2008, FDI firms in the technology-intensive sector held 42.15 per cent of the sector's total assets, while FDI firms in the labour-intensive sector held 33.79 per cent of the sector's total assets. Second, the investment pattern of FDI firms in manufacturing has been changing gradually, especially after China's entry into the WTO. FDI inflows into manufacturing have shifted from being concentrated in the labour-intensive sector in the 1980s and the early 1990s towards increasing investment in the technology-intensive sector and the capital-intensive sector in the late 1990s and the 2000s. As a result, the technology-intensive and capital-intensive sectors have become more and more important to FDI, and by 2008 their combined share reached 68.89 per cent of the total assets of FDI firms in manufacturing.

Second, several differences in investment and production behaviour between the two major groups of investors, the overseas Chinese investors and the foreign country investors, have been identified:

- The overseas Chinese investors tend to invest more in the labour-intensive sector while the foreign country investors tend to invest more in the capital-intensive and technology-intensive sectors. This is clearly revealed by the relative sector investment intensity indexes, which measure the relative importance of a sector as a host for an investor's investments as compared to all manufacturing sectors. For the overseas Chinese investors, only the labour-intensive sector's index is above 100 per cent, indicating that the labour-intensive sector is a more important host sector for the overseas Chinese investors' investments as compared to the capital-intensive sector and technology-intensive sector in Chinese manufacturing. By contrast, for the foreign country investors, the relative sector investment intensity indexes are above 100 per cent both for the capital-intensive sector and the technology-intensive sector, indicating that these sectors are more important as host sectors for foreign country investors' investments than the labour-intensive sector in Chinese manufacturing.

- In terms of the types of entry, the study finds that for both foreign country investors and the overseas Chinese investors the more technology-intensive a sector is, the more likely it is to set up wholly owned enterprises. This is consistent with the theoretical predictions that the greater the high-technology intensity of the intangible assets, the more important it is for the MNEs to protect such assets, and the more likely it is for the MNEs to set up wholly owned enterprises rather than to enter into joint ventures with local partners.

- One interesting finding is that the overseas Chinese investors tend to have stronger incentives to secure control over their business than the foreign country investors. This is reflected by the higher propensity by the overseas Chinese investors to set up wholly owned enterprises. It seems contradictory with the theoretical predictions that the foreign country investors possessing more intangible assets should have a higher propensity to set up wholly owned enterprises than the overseas Chinese investors. In fact, given the high transaction costs of doing business in China for the foreign country investors compared to the overseas Chinese investors, it is a rational choice for foreign country investors to enter into joint ventures with local Chinese partners in order to reduce the costs of doing business. However, this may imply that foreign country investors might not bring in the most advanced technologies when entering into joint ventures with local Chinese partners for the purpose of reducing the costs of protecting their intangible assets. However, the study also finds that the shares of wholly owned enterprises for both the overseas Chinese affiliates and the foreign country affiliates have been increasing over time, and the gap between the overseas Chinese investors and the foreign countries investors in the propensity to set up wholly owned enterprises has been greatly reduced, indicating that the two groups of investors have been increasingly choosing wholly owned enterprises as the main entry mode to invest in China. This implies that China's business environment has been improving and the transaction costs of doing business in China for FDI firms in general and for foreign country investors in particular have been greatly reduced. The increasing propensity of foreign country investors to set up wholly owned enterprises also implies that foreign country investors have increasingly brought more intangible assets and advanced technology into China.

- The overseas Chinese affiliates have a higher export propensity than the foreign country affiliates. This is consistent with the revealed investment patterns of the two groups of investors. It is also interesting to note that both the overseas Chinese affiliates and the foreign country affiliates have a much higher propensity to export than Chinese domestic enterprises. This implies that using China as a low cost of production export platform is one of the main motives for FDI in China.

- The overseas Chinese investors in China tend to adopt more labour-intensive technologies than the foreign country investors. As revealed by the capital intensity and the scale of capital, the overseas Chinese affiliates not only have a lower capital to labour ratio but also are much smaller than the foreign country affiliates. As a result, the overseas Chinese affiliates have lower average labour productivity than the foreign country affiliates.

- Finally, the comparison between foreign country affiliates and the overseas Chinese affiliates with Chinese domestic enterprises also reveals some interesting findings. FDI firms on average are more advanced than, and superior to, Chinese domestic firms in terms of firm size, capital intensity and labour productivity. However, the relative superiority of FDI firms over Chinese domestic enterprises in capital intensity and labour productivity has been lessening.

In the labour-intensive sector, both capital intensity and labour productivity of the overseas Chinese affiliates have fallen below those of Chinese domestic enterprises, though FDI firms still have relatively higher capital intensity and labour productivity in the capital-intensive and technology-intensive sectors than the Chinese domestic enterprises. These changes indicate that through enterprise reform and competition, Chinese domestic enterprises have been catching up with FDI firms, especially in the labour-intensive sector.

Through the analyses of Chapters 6 and 7, the Chinese case has offered valuable evidence on the differences among the main groups of investors. The distinctive features of the overseas Chinese investments as compared to the foreign country investments are confirmed. The diversity of foreign investors suggests that there is considerable scope for China to introduce and absorb foreign capital, technology, and modern management skills in many industries from the world.

In terms of the economic impacts of FDI on China's economy, theoretically, because FDI brings into the host country a package of capital, technology, production know-how, management skills, marketing skills and information, competition and so on, it is expected that FDI can increase host countries' economic growth, via capital formation, the creation of employment opportunity, promotion of international trade, technology transfer and spillover effects to the domestic economy. During the past three decades, China has attracted a huge amount of FDI inflows and at the same time it has achieved remarkable economic growth with an annual growth rate around 10 per cent. What has been the contribution of FDI to China's economic growth? Chapter 8 investigated empirically the contribution of FDI, with a special emphasis on whether FDI has generated spillover effects on China's economic growth. Based on theoretical foundations, an augmented empirical growth model was specified, and a panel dataset containing China's 30 provinces over the period from 1986 to 2005 was used under the fixed effects regression model.

The regression results provide strong evidence that FDI contributes to China's economic growth both directly through increasing capital input and indirectly through positive spillover effects. This implies that provinces with higher FDI inflows will have higher economic growth contributed to directly by the increase in foreign capital input associated with the high productivity of FDI firms and indirectly by the diffusion of technology spillovers from FDI to the local economy. The study reveals that FDI has made a significant contribution to China's economic growth. During the period from 1986 to 2005, out of the 11.77 per cent average growth rate of China's real GDP, 1.46 percentage points came from direct and indirect contributions of FDI, which constitute 12.43 per cent of the total growth rate in that period.

The study also reveals that the impact of FDI on economic growth varies between China's regions. The regression results show that both the direct and indirect contributions of FDI to economic growth are higher in the eastern coastal region than those in the central and western regions. This implies that, given the level of FDI stock, provinces with higher human capital stock, a higher level of economic development (per capita GDP), a higher level of R&D activities, a higher level of infrastructure, and a higher level of economic interactions with the rest of the world, will facilitate and enhance the diffusion of technology spillovers from FDI to the local economy, and therefore will benefit more from FDI in promoting provincial economic growth.

Finally, the study finds that although the empirical regression results show a positive and statistically significant impact of the spillover effects of FDI on economic growth, the magnitude of the contribution from the spillover effects of FDI to China's economic growth was still very small. This implies that China still has a lot of benefits to gain from FDI.

According to the OLI framework explaining FDI, FDI firms can compete locally with more informed domestic firms because they possess firm-specific ownership advantages, such as advanced technology and know-how, mature marketing and managerial skills, well-organized international distribution channels, coordinated relationships with suppliers and good reputation. Since both FDI firms and domestic firms can imitate each other in the same market, domestic firms are usually expected to obtain an additional increase in productivity. This positive impact of foreign presence on domestic firms' productivity is called technology spillovers of FDI. What would be the impact of FDI on China's domestic firms' productivity through technology spillovers? The question is significant in a theoretical sense as it is hypothesized that FDI contributes positively to the host country's productivity growth through its technology spillovers to domestic firms. The question is also significant in an empirical sense as evidence from both developed and developing countries varies in supporting the existence of positive externalities generated by FDI. Therefore, Chapter 9, using the firm-level census data of China's manufacturing industries during the period from 2000 to 2003, investigated empirically the impact of FDI on China's domestic firms' productivity by focusing on examining the horizontal technology spillovers of FDI on China's domestic firms' productivity.

After controlling for the inter-industry linkages between FDI presence and domestic firms, the sources of FDI from Hong Kong and Taiwan, the dummy variables of region, industry and time, and dealing with the selection bias from firms' exit and entry with the neighbourhood matching technique, and the endogeneity problem with the FD technique, the study finds that there is a non-linear relationship between FDI presence and domestic firms' productivity in the same industry. Foreign direct investment initially has significant positive spillovers on the productivity of domestic firms within the same industry, however, the marginal positive spillovers effect decreases as the share of FDI increases, and it even becomes negative when the share of FDI in an industry reaches a critical value (a turning point). The regression results also show that the share of FDI in Chinese manufacturing on average has not reached the turning point during the period of analysis, 2000 to 2003. This means that a further increase in FDI would continue to benefit China's domestic manufacturing firms in terms of further improvement in their productivity.

However, the study finds that FDI does not have significant spillover effects on China's domestic firms' productivity through backward and forward industrial linkages, and also finds that overseas Chinese investment on average does not have higher spillovers than FDI from other foreign investors on China's domestic firms' productivity.

Since the early 1980s, China's exports have grown rapidly and, as a result, China has become the largest exporting nation in the world. Apart from the market-oriented economic reforms and trade liberalization particularly since the 1990s and after China's accession to the WTO in 2001, one of the main sources of China's rapid export expansion is the massive inflows of FDI associated with the fast export growth of FDI firms, whose export share in China's total exports increased from 0.05 per cent in 1980 to 55.25 per cent in 2008. What, however, are the impacts of FDI on China's domestic firms' exports? This question is worthy of both theoretical analysis and empirical investigation because it is expected that export spillovers are one of the main benefits generated by FDI to host country economies, which not only can help domestic firms improve productivity, promote specialization and increase exports, but can also help host countries improve resource allocation and play their comparative advantages in international trade. Therefore, Chapter 10, using the firm-level census data of China's manufacturing industries during the 2000 to 2003 period, investigated empirically the impact of FDI on China's domestic firms' exports.

After controlling for the impact of firm-specific characteristics of productivity, capital to labour ratio, R&D activities, scale, age and indirect foreign investment of domestic firms, and dealing with some econometric problems of endogeneity and sample selection, the empirical regressions reveal that FDI firms have a positive and statistically significant impact on the export propensity of domestic firms in the same industry through demonstration effects, and this positive impact is mainly generated by high-exporting FDI firms. The study also finds some evidence that FDI firms, in particular high-exporting FDI firms, have positive export spillovers on domestic firms in the downstream industries through forward linkage, meaning that domestic firms can get intermediate inputs of good quality from upstream FDI firms. Thus, domestic firms can improve competitiveness and increase exports.

However, the study does not find significant evidence that FDI firms, particularly high-exporting FDI firms, generate export spillovers to domestic firms through backward industrial linkage. An explanation is that FDI firms, particularly high-exporting FDI firms, are highly engaged in the processing trade in China. Because they are concentrated in the special export-processing zones and the import duty-free zones specifically designed for export-oriented FDI firms, import almost all of the materials and intermediate inputs from overseas, and export the processed and assembled products abroad, they have very few industrial linkages with domestic firms. Therefore, these FDI firms generate no significant inter-industry spillovers to domestic firms. This finding is consistent with the findings in Chapter 9, in which we do not find significant inter-industry productivity spillovers from FDI firms to China's domestic firms.

POLICY IMPLICATIONS

Referring to the results of this study, the following policy implications are relevant to China's further attraction and utilization of FDI.

First, although China has achieved substantial progress in its FDI policy reform within a relatively short period, comparing China's current FDI policy to the WTO's investment-related principles, China's current FDI policy can be further improved, particularly in respect of transparency, national treatment and the protection of intellectual property rights. With respect to the principle of transparency, China still maintains a complex application process for FDI approval, which can be simplified and made more transparent through further policy reform.

In terms of national treatment, on the one hand, since the initial offer in the early 1980s of tax incentives to FDI firms in the SEZs and open coastal cities, China has extensively but selectively used tax incentives as 'economic levers' to guide FDI into its designated regions, economic sectors and industries. The extensive tax incentives offered to FDI firms not only distorted the global capital markets, causing potential diversion of global FDI flows, but also distorted domestic capital markets, creating incentives for round-tripping FDI, and at the same time created unfair competition between domestic firms and FDI firms. Not until January 2008 did the Chinese government unified the tax rates for FDI firms and domestic firms at 25 per cent, and in December 2010 China began levying the city maintenance and construction tax as well as the education surcharge on FDI firms and foreign individuals, symbolizing the end of 'super national treatment' offered to FDI firms and marking the beginning of a fully unified national tax system for domestic and foreign companies. This is a very important move in the right direction to bring China's tax laws more in line with international standards and create a more consistent tax climate for the operations of FDI firms. The unification of the tax system is a fulfilment of China's commitment to the WTO for equal treatment of domestic and overseas investors and it will certainly and substantially reduce the incentive for round-tripping FDI.

On the other hand, to protect some industries and domestic firms the Chinese government has introduced regulations to prohibit or restrict FDI participation in some sectors and industries. For example, in the 2007 Catalogue for the Guidance of Foreign Investment Industries, in order to protect national economic and spiritual security, China takes a prudent attitude towards the liberalization of certain strategic and sensitive industries. Under the 2007 Catalogue, many encouraged items for FDI are still limited to cooperative joint ventures or equity joint ventures, especially the survey and exploration of important mineral resources which is limited to joint venture or Sino-foreign cooperation, restricted or even prohibited. FDI in survey and exploration of tungsten, molybdenum, tin, antimony and fluorite was formerly restricted, but is completely forbidden now. Many restricted items are limited to joint venture rather than wholly foreign-owned enterprise and the Chinese partner must hold the controlling interests in the joint venture. Participation in the publishing and media industry is still prohibited. In recognition of the Internet as an alternative to publishing, various Internet-based businesses, such as news websites, web-streaming audio-visual services, e-commerce and culture-related websites, have been newly added as a prohibited category in the 2007 Catalogue.

Therefore, foreign investors are not treated equally in accessing and doing business in certain areas in China. The application of national treatment will not only level the playing field between foreign and domestic firms but also provide equal incentives and opportunities for various types of FDI and different groups of foreign investors, as well as provide equal access to China's domestic market and more business opportunities for foreign investors.

Protection of intellectual property rights has long been an issue in China. The weak legal framework and particularly the weak enforcement for intellectual property rights protection in China will not only deter the inflows of FDI with high technology but will also have a negative impact on foreign investors' decisions to bring technology into China. This could be one of the main reasons for the low level of FDI inflows from developed countries into China. Although there has been some improvement, it is still very important for China to further improve the legal framework and strengthen the enforcement for intellectual property rights protection if it wants to attract more FDI inflows with high technology from the world especially from the developed countries.

Second, the uneven regional distribution of FDI concentrated in the coastal areas has greatly contributed to the economic growth of coastal provinces. However, we should point out that this kind of regional distribution of FDI is not compatible with the regional distribution of China's natural resource endowments. China's natural resources are mainly located in the inland areas, particularly in the western region, and a large number of China's heavy industrial projects established since the 1950s are located in the inland provinces. Therefore, if China wanted to help the economic development of inland provinces, particularly the western less developed areas, it could: (1) shift the preferential policies for FDI from regional priority to industrial priority, namely, to encourage those FDI projects engaged in technologically advanced, infrastructure-based, transportation, communication, agriculture, environmental protection, energy and raw materials industries, and modern service industries; (2) adjust its regional development strategy by offering special economic and industrial development policies to the central and western regions, and the launch of the west development strategy in 1998 was an important step in the right direction; and (3) encourage coastal areas to transfer managerial skills and technology accumulated and obtained from attracting and utilizing FDI to the inland regions in order to benefit more from FDI nationwide.

Third, the current composition of FDI sources in China has both advantages and disadvantages. The major advantage is that the overwhelming dominance of FDI from developing source countries and economies, particularly from the overseas Chinese investors, is well matched with China's abundant labour resource endowments and comparative advantage in labour-intensive activities, which will help China to play its comparative advantage in international trade, thus promoting China's exports. However, the main disadvantage is that since the overseas Chinese investments are mainly in labour-intensive activities and relatively low in technology, as well as small in scale, their roles in upgrading China's overall technological level and industrial structure are limited and much less than that of the investments from developed source countries. This may constrain China's participation in the international division of production and may also increase the risks and vulnerability of China in international competition as its specialization becomes narrower and is more based on the costs of labour.

There are many reasons for the low level of FDI inflows from the developed countries into China. First, the economic and technological gap between the developed countries and China is relatively large and the transfer of technology is hampered, to a certain extent, by the appropriateness of the technology. Second, the firms of developed countries usually possess more advanced technology and production techniques. Since the legal framework for protecting intellectual property rights in China is relatively weak, the firms from the developed countries possessing advanced technology and production techniques are reluctant to invest in China. Third, the service sector in developed countries is advanced and has recorded the highest growth rates in global FDI flows over the last three decades. However, most of China's service industries were closed to FDI before its 2001 accession to the WTO. Fourth, the large MNEs are the main carriers of FDI from developed countries and cross-border M&As are the increasingly important means by which they carry out FDI. However, cross-border M&As transactions by foreign investors in China have only been allowed in an experimental fashion in recent years. All of these factors have had a negative impact on the investment decision of the developed country investors.

The current composition of FDI sources in China needs to be diversified if China wants to benefit more from FDI. The diversification of FDI sources is not only necessary for China to attract a high level of FDI, but is also very important for it to attract high quality FDI from the developed countries. In general, enterprises from developed countries with high technological and innovative capabilities have advantages in high technology, product differentiation, managerial and entrepreneurial skills, and knowledge-based intangible assets. Because of these advantages, investors from developed countries are more interested in the Chinese market. The general implication is that host countries with larger market size, faster economic growth and higher income will attract more market-oriented FDI. China's huge domestic market, fast growth and rising income are very attractive to market-oriented FDI from developed countries. Therefore, China has a great potential to attract FDI from developed countries. However, to realize its potential, China should fulfil its commitments to the WTO in trade and investment liberalization, particularly in strengthening the intellectual property rights protection, opening more service sectors to FDI, and relaxing restrictions in cross-border M&As.

Fourth, over the past three decades the large amount of FDI inflows into China has made great contributions to China's economy directly through capital formation, employment creation and export expansion. However, in terms of the spillover effects of FDI on China's economy, although the study finds positive and statistically significant spillover effects of FDI on China's economic growth and on domestic firms' productivity and exports through intra-industry demonstration effects, the study also reveals that the spillover effects of FDI were not only very small in terms of the magnitude of the contribution to China's economic growth, but were also weak or absent in terms of forward and particularly backward spillovers through inter-industrial linkages to domestic firms' productivity and exports. An explanation is that FDI firms, particularly high-exporting FDI firms, are highly engaged in processing trade in China. They are not only geographically isolated from China's domestic firms by locating in the export-processing zones and import duty-free zones, but also have little economic contact with China's domestic firms due to their strong outward sourcing and marketing operation behaviours. Because they are concentrated in the special export-processing zones and the import duty-free zones specifically designed for export-oriented FDI firms and import almost all the materials and intermediate inputs from overseas and export the processed and assembled products abroad, they have very little inter-industrial linkages with China's domestic firms. Therefore, these FDI firms generate no significant forward and backward spillovers to domestic firms through inter-industrial linkages.

The results of this study raise a very important policy implication for the Chinese government's FDI policies. For the past three decades, the Chinese government's FDI policies have been deliberately biased towards attracting export-oriented FDI aiming to boost its exports. Undoubtedly, the export-oriented FDI policies have been very successful in terms of promoting China's export growth. As a result, China has become the largest exporting nation and the largest holder of foreign reserves in the world. However, China's domestic firms have benefited very little from the export-oriented FDI policies in terms of the positive spillovers from the export-oriented FDI firms through inter-industrial linkages. Therefore, the Chinese government should adjust its FDI policies to encourage contact, information exchange, production and technological cooperation, joint R&D activities, industrial linkages and competition between domestic firms and FDI firms, in order to enhance and accelerate the diffusion of positive spillovers from FDI to China's economy.

PROSPECTS FOR FDI INFLOWS INTO CHINA

To conclude this study, we cannot escape the question of the prospects for FDI inflows into China especially given the current global financial crisis.

The current global financial crisis started in 2008 and has severely affected the world economy as well as world FDI flows. Global FDI inflows declined from a historic record of US$2.10 trillion in 2007 to US$1.77 trillion in 2008, decreasing by 15.71 per cent, and further declined to US$1.11 trillion in 2009, dropping by 37.29 per cent. China is not immune from this crisis. Foreign direct investment inflows into China have also been affected by the crisis.

Foreign direct investment inflows into China's non-financial sectors dropped from US$92.4 billion in 2008 to US$90 billion in 2009, declining by 2.67 per cent. Foreign direct investment inflows into China's financial sector dropped sharply, from US$15.92 billion in 2008 to US$4.97 billion in 2009, declining by 68.78 per cent. This sharp decline was mainly attributed to two factors. First, the financial crisis has severely weakened the ability of foreign financial institutions, especially those of developed countries, to undertake strategic investment in China's financial sector. Second, some foreign strategic investors sold stakes in Chinese banks in order to improve their own balance sheets. For example, in January 2009, the United Bank of Switzerland (UBS) sold its entire 3.378 billion shares in the Bank of China (BOC) for US$800 million; and the Bank of America (BOA) cut its 19.13 per cent stake in the China Construction Bank (CCB) to 16.72 per cent by selling 5.62 billion shares for US$2.8 billion (*ETCN*, 2009). Also in January 2009, the Royal Bank of Scotland (RBS) sold its entire stake in BOC for US$2.43 billion. In April 2009, American Express Co. and German insurer Allianz sold half of their shares in the Industrial and Commercial Bank of China (ICBC) for US$318 million and US$1.6 billion respectively (*The Sydney Morning Herald*, 2009). In May 2009, BOA again sold 5.7 per cent of its stake in CCB for US$7.3 billion (*The Wall Street Journal*, 2009). In June 2009, Goldman Sachs Group Inc. sold 20 per cent of its shares in ICBC for US$2 billion (*Caijing*, 2009). The above transactions amounted to around US$18 billion of divestments by foreign strategic investors in Chinese banks in 2009.

Undoubtedly, the global financial crisis has had a negative impact on FDI inflows into China. However, compared to the sharp decline of world FDI inflows, its negative impact on FDI inflows into China has been moderate. There are a number of reasons why FDI inflows into China have been resilient and why MNEs remain committed to investing in China.

First, China's overall investment environment remains attractive, with relatively efficient public services, good infrastructure, abundant and well-educated human resources, low labour costs, and macroeconomic and political stability. This makes China one of the most attractive locations for FDI.

Second, China, as the largest developing economy and a fast-growing

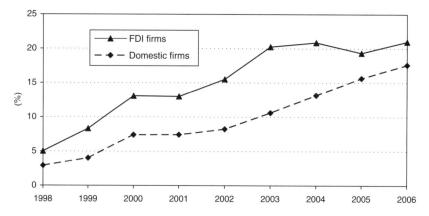

Sources: Calculated from National Bureau of Statistics of China (various issues), *China Statistical Yearbook*, Beijing: China Statistics Press.

Figure 11.1   *Profit rates of domestic firms and FDI firms in manufacturing sector in China, 1998–2006*

economy, has remained attractive to FDI, particularly to the market-seeking FDI. Foreign direct investment firms in China are very profitable. As shown in Figure 11.1, the profit rate (measured by the ratio of profits to the net value of fixed assets) of FDI firms is not only higher than that of domestic firms but has been increasing over time and has been over 20 per cent since 2003. A survey by the United States–China Business Council in March 2009 revealed that 88 per cent of foreign businesses in China are profitable, 81 per cent have a higher profit margin in China than elsewhere, and 89 per cent select China as their first-time investment location (*Xinhuanet*, 2009). China maintained high economic growth during the period of 2008 to 2010, with a real GDP growth rate of 9.6 per cent, 9.2 per cent and 10.3 per cent respectively. Therefore, China is very attractive to market-oriented FDI and provides huge market opportunities for MNEs.

Third, China's abundant and relatively well-educated labour force with low labour costs is attractive to labour-intensive and export-oriented FDI projects. Despite the global economic recession, China's labour-intensive products are still very competitive in the world markets. On the one hand, with good quality and low prices, China's labour-intensive products are preferred by consumers. On the other, China's labour-intensive products are mainly daily consumer goods with low elasticities of demand. Therefore, the negative impact of the economic recession on demand for China's labour-intensive products is relatively small. China's exports increased from US$1201.66 billion in 2009 to US$1577.93 billion in 2010, up 31.31 per cent. This is a good sign of recovery of China's exports and is also a positive signal to export-oriented FDI to increase investment in China.

Fourth, in the face of the global financial crisis, in November 2008, the Chinese government announced a 4 trillion yuan (about US$600 billion) economic stimulus package to boost economic growth through public investment for three years. It may help keep the annual GDP growth rate of China at 9 to 10 per cent for this period. By enhancing growth prospects and increasing investor confidence, the plan may help maintain FDI inflows into China.

Fifth, China has implemented a series of favourable FDI and trade policies to promote FDI inflows. China decentralized FDI approval rights in March 2009, allowing provincial authorities to approve FDI projects under US$100 million. China has adjusted six times the tax rebate rates for exports to increase tax rebate for some export products since 2008. As a result, the comprehensive tax rebate rates reached 12.4 per cent.[1] These policy changes are necessary to cope with the global financial crisis and will help attract FDI inflows.

In April 2010, the Chinese State Council released new regulations on foreign investment (State Council, 2010). According to the new regulations, China will improve good business conditions, welcome foreign investment in high-technology industries, service sectors, energy-saving and environmental protection, but FDI into pollution- and energy-intensive projects or industries running at overcapacity are strictly prohibited. China will continue to support Chinese A-share listed companies in further introducing strategic investors from home and abroad, and standardize foreign companies' investment in domestic securities and cross-border M&A transactions. Qualified foreign-funded companies are allowed to go public, and issue corporate bonds or medium-term bills in China. Multinationals are encouraged to set up regional headquarters, R&D centres, procurement hubs, financial management and other functional offices in China. Importing items for scientific and technological development by qualified foreign-funded R&D centres will be exempt from tariffs, importing value-added tax, and goods and services tax by the end of 2010. Foreign direct investment firms are also encouraged to increase their investment in China's central and western regions, particularly in environmentally friendly and labour-intensive companies (*People's Daily Online*, 2010a). The new regulations are expected not only to increase FDI inflows into China but also to improve the industrial and sectoral structure, regional distribution, and the quality of FDI inflows.

All of these factors have contributed positively to attracting FDI inflows into China. As a result, FDI inflows increased from US$90 billion in 2009 to US$105.74 billion in 2010, up 17.45 per cent and reaching the highest level in China's inward FDI history.

However, one policy factor that may create some uncertainties for FDI inflows is China's foreign exchange rate policy. Since the beginning of 2010, the developed countries led by the USA have renewed the pressure on China to reform its foreign exchange rate policy and to appreciate the RMB, as it is assumed to be 40 per cent undervalued by C. Fred Bergsten, head of the Peterson Institute for International Economics (Cleveland. com, 2010). Paul Krugman claimed that China's policy to keep its currency undervalued has become a significant drag on global economic recovery (*The New York Times*, 2010). However, the Chinese government rejected the claim and resists the pressure to revalue its currency.

What would be the possible impacts of RMB appreciation on FDI inflows into China? First, as the value of the RMB increases, so does the value of Chinese assets in terms of foreign currency. As a result, it will be more expensive for foreign investors to invest in China, thus having a negative impact on FDI inflows into China. Second, as the RMB appreciates, Chinese-made products become more expensive, which will reduce the competitiveness of Chinese products in international markets. As a result, the profit margin of export firms will be reduced, thus having a negative impact on export-oriented FDI inflows into China. Third, there might be a capital flight out of China soon after the sharp appreciation of the RMB. Some foreign investors might sell their assets (especially in the real estate sector) and repatriate their profits abroad so as to make windfalls from the sharp change in the exchange rate. Undoubtedly, in the short term, a sharp appreciation of the RMB will have a negative impact on FDI inflows into China.

As China's economy grows faster and larger, China will play a more important role in the global economy. So, it is inevitable that the RMB will appreciate. The question is how fast and by how much the RMB will appreciate. During a visit in April 2010 by the Chinese President Hu Jintao to Washington, DC, the USA and China seem to have reached an agreement with regard to the exchange rate between their two currencies. The agreement is that the US government will stop complaining about it, and China will do whatever it can to reform its exchange rate regime, including a modest rise in the RMB some time in the near future (China. org.cn, 2010).

In summary, the prospects for FDI inflows into China are promising. Although the global financial crisis has had a negative impact on FDI inflows into China, especially into the financial sector, compared with the large decline of world FDI inflows, the negative impact of the crisis on FDI inflows into China has been moderate. China's sound and competitive overall investment environment, a large and fast-growing domestic market, abundant and relatively well-educated labour resources, macroeconomic and political stability, and its government's strong policy response to counter the crisis and to further liberalize trade and investment, have all made China one of the most attractive locations for FDI. Therefore, China will remain one of the top FDI destinations in the world, and FDI will continue to play a significant role in China's economy.

NOTE

1. The full tax rebate rate for export is 17 per cent.

References

A.T. Kearney (2007), '2005 Foreign Direct Investment Confidence Index', available at http://www.atkearney.com/images/global/pdf/FDICI_2005.pdf (accessed 19 February 2011).

A.T. Kearney (2010), '2010 Foreign Direct Investment Confidence Index', available at http://www.atkearney.com/index.php/Publications/foreign-direct-investment-confidence-index.html (accessed 19 February 2011).

Aitken, B., H. Hanson and A. Harrison (1997), 'Spillovers, foreign direct investment, and export behaviour', *Journal of International Economics*, **43** (1), 103–32.

Aitken, B. and A. Harrison (1999), 'Do domestic firms benefit from foreign direct investment? Evidence from panel data', *American Economic Review*, **89** (3), 605–18.

Amiti, M. and B. Javorcik (2008), 'Trade costs and location of foreign firms in China', *Journal of Development Economics*, **85** (1–2), 129–49.

Anderson, J. (1979), 'A theoretical foundation for the gravity equation', *American Economic Review*, **69** (1), 106–16.

Anderson, J. and E. van Wincoop (2003), 'Gravity with gravitas: a solution to the border puzzle', *American Economic Review*, **93** (1), 170–92.

Anderson, K. (1990), *Changing Comparative Advantages in China: Effects on Food, Feed, and Fibre Markets*, Paris: Development Centre of the OECD.

Anderson, M. and S. Smith (1999a), 'Canadian provinces in world trade: engagement and detachment', *Canadian Journal of Economics*, **32** (1), 23–37.

Anderson, M. and S. Smith (1999b), 'Do national borders really matter? Canada–U.S. regional trade reconsidered', *Review of International Economics*, **7** (2), 219–27.

Ash, R. and Y. Kueh (1993), 'Economic integration within greater China: trade and investment flows between China, Hong Kong and Taiwan', *The China Quarterly*, **136**, 711–45.

Barrios, S., H. Gorg and E. Strobl (2003), 'Explaining firms' export behaviour: R&D, spillovers and the destination market', *Oxford Bulletin of Economics and Statistics*, **65** (4), 475–96.

Barro, R. and X. Sala-i-Martin, (1995), *Economic Growth*, New York: McGraw-Hill.

Bergstrand, J. (1989), 'The generalized gravity equation, monopolistic competition, and the factor-proportions theory in international trade', *Review of Economics and Statistics*, **71** (1), 143–52.

Beijing Review (1986), 'Wholly foreign-owned enterprises', 5 May, p.16.

Bevan, A. and S. Estrin (2000), 'The determinants of foreign direct investment in transition economies', Working Paper No.342, Centre for New Emerging Markets, London Business School.

Blalock, G. and P. Gertler (2008), 'Welfare gains from foreign direct investment through technology transfer to local suppliers', *Journal of International Economics,* **74** (2), 402–21.

Blanchard, J. (2007), 'China, multinational corporations, and globalization: Beijing and Microsoft battle over the opening of China's gates', *Asian Perspective*, **31** (3), 67–102.

Blomstrom, M. (1986), 'Foreign investment and productive efficiency: the case of Mexico', *Journal of Industrial Economics*, **35** (1), 97–110.

Blomstrom, M. and M. Zejan (1991), 'Why do multinational firms seek out joint ventures', *Journal of International Development*, **3** (1), 53–63.

Blomstrom, M. and A. Kokko (1998), 'Multinational corporations and spillovers', *Journal of Economic Surveys*, **12** (3), 247–77.

Braga, C. and G. Bannister (1994), 'East Asian investment and trade: prospects for growing regionalisation in the 1990s', *Transnational Corporations*, **3** (1), 97–136.

Branstetter, G. and R. Feenstra (1999), 'Trade and foreign direct investment in China: a political economy approach', NBER Working Paper No. 7100, Cambridge, MA: National Bureau of Economic Research.

Breslin, S. (2003), 'Foreign direct investment in China: what the figures don't tell us', paper presented at Asia-Link Conference, 'Regional governance: greater China in the 21st century', 24–25 October, University of Durham, available at http://www2.warwick.ac.uk/fac/soc/pais/staff/breslin/research/fdi.pdf (accessed 19 February 2011).

Broadman, G. and X. Sun (1997), 'The distribution of foreign direct investment in China', *The World Economy*, **20** (3), 339–61.

Brown, A. (1949), *Applied Economics, Aspects of the World Economy in War and Peace*, London: George Allen and Unwin.

Buck, T., X. Liu, Y. Wei and X. Liu (2007), 'The trade development path and export spillovers in China: a missing link?', *Management International Review*, **47** (5), 683–706.

Buckley, P. (1987), *The Theory of the Multinational Enterprise*, Acta Universitas Upsalienis, Uppsala: Almquist and Wiksell International.

Buckley, P. and M. Casson (1976), *The Future of the Multinational Enterprise*, London: Macmillan.

Buckley, P., J. Clegg and A. Cross (2007), 'The determinants of Chinese outward foreign direct investment', *Journal of International Business Studies*, **38** (4), 499–518.

Buckley, P., J. Clegg, C. Wang and A. Cross (2002), 'FDI, regional differences and economic growth: panel data evidence from China', *Transnational Corporations*, **2** (1), 1–28.

Caijing (2009), 'Goldman Sachs selling 0.9% stake in ICBC for US$2 billion', 2 June, available at http://english.caijing.com.cn/2009-06-02/110174882.html (accessed 19 February 2011).

Campos, N. and Y. Kinoshita (2002), 'Foreign direct investment as technology transferred: some panel evidence from the transition economies', *Manchester School*, **70** (3), 398–419.

Casson, M. (1987), *The Firm and the Market*, Oxford: Basil Blackwell.

Caves, R. (1971), 'Industrial corporations: the industrial economics of foreign investment', *Economica*, **38** (1), 1–27.

Caves, R. (1974a), 'Causes of direct investment: foreign firms' shares in Canadian and United Kingdom manufacturing industries', *Review of Economics and Statistics*, **56**, 272–93.

Caves, R. (1974b), 'Multinational firms, competition and productivity in host country markets', *Economica*, **41** (162), 176–93.

Caves, R. (1982), *Multinational Enterprise and Economic Analysis*, Cambridge: Cambridge University Press.

Caves, R. (1996), *Multinational Enterprise and Economic Analysis*, 2nd edition, Cambridge: Cambridge University Press.

Caves, R. (2007), *Multinational Enterprise and Economic Analysis*, 3rd edition, Cambridge: Cambridge University Press.

Chantasasawat, B., K. Fung, H. Iizaka and A. Siu (2004), 'Foreign direct investment in China and East Asia', available at http://www.hiebs.hku.hk/working_paper_updates/pdf/wp1135.pdf (accessed 19 February 2011).

Chen, C. (1996), 'Recent development in foreign direct investment in China', Chinese Economies Research Centre Working Paper, No. 3, University of Adelaide.

Chen, C. (1997a), 'The evolution and main features of China's foreign direct investment policies', Chinese Economies Research Centre Working Paper, No. 15, University of Adelaide.

Chen, C. (1997b), 'The location determinants of foreign direct investment in developing countries', Chinese Economies Research Centre Working Paper, No. 12, University of Adelaide.

Chen, C. (1997c), 'Comparison of investment behaviour of source countries in China', Chinese Economies Research Centre Working Paper, No. 14, University of Adelaide.

Chen, C. (1997d), 'Foreign direct investment and trade: an empirical investigation of the evidence from China', Chinese Economies Research Centre Working Paper, No. 11, University of Adelaide.

Chen, C. (1999), 'The impact of FDI and trade', in Y. Wu (ed.), *Foreign Direct Investment and Economic Growth in China*, Cheltenham, UK and Northampton, MA, USA: Edward Elgar Publishing, pp. 71–99.

Chen, C. (2002), 'Foreign direct investment: prospects and policies', in C. Pigott (ed.), *China in the World Economy: The Domestic Policy Challenges*, Paris: OECD, pp. 321–58.

Chen, C. (2003), 'Location determinants and provincial distribution of FDI', in R. Garnaut and L. Song (eds), *China New Engine of World Growth*, Canberra: Asia Pacific Press, pp. 189–216.

Chen, C. (2006), 'Changing patterns in China's agricultural trade after WTO accession', in R. Garnaut and L. Song (eds), *The Turning Point in China's Economic Development*, Canberra: Asia Pacific Press, pp. 197–224.

Chen, C. (2007), 'Foreign direct investment in China: trends and characteristics after WTO accession', in R. Garnaut and L. Song (eds), *China – Linking Markets for Growth*, Canberra: Asia Pacific Press, pp. 197–224.

Chen, C. (2010a), 'Foreign direct investment in China: trends, characteristics and impacts', in C. Findlay, M. Pangestu and D. Parsons (eds), *Light The Lamp: Papers on World Trade and Investment in Memory of Bijit Bora*, Singapore: World Scientific, pp. 179–218.

Chen, C. (2010b), 'Asia foreign direct investment and the "China effect"', in R. Garnaut, J. Golley and L. Song (eds), *China: The Next 20 Years of Reform and Development*, Canberra: ANU E Press and Social Sciences Academic Press (China), pp. 221–40.

Chen, C., L. Chang and Y. Zhang (1995), 'The role of foreign direct investment in China's post-1978 economic development', *World Development*, **23** (4), 691–703.

Chen, C., J. Yang and C. Findlay (2008), 'Measuring the effect of food safety standards on China's agricultural exports', *Review of World Economics*, **144** (1), 83–106.

Chen, C.H. (1996), 'Regional determinants of foreign direct investment in mainland China', *Journal of Economic Studies*, **23** (2), 18–30.

Chen, C.Y. (1982), *China's Economic Development, Growth and Structural Changes*, Boulder, CO: Westview Press.

Chen, N. (2004), 'Intra-national versus international trade in the European Union: why do national borders matter?', *Journal of International Economics*, **63** (1), 93–118.

Chen, Y. (2007), 'The upgrading of multinational regional innovation networks in China', *Asia Pacific Business Review*, **13** (3), 373–403.

Cheung, K. (2010), 'Spillover effects of FDI via exports on innovation performance of China's high-technology industries', *Journal of Contemporary China*, **19** (65), 541–57.

China.org.cn (2010), 'US, China "agree" on RMB, Iran', 16 April, available at http://www.china.org.cn/opinion/2010-04/16/content_19832000.htm (accessed 19 February 2011).

Choong, C. and S. Lam (2010), 'The determinants of foreign direct investment in Malaysia: a revisit', *Global Economic Review*, **39** (2), 175–95.

Christofides, L., Q. Li, Z. Liu and I. Min (2003), 'Recent two-stage sample selection procedures with an application to the gender wage gap', *Journal of Business and Economic Statistics*, **21** (3), 396–405.

Chu, B. (ed.) (1987), *Foreign Investment in China: A Question and Answer Guide*, Hong Kong: University Publisher & Printer.

Cleveland.com (2010), 'Pressure growing on China to revalue currency', 24 March, available at http://www.cleveland.com/business/index.ssf/2010/03/pressure_growing_on_china_to_r.html (accessed 19 February 2011).

Cole, M., R. Elliott and J. Zhang (2009), 'Corruption, governance and FDI location in China: a province-level analysis', *Journal of Development Studies*, **45** (9), 1494–512.

Coughlin, C., J. Terza and V. Arromdee (1991), 'State characteristics and the location of foreign direct investment within the United States', *The Review of Economics and Statistics*, **73** (4), 675–83.

Cravino, J., D. Lederman and M. Olarreaga (2007), 'Foreign direct investment in Latin America during the emergence of China and India: stylized facts', World Bank, Policy Research Working Paper 4360, available at http://ideas.repec.org/p/wbk/wbrwps/4360.html (accessed 19 February 2011).

Croix, S., M. Plummer and K. Lee (eds) (1995), *Emerging Patterns of East Asian Investment in China*, Armonk, NY: East Gate.

Damijan J., B. Majcen, M. Knell and M. Rojec (2003), 'The role of FDI, absorptive capacity and trade in transferring technology to transition countries: evidence from firm panel data for eight transition countries', *Economic Systems*, **27** (2), 189–204.

de Mello (1997), 'Foreign direct investment in developing countries and growth: a selective survey', *The Journal of Development Studies*, **34** (1), 1–34.

Deardorff, A. (1984), 'Testing trade theories and predicting trade flows', in R. Jones and P. Kenen (eds), *Handbook of International Economics*, Amsterdam: Elsevier Science.

Deardorff, A. (1995), 'Determinants of bilateral trade: does gravity work in a neo-classical world?', NBER Working Paper No. 5377, Cambridge, MA: National Bureau of Economic Research.

Dees, S. (1998), 'Foreign direct investment in China: determinants and effects', *Economics of Planning*, **31** (2), 175–94.

Deng, Xiaoping (1984), *Selected Works of Deng Xiaoping (1975–1982)*, Beijing: Foreign Language Press.

Dobson, W. (1993), *Japan in East Asia: Trading and Investment Strategies*, Singapore: Institute of Southeast Asian Studies.

Driffield, N. (2000), 'The impact on domestic productivity of inward investment into the UK', *Manchester School*, **69** (1), 103–19.

Drysdale, P. and R. Garnaut (1994), 'Trade intensities and the analysis of bilateral trade flows in a many-country world: a survey', in R. Garnaut and P. Drysdale (eds), *Asia Pacific Regionalism: Readings in International Economic Relations*, Pymble, NSW, Australia: Harper Educational, pp. 20–35.

Dunning, J. (1977), 'Trade, location of economic activity and the multinational enterprise: a search for an eclectic approach', in B. Ohlin, P. Hesselborn and P. Wijkman (eds), *The International Allocation of Economic Activity*, London: Macmillan, pp. 395–418.

Dunning, J. (1980), 'Towards an eclectic theory of international production: some empirical tests', *Journal of International Business Studies*, **11** (1), 9–31.

Dunning, J. (1981a), *International Production and the Multinational Enterprise*, London: Allen and Unwin.

Dunning, J. (1981b), 'Explaining the international direct investment position of countries: towards a dynamic or development approach', *Weltwirtschaftliches Archiv*, **117** (1), 30–64.

Dunning, J. (1986), 'The investment development cycle revisited', *Weltwirtschaftliches Archiv*, **122**, 667–77.

Dunning, J. (1988a), *Multinationals, Technology and Competitiveness*, London: Allen and Unwin.

Dunning, J. (1988b), 'The eclectic paradigm of international production: a restatement and some possible extensions', *Journal of International Business Studies*, **19** (1), 1–32.

Dunning, J. (1993), *Multinational Enterprises and the Global Economy*, Wokingham: Addison-Wesley.

Dunning, J. and S. Lundan (2008), *Multinational Enterprises and the Global Economy*, Cheltenham, UK and Northampton, MA, USA: Edward Elgar Publishing.

East Asia Analytical Unit (EAAU) (1995), *Overseas Chinese Business Networks in Asia*, Canberra: Department of Foreign Affairs and Trade.

Eichengreen, B. and H. Tong (2005), 'Is China's FDI coming at the expense of other countries?', NBER Working Paper No. 11335, Cambridge, MA: National Bureau of Economic Research.

ETCN (2009), 'Share sales "don't shake relations" between Chinese, foreign banks', 14 January, available at http://www.e-to-china.com/financial_crisis/analysis_comments/Authoritative_interpretation/2009/0114/15669.html (accessed 19 February 2011).

Fan, Y. (1992), *China's Industrialization and Foreign Direct Investment*, Shanghai: Shanghai Social Science Press.

Foreign Investment Administration of the Ministry of Foreign Trade and Economic Cooperation (MOFTEC) (1998), *Tax Exemption Policies on Importation of*

Equipment by Enterprises with Foreign Investment, Beijing: Foreign Investment Administration of MOFTEC.

Frankel, J. (1994), 'Is Japan creating a yen bloc in East Asia and the Pacific?', in J. Frankel and M. Kahler (eds), *Regionalism and Rivalry: Japan and the U.S. in Pacific Asia*, Chicago, IL: University of Chicago Press.

Girma, S. and K. Wakelin (2001), 'Regional underdevelopment: is FDI the solution? A semiparametric analysis', CEPR Discussion Paper No. 2995.

Gorg, H. and D. Greenaway (2004), 'Much ado about nothing? Do domestic firms really benefit from foreign direct investment?', *World Bank Research Observer*, **19** (2), 171–97.

Graham, E. and P. Krugman (1991), *Foreign Direct Investment in the United States*, 2nd edition, Washington, DC: Institute for International Economics.

Greenaway, D., N. Sousa and K. Wakelin (2004), 'Do domestic firms learn to export from multinationals?', *European Journal of Political Economy*, **20** (4), 1027–43.

Guisinger, S. and Associates (1985), *Investment Incentives and Performance Requirements: Patterns of International Trade, Production, and Investment*, New York: Praeger.

Haddad M. and A. Harrison (1993), 'Are there positive spillovers from direct foreign investment? Evidence from panel data for Morocco', *Journal of Development Economics*, **42** (1), 51–74.

Hahn, J., P. Todd and W. Van der Klaauw (2001), 'Identification and estimation of treatment effects with a regression-discontinuity design', *Econometrica*, **69** (1), 201–9.

Harrold, P. and R. Lall (1993), 'China reform and development in 1992–93', World Bank Discussion Paper No. 215, Washington, DC: The World Bank.

Haskel, J., S. Pereira and M. Slaughter (2007), 'Does inward foreign direct investment boost the productivity of domestic firms?', *The Review of Economics and Statistics*, **89** (3), 482–96.

Head, K. and J. Ries (2001), 'Increasing returns versus national product differentiation as an explanation for the pattern of U.S.–Canada trade', *American Economic Review*, **91** (4), 858–76.

Heckman, J. (1979), 'Sample selection bias as a specification error', *Econometrica*, **47** (1), 153–61.

Helliwell, J. (1996), 'Do national borders matter for Quebec's trade?', *Canadian Journal of Economics*, **29** (3), 507–22.

Helliwell, J. (1997), 'National borders, trade and migration', *Pacific Economic Review*, **2** (3), 165–85.

Helliwell, J. (1998), *How Much Do National Borders Matter?*, Washington, DC: Brookings Institution.

Helliwell, J. and J. McCallum (1995), 'National borders still matter for trade', *Policy Options*, **16** (5), 44–8.

Helpman, E. and P. Krugman (1985), *Market Structure and Foreign Trade*, Cambridge, MA: The MIT Press.

Henley, J., C. Kirkpatrick and G. Wilde (1999), 'Foreign direct investment in China: recent trends and current issues', *The World Economy*, **22** (2), 223–43.

Hillberry, R. (1998), 'Regional trade and the medicine line: the national border effect in U.S. commodity flow data', *Journal of Borderlands Studies*, **8** (2), 1–17.

Hillberry, R. (2002), 'Aggregation bias, compositional change and the border effect', *Canadian Journal of Economics*, **35** (3), 517–30.

Hillberry, R. and D. Hummels (2002), 'Explaining home bias in consumption: the rule of intermediate input trade', NBER Working Paper No. 9020, Cambridge, MA: National Bureau of Economic Research.

Hu, X. and Y. Ma (1999), 'International intra-industry trade of China', *Review of World Economics*, **135** (1), 82–101.

Huang, Y. (2003a), *Selling China: Foreign Direct Investment during the Reform Era*, Cambridge: Cambridge University Press.

Huang, Y. (2003b), 'One country two systems: foreign-invested enterprise and domestic firms in China', *China Economic Review*, **14** (4), 404–16.

Huang, Y. (2010), 'Ownership biases and foreign direct investment in China', in P. Athukorala (ed.), *The Rise of Asia: Trade and Investment in Global Perspective*, New York: Routledge, pp. 161–81.

Hultman, C. and L. McGee (1988), 'Factors influencing foreign investment in the U.S., 1970–1986', *Rivista Internazionale di Scienze Economiche e Commerciali*, **35** (10–11), 1061–6.

Hymer, S. (1976), *The International Operations of National Firms: A Study of Direct Foreign Investment*, Cambridge, MA: The MIT Press.

Imbens, G. and J. Angrist (1994), 'Identification and estimation of local average treatment effects', *Econometrica*, **62** (2), 467–75.

Institutional Investor, Global Credit Rating, available at http://www.iimagazine rankings.com/countrycredit/GlobalRankingP6.asp.

International Labour Organization (ILO), LABORSTA Internet, available at http://laborsta.ilo.org/.

International Monetary Fund (IMF) (2004), 'Definition of foreign direct investment (FDI) terms', IMF Committee on Balance of Payments Statistics and OECD Workshop on International Investment Statistics, available at http://www.imf.org/External/NP/sta/bop/pdf/diteg20.pdf (accessed 19 February 2011).

Janicki, H. and P. Wunnava (2004), 'Determinants of foreign direct investment: empirical evidence from EU accession candidates', *Applied Economics*, **36** (5), 505–9.

Javorcik, B. (2004), 'Does foreign direct investment increase the productivity of domestic firms? In search of spillovers through backward linkages', *American Economic Review*, **94** (3), 605–27.

Kamath, S. (1990), 'Foreign direct investment in a centrally planned developing economy: the Chinese case', *Economic Development and Cultural Change*, **39** (1), 107–30.

Kamath, S. (1994), 'Property rights and the evolution of foreign direct investment in a centrally planned developing economy: reply to Pomfret', *Economic Development and Cultural Change*, **42** (2), 419–26.

Kang, S. and H. Lee (2007), 'The determinants of location choice of South Korean FDI in China', *Japan and the World Economy*, **19** (4), 441–60.

Kaynak, E., M. Demirbag and E. Tatoglu (2007), 'Determinants of ownership-based entry mode choice of MNEs: evidence from Mongolia', *Management International Review*, **47** (4), 505–30.

Keller, W. and S. Yeaple (2003), 'Multinational enterprises, international trade and productivity growth: firm-level evidence from the United States', NBER Working Paper No. 9504, Cambridge, MA: National Bureau of Economic Research.

Kindleberger, C. (1969), *American Business Abroad*, New Haven, CT: Yale University Press.

Kindleberger, C. (ed.) (1970), *The International Corporation*, Cambridge, MA: The MIT Press.

Kindleberger, C. (1974), 'Size of firm and size of nation state', in J. Dunning (ed.), *Economic Analysis and the Multinational Enterprise*, London: Allen and Unwin.

Kneller, R. and M. Pisu (2007), 'Industrial linkages and export spillovers from FDI', *The World Economy*, **30** (1), 105–34.

Kojima, K. (1964), 'The pattern of international trade among advanced countries', *Hitotsubashi Journal of Economics*, **5** (1), 16–36.

Kokko, A., M. Zejan and R. Tansini (2001), 'Trade regimes and spillover effects of FDI: evidence from Uruguay', *Weltwirtschaftliches Archiv*, **137** (1), 124–49.

Kueh, Y. (1992), 'Foreign investment and economic change in China', *The China Quarterly*, **131**, 637–90.

Lardy, N. (1995), 'The role of foreign trade and investment in China's economic transformation', *The China Quarterly*, **144**, 1065–82.

Leamer, E. (1974), 'The commodity composition of international trade in manufactures: an empirical analysis', *Oxford Economic Papers*, **26** (3), 350–74.

Leamer, E. (1984), *Sources of International Comparative Advantage: Theory and Evidence*, Cambridge, MA: The MIT Press.

Leamer, E. and R. Stern (1970), *Quantitative International Economics*, Boston: Allyn and Bacon.

Lever-Tracy, C., D. Ip and N. Tracy (1996), *The Chinese Diaspora and Mainland China: An Emerging Economic Synergy*, London: Macmillan and New York: St. Martin's Press.

Levin, A. and L. Raut (1997), 'Complementarities between exports and human capital in economic growth: evidence from the semi-industrialized countries', *Economic Development and Cultural Change*, **46** (1), 155–74.

Levinsohn, J. and A. Petrin, (2003), 'Estimating production functions using inputs to control for unobservables', *Reviews of Economic Studies*, **70** (2), 317–42.

Li, J. and C. Zhou (2008), 'Dual-edged tools of trade: how international joint ventures help and hinder capability building of Chinese firms', *Journal of World Business*, **43** (4), 463–74.

Li, F. and J. Li (1999), *Foreign Direct Investment in China*, London: Macmillan and New York: St. Martin's Press.

Li, Y. (2003), 'The impact of FDI on trade: evidence from China's bilateral trade', *Journal of the Academy of Business and Economics*, **2** (2), 1–11.

Lim, D. (1983), 'Fiscal incentives and direct foreign investment in less developed countries', *The Journal of Development Studies*, **19** (2), 207–12.

Lin, P. and K. Saggi (2005), 'Multinational firms and backward linkages: a critical survey and a simple model', in T. Moran, E. Graham and M. Blomstrom (eds), *Does Foreign Direct Investment Promote Development?*, Washington, DC: Institute for International Economics, pp. 159–74.

Linnemann, H. (1966), *An Econometric Study of World Trade Flows*, Amsterdam: North-Holland.

Lipsey, R. (2002), 'Home and host country effects of FDI', NBER Working Paper No. 9293, Cambridge, MA: National Bureau of Economic Research.

Lipsey, R. (2006), 'Measuring the impacts of FDI in Central and Eastern Europe', NBER Working Paper No. 12808, Cambridge, MA: National Bureau of Economic Research.

Liu, T. (2008), 'Impact of regional trade agreements on Chinese foreign direct investment', *Chinese Economy*, **41** (5), 68–102.

Liu, X., C. He, Z. Lu, B. Fan and J. Zhou (eds) (1993), *Guide to China's Foreign Economic and Trade Policies*, Beijing: Economic Management Press.

Liu, X., Wang, C. and Y. Wei (2001), 'Causal links between FDI and trade in China', *China Economic Review*, **12** (2-3), 190–202.

Lo, V. and X. Tian (2009), *Law for Foreign Business and Investment in China*, Abington, NY: Routledge.

Lucas, R. (1993), 'On the determinants of direct foreign investment: evidence from East and Southeast Asia', *World Development*, **21** (3), 391–406.

Lundgren, N. (1977), 'Comment (on a chapter by J. Dunning)', in B. Ohlin, P. Hesselborn and P. Wijkman (eds), *The International Allocation of Economic Activity: Proceedings of a Nobel Symposium Held at Stockholm*, London: Macmillan.

Ma, A. (2006), 'Export spillovers to Chinese firms: evidence from provincial data', *Journal of Chinese Economic and Business Studies*, **4** (2), 127–49.

Markusen, J. (1995), 'The boundaries of multinational enterprises and the theory of international trade', *Journal of Economic Perspectives*, **9** (2), 169–89.

Markusen, J. and A. Venables (1999), 'Foreign direct investment as a catalyst for industrial development', *European Economic Review*, **43** (2), 335–56.

McCallum, J. (1995), 'National borders matter: Canada–U.S. regional trade patterns', *American Economic Review*, **85** (3), 615–23.

McKibben, W. and P. Wilcoxen (1998), 'The global impacts of trade and financial reform in China', Asia Pacific School of Economics and Management, Working Paper 98-3, The Australian National University.

Melitz, M. (2003), 'The impact of trade on intra-industry reallocations and aggregate industry productivity', *Econometrica*, **71** (6), 1695–725.

Mercereau, B. (2005), 'FDI flows to Asia: did the dragon crowd out the tigers?', (September), IMF Working Paper, WP/05/189, available at http://zunia.org/uploads/media/knowledge/wp051891.pdf (accessed 19 February 2011).

Ministry of Commerce of China (MOFCOM), Invest in China, FDI Statistics, available at http://www.fdi.gov.cn/pub/FDI_EN/Statistics/FDIStatistics/default.htm.

Ministry of Commerce of China (MOFCOM) (various issues), *China Foreign Investment Report*, Beijing: MOFCOM.

Moran, T. (2001), *Parental Supervision: The New Paradigm for Foreign Direct Investment and Development*, Washington, DC: Institute for International Economics.

Morck, R. and B. Yeung (1991), 'Why investors value multinationality', *Journal of Business*, **64** (2), 165–87.

National Bureau of Statistics of China (NBS) (various issues), *China Statistical Yearbook*, Beijing: China Statistics Press.

National Bureau of Statistics of China (NBS) (various issues), *China Foreign Economic Statistical Yearbook*, Beijing: China Statistics Press.

Niedercorn, J. and B. Bechdolt (1969), 'An economic derivation of the "Gravity Law" of spatial interaction', *Journal of Regional Science*, **9** (2), 273–82.

Office of the Third National Industrial Census (1997a), *Data of the 1995 Third National Industrial Census of the PRC: All Enterprises*, Beijing: China Statistics Press.

Office of the Third National Industrial Census (1997b), *Data of the 1995 Third National Industrial Census of the PRC: State-owned, Foreign-funded, and Township and Village Enterprises*, Beijing: China Statistics Press.

Office of the West Development Leading Group of the State Council (2000), 'State's relevant policies and measures on supporting the development of western areas', unpublished internal document.

Oxelheim, L. and P. Ghauri (2008), 'EU–China and the non-transparent race for inward FDI', *Journal of Asian Economics*, **19** (4), 358–70.

People's Daily Online (2010a), 'China unveils new rules for foreign investment', 14 April, available at http://english.peopledaily.com.cn/90001/90778/90861/6949654.html (accessed 19 February 2011).

People's Daily Online (2010b), 'China ends foreign firms' "super-national treatment"', 1 December, available at http://english.peopledaily.com.cn/90001/90778/90861/7217484.html (accessed 19 February 2011).

Petri, P. (1995), 'The interdependence of trade and investment in the Pacific', in E. Chen and P. Drysdale (eds), *Corporate Links and Foreign Direct Investment in Asia and the Pacific*, Pymble, NSW, Australia: Harper Educational, pp. 29–54.

Pomfret, R. (1989), *Equity Joint Ventures in Jiangsu Province: A Specially Commissioned Report*, Hong Kong: Longman.

Pomfret, R. (1991), *Investing in China: Ten Years of the 'Open Door' Policy*, Ames, IA: Iowa State University Press.

Pomfret, R. (1994), 'Foreign direct investment in a centrally planned economy: lessons from China: comment on Kamath', *Economic Development and Cultural Change*, **42** (2), 413–18.

Pomfret, R. (1997), 'Growth and transition: why has China's performance been so different?', *Journal of Comparative Economics*, **25**, 422–40.

Qi, L. and C. Howe (1993), 'Direct investment and economic integration in the Asia Pacific: the case of Taiwanese investment in Xiamen', *The China Quarterly*, **136**, 746–69.

Ramasamy, B. and M. Yeung (2010), 'A causality analysis of the FDI-wages-productivity nexus in China', *Journal of Chinese Economic and Foreign Trade Studies*, **3** (1), 5–23.

Ran, J., J. Voon and G. Li (2007), 'How does FDI affect China? Evidence from industries and provinces', *Journal of Comparative Economics*, **35** (4), 774–99.

Resmini, L. and I. Siedschlag (2008), 'Is FDI into China crowding out the FDI into the European Union?', available at http://www.etsg.org/ETSG2008/Papers/Siedschlag.pdf (accessed 19 February 2011).

Rodriguez-Clare, A. (1996), 'Multinationals, linkages, and economic development', *American Economic Review*, **86** (4), 852–73.

Ruane, F. and J. Sutherland (2005), 'Foreign direct investment and export spillovers: how do export platforms fare?', IIIS Discussion Paper No. 58, Institute for International Integration Studies, Trinity College Dublin, Ireland.

Rugman, A. (1986), 'New theories of the multinational enterprise: an assessment of internalization theory', *Bulletin of Economic Research*, **38** (2), 101–18.

Scaperlanda, A. and L. Mauer (1969), 'The determinants of U.S. direct investment in the E.E.C.', *American Economic Review*, **59** (4), 558–68.

Shirk, S. (1994), *How China Opened Its Door, The Political Success of the PRC's Foreign Trade and Investment Reforms*, Washington, DC: Brookings Institution.

Singh, H. and K. Jun (1995), 'Some new evidence on determinants of foreign direct investment in developing countries', Policy Research Working Paper, No. 1531, the World Bank, available at http://ideas.repec.org/p/wbk/wbrwps/1531.html (accessed 19 February 2011).

Song, L. (1996), *Changing Global Comparative Advantage: Evidence from Asia and the Pacific*, Melbourne: Addison-Wesley Longman Australia.

State Council (2010), State Council's Regulations on Further Improvement on the Work of Utilising Foreign Direct Investment, 13 April, available at http://www.gov.cn/zwgk/2010-04/13/content_1579732.htm (accessed 19 February 2011).

Sun, H. (1995), 'Foreign investment and regional economic development in China', *Australian Journal of Regional Studies*, **1** (2), 133–48.

Sun, H. and A. Parikh (2001), 'Exports, inward foreign direct investment (FDI) and regional economic growth in China', *Regional Studies*, **35** (3), 187–96.

Sun, S. (2009), 'How does FDI affect domestic firms' exports? Industrial evidence', *World Economy*, **32** (8), 1203–22.

Sung, Y. (2007), 'Made in China: from world sweatshop to a global manufacturing centre?', *Asian Economic Paper*, **6** (3), 43–72.

Suyanto, R. Salim and H. Bloch (2009), 'Does foreign direct investment lead to productivity spillovers? Firm level evidence from Indonesia', *World Development*, **37** (12), 1861–76.

Swedenborg, B. (1979), *The Multinational Operations of Swedish Firms: An Analysis of Determinants and Effects*, Stockholm: Industrial Institute for Economic and Social Research.

Tang, S., E. Selvanathan and S. Selvanathan (2008), 'Foreign direct investment, domestic investment and economic growth in China: a time series analysis', *World Economy*, **31** (10), 1292–309.

The New York Times (2010), 'Taking on China', 14 March, available at http://www.nytimes.com/2010/03/15/opinion/15krugman.html (accessed 19 February 2011).

The Sydney Morning Herald (2009), 'Allianz, AmEx sell half of stakes in China's ICBC', 28 April, available at http://news.smh.com.au/breaking-news-world/allianz-amex-sell-half-of-stakes-in-chinas-icbc-20090429-am6m.html (accessed 19 February 2011).

The Wall Street Journal (2009), 'BofA gets $7.3 billion in CCB sale', 13 May, available at http://online.wsj.com/article/SB124210827820109929.html (accessed 19 February 2011).

Thoburn, J., H. Leung, E. Chau and S. Tang (1990), *Foreign Investment in China Under the Open Policy – the Experience of Hong Kong Companies*, Avebury: Gower.

Tinbergen, J. (1962), *Shaping the World Economy – Suggestions for an International Economic Policy*. New York: Twentieth Century Fund.

Torrisi, C. (1985), 'The determinants of direct foreign investment in a small LDC', *Journal of Economic Development*, **10** (1), 29–45.

Tse, D., Y. Pan and K. Au (1997), 'How MNCs choose entry modes and form alliances: the China experience', *Journal of International Business Studies*, **28** (4), 779–805.

Tuan, C., L. Ng and B. Zhao (2009), 'China's post-economic reform growth: the role of FDI and productivity progress', *Journal of Asian Economics*, **20** (3), 280–93.

United Nations Common Database (UNCDB), available at http://data.un.org/Search.aspx?q=Literacy+rate.

United Nations Conference on Trade and Development (UNCTAD) (2007), 'Rising FDI into China: the facts behind the numbers', UNCTAD Investment

Brief, Number 2, available at http://www.unctad.org/en/docs/iteiiamisc20075_en.pdf (accessed 19 February 2011).

United Nations Conference on Trade and Development (UNCTAD) (various issues), *World Investment Report*, New York and Geneva: United Nations Publication.

United Nations Statistics Division, Commodity Trade Statistics Database, COMTRADE, available at http://comtrade.un.org/db/default.aspx.

United Nations Statistics Division, National Accounts, available at http://unstats.un.org/unsd/snaama/dnllist.asp.

Uttama, N. and N. Peridy (2009), 'The impact of regional integration and third-country effects on FDI: evidence from ASEAN', *ASEAN Economic Bulletin*, **26** (3), 239–52.

Vernon, R. (1966), 'International investment and international trade in the product cycle', *Quarterly Journal of Economics*, **80** (2), 190–207.

Vogiatzoglou, K. (2007), 'Vertical specialisation and new determinants of FDI: evidence from South and East Asia', *Global Economic Review*, **36** (3), 245–66.

Vogiatzoglou, K. (2008), 'The triad in Southeast Asia: what determines U.S., EU and Japanese FDI within AFTA?', *ASEAN Economic Bulletin*, **25** (2), 140–60.

Vu, T., B. Gangnes and I. Noy (2008), 'Is foreign direct investment good for growth? Evidence from sectoral analysis of China and Vietnam', *Journal of the Asia Pacific Economy*, **13** (4), 542–62.

Walmsley, T. and T. Hertel (2001), 'China's accession to the WTO: timing is everything', *The World Economy*, **24** (8), 1019–49.

Wang, C., Y. Wei and X. Liu (2007), 'Does China rival its neighbouring economies for inward FDI', *Transnational Corporation*, **16** (3), 35–60.

Wang, R. (ed.) (1997), *Report on Foreign Direct Investment in China: Industrial Distribution of Foreign Direct Investment*, Beijing: Economic and Management Press.

Wei, J. (1994), *Chinese Foreign Investment Laws and Policies: Evolution and Transformation*, Westport, CT: Quorum Books.

Wei, S. (1995), 'Attracting foreign direct investment: has China reached its potential?', *China Economic Review*, **6** (2), 187–99.

Wei, S. (1996a), 'Foreign direct investment in China: sources and consequences', in T. Ito and A. Krueger (eds), *Financial Deregulation and Integration in East Asia*, NBER-EASE vol. 5, Chicago, IL: University of Chicago Press, pp. 77–105.

Wei, S. (1996b). 'Intra-national versus inter-national trade: how stubborn are nations in global integration', NBER Working Paper No. 5531, Cambridge, MA: National Bureau of Economic Research.

Wei, S. and J. Frankel (1994), 'A "Greater China" trade bloc?', *China Economic Review*, **5** (2), 179–90.

Whalley, J. and X. Xin (2010), 'China's FDI and non-FDI economies and the sustainability of future high Chinese growth', *China Economic Review*, **21** (1), 123–35.

Wheeler, D. and A. Mody (1992), 'International investment location decisions: the case of U.S. firms', *Journal of International Economics*, **33** (1–2), 57–76.

Wilson, S. (2009), *Remade in China: Foreign Investors and Institutional Change in China*, Oxford: Oxford University Press.

Wolf, C. and D. Weinschrott (1973), 'International transactions and regionalism: distinguishing "insiders" from "outsiders"', *American Economic Review*, **63** (2), 52–60.

Wooldridge, J. (1995), 'Selection corrections for panel data model under conditional mean independent assumptions', *Journal of Econometrics*, **68** (1), 115–32.

Wooldridge, J. (2002), *Econometric Analysis of Cross Section and Panel Data*, Cambridge, MA: The MIT Press.

Wooldridge, J. (2006), 'Cluster-sample methods in applied econometrics: an extended analysis', mimeo, available at https://www.msu.edu/~ec/faculty/wooldridge/current%20research/clus1aea.pdf (accessed 19 February 2011).

Wu, F., P. Siaw, Y. Sia and P. Keong (2002), 'Foreign direct investments to China and Southeast Asia: has ASEAN been losing out?', *Economic Survey of Singapore* (Third Quarter), 96–115, available at http://unpan1.un.org/intradoc/groups/public/documents/apcity/unpan010347.pdf (accessed 19 February 2011).

Wu, Y. (2009), 'China's capital stock series by region and sector', Business School, University of Western Australia, Discussion Paper No. 09.02, available at http://www.business.uwa.edu.au/__data/assets/pdf_file/0009/260487/09_02_Wu.pdf (accessed 19 February 2011).

Xiao, G. (2004), 'People's Republic of China's round-tripping FDI: scale, causes and implications', ADB Institute Discussion Paper, No. 7, available at http://www.adbi.org/files/2004.06.dp7.foreign.direct.investment.people.rep.china.implications.pdf (accessed 19 February 2011).

Xinhua News Agency (2007), 'Parliament adopts corporate income tax', 16 March, available at http://news.xinhuanet.com/english/2007-03/16/content_5854950.htm (accessed 19 February 2011).

Xinhuanet (2009), 'China's FDI decline slows in March', 14 April, available at http://news.xinhuanet.com/english/2009-04/14/content_11181782.htm (accessed 19 February 2011).

Xu, B. and J. Lu (2009), 'Foreign direct investment, processing trade, and the sophistication of China's exports', *China Economic Review*, **20** (3), 425–39.

Yu, J. and W. Zhao (2008), 'The impacts of Japanese direct investment in China on the Sino-Japanese bilateral trade', *Journal of Chinese Economic and Foreign Trade Studies*, **1** (3), 185–99.

Zhan, J. (1993), 'The role of foreign direct investment in market-oriented reforms and economic development: the Case of China', *Transnational Corporation*, **2** (3), 121–48.

Zhang, K. (2006), 'Foreign direct investment and economic growth in China: a panel data study for 1992–2004', paper prepared for the conference of 'WTO, China and Asian Economies', 24–26 June, University of International Business and Economics, Beijing, China, available at http://faculty.washington.edu/karyiu/confer/beijing06/papers/zhang.pdf (accessed 19 February 2011).

Zhang, L. (1994), 'Location-specific advantages and manufacturing direct foreign investment in South China', *World Development*, **22** (1), 45–53.

Zheng, P., P. Siler and G. Giorgioni (2004), 'FDI and the export performance of Chinese indigenous firms: a regional approach', *Journal of Chinese Economic and Business Studies*, **2** (1), 55–71.

Zhou, Y. and S. Lall (2005), 'The impact of China's surge on FDI in South-East Asia: panel data analysis for 1986–2001', *Transnational Corporation*, **14** (1), 41–65.

Index